ST. MARY'S COLLEGE OF MARYLAND LIBRARY
ST. MARY'S CITY, MARYLAND

ADDRESSES ON
INTERNATIONAL SUBJECTS

ADDRESSES ON INTERNATIONAL SUBJECTS

BY

ELIHU ROOT

COLLECTED AND EDITED BY

ROBERT BACON

AND

JAMES BROWN SCOTT

Essay Index Reprint Series

BOOKS FOR LIBRARIES PRESS
FREEPORT, NEW YORK

First Published 1916
Reprinted 1969

STANDARD BOOK NUMBER:
8369-1191-1

LIBRARY OF CONGRESS CATALOG CARD NUMBER:
74-86780

PRINTED IN THE UNITED STATES OF AMERICA

CONTENTS

	PAGE
INTRODUCTORY NOTE	vii

THE NEED OF POPULAR UNDERSTANDING OF INTERNATIONAL LAW 3
An Article contributed to the first issue of the *American Journal of International Law*, 1907.

THE REAL QUESTIONS UNDER THE JAPANESE TREATY AND THE SAN FRANCISCO SCHOOL BOARD RESOLUTION . . 7
Presidential Address at the first annual meeting of the American Society of International Law, Washington, D. C., April 19, 1907.

THE SANCTION OF INTERNATIONAL LAW 25
Presidential Address at the second annual meeting of the American Society of International Law, Washington, D. C., April 24, 1908.

THE RELATIONS BETWEEN INTERNATIONAL TRIBUNALS OF ARBITRATION AND THE JURISDICTION OF NATIONAL COURTS 33
Presidential Address at the third annual meeting of the American Society of International Law, Washington, D. C., April 23, 1909.

THE BASIS OF PROTECTION TO CITIZENS RESIDING ABROAD 43
Presidential Address at the fourth annual meeting of the American Society of International Law, Washington, D. C., April 28, 1910.

THE FUNCTION OF PRIVATE CODIFICATION IN INTERNATIONAL LAW 57
Presidential Address at the fifth annual meeting of the American Society of International Law, Washington, D. C., April 27, 1911.

THE REAL SIGNIFICANCE OF THE DECLARATION OF LONDON . 73
Presidential Address at the sixth annual meeting of the American Society of International Law, Washington, D. C., April 25, 1912.

FRANCIS LIEBER 89
Presidential Address at the seventh annual meeting of the American Society of International Law, Washington, D. C., April 24, 1913.

CONTENTS

THE REAL MONROE DOCTRINE 105
Presidential Address at the eighth annual meeting of the American Society of International Law, Washington, D. C., April 22, 1914.

ADDRESS AT A CONFERENCE OF TEACHERS OF INTERNATIONAL LAW 125
Opening Remarks at a conference held in Washington, D.C., April 23–25, 1914, under the auspices of the American Society of International Law.

THE HAGUE PEACE CONFERENCES 129
Address in the National Arbitration and Peace Congress, New York, April 15, 1907.

THE IMPORTANCE OF JUDICIAL SETTLEMENT 145
Opening Address at the International Conference of the American Society for Judicial Settlement of International Disputes, Washington, D.C., December 15, 1910.

NOBEL PEACE PRIZE ADDRESS 153
A Speech prepared in acceptance of the Nobel Peace Prize of 1912.

THE ETHICS OF THE PANAMA QUESTION 175
Address before the Union League Club of Chicago, February 22, 1904.

THE OBLIGATIONS OF THE UNITED STATES AS TO PANAMA CANAL TOLLS 207
Address in the Senate of the United States, January 21, 1913.

PANAMA CANAL TOLLS 241
Speech in reply in the Senate of the United States, May 21, 1914.

THE TREATY OF 1832 WITH RUSSIA 313
Address in the Senate of the United States, December 19, 1911.

THE MEXICAN RESOLUTION 327
Address in the Senate of the United States, April 21, 1914.

THE SHIP PURCHASE BILL 337
An Address delivered in the United States Senate, January 4, 1915.

SECOND SPEECH ON THE SHIP PURCHASE BILL 341
An Address delivered in the United States Senate, January 25, 1915.

CONTENTS

THE OUTLOOK FOR INTERNATIONAL LAW   391
  Presidential Address at the ninth annual meeting of the
  American Society of International Law, Washington, D. C.,
  December 28, 1915.

SHOULD INTERNATIONAL LAW BE CODIFIED?   405
  Address at the joint meeting of the Subsection on International Law of the Second Pan-American Scientific Congress,
  Washington, D. C., December 30, 1915.

THE DECLARATION OF THE RIGHTS AND DUTIES OF NATIONS
    OF THE AMERICAN INSTITUTE OF INTERNATIONAL LAW   413
  Presidential Address at the tenth annual meeting of the
  American Society of International Law, Washington, D. C.,
  April 27, 1916.

FOREIGN AFFAIRS, 1913–1916   427
  Address as Temporary Chairman of the New York Republican
  State Convention, New York, February 15, 1916.

INDEX   449

INTRODUCTORY NOTE

THE collected addresses and state papers of Elihu Root, of which this is one of several volumes, cover the period of his service as Secretary of War, as Secretary of State, and as Senator of the United States, during which time, to use his own expression, his only client was his country.

The many formal and occasional addresses and speeches, which will be found to be of a remarkably wide range, are followed by his state papers, such as the instructions to the American delegates to the Second Hague Peace Conference and other diplomatic notes and documents, prepared by him as Secretary of State in the performance of his duties as an executive officer of the United States. Although the official documents have been kept separate from the other papers, this plan has been slightly modified in the volume devoted to the military and colonial policy of the United States, which includes those portions of his official reports as Secretary of War throwing light upon his public addresses and his general military policy.

The addresses and speeches selected for publication are not arranged chronologically, but are classified in such a way that each volume contains addresses and speeches relating to a general subject and a common purpose. The addresses as president of the American Society of International Law show his treatment of international questions from the theoretical standpoint, and in the light of his experience as Secretary of War and as Secretary of State, unrestrained and uncontrolled by the limitations of official position, whereas his addresses on foreign affairs, delivered while Secretary of State or as United States Senator, discuss these questions under the reserve of official responsibility.

Mr. Root's addresses on government, citizenship, and legal procedure are a masterly exposition of the principles of the Constitution and of the government established by it; of the duty of the citizen to understand the Constitution and to conform his conduct to its requirements; and of the right of the people to reform or to amend the Constitution in order to make representative government more effective and responsive to their present and future needs. The addresses on law and its administration state how legal procedure should be modified and simplified in the interest of justice rather than in the supposed interest of the legal profession.

The addresses delivered during the trip to South America and Mexico in 1906, and in the United States after his return, with their message of good will, proclaim a new doctrine — the Root doctrine — of kindly consideration and of honorable obligation, and make clear the destiny common to the peoples of the Western World.

The addresses and the reports on military and colonial policy made by Mr. Root as Secretary of War explain the reorganization of the army after the Spanish-American War, the creation of the General Staff, and the establishment of the Army War College. They trace the origin of and give the reason for the policy of this country in Cuba, the Philippines, and Porto Rico, devised and inaugurated by him. It is not generally known that the so-called Platt Amendment, defining our relations to Cuba, was drafted by Mr. Root, and that the Organic Act of the Philippines was likewise the work of Mr. Root as Secretary of War.

The argument before The Hague Tribunal in the North Atlantic Fisheries Case is a rare if not the only instance of a statesman appearing as chief counsel in an international arbitration, which, as Secretary of State, he had prepared and submitted.

INTRODUCTORY NOTE

The political, educational, historical, and commemorative speeches and addresses should make known to future generations the literary, artistic, and emotional side of a statesman of our time, and the publication of these collected addresses and state papers will, it is believed, enable the American people better to understand the generation in which Mr. Root has been a commanding figure and better to appreciate during his lifetime the services which he has rendered to his country.

ROBERT BACON.
JAMES BROWN SCOTT.

APRIL 15, 1916.

ADDRESSES ON
INTERNATIONAL SUBJECTS

THE NEED OF POPULAR UNDERSTANDING OF INTERNATIONAL LAW

At the eleventh annual meeting of the Lake Mohonk Conference on International Arbitration the advisability of forming an American society of international law was considered on June 2, 1905, by those gentlemen present who were interested in international law as such. The idea was approved and a committee was appointed to take the necessary steps. On January 12, 1906, the American Society of International Law was organized in the rooms of the Bar Association of the City of New York. A constitution was adopted and officers selected. Mr. Root was elected the first president of the Society, and he has since been continued in that position. To the first issue of the *American Journal of International Law* (1907), the organ of the Society, Mr. Root contributed the following article:

THE increase of popular control over national conduct, which marks the political development of our time, makes it constantly more important that the great body of the people in each country should have a just conception of their international rights and duties.

Governments do not make war nowadays unless assured of general and hearty support among their people; and it sometimes happens that governments are driven into war against their will by the pressure of strong popular feeling. It is not uncommon to see two governments striving in the most conciliatory and patient way to settle some matter of difference peaceably, while a large part of the people in both countries maintain an uncompromising and belligerent attitude, insisting upon the extreme and uttermost view of their own rights in a way which, if it were to control national action, would render peaceable settlement impossible.

One of the chief obstacles to the peaceable adjustment of international controversies is the fact that the negotiator or arbitrator who yields any part of the extreme claims of his own country and concedes the reasonableness of any argument of the other side is quite likely to be violently condemned by great numbers of his own countrymen who have never taken the pains to make themselves familiar with the merits of the controversy or have considered only the arguments on their own side. Sixty-four years have passed since the northeastern boundary between the United States and Canada was settled by the Webster-Ashburton Treaty of 1842; yet to this day there are many people on our side of the line who condemn Mr. Webster for sacrificing our rights, and many people on the Canadian side of the line who blame Lord Ashburton for sacrificing their rights, in that treaty. Both sets of objectors cannot be right; it seems a fair inference that neither of them is right; yet both Mr. Webster and Lord Ashburton had to endure reproach and obloquy as the price of agreeing upon a settlement which has been worth to the peace and prosperity of each country a thousand times as much as the value of all the territory that was in dispute.

In the great business of settling international controversies without war, whether it be by negotiation or arbitration, essential conditions are reasonableness and good temper, a willingness to recognize facts and to weigh arguments which make against one's own country as well as those which make for one's own country; and it is very important that in every country the people whom negotiators represent and to whom arbitrators must return, shall be able to consider the controversy and judge the action of their representatives in this instructed and reasonable way.

One means to bring about this desirable condition is to increase the general public knowledge of international rights and duties and to promote a popular habit of reading and thinking about international affairs. The more clearly the people of a country understand their own international rights the less likely they are to take extreme and extravagant views of their rights and the less likely they are to be ready to fight for something to which they are not really entitled. The more clearly and universally the people of a country realize the international obligations and duties of their country, the less likely they will be to resent the just demands of other countries that those obligations and duties be observed. The more familiar the people of a country are with the rules and customs of self-restraint and courtesy between nations which long experience has shown to be indispensable for preserving the peace of the world, the greater will be the tendency to refrain from publicly discussing controversies with other countries in such a way as to hinder peaceful settlement by wounding sensibilities or arousing anger and prejudice on the other side.

In every civil community it is necessary to have courts to determine rights and officers to compel observance of the law; yet the true basis of the peace and order in which we live is not fear of the policeman; it is the self-restraint of the thousands of people who make up the community and their willingness to obey the law and regard the rights of others. The true basis of business is not the sheriff with a writ of execution; it is the voluntary observance of the rules and obligations of business life which are universally recognized as essential to business success. Just so while it is highly important to have controversies between nations settled by arbitration rather than by war, and the growth of sentiment in favor of that peaceable method of settlement is one of the great advances in civilization to the credit of this generation; yet the true basis of peace among men is to be found in a just and considerate spirit among the people who rule our modern democracies, in their regard for the rights of other countries, and in their desire to be fair and kindly in the treatment of the subjects which give rise to international controversies.

Of course it cannot be expected that the whole body of any people will study international law; but a sufficient number can readily become sufficiently familiar with it to lead and form public opinion in every community in our country upon all important international questions as they arise.

For these reasons it seems to me that the influence of the new American Society of International Law and the publication of its *Quarterly* will be of practical benefit to the people of the United States; and I commend the Association and the *Quarterly* to the support of thoughtful men and women who wish to help in promoting the cause of international justice and peace.

THE REAL QUESTIONS UNDER THE JAPANESE TREATY AND THE SAN FRANCISCO SCHOOL BOARD RESOLUTION

PRESIDENTIAL ADDRESS AT THE FIRST ANNUAL MEETING OF THE AMERICAN SOCIETY OF INTERNATIONAL LAW WASHINGTON, D.C., APRIL 19, 1907

IN opening this meeting of the American Society of International Law, which I hope will be the first of many meetings in unbroken succession to continue long after we personally have ceased to take part in affairs, let me welcome you to the beginning of your labors for a more thorough understanding of this important and fascinating subject. It is impossible that the human mind should be addressed to questions better worth its noblest efforts, offering a greater opportunity for usefulness in the exercise of its powers, or more full of historical and contemporary interest, than in the field of international rights and duties. The change in the theory and practice of government which has marked the century since the establishment of the American Union has shifted the determination of great questions of domestic national policy from a few rulers in each country to the great body of the people, who render the ultimate decision under all modern constitutional governments. Coincident with that change the practice of diplomacy has ceased to be a mystery confined to a few learned men who strive to give effect to the wishes of personal rulers, and has become a representative function answering to the opinions and the will of the multitude of citizens, who themselves create the relations between states and determine the issues of friendship and estrangement, of peace and war. Under the new system there are many dangers from which the old system was free. The rules and customs which the experience of centuries had shown to be essential to the maintenance of peace and good understanding between nations have little weight with the new popular masters of diplomacy; the precedents and agreements of opinion which have carried so great a part of the rights and duties of nations toward each other beyond the pale of discussion are but little understood. The education of public opinion, which should lead the sovereign people in each country to understand the definite limitations upon national rights and the full scope and responsibility of national duties, has only just begun. Information, understanding, leadership of opinion in these matters, so vital to wise judgment and right action in international affairs, are much needed. This society may serve as a *collegium*, in the true sense of the word, in which all who choose to seek a broader knowledge of the law that governs the affairs of nations may give each to the other the incitement of earnest and faithful study and may give to the great body of our countrymen a clearer view of their international rights and responsibilities.

I shall detain you from the interesting program of instruction and discussion which has been arranged for this meeting only by trying to illustrate the kind of service that the society may render, in a few remarks intended to clear away a somewhat widespread popular misapprehension regarding a question arising under a treaty of the United States.

The treaty of November 22, 1894, between the United States and Japan provided, in the first article:

> The citizens or subjects of each of the two high contracting parties shall have full liberty to enter, travel, or reside in any part of the territory of the other contracting party, and shall enjoy full and perfect protection for their persons and property. . . .
>
> In whatever relates to rights of residence and travel; to the possession of goods and effects of any kind; to the succession to personal estate, by will or otherwise, and the disposal of property of any sort and in any man-

ner whatsoever which they may lawfully acquire, the citizens or subjects of each contracting party shall enjoy in the territories of the other the same privileges, liberties, and rights, and shall be subject to no higher imposts or charges in these respects than native citizens or subjects or citizens or subjects of the most favored nation.

The constitution of the state of California provides, in article 9:

SECTION 1. A general diffusion of knowledge and intelligence being essential to the preservation of the rights and liberties of the people, the legislature shall encourage by all suitable means the promotion of intellectual, scientific, moral and agricultural improvement.

SEC. 5. The legislature shall provide for a system of common schools, by which a free school shall be kept up and supported in each district at least six months in every year, after the first year in which a school has been established.

SEC. 6. The public school system shall include primary and grammar schools, and such high schools, evening schools, normal schools and technical schools as may be established by the legislature, or by municipal or district authority. The entire revenue derived from the state school fund and from the general state school tax shall be applied exclusively to the support of the primary and grammar schools.

The statutes of California establish the public school system required by the constitution. They provide that the State Comptroller must each year

estimate the amount necessary to raise the sum of seven dollars for each census child between the ages of five and seventeen years in the said state of California, which shall be the amount necessary to be raised by ad valorem tax for the school purposes during the year.

The statutes further provide that the Board of Education of San Francisco shall have authority

to establish and enforce all necessary rules and regulations for the government and efficiency of the schools [in that city] and for the carrying into effect the school system; to remedy truancy; and to compel attendance at school of children between the ages of six and fourteen years, who may be found idle in public places during school hours.

The statutes further provide, in section 1662 of the school law:

Every school, unless otherwise provided by law, must be open for the admission of all children between six and twenty-one years of age residing in the district, and the board of school trustees, or city board of education, have power to admit adults and children not residing in the district, whenever good reasons exist therefor. Trustees shall have the power to exclude children of filthy or vicious habits, or children suffering from contagious or infectious diseases, and also to establish separate schools for Indian children and for children of Mongolian or Chinese descent. When such separate schools are established, Indian, Chinese, or Mongolian children must not be admitted into any other school.

On October 11, 1906, the Board of Education of San Francisco adopted a resolution in these words:

Resolved: That in accordance with article X, section 1662, of the school law of California, principals are hereby directed to send all Chinese, Japanese, or Korean children to the Oriental Public School, situated on the south side of Clay Street, between Powell and Mason Streets, on and after Monday, October 15, 1906.

The school system thus provided school privileges for all resident children, whether citizen or alien; all resident children were included in the basis for estimating the amount to be raised by taxation for school purposes; the fund for the support of the school was raised by general taxation upon all property of resident aliens as well as of citizens; and all resident children, whether of aliens or of citizens, were liable to be compelled to attend the schools. So that, under the resolution of the Board of Education, the children of resident aliens of all other nationalities were freely admitted to the schools of the city in the neighborhood of their homes, while the children of Indians, Chinese and Japanese were excluded from those schools, and were not only deprived of education unless they consented to go to the special oriental school on Clay Street, but were liable to be forcibly compelled to go to that particular school.

After the passage of this resolution, admission to the ordinary primary schools of San Francisco was denied to Japanese children, and thereupon the Government of Japan made representations to the Government of the United States that inasmuch as the children of residents who were citizens of all other foreign countries were freely admitted to the schools, the citizens of Japan residing in the United States were, by that exclusion, denied the same privileges, liberties, and rights relating to the right of residence which were accorded to the citizens or subjects of the most favored nation. The questions thus raised were promptly presented by the Government of the United States to the federal court in California, and also to the state court of California, in appropriate legal proceedings. The matter has been happily disposed of without proceeding to judgment in either case; but in the meantime there was much excited discussion of the subject in the newspapers and in public meetings and in private conversation.

It is a pleasure to be able to say that never for a moment was there as between the Government of the United States and the Government of Japan, the slightest departure from perfect good temper, mutual confidence, and kindly consideration; and that no sooner had the views and purposes of the Governments of the United States, the state of California, and the city of San Francisco been explained by each to the other than entire harmony and good understanding resulted, with a common desire to exercise the powers vested in each, for the common good of the whole country, of the state, and of the city.

The excitement has now subsided, so that it may be useful to consider what the question really was, not because it is necessary for the purposes of that particular case, but because of its bearing upon cases which may arise in the future under the application of the treaty-making power of the United States to other matters and in other parts of the national domain.

It is obvious that three distinct questions were raised by the claim originating with Japan and presented by our national government to the courts in San Francisco. The first and second were merely questions of construction of the treaty. Was the right to attend the primary schools a right, liberty, or privilege of residence ? and, if so, was the limitation of Japanese children to the oriental school and their exclusion from the ordinary schools a deprivation of that right, liberty, or privilege ? These questions of construction, and especially the second, are by no means free from doubt; but as they concern only the meaning of a particular clause in a particular treaty they are not of permanent importance, and, the particular occasion for their consideration having passed, they need not now be discussed.

The other question was whether, if the treaty had the meaning which the Government of Japan ascribed to it, the Government of the United States had the constitutional power to make such a treaty agreement with a foreign nation which should be superior to and controlling upon the laws of the state of California. A correct understanding of that question is of the utmost importance not merely as regards the state of California, but as regards all states and all citizens of the Union.

There was a very general misapprehension of what this treaty really undertook to do. It was assumed that in making and asserting the validity of the treaty of 1894 the United States was asserting the right to compel the state of California to admit Japanese children to its schools. No such question was involved. That treaty did not, by any possible construction, assert the authority of the United States to compel any state to maintain public schools, or to extend the privileges of its public schools to Japanese children or to the children of any alien residents. The treaty did assert the right of the United States, by treaty, to assure to the citizens of a foreign nation residing in American territory equality of treatment with the citizens of other foreign nations, so that if any state chooses to extend privileges to alien residents as well as to citizen residents, the state will be forbidden by the obligation of the treaty to discriminate against the resident citizens of the particular country with which the treaty is made and will be forbidden to deny to them the privileges which it grants to the citizens of other foreign countries. The effect of such a treaty, in respect of education, is not positive and compulsory; it is negative and prohibitory. It is not a requirement that the state shall furnish education; it is a prohibition against discrimination when the state does choose to furnish education. It leaves every state free to have public schools or not, as it chooses, but it says to every state: " If you provide a system of education which includes alien children, you must not exclude these particular alien children."

It has been widely asserted or assumed that this treaty provision and its enforcement involved some question of state's rights. There was and is no question of state's rights involved, unless it be the question which was settled by the adoption of the Constitution.

This will be apparent upon considering the propositions which I will now state:

1. The people of the United States, by the Constitution of 1787, vested the whole treaty-making power in the national government. They provided:

The president shall have power, by and with the advice and consent of the senate, to make treaties, provided two-thirds of the senators present concur. (Art. II, sec. 2.)

No state shall enter into any treaty, alliance or confederation; . . . No state shall, without the consent of congress, . . . enter into any agreement or compact with another state, or with a foreign power. (Art. I, sec. 10.)

This constitution, and the laws of the United States which shall be made in pursuance thereof, and all treaties made, or which shall be made under the authority of the United States, shall be the supreme law of the land; and the judges in every state shall be bound thereby, anything in the constitution or laws of any state to the contrary notwithstanding. (Art. VI.)

Legislative power is distributed: upon some subjects the national legislature has authority; upon other subjects the state legislature has authority. Judicial power is distributed: in some cases the federal courts have jurisdiction, in other cases the state courts have jurisdiction. Executive power is distributed: in some fields the national executive is to act; in other fields the state executive is to act. The treaty-making power is not distributed; it is all vested in the national government; no part of it is vested in or reserved to the states. In international affairs there are no states; there is but one nation, acting in direct relation to and representation of every citizen in every state. Every treaty made under the authority of the United States is made by the national government, as the direct and sole representative of every citizen of the United States residing in California equally with every citizen of the United States residing elsewhere. It is, of course, conceivable that, under pretense of exercising the treaty-making power, the President and Senate might attempt to make provisions regarding matters which are not proper subjects of international agreement, and which would be only a colorable — not a real — exercise of the treaty-making power; but so far as the real exercise of the power goes, there can be no question of state rights, because the Constitution itself, in the most explicit terms, has precluded the existence of any such question.

2. Although there are no express limitations upon the treaty-making power granted to the national government, there are certain implied limitations arising from the nature of our government and from other provisions of the Constitution; but those implied limitations do not in the slightest degree touch the making of treaty provisions relating to the treatment of aliens within our territory.

In the case of Geofroy *v.* Riggs, which, in 1889, sustained the rights of French citizens under the treaty of 1800 to take and hold real and personal property in contravention of the common law and the statutes of the state of Maryland, the Supreme Court of the United States said:

> That the treaty power of the United States extends to all proper subjects of negotiation between our government and the governments of other nations is clear. . . . The treaty power, as expressed in the constitution, is in terms unlimited except by those restraints which are found in that instrument against the action of the government or of its departments, and those arising from the nature of the government itself and of that of the states. It would not be contended that it extends so far as to authorize what the constitution forbids, or a change in the character of the government, or in that of one of the states, or a cession of any portion of the territory of the latter without its consent. But with these exceptions it is not perceived that there is any limit to the questions which can be adjusted touching any matter which is properly the subject of negotiation with a foreign country.

3. Reciprocal agreements between nations regarding the treatment which the citizens of each nation shall receive in the territory of the other nation are among the most familiar, ordinary and unquestioned exercises of the treaty-making power. To secure the citizens of one's country against discriminatory laws and discriminatory administration in the foreign countries where they may travel or trade or reside is, and always has been, one of the chief objects of treaty making, and such provisions always have been reciprocal.

During the entire history of the United States provisions of this description have been included in our treaties of friendship, commerce and navigation with practically all the other nations of the world. Such provisions had been from time immemorial the subject of treaty agreements among the nations of Europe before American independence; and the power to make such provisions was exercised without question by the Continental Congress in the treaties which it made prior to the adoption of our Constitution. The treaty of 1778 with France, made between the Most Christian King and the thirteen United States of North America by name, contained such provisions. So did the treaty of 1782 between Their High Mightinesses the States-General of the United Netherlands and the thirteen United States of America by name.

The treaty of 1785 with Prussia, ratified by the Continental Congress on May 17, 1786, contained an exercise of the same kind of power. Mr. Bancroft Davis summarizes the provisions of this character in the Prussian treaty in these words:

> The favored nation clause put Prussia on the best footing in the ports of Charleston, Boston, Philadelphia and New York, no matter what the legislatures of South Carolina, Massachusetts, Pennsylvania, or New York might say. Aliens were permitted to hold personal property and dispose of it by testament, donation, or otherwise, and the exaction of state dues in excess of those exacted from citizens of the state in like cases were forbidden. The right was secured to aliens to frequent the coasts of each and all the states, and to reside and trade there. Resident aliens were assured against state legislation to prevent the exercise of liberty of conscience and the performance of religious worship; and when dying, they were guaranteed the right of decent burial and undisturbed rest for their bodies.

It is not open to doubt that when the delegates of these thirteen states conferred the power to make treaties upon the new national government in the broadest possible terms and without any words of limitation, the subjects about which they themselves had been making the treaties then in force were included in the power.

The treaty of July 28, 1868, between the United States and China — the celebrated Burlingame Treaty — contained, in the sixth article, a provision in the very words of the Japanese treaty. That article provided:

> Citizens of the United States visiting or residing in China shall enjoy the same privileges, immunities or exemptions in respect to travel or residence as may there be enjoyed by the citizens or subjects of the most favored nation. And, reciprocally, Chinese subjects visiting or residing in the United States, shall enjoy the same privileges, immunities, and exemptions in respect to travel or residence, as may there be enjoyed by the citizens or subjects of the most favored nation.

In the case of Tiburicio Parrot (6 Sawyer, 368) the Circuit Court of the United States said, Mr. Justice Sawyer reading the opinion:

As to the point whether the provision in question is within the treaty-making power, I have as little doubt as upon the point already discussed. Among all civilized nations, in modern times at least, the treaty-making power has been accustomed to determine the terms and conditions upon which the subjects of the parties to the treaty shall reside in the respective countries, and the treaty-making power is conferred by the Constitution in unlimited terms. Besides, the authorities cited on the first point fully cover and determine this question. If the treaty-making power is authorized to determine what foreigners shall be permitted to come into and reside within the country, and who shall be excluded, it must have the power generally to determine and prescribe upon what terms and conditions such as are admitted shall be permitted to remain.

And regarding the same treaty the Supreme Court of the United States remarked, in the case of Baldwin v. Franks (120 U. S., 679):

That the United States have power under the Constitution to provide for the punishment of those who are guilty of depriving Chinese subjects of any of the rights, privileges, immunities, or exemptions guaranteed to them by this treaty we do not doubt.

4. It has been settled for more than a century that the fact that a treaty provision would interfere with or annul the laws of a state as to the aliens concerning whom the provision is made, is no impeachment of the treaty's authority.

The very words of the Constitution, that the judges in every state shall be bound by a treaty " anything in the constitution or laws of any state to the contrary notwithstanding," necessarily imply an expectation that some treaties will be made in contravention of laws of the states. Far from the treaty-making power being limited by state laws, its scope is entirely independent of those laws; and whenever it deals with the same subject, if inconsistent with the law, it annuls the law. This is true as to any laws of the states, whether the legislative authority under which they are passed is concurrent with that of Congress, or exclusive of that of Congress.

In the case of Ware *v.* Hylton the Supreme Court of the United States, in the year 1796, considered the effect under the Constitution of the treaty of peace with England of 1783, which provided that

creditors on either side should meet with no lawful impediment to the recovery of the full value in stirling money, of all *bona fide* debts, theretofore contracted,

as against a law of the state of Virginia, which confiscated to the state of Virginia the debts due from its citizens to British subjects.

The court said:

There can be no limitation on the power of the people of the United States. By their authority the state constitutions were made, and by their authority the Constitution of the United States was established; and they had the power to change or abolish the state constitutions, or to make them yield to the general government and to treaties made by their authority. A treaty cannot be the supreme law of the land — that is, of all the United States — if any act of a state legislature can stand in its way. If the constitution of a state (which is the fundamental law of the state, and paramount to its legislature) must give way to a treaty and fall before it, can it be questioned whether the less power, an act of the state legislature, must not be prostrate ? It is the declared will of the people of the United States that every treaty made by the authority of the United States shall be superior to the constitution and laws of any individual state; and their will alone is to decide. . . .

Four things are apparent on a view of this sixth article of the national Constitution: 1st. That it is retrospective, and is to be considered in the same light as if the Constitution had been established before the making of the treaty of 1783. 2d. That the constitution or laws of any of the states, so far as either of them shall be found contrary to that treaty, are by force of the said article prostrated before the treaty. 3d. That, consequently, the treaty of 1783 has superior power to the legislature of any state, because no legislature of any state has any kind of power over the Constitution, which was its creator. 4th. That it is the declared duty of the state judges to determine any constitution or laws of any state contrary to that treaty (or any other), made under the authority of the United States, null and void. National or federal judges are bound by duty and oath to the same conduct.

In the case of Fairfax *v*. Hunter, in 1812, Mr. Justice Story delivering the opinion, the supreme court of the United States sustained the title of a British subject, under the provisions of the treaty of 1794, in direct contravention of the laws of the state of Virginia. In the case of Chirac *v*. Chirac, in 1817, Chief Justice Marshall delivering the opinion, the Supreme Court of the United States sustained the title of a French subject to real estate in Maryland, in direct contravention of the laws of that state. A long line of cases have followed in the Supreme Court applying the provisions of various treaties and maintaining without exception the unvarying rule that the state statute falls before the treaty.

It equally appears from these cases that the treaty provisions which were sustained by the Supreme Court and the state laws which were declared void, so far as they conflicted with a treaty, related to matters regarding which Congress had no power to legislate, but upon which, in the distribution of legislative powers under the Constitution, the states, and the states alone, had power to legislate.

5. Since the rights, privileges, and immunities, both of person and property, to be accorded to foreigners in our country and to our citizens in foreign countries are a proper subject of treaty provision and within the limits of the treaty-making power, and since such rights, privileges, and immunities may be given by treaty in contravention of the laws of any state, it follows of necessity that the treaty-making power alone has authority to determine what those rights, privileges, and immunities shall be. No state can set up its laws as against the grant of any particular right, privilege, or immunity any more than against the grant of any other right, privilege, or immunity. No state can say a treaty may grant to alien residents equality of treatment as to property but not as to education, or as to the exercise of religion and as to burial but not as to education, or as to education but not as to property

or religion. That would be substituting the mere will of the state for the judgments of the President and Senate in exercising a power committed to them and prohibited to the states by the Constitution.

There was, therefore, no real question of power arising under this Japanese treaty and no question of state rights.

There were, however, questions of policy, questions of national interests and of state interests, arising under the administration of the treaty and regarding the application of its provisions to the conditions existing on the Pacific coast.

In the distribution of powers under our composite system of government the people of San Francisco had three sets of interests committed to three different sets of officers — their special interest as citizens of the principal city and commercial port of the Pacific coast represented by the city government of San Francisco; their interest in common with all the people of the state of California represented by the governor and legislature at Sacramento; and their interests in common with all the people of the United States represented by the national government at Washington. Each one of these three different governmental agencies had authority to do certain things relating to the treatment of Japanese residents in San Francisco. These three interests could not be really in conflict; for the best interest of the whole country is always the true interest of every state and city, and the protection of the interests of every locality in the country is always the true interest of the nation. There was, however, a supposed or apparent clashing of interests, and, to do away with this, conference, communication, comparison of views, explanation of policy and purpose were necessary. Many thoughtless and some mischievous persons have spoken and written regarding these conferences and communications as if they were the parleying and compromise of enemies. On the contrary, they were an example of the way in which the public business ought always to be conducted; so that the different public officers respectively charged with the performance of duties affecting the same subject-matter may work together in furtherance of the same public policy and with a common purpose for the good of the whole country and every part of the country. Such a concert of action with such a purpose was established by the conferences and communications between the national authorities and the authorities of California and San Francisco which followed the passage of the Board of Education resolution.

There was one great and serious question underlying the whole subject which made all questions of construction and of scope and of effect of the treaty itself — all questions as to whether the claims of Japan were well founded or not, all questions as to whether the resolution of the School Board was valid or not — seem temporary and comparatively unimportant. It was not a question of war with Japan. All the foolish talk about war was purely sensational and imaginative. There was never even friction between the two governments. The question was, What state of feeling would be created between the great body of the people of the United States and the great body of the people of Japan as a result of the treatment given to the Japanese in this country?

What was to be the effect upon that proud, sensitive, highly civilized people across the Pacific, of the discourtesy, insult, imputations of inferiority and abuse aimed at them in the columns of American newspapers and from the platforms of American public meetings? What would be the effect upon our own people of the responses that natural resentment for such treatment would elicit from the Japanese?

The first article of the first treaty Japan ever made with a western power provided:

> There shall be a perfect, permanent, and universal peace and a sincere and cordial amity between the United States of America on the one part,

and the empire of Japan on the other part, and between their people respectively, without exception of persons or places.

Under that treaty, which bore the signature of Matthew Calbraith Perry, we introduced Japan to the world of western civilization. We had always been proud of her wonderful development — proud of the genius of the race that in a single generation adapted an ancient feudal system of the far East to the most advanced standards of modern Europe and America. The friendship between the two nations had been peculiar and close. Was the declaration of that treaty to be set aside ? At Kurihama, in Japan, stands a monument to Commodore Perry, raised by the Japanese in grateful appreciation, upon the site where he landed and opened negotiations for the treaty. Was that monument henceforth to represent dislike and resentment ? Were the two peoples to face each other across the Pacific in future years with angry and resentful feelings ? All this was inevitable if the process which seemed to have begun was to continue, and the government of the United States looked with the greatest solicitude upon the possibility that the process might continue.

It is hard for democracy to learn the responsibilities of its power; but the people now, not governments, make friendship or dislike, sympathy or discord, peace or war, between nations. In this modern day, through the columns of the myriad press and messages flashing over countless wires, multitude calls to multitude across boundaries and oceans in courtesy or insult, in amity or in defiance. Foreign offices and ambassadors and ministers no longer keep or break the peace, but the conduct of each people toward every other. The people who permit themselves to treat the people of other countries with discourtesy and insult are surely sowing the wind to reap the whirlwind, for a world of sullen and revengeful hatred can never be a world of peace. Against such a feeling treaties are waste paper and diplomacy the empty routine of idle form. The great question which overshadowed all discussion of the treaty of 1894 was the question: Are the people of the United States about to break friendship with the people of Japan? That question, I believe, has been happily answered in the negative.

THE SANCTION OF INTERNATIONAL LAW

PRESIDENTIAL ADDRESS AT THE SECOND ANNUAL MEETING
OF THE AMERICAN SOCIETY OF INTERNATIONAL LAW
WASHINGTON, APRIL 24, 1908

ONE accustomed to the administration of municipal law who turns his attention for the first time to the discussion of practical questions arising between nations and dependent upon the rules of international law, must be struck by a difference between the two systems which materially affects the intellectual processes involved in every discussion, and which is apparently fundamental.

The proofs and arguments adduced by the municipal lawyer are addressed to the object of setting in motion certain legal machinery which will result in a judicial judgment to be enforced by the entire power of the state over litigants subject to its jurisdiction and control. Before him lies a clear, certain, definite conclusion of the controversy, and for the finality and effectiveness of that conclusion the sheriff and the policeman stand always as guarantors in the last resort.

When the international lawyer, on the other hand, passes from the academic discussion in which he has no one to convince but himself, and proceeds to seek the establishment of rights or the redress of wrongs in a concrete case, he has apparently no objective point to which he can address his proofs or arguments, except the conscience and sense of justice of the opposing party to the controversy. In only rare, exceptional and peculiar cases, do the conclusions of the international lawyer, however clearly demonstrated, have behind them the compulsory effect of possible war. In the vast majority of practical questions arising under the rule of international law there does not appear on the surface to be any reason why either party should abandon its own contention or yield against its own interest to the arguments of the other side. The action of each party in yielding or refusing to yield to the arguments of the other appears to be entirely dependent upon its own will and pleasure. This apparent absence of sanction for the enforcement of the rules of international law has led great authority to deny that those rules are entitled to be called law at all; and this apparent hopelessness of finality carries to the mind which limits its consideration to the procedure in each particular case, a certain sense of futility of argument.

Nevertheless, all the foreign offices of the civilized world are continually discussing with each other questions of international law, both public and private, cheerfully and hopefully marshaling facts, furnishing evidence, presenting arguments, and building up records, designed to show that the rules of international law require such and such things to be done or such and such things to be left undone. And in countless cases nations are yielding to such arguments and shaping their conduct against their own apparent interests in the particular cases under discussion, in obedience to the rules which are shown to be applicable.

Why is it that nations are thus continually yielding to arguments with no apparent compulsion behind them, and before the force of such arguments abandoning purposes, modifying conduct, and giving redress for injuries ? A careful consideration of this question seems to lead to the conclusion that the difference between municipal and international law, in respect of the existence of forces compelling obedience, is more apparent than real, and that there are sanctions for the enforcement of international law no less real and substantial than those which secure obedience to municipal law.

It is a mistake to assume that the sanction which secures obedience to the laws of the state consists exclusively or chiefly of the pains and penalties imposed by the law itself for its violation. It is only in exceptional cases that men refrain from crime through fear of fine or imprisonment. In the vast majority of cases men refrain from criminal conduct because they are unwilling to incur in the community in which they live the public condemnation and obloquy which would follow a repudiation of the standard of conduct prescribed by that community for its members. As a rule, when the law is broken the disgrace which follows conviction and punishment is more terrible than the actual physical effect of imprisonment or deprivation of property. Where it happens that the law and public opinion point different ways, the latter is invariably the stronger. I have seen a lad grown up among New York toughs break down and weep because sent to a reformatory instead of being sentenced to a state's prison for a violation of law. The reformatory meant comparative ease, comfort, and opportunity for speedy return to entire freedom; the state's prison would have meant hard labor and long and severe confinement. Yet in his community of habitual criminals a term in state's prison was a proof of manhood and a title to distinction, while consignment to a reformatory was the treatment suited to immature boyhood. He preferred the punishment of manhood with what he deemed honor to the opportunity of youth with what he deemed disgrace. Not only is the effectiveness of the punishments denounced by law against crime derived chiefly from the public opinion which accompanies them, but those punishments themselves are but one form of the expression of public opinion. Laws are capable of enforcement only so far as they are in agreement with the opinions of the community in which they are to be enforced. As opinion changes old laws become obsolete and new standards force their way into the statute books. Laws passed, as they sometimes are, in advance of public opinion ordinarily wait for their enforcement until the progress of opinion has reached recognition of their value. The force of law is in the public opinion which prescribes it.

The impulse of conformity to the standard of the community and the dread of its condemnation are reënforced by the practical considerations which determine success or failure in life. Conformity to the standard of business integrity which obtains in the community is necessary to business success. It is this consideration far more frequently than the thought of the sheriff with a writ of execution that leads men to pay their debts and to keep their contracts. Social esteem and standing, power and high place in the professions, in public office, in all associated enterprise, depend upon conformity to the standards of conduct in the community. Loss of these is the most terrible penalty society can inflict. It is only for the occasional nonconformist that the sheriff and policeman are kept in reserve; and it is only because the nonconformists are occasional and comparatively few in number that the sheriff and the policeman can have any effect at all. For the great mass of mankind laws established by civil society are enforced directly by the power of public opinion, having, as the sanction for its judgments, the denial of nearly everything for which men strive in life.

The rules of international law are enforced by the same kind of sanction, less certain and peremptory, but continually increasing in effectiveness of control. "A decent respect to the opinions of mankind" did not begin or end among nations with the American Declaration of Independence; but it is interesting that the first public national act in the New World should be an appeal to that universal international public opinion, the power and effectiveness of which the New World has done so much to promote.

In former times, each isolated nation, satisfied with its own opinion of itself and indifferent to the opinion of others, separated from all others by mutual ignorance and misjudgment, regarded only the physical power of other nations. Gibbon could say of the Byzantine Empire: " Alone in the universe, the self-satisfied pride of the Greeks was not disturbed by the comparison of foreign merit; and it is no wonder if they fainted in the race, since they had neither competitors to urge their speed nor judges to crown their victory." Now, however, there may be seen plainly the effects of a long-continued process which is breaking down the isolation of nations, permeating every country with better knowledge and understanding of every other country, spreading throughout the world a knowledge of each government's conduct to serve as a basis for criticism and judgment, and gradually creating a community of nations, in which standards of conduct are being established, and a world-wide public opinion is holding nations to conformity or condemning them for disregard of the established standards. The improved facilities for travel and transportation, the enormous increase of production and commerce, the revival of colonization and the growth of colonies on a gigantic scale, the severance of the laborer from the soil, accomplished by cheap steamship and railway transportation and the emigration agent, the flow and return of millions of emigrants across national lines, the amazing development of telegraphy and of the press, conveying and spreading instant information of every interesting event that happens in regions however remote — all have played their part in this change.

Pari passu with the breaking down of isolation, that makes a common public opinion possible, the building up of standards of conduct is being accomplished by the formulation and establishment of rules that are being gradually taken out of the domain of discussion into that of general acceptance, a process in which the recent conferences at The Hague have played a great and honorable part. There is no civilized country now which is not sensitive to this general opinion, none that is willing to subject itself to the discredit of standing brutally on its power to deny to other countries the benefit of recognized rules of right conduct. The deference shown to this international public opinion is in due proportion to a nation's greatness and advance in civilization. The nearest approach to defiance will be found among the most isolated and least civilized of countries, whose ignorance of the world prevents the effect of the world's opinion; and in every such country internal disorder, oppression, poverty, and wretchedness mark the penalties which warn mankind that the laws established by civilization for the guidance of national conduct cannot be ignored with impunity.

National regard for international opinion is not caused by *amour propre* alone — not merely by desire for the approval and good opinion of mankind. Underlying the desire for approval and the aversion to general condemnation with nations as with the individual, there is a deep sense of interest, based partly upon the knowledge that mankind backs its opinions by its conduct and that nonconformity to the standard of nations means condemnation and isolation, and partly upon the knowledge that in the give and take of international affairs it is better for every nation to secure the protection of the law by complying with it than to forfeit the law's benefits by ignoring it.

Beyond all this there is a consciousness that in the most important affairs of nations, in their political status, the success of their undertakings and their processes of development, there is an indefinite and almost mysterious influence exercised by the general opinion of the world regarding the nation's character and conduct. The greatest and strongest governments recognize this influence and act with reference to it. They dread the moral isolation created by general adverse opinion and the unfriendly feeling that accompanies it, and they desire general approval and the kindly feeling that goes with it.

This is quite independent of any calculation upon a physical enforcement of the opinion of others. It is difficult to say just why such opinion is of importance, because it is always difficult to analyze the action of moral forces; but it remains true and is universally recognized that the nation which has with it the moral force of the world's approval is strong, and the nation which rests under the world's condemnation is weak, however great its material power.

These are the considerations which determine the course of national conduct regarding the vast majority of questions to which are to be applied the rules of international law. The real sanction which enforces those rules is the injury which inevitably follows nonconformity to public opinion; while, for the occasional and violent or persistent law-breaker, there always stands behind discussion the ultimate possibility of war, as the sheriff and the policeman await the occasional and comparatively rare violators of municipal law.

Of course, the force of public opinion can be brought to bear only upon comparatively simple questions and clearly ascertained and understood rights. Upon complicated or doubtful questions, as to which judgment is difficult, each party to the controversy can maintain its position of refusing to yield to the other's arguments without incurring public condemnation. Upon this class of questions the growth of arbitration furnishes a new and additional opportunity for opinion to act; because, however complicated the question in dispute may be, the proposition that it should be submitted to an impartial tribunal is exceedingly simple, and the proposition that the award of such a tribunal shall be complied with is equally simple, and the nation which refuses to submit a question properly the subject of arbitration naturally invites condemnation.

Manifestly, this power of international public opinion is exercised not so much by governments as by the people of each country whose opinions are interpreted in the press and determine the country's attitude towards the nation whose conduct is under consideration. International opinion is the consensus of individual opinion in the nations. The most certain way to promote obedience to the law of nations and to substitute the power of opinion for the power of armies and navies is, on the one hand, to foster that " decent respect to the opinions of mankind " which found place in the great Declaration of 1776, and, on the other hand, to spread among the people of every country a just appreciation of international rights and duties and a knowledge of the principles and rules of international law to which national conduct ought to conform; so that the general opinion, whose approval or condemnation supplies the sanction for the law, may be sound and just and worthy of respect.

THE RELATIONS BETWEEN INTERNATIONAL TRIBUNALS OF ARBITRATION AND THE JURISDICTION OF NATIONAL COURTS

PRESIDENTIAL ADDRESS AT THE THIRD ANNUAL MEETING OF
THE AMERICAN SOCIETY OF INTERNATIONAL LAW
WASHINGTON, APRIL 23, 1909

THE growing tendency towards international arbitration brings into special consideration and importance the relation between the jurisdiction of national courts of justice and international tribunals of arbitration.

When one nation urges claims in behalf of its citizens upon the government of another nation and proposes arbitration, how far does that other nation's respect for its own independent sovereignty and for the integrity of its own judicial system require it to insist that the claims be submitted for final decision to its own national courts?

The true basis for the consideration of this question is in the nature of the obligation which constrains a nation to submit questions to any tribunal whatever.

That there is no legal obligation to make any submission, that is to say, that it is not required by any rule imposed by a superior power, is a corollary from our conception of sovereignty. Sovereignty involves the right to determine one's own actions — to pay or not to pay, to redress injury or not to redress it, at the will of the sovereign, subject only to the necessary conditions created by the existence of other equally independent states. So far as questions arise out of contract, Alexander Hamilton states the strongest view of national freedom from restraint in a passage often quoted in recent years:

Contracts between a nation and private individuals are obligatory, according to the conscience of the sovereign, and may not be the object of compelling force. They confer no right of action contrary to the sovereign will.

So far as questions arise out of alleged wrongs by one government against a citizen of another, the sovereignty of one nation is merely confronted by another sovereignty, which is itself equally supreme within its own limits. Wherever the true lines are to be drawn between two mutually exclusive sovereignties, each is supreme and subject to no compulsion on its own side of the line. Wherever there is infringement by one on the other there exists the right of adverse action, which involves no impeachment of independent sovereignty, but follows necessarily from the contact of two independent powers. Whatever modifications international lawyers urge to the broad statement of doctrine to which Doctor Calvo has given his name, so ably enforced by his successor, Dr. Drago, there is no effective dispute regarding the foundation of his main proposition, regarding the essential nature of sovereignty.

The conditions under which this sovereign power is exercised among civilized nations do, however, impose upon it important limitations, just as the conditions under which individual liberty is enjoyed in a free civil community impose limitations upon individual conduct in matters not at all controlled by law. Municipal law does not, in general, undertake to compel men to be virtuous, truthful, sober, fair, polite, and considerate of others. Yet the existence of civil liberty is conditioned upon the existence of a community standard of conduct quite independent of legal compulsion, and extending far beyond the limits touched by any statute. The member of a community who chooses to use his individual liberty to violate that standard conspicuously, meets severe punishment in the loss of respect, confidence, and esteem, and in the consequences of that loss. Another very

ARBITRATION AND NATIONAL COURTS

effective limitation upon conduct is the knowledge that certain courses of conduct quite within one's legal rights may lead some other man to use his individual freedom, to do one injury. The compulsion which such considerations produce upon individual action is no more an infringement upon individual liberty than is the effect caused by the knowledge that fire will burn and water will drown. The individual in each case regulates his own conduct in accordance with his own will.

The assertion of independent sovereignty of nations is but another expression of the individual liberty of each nation in the community of nations. In its practical application it is of modern acceptance, superseding the old idea that each nation, tribe or group of people under whatever chieftain, leader, sovereign, or government, was entitled to hold such territory and exercise such control over its own conduct, as it could maintain by force of arms, and no more.

The theory of independent sovereignty, entitled to be respected by all mankind without regard to its power to maintain itself by force, could find no place in the world except in coincidence with a standard of international conduct to which the nations generally, in the exercise of their individual sovereignty, conform, each without compulsion of any other power, but voluntarily.

The chief principle entering into this standard of conduct is that every sovereign nation is willing at all times and under all circumstances to do what is just. That is the universal postulate of all modern diplomatic discussion. No nation would for a moment permit its own conformity to the standard in this respect, to be questioned. The obligation which this willingness implies is no impeachment of sovereignty. It is voluntarily assumed as an incident to the exercise of sovereignty because it is essential to a continuance of the conditions under which the independence of sovereignty is possible. This obligation is by universal consent interpreted according to established and accepted rules as to what constitutes justice under certain known and frequently recurring conditions; and these accepted rules we call international law. No demand can ever be made by one nation upon another to give redress in any case but that the demand is met by an avowed readiness to do justice in that case, and upon that demand in accordance with the rules of international law. No compulsion upon sovereignty is needed to reach that result.

The only question that can arise upon such a demand is the question, "What is just in this case?" In that necessary condition of agreement upon the underlying principle to be followed, a common duty is presented to both nations to ascertain and determine what is just.

It is not usually a simple or easy thing to determine what is just as between a nation and either its own citizens or the citizens of other nations. Upon one conclusion all civilized nations are in accord — that the executive and administrative officers of government cannot be depended upon to make such determinations. Civilized nations uniformly provide machinery for judicial decision of such questions so that the views of executive and administrative officers in rejecting claims may be reviewed and controlled. The grant of jurisdiction to courts or the creation of courts to exercise such jurisdiction is no disparagement of the officers whose views of what is just are thus called in question. Sovereigns and presidents and ministers and department officers are not insulted by such provisions, or because the common sense of justice recognizes that their relation to the questions which arise between the government which they conduct, and others, is such that they cannot well be impartial.

The whole system by which sovereign states permit themselves to be sued in courts vested with jurisdiction for that purpose is in recognition of the fundamental rule of right that none shall be a judge in his own case.

That same great rule cannot be ignored when the question is whether the decision of a national court is to be taken as a final and satisfactory determination of what is just in an international case, to which the judge's own country is a party. For after all judges are but men. They are part of the government that is called in question. They are subject to the influence of their environment. They cannot always escape all the influences of popular feeling and prejudice in their own communities. The political fortunes of the very officials who appointed them to the bench, or their own tenure of office may perhaps be at stake upon their action. They cannot help bringing to the bench strong tendencies and predilections in favor of their own countrymen's ways of acting and thinking. They desire the approbation of their fellow-citizens, and in cases of public interest it may be much harder to decide against than for, their own country. It is difficult for a foreigner to understand and avail himself of their modes of reasoning, their rules of evidence and of procedure, and the precedents they follow. If there is a difference of languages a stranger is at a great disadvantage. He may often lose his case through not knowing how to do his part towards maintaining it.

There are many circumstances varying in different countries and in different cases which tend to strengthen or to weaken these obstacles to a satisfactory attainment of justice. The general state of feeling in the country of trial towards the country of the complainant and its effect upon the atmosphere of the court room, that every experienced lawyer knows to be so important, is one of these circumstances. The relative importance of the case in proportion to the resources of the country — whether an adverse decision would make a slight or a great difference to the government or the people, is another. Whether the action of the executive has been generally discussed and has assumed political importance is another.

Every country is entitled to follow its own judgment and is not subject to criticism for following its own judgment, as to the degree of independence it shall give to its judiciary, yet it cannot well be denied that with human nature as it is, there is less certainty of an impartial decision from judges removable at will in a case calling in question the acts of the appointing and removing power, than from judges whose tenure of office is not dependent upon the executive. The decision of such a dependent court is liable to be affected by the same infirmities which the whole world recognizes as making the determination of the executive itself an unsatisfactory method of concluding the search for justice.

It should not be forgotten that it is not only desirable to have justice done; but also to have men believe that justice is done. That belief is important to respect for law among the people within each nation and to the maintenance and growth of respect and friendship between the peoples of different nations.

Of course there are many cases falling naturally into the ordinary routine of national judicial procedure — cases plainly not presenting the elements of prejudice which would prevent reaching justice through that procedure. Of course there are many great international questions which no one would ever propose to lay before a national tribunal. Between these two extremes there is a wide range of cases in which national courts may exercise jurisdiction, but to which the considerations that I have suggested apply. When such cases arise the international question is not one of compulsion or derogation from sovereignty, but it is: How shall two nations desiring to ascertain what is the truth of justice in

ARBITRATION AND NATIONAL COURTS

this case reach a decision? By what procedure and before what tribunal can that end best be attained?

If recourse to arbitration is a reflection upon national courts, the people of the United States have been strangely obtuse, for nowhere in the world, surely, is greater honor paid to the courts of justice, yet we have embodied in the fundamental law which binds our states together a recognition of the liability of courts to be affected by local sentiment, prejudice, and pressure. We have provided in the third article of the Constitution of the United States that in controversies between states or between citizens of different states the determination of what is just shall not be confined to the courts of justice of either state, but may be brought in the Federal tribunals, selected and empowered by the representatives of both states and of all the states — true arbitral tribunals in the method of their creation and the office they perform.

Alexander Hamilton explains this provision in *The Federalist* in these words:

> The reasonableness of the agency of the National courts in cases in which the state tribunals cannot be supposed to be impartial, speaks for itself. No man ought certainly to be a judge in his own cause, or in any cause in respect to which he has the slightest interest or bias. This principle has no inconsiderable weight in designating the Federal courts as the proper tribunals for the determination of controversies between different states and their citizens. And it ought to have the same operation in regard to some cases between the citizens of the same state. Claims to lands under grants of different states founded upon adverse pretension of boundary are of this description. The courts of neither of the granting states could be expected to be unbiased. The laws may have even prejudged the question and tied the courts down to decisions in favor of the grant of the state to which they belonged. And where this has not been done it would be natural that judges as men should feel a strong predilection to the claims of their own government.

The whole world owes too much to the Constitution of the United States to think little of its example. Especially the

American nations, which have drawn from that great instrument their forms of government and the spirit of their free institutions, must regard with respect the lesson which it teaches.

The proud independent sovereign commonwealths like Virginia and Pennsylvania and New York and Massachusetts, which formed the American Union, revered their judges. They were prepared to give, and did give to their courts a degree of authority over them and over their executives and legislatures without precedent in the history of free government; but they also revered justice; they prized peace and concord and friendship and brotherhood between the states and their citizens. A century and a half of free self-government had brought to them the lessons and the self-restraint of experience. They knew the limitations of good men and the essential conditions of doing justice. In that great cause they allowed no small local jealousies to bar the way. When the ever-recurring question arises between submission of controversies to international arbitration on the one hand and insistence upon the jurisdiction of national tribunals on the other, the nations who look to the framers of the American Constitution as an example of high constructive statesmanship and wisdom, should not fail to find in this judgment, matter to arrest their attention and influence their action.

No court in the world has greater power and independence and honor than the Supreme Court, established under the Constitution of the United States, yet our Government, by international agreement, has submitted to international tribunals many cases which could have been, and many cases which already had been, decided by that great court. For example, the cases of the *Peterhof*, reported in Wallace's Reports, Volume 5, the *Dashing Wave* (5 Wallace), the *Georgia* (7 Wallace), the *Isabella Thompson* (3 Wallace), the *Pearl* (5 Wallace), the *Adela* (6 Wallace), had all been decided by the Supreme Court, and they were re-submitted to an international tribunal, which decided them in the same way the court had decided them.

The cases of the *Hiawatha* (2 Black), the *Circassian* (2 Wallace); the *Springbock* (5 Wallace), the *Sir William Peel* (5 Wallace), the *Volant* (5 Wallace), the *Science* (5 Wallace), had all been decided by the Supreme Court, and they were re-submitted to an international tribunal, which decided them adversely to the decisions of the court, and the United States complied with the decisions of the arbitral tribunal.

It is true that the rule is undisputed that where there has been a denial of justice in national courts their decisions are not to be held conclusive, and arbitration or other further action may be called for. Unfortunately it has been necessary often in the past, to invoke this rule; but it is an unsatisfactory rule and injurious in its effects. It involves an indictment and trial of the judicial system under which the denial of justice is alleged to have occurred. It involves aspersions upon government, imputations upon high officials, incitement to anger and resentment, and tends to destroy rather than to preserve good feeling and friendship between the nations concerned.

The better rule would be, to avoid the danger of denials of justice, and to prevent the belief that justice has not been done, which must always possess the parties defeated in a tribunal suspected of partiality, by submitting in the first instance to an impartial arbitral tribunal all such cases as are liable to be affected by the considerations I have mentioned.

And the reason of such a rule would require that when such cases have been decided already by national courts, and the impartial justice of the decision is seriously questioned, upon substantial grounds, they should be re-submitted to an arbitral tribunal, not for proof that justice has been denied, but for rehearing upon the merits because self-respect and intelligent self-interest forbid a nation to shelter itself behind decisions of its own courts that rest under the imputation of partiality, or to be content with any but the best means and the most sincere effort to learn what is just in order that the nation may do what is just.

THE BASIS OF PROTECTION TO CITIZENS RESIDING ABROAD

PRESIDENTIAL ADDRESS AT THE FOURTH ANNUAL MEETING
OF THE AMERICAN SOCIETY OF INTERNATIONAL LAW
WASHINGTON, APRIL 28, 1910

I SHALL ask you to listen for a few minutes to some remarks regarding the protection which a nation should extend over its citizens in foreign countries. I do not select this topic because I have anything new to say about it, or because there is any real controversy among international lawyers concerning the principles involved or concerning the fundamental rules to be applied, but because there is a considerable degree of public misunderstanding about the subject, and situations are continually arising in which a failure of the public in one country or another to appreciate justly the extent and nature of international obligation leads to resentment and unfriendly feeling that ought to be avoided.

The subject has grown in importance very rapidly during recent years. The world policy of commercial exclusiveness prevailing in the early part of the last century has practically disappeared. The political relations on the one hand and the commercial and industrial relations on the other hand of different parts of the earth to each other are quite separate and distinct. It is not uncommon to find that a nation has commercial colonies which bear no political relation to her whatever, and political colonies which are industrially allied most closely to other countries.

The increase in facilities for transportation and communication — steamships and railroads and telegraphs and telephones — has set in motion vast armies of travelers who are making their way into the most remote corners of foreign countries to a degree never before known.

The general diffusion of intelligence among the people of all civilized, and to a considerable degree of semi-civilized, countries, has carried to the great mass of the people — the working people of the world — a knowledge of the affairs and the conditions of life in other lands; and this, with the cheapness and ease of transportation, has led to enormous emigration and shifting of population. One of the salient features of modern political development has been the severance of the people from the soil of their native countries. The peasant, who was formerly a fixture in his native valley, unable to conceive of himself as a part of any life beyond the circle of the surrounding hills, now moves freely to and fro, not only from one community to another but from one country to another. Labor is becoming fluid, and, like money, flows towards the best market without paying much attention to political lines. The doctrine of inalienable allegiance so inconsistent with the natural course of development of the new world, and so long and so stoutly contested by the United States, has been almost universally abandoned. It is manifest that the few nations which have not given their assent to the right of their citizens to change their citizenship and allegiance as they change their residence will not long maintain their position. This change has led to a new class of citizens traveling or residing abroad; that is, the naturalized citizen, who, returning to his country of origin or going to still other countries, claims the protection not of his native but of his adopted government. Among the great throngs of emigrants to other countries may be distinguished two somewhat different classes — one composed of those who have transferred their substantial interests to the new country and are building up homes for themselves; the other class composed of those who still continue their principal interests in the country from which they have come and under their new conditions are engaged in accumulating means for the better support of the families and friends they have left behind them, or for their own future support after the return to which they look forward.

The great accumulation of capital in the money centers of the world, far in excess of the opportunities for home investment, has led to a great increase of international investment extending over the entire surface of the earth, and these investments have naturally been followed by citizens from the investing countries prosecuting and caring for the enterprises in the other countries where their investments are made. For example, it was estimated three or four years ago that within the preceding ten years over seven hundred millions of capital had gone from the United States alone into Mexico for investment; and this capital had been followed by more than forty thousand citizens of the United States who had become resident in Mexico. This same process has been going on all over the world.

All these forms of peaceful interpenetration among the nations of the earth naturally contribute their instances of citizens justly or unjustly dissatisfied with the treatment they receive in foreign countries and calling upon their own governments for protection.

In two directions the process has gone so far as to justify and receive limitation. On the one hand, there has come to be a recognition of the essential difference between emigration *en masse*, by means of which the people of one country may virtually take possession of considerable portions of the territory of another country to the practical exclusion of its own citizens, and the ordinary travel and residence upon individual initiative to which the usual conventions concerning reciprocal rights of travel and residence relate. The occasion for considering this difference naturally depends very much upon the capacity of the emigrants for assimilation with the people of the country to which they go. The wider the differences in race, customs, traditions, and standards of living, the less is the probability of assimilation and the greater the certainty that emigration of large bodies of people will assume the character of peaceful invasion and occupation of territory. After many years of discussion China has come to recognize the existence of such a distinction in respect of Chinese emigration to North America. Japan has recognized it from the first, and there has never been any question between the governments of Japan and the United States upon that subject.

On the other hand, the United States has itself put a limit upon the practice, which had already reached the point of serious abuse, of permitting the natives of other countries to become naturalized here for the purpose of returning to their homes or seeking a residence in third countries with the benefit of American protection. Several years ago it was estimated that there were in Turkey seven or eight thousand natives of Turkey who had in one way and another secured naturalization in the United States and had gone home to live with the advantage over their friends and neighbors of being able to call upon the American embassy for assistance whenever they were not satisfied with the treatment they received from their own government. At the time of the troubles in Morocco, which were disposed of at the Algeciras Conference, an examination of the list of American citizens in Morocco showed that one half of the list consisted of natives of Morocco who had been naturalized in the United States and had left this country and gone back to Morocco within three months after obtaining their naturalization papers. We have now adopted a rule, which has been embodied in a number of treaties and in the Act of Congress of March 2, 1907, for the purpose of checking this abuse.

The new rule is, that when a naturalized citizen leaves this country instead of residing in it, two years' residence in the country of his origin or five years' residence in any other country creates a presumption of renunciation of the citizenship which he had acquired here, and unless that presumption is rebutted by showing some special and temporary reason for the change of residence, the obligation of protection by the United States is deemed to be ended.

I have dwelt upon the magnitude and diversity of the causes which are resulting in the presence in each civilized country of great numbers of citizens of other countries, because conditions so universal plainly must be dealt with pursuant to fixed, definite, certain, and universally recognized rules of international action.

The simplest form of protection is that exercised by strong countries whose citizens are found in parts of the earth under the jurisdiction of governments whose control is inadequate for the preservation of order. Under such circumstances in times of special disturbance it is an international custom for the countries having the power to intervene directly for the protection of their own citizens, as in the case of the Boxer rebellion in China, when substantially all the Western powers were concerned in the march to Peking and the forcible capture of that city for the protection of the legations. On a smaller scale, armed forces have often been landed from men-of-war for the protection of the life and property of their national citizens during revolutionary disturbances, as, for example, in Central America and the West Indies. Such a course is undoubtedly often necessary, but it is always an impeachment of the effective sovereignty of the government in whose territory the armed demonstration occurs, and it can be justified only by unquestionable facts which leave no practical doubt of the incapacity of the government of the country to perform its international duty of protection. It leads to many abuses, especially in the conduct of those nationals who, feeling that they are backed up by a navy, act as if they were superior to the laws of the country in which they are residing and permit their sense of immunity to betray them into arrogant and offensive disrespect.

Similar in principle to the method of direct protection which I have mentioned is the practice of exercising extraterritorial jurisdiction, under conventional arrangements, in countries whose methods of administering justice are very greatly at variance with the methods to which the people of the great body of civilized states are accustomed, such, for example, as China and Turkey.

Between countries which maintain effective government for the maintenance of order within their territories, the protection of one country for its nationals in foreign territory can be exercised only by calling upon the government of the other country for the performance of its international duty, and the measure of one country's international obligation is the measure of the other country's right. The rule of obligation is perfectly distinct and settled. Each country is bound to give to the nationals of another country in its territory the benefit of the same laws, the same administration, the same protection and the same redress for injury which it gives to its own citizens, and neither more nor less: provided the protection which the country gives to its own citizens conforms to the established standard of civilization.

There is a standard of justice, very simple, very fundamental, and of such general acceptance by all civilized countries as to form a part of the international law of the world. The condition upon which any country is entitled to measure the justice due from it to an alien by the justice which it accords to its own citizens is that its system of law and administration shall conform to this general standard. If any country's system of law and administration does not conform to that standard, although the people of the country may be content or compelled to live under it, no other country can be compelled to accept it as furnishing a satisfactory measure of treatment to its citizens. In the famous Don Pacifico case, Lord Palmerston said, in the House of Commons:

If our subjects abroad have complaints against individuals, or against the government of a foreign country, if the courts of law of that country can afford them redress, then, no doubt, to those courts of justice the British subject ought in the first instance to apply; and it is only on a denial of justice, or upon decisions manifestly unjust, that the British Government should be called upon to interfere. But there may be cases in which no confidence can be placed in the tribunals, those tribunals being, from their composition and nature, not of a character to inspire any hope of obtaining justice from them. It has been said: ' We do not apply this rule to countries whose governments are arbitrary or despotic, because there the tribunals are under the control of the government, and justice cannot be had; and, moreover, it is not meant to be applied to nominally constitutional governments, where the tribunals are corrupt.'

I say, then, that our doctrine is, that, in the first instance, redress should be sought from the law courts of the country; but that in cases where redress cannot be so had — and those cases are many — to confine a British subject to that remedy only, would be to deprive him of the protection which he is entitled to receive. . . .

We shall be told, perhaps, as we have already been told, that if the people of the country are liable to have heavy stones placed upon their breasts, and police officers to dance upon them; if they are liable to have their heads tied to their knees, and to be left for hours in that state; or to be swung like a pendulum, and to be bastinadoed as they swing, foreigners have no right to be better treated than the natives, and have no business to complain if the same things are practised upon them. We may be told this, but that is not my opinion, nor do I believe it is the opinion of any reasonable man.

Nations to which such observations apply must be content to stand in an intermediate position between those incapable of maintaining order, and those which conform fully to the international standard. With this understanding there are no exceptions to the rule and no variations from it. There may be circumstances at particular times and places such that the application of the rule calls for action regarding foreign citizens quite unlike the action ordinarily taken for the benefit of native citizens, but it is always action which would be equally required in case a native citizen were placed under the same circumstances of exigency. It is plain that no other rule is practicable. Upon any other basis every country would be obliged to have two systems of law and administration and police regulations, and the existence of great numbers of foreigners in a country would be an intolerable burden. The standard to which the rule applies is a standard of right, and not necessarily of actual performance. The foreigner is entitled to have the protection and redress which the citizen is entitled to have, and the fact that the citizen may not have insisted upon his rights, and may be content with lax administration which fails to secure them to him, furnishes no reason why the foreigner should not insist upon them and no excuse for denying them to him. It is a practical standard and has regard always to the possibilities of government under existing conditions. The rights of the foreigner vary as the rights of the citizen vary between ordinary and peaceful times and times of disturbance and tumult; between settled and ordinary communities and frontier regions and mining camps.

The diplomatic history of this country presents a long and painful series of outrages on foreigners by mob violence. These have uniformly been the subject of diplomatic claims and long-continued discussion, and ultimately of the payment of indemnity. An examination of these discussions will show that in every case the indemnity was in fact paid because the United States had not done in the particular case what it would have done for its own citizens if our laws had been administered as our citizens were entitled to have them administered. Of course, no government can guarantee all the inhabitants of its territory against injury inflicted by individual crime and no government can guarantee the certain punishment of crime; but every citizen is entitled to have police protection accorded to him commensurate with the exigency under which he may be placed. If he is able to give notice to the government of intended violence against him he is entitled to have due measures taken for its prevention, and he is entitled always to have such vigorous prosecution and punishment of those who are guilty of criminal violation of his rights that it will be apparent to all the world that he cannot be misused with impunity and that he will have the benefit of the deterrent effect of punishment.

It is a distressing fact that in one important respect the Government of the United States fails to comply with its international obligation in giving the same degree of protection and opportunity for redress of wrong to foreigners that it gives to its own citizens. The difficulties which beset aliens in a strange land are ordinarily local difficulties. The government and the people of the foreign country are usually quite ready, in a broad and abstract way, to accord to foreigners the fullest toleration, equality before the law, and protection. But the people of the particular community with whom the alien comes in contact too often fail of understanding and sympathy. They misunderstand and resent the foreign customs with which they are unfamiliar. They are aroused to anger by the competition to which the foreigner subjects them. Immediate contact is too apt at first to breed dislike and intolerance towards what Bret Harte describes as the " defective moral quality of being a foreigner." Our Constitution recognizes this natural and often inevitable prejudice by giving to our national courts jurisdiction over all civil suits between aliens and citizens of the United States. We fail to recognize the same conditions, however, in respect of the security of the persons and property of aliens. The Revised Statutes of the United States aim to protect citizens of the United States against local prejudice and injury, by providing in Section 5508:

> If two or more persons conspire to injure, oppress, threaten, or intimidate any citizen in the free exercise or enjoyment of any right or privilege secured to him by the Constitution or laws of the United States, or because of his having so exercised the same; or if two or more persons go in disguise on the highway, or on the premises of another, with intent to prevent or hinder his free exercise or enjoyment of any right or privilege so secured, they shall be fined not more than five thousand dollars and imprisoned not more than ten years; and shall, moreover, be thereafter ineligible to any office, or place of honor, profit, or trust created by the Constitution or laws of the United States.

This provision, however, does not apply to aliens, and no similar provision applies to them. Accordingly, defenseless Chinamen were mobbed at Denver in 1880, and at Rock Springs, Wyoming, in 1885; Italians were lynched in New Orleans in 1891, and again at Rouse, Colorado, in 1895; and Mexicans were lynched at Yreka, California, in 1895; and Italians at Tallulah, Louisiana, in 1899, and again at Erwin, Mississippi, in 1901. Our Government was practically defenseless against claims for indemnity because of our failure to extend over these aliens the same protection that we extend over our own citizens, and the final result of long diplomatic correspondence in each case was the payment of indemnity for the real reason that we had not performed our international duty. In these discussions our State Department from time to time undertook to shelter itself behind the distribution of power in our constitutional system, and the fact that there was no law of the United States providing for any redress except at the hands of the State officials in the very locality where prejudice led to the injury. Yet when an American citizen was injured by a mob in Brazil in 1875, the dispatch of Secretary Fish to the American Minister at Rio de Janeiro said:

> You represent that the facts as set forth in the memorial of the claimant are admitted by that Government, which, however, denies its accounta-

bility and says that the province where the injury to Mr. Smyth took place is alone answerable. Supposing, however, the case to be a proper one for the interposition of this Government, the reference of the claimant to the authorities of the province for redress will not be acquiesced in. Those authorities cannot be officially known to this Government. It is the Imperial Government at Rio de Janeiro only which is accountable to this Government for any injury to the person or property of a citizen of the United States committed by the authorities of a province. It is with that Government alone that we hold diplomatic intercourse. The same rule would be applicable to the case of a Brazilian subject who, in this country, might be wronged by the authorities of a State.

And President Harrison, in his message to Congress of December 9, 1891, relating to the lynching of Italians at New Orleans in that year, said:

Some suggestions growing out of this unhappy incident are worthy the attention of Congress. It would, I believe, be entirely competent for Congress to make offenses against the treaty rights of foreigners domiciled in the United States cognizable in the Federal Courts. This has not, however, been done, and the Federal officers and Courts have no power in such cases to intervene either for the protection of a foreign citizen or for the punishment of his slayers. It seems to me to follow, in this state of the law, that the officers of the State charged with police and judicial powers in such cases must, in the consideration of international questions growing out of such incidents, be regarded in such sense as Federal agents as to make this Government answerable for their acts in cases where it would be answerable if the United States had used its constitutional power to define and punish crimes against treaty rights.

It is to be hoped that our Government will never again attempt to shelter itself from responsibility for the enforcement of its treaty obligations to protect foreigners by alleging its own failure to enact the laws necessary to the discharge of those obligations.

The most frequent occasions of appeal by citizens for protection in other countries arise upon the assertion that justice has been denied them in the courts, and this appears, unfortunately, to be a frequent occurrence. The justification of such complaints does not rest upon any obligation of another country to furnish any better or different judicial relief or procedure to foreigners than is provided for the citizens of the country itself, but it results from the fact that in many countries the courts are not independent; the judges are removable at will; they are not superior, as they ought to be, to local prejudices and passions, and their organization does not afford to the foreigner the same degree of impartiality which is accorded to citizens of the country, or which is required by the common standard of justice obtaining throughout the civilized world. When justice is denied for such reasons there is a failure on the part of the government to perform its international duty, and a right on the part of the government whose citizen has failed to secure justice to demand reparation.

A large proportion of such complaints are, however, without just foundation. Citizens abroad are too apt to complain that justice has been denied them whenever they are beaten in a litigation, forgetting that, as a rule, they would complain just the same if they were beaten in a litigation in the courts of their own country. When a man goes into a foreign country to reside or to trade he submits himself, his rights, and interests to the jurisdiction of the courts of that country. He will naturally be at a disadvantage in litigation against citizens of the country. He is less familiar than they with the laws, the ways of doing business, the habits of thought and action, the methods of procedure, the local customs and prejudices, and often with the language in which the business is done and the proceedings carried on. It is not the duty of a foreign country in which such a litigant finds himself to make up to him for these disadvantages under which he labors. They are disadvantages inseparable from his prosecuting his business in a strange land. A large part of the dissatisfaction which aliens feel and express regarding their treatment by foreign tribunals results from these causes, which furnish no just ground for international complaint. It is very desirable that people who go into other countries shall realize that they are not entitled to have the laws and police regulations and methods of judicial procedure and customs of business made over to suit them, or to have any other or different treatment than that which is accorded to the citizens of the country into which they have gone; so long as the government of that country maintains, according to its own ideas and for the benefit of its own citizens, a system of law and administration which does not violate the common standard of justice that is a part of international law; and so long as, in conformity with that standard, the same rights, the same protection, and the same means of redress for wrong are given to them as are given to the citizens of the country where they are. On the other hand, every one who goes into a foreign country is bound to obey its laws, and if he disobeys them he is not entitled to be protected against punishment under those laws. It follows, also, that one in a foreign country must submit to the inconvenience of proceedings that may be brought in accordance with law upon any *bona fide* charge that an offense has been committed, even though the charge may not be sustained. Nevertheless, no violation of law can deprive a citizen in a foreign country of the right to protection from the government of his own country. There can be no crime which leaves a man without legal rights. One is always entitled to insist that he shall not be punished except in accordance with law, or without such a hearing as the universally accepted principles of justice demand. If that right be denied to the most desperate criminal in a foreign country, his own government can and ought to protect him against the wrong.

Happily, the same causes which are making questions of alien protection so frequent are at the same time bringing about among all civilized peoples a better understanding of the rights and obligations created by the presence of the alien in a foreign country; a fuller acceptance of the common international standard of justice, and a gradual reduction of the local prejudices and misunderstandings which are in the way of the alien's getting his full rights. Discussions between governments upon complaints of wrong to their citizens tend more and more to relate to questions of fact upon the determination of which accepted and settled rules can be readily applied. And in all nations the wise and sound policy of equal protection and impartial justice to the alien is steadily gaining acceptance in the remotest parts and throughout even the least instructed communities.

THE FUNCTION OF PRIVATE CODIFICATION IN INTERNATIONAL LAW [1]

PRESIDENTIAL ADDRESS AT THE FIFTH ANNUAL MEETING
OF THE AMERICAN SOCIETY OF INTERNATIONAL LAW
WASHINGTON, APRIL 27, 1911

THE increasing frequency of arbitration and the pressure for a regular Court of International Justice composed of permanent judges, have given new emphasis to the demand for what is called the codification of international law.

The process and the result intended to be described when the term codification is applied to international law involves something very different from the codification of municipal law. The codifier of any part of the law of a nation finds the law with which he is to deal already in existence and authenticated. It may be confused in form and apparently unrelated in its parts: it may be scattered through the statutory enactments of many years and the declarations of a multitude of judicial decisions; the codifier may have to struggle with difficult questions of apparent inconsistency, of doubtful repeal, of obscurities in expression calling for interpretation and construction, and with conflicts of judicial opinion; but the expressions which he considers all come from the same law-making power. Somewhere in the mass of material is to be found the final expression of legislative will, the controlling decision of the courts, and when these are

[1] The reader's attention is called to the fact that a second address on the subject of the Codification of International Law, was delivered by Mr. Root at the joint meeting of the Subsection on International Law and the American Institute of International Law at the Second Pan-American Scientific Congress, Washington, D. C., December 30, 1915, which appears at page 429 of this volume.

found everything inconsistent with them may be rejected as repealed or overruled. The codifier's task is to find what the rules really are; to put them in due relations to each other under appropriate heads in accordance with some systematic scheme of arrangement; to bring order out of confusion; to furnish a methodical statement of the results of his researches which may make the law plain to the people who live under it and may relieve countless lawyers from the necessity of going through the same wearisome process of inquiry in each separate case. When the work is complete, if it is acceptable, the legislative power of the State puts its stamp of approval upon it and resolves any doubts or uncertainties by its acceptance of the codifier's conclusions. It may indeed be that the research of the codifier and the clearer view presented by a systematic arrangement will have revealed inadequacies of expression, incongruities, and omissions in the existing law, but, as to these, the suggestions of the codifier for remedying the defects discovered will be accepted or rejected by the single fiat of the legislative body which enacts the code.

In the main, to codify municipal law is to produce a systematic, and authoritative statement of the law already prescribed by a sovereign.

An attempt to codify international law must deal with entirely different material and must involve a very different process. Lord Mansfield has described the law of nations as "founded upon justice, equity, convenience, the reason of the thing and confirmed by long usage."

When any one undertakes to produce a systematic statement of the rules of international law, having no statutes embodying it, no binding judicial decisions declaring it, no deliverance of any law-making power establishing it, he must have recourse to a vast mass of conflicting opinion expressed by a multitude of text-writers, of publicists, of the authors of diplomatic correspondence, as to what is just, what is equitable, reasonable, convenient, with very defective and partial evidence of acceptance by the civilized nations of opinions one way or another upon these questions. He will find it possible by research to secure evidence of the acceptance of certain very general rules of conduct, of certain ethical principles, of many partial and a few general usages and precedents, and the conventional acceptance of a few specific rules designed to make certain the practical application of general principles. A very great part, however, of the so-called rules of international law, the relevancy of which to the practical affairs of life has been perceived, and which have been the subject of discussion among international lawyers, he will find to be of such doubtful authority, to rest upon such uncertain and partial acceptance by governmental authority, or upon such vague and unsatisfactory evidence of usage, that they will certainly be open to dispute whenever cases involving diverse interests arise; and any proper statement of them must be, not that this is the law, but that this ought to be the law, or this is the better opinion, or this is more generally received as being the rule which should govern. The substantial work of international codification is, not merely to state rules but to secure agreement as to what the rules are, by the nations whose usage must confirm them. Except as a means to this end, any codification of international law can be of little value except as a topical index and guide to the student. As a means to this end, to be properly used and followed out, it is of very great importance to press forward the work of codifying international law.

To codify municipal law is to state in systematic form the results of the law-making process already carried on by a nation through its established institutional forms. To codify international law is primarily to set in motion and promote the law-making process itself in the community of nations in which the institutional forms appropriate for the carrying on of such a process have been so vague, indistinct, uncertain, and irregular that they could hardly be said to exist at all.

The nations are a law-making power. When by their confirmation of a rule of justice they make it a law of nations, it is truly a law and cannot be violated without punishment. But no government ever has been or can be conducted successfully except through the creation of institutions by the orderly working of which the will of the governing power becomes transmuted into specific rules of action made effective and applied to the affairs of life. In the absence of institutional forms through which the process of international law-making may be carried on with regularity, the process is very slow and difficult. It is hindered by two facts resting in human nature. The first is, that while international law can be made only by the assent of governments, governments ordinarily concentrate their attention on propositions of international law affecting any given subject only when there is some practical, concrete case arising in their own international relations and requiring the application of a rule. Governments are practical organizations dealing with actual conditions, continually pressed by immediate difficulties, and the men engaged in them ordinarily have but little time and strength to devote to questions which for practical purposes, so far as they themselves are concerned, seem academic because they have not yet arisen or may possibly never arise.

Every foreign office is fully occupied with questions that it must decide, and, as a rule, foreign offices will not concern themselves with any other question unless they are moved by some special impulse of external pressure or by the promptings of exceptionally far-sighted policy.

On the other hand, it is a matter of common observation that the only way to secure a general agreement upon a rule of action is to secure consideration of it at a time when there

FUNCTION OF PRIVATE CODIFICATION   61

is no concrete case calling for its application; when there are no diverse interests tending to produce different views as to what the rule should be.

This is very well illustrated by the experience of all the States which live under written constitutions. For example, in all the States of our American union there is a substantial similarity in a series of constitutional provisions not merely expressing general principles of justice but stating specific rights designed practically to insure the benefit of those principles to the individual citizen, such as the prohibition against taking private property for public use without compensation; against depriving one of life, liberty, or property, without due process of law; against being put twice in jeopardy for the same offense; against being compelled to testify against one's self; against unreasonable searches and seizures; against excessive bail and cruel and unusual punishment; against State action impairing the obligation of contracts, etc. These rules are adopted through a process which does not deal at all with concrete cases. They are agreed upon by the people of the States as rules of abstract justice. There is no American State in which the people would under any condition abandon them; yet it would be difficult to find any State in which there are not attempts made every year on the part of the officers of government to evade and override these very rules in concrete cases. Indeed the reason why our people put such provisions into our constitutions is that they feel that if they do not make such rules of action binding when there is no practical question at issue, they themselves will not observe the rules when a practical question is presented. They know that the time for agreeing upon a just rule of action and the occasion for applying a rule of action must be separate and distinct, or the interest of the particular occasion will override and control the law-maker's sense of justice. Of course these considerations apply much more strongly in the making of an international law; because the particular occasion for the application of an international rule ordinarily is created by the existence of diverse interests which make very difficult any agreement as to what the rule of justice is.

It thus appears that in the ordinary course of international affairs the only occasions when it is possible to secure the attention of a law-making power to questions as to what the rules of law are or ought to be, are the very occasions when it is most difficult for the law-making powers to agree upon such rules, that is, the most difficult for them to establish a rule as law. The movement for codification of international law is an expression of a natural impulse on the part of those who are interested in international relations to remedy this failure of national governments to function as an international law-making power. The movement has proceeded along several apparently distinct lines. The first has been the line of individual codification by temperamental successors to Jeremy Bentham — men whose natures moved them to evoke order out of confusion and to give system and definiteness to the subject-matter contained in the vast mass of writings by publicists upon international law, often vague and indefinite, often repetitious and prolix, often contentious and prejudiced. The forty-five years which have passed since, at the instance of **Mr. David Dudley Field**, the British Association for the Promotion of Social Science appointed a committee to prepare and report the outline of an international code have been a period not of stagnation but of extraordinary growth in the direction of international law-making. Although Mr. Field alone did anything under the committee appointment, he produced his own admirable draft outlines of an international code in 1872. In the meantime the codification by Professor Bluntschli of Heidelberg, had been published in 1868. The code of Pasquale Fiore, of the

FUNCTION OF PRIVATE CODIFICATION   63

University of Naples, was published in 1888, and in 1906 the project for a code of public international law by M. Duplessix was published at Paris and crowned by the Bureau of International Peace. A comprehensive draft of a statute has thus been made in four different countries from four different national points of view at different times and upon independent, individual initiative.

In the meantime also another process has been going on much like the discussion to which the provisions of proposed laws are subject in committee under ordinary methods of legislative procedure. That process has been carried on by voluntary international associations of great dignity and consequence.

The Institute of International Law established at Ghent in 1873 has devoted itself to the scientific study and discussion of the law. Closely limited in number, composed entirely of eminent experts whose qualifications have already been demonstrated by their individual writings, filling the vacancies in its number by its own selection, it has rendered very great services in the systematic development of the science of international law. It has drafted and adopted, after full discussion and mature deliberation, model codes upon a great number of subjects and has bestowed great benefits upon mankind by leading the way in the study of international law from the philosophical and historical point of view.

The Association for the Reform and Codification of the Law of Nations, organized at Brussels in the same year, 1873, under the initiative of James B. Miles, the Secretary of the American Peace Society, and with the coöperation of David Dudley Field, Theodore Dwight Woolsey, William Beach Lawrence, Emory Washburn, Elihu Burritt, and many other distinguished Americans, is still active under its new title of the International Law Association. Unlimited in number, welcoming to its lists all competent persons, including not merely scientific students of the law from all countries, but merchants, men of affairs, underwriters, ship owners, economists, municipal lawyers, politicians, representatives of chambers of commerce and peace societies, it has discussed questions of international law from many practical and popular points of view and has dealt with the application of scientific principles to the actual conditions of international trade and intercourse.

In the meantime also a great number and variety of international societies for specific purposes have arisen, associations devoted to political economy; to the promotion of commerce and industry; to navigation and railroads; to penology and criminal anthropology; to the legal protection of travellers and of children and of animals; to the protection of industrial property and of artistic and literary property; to reforming the abuse of alcoholic drinks and the suppression of immoral literature; to libraries and bibliography; to education and insurance; to sanitation and hygiene and demography; to universal peace, and a universal language; to engineering and architecture and agriculture; to more separate sciences and more different reforms than one can well recall without a memorandum. The recently established Central Office of International Institutions at Brussels invited a congress of representatives of such associations to meet at Brussels in the year 1910, and representatives of one hundred and thirty-four international associations attended the congress. The investigation of the Central Office develops the fact that there are about three hundred such international associations, a large part of them quite ignorant of the others' existence.

Most of them are not consciously endeavoring to develop international law, but they are building up customs of private international action. They are establishing precedents, formulating rules for their own guidance, many of them pressing for uniformity of national legislation and many of them urging treaties and conventions for the furtherance of their common purposes. A great part of them represent a multitude of national associations of which the international association is a federation. Their activity is making a multitude of leaders of thought in almost every department of human effort familiar with a field which transcends the limits of any national law and in which, if regulation be needed at all, it must be found in international agreement.

I have not endeavored to make an exhaustive enumeration, but merely to give instances indicating the existence during the last half-century of widespread, continuous, and intense private, unofficial action tending in the direction of international law-making.

But all of this private activity did not of itself make international law. However plainly founded upon justice, equity, convenience, and the reason of the thing a rule might be, in order to be law it must be confirmed by the nations. And until the Peace Conference at The Hague in 1899, governments, that is to say, the only powers that could really make international law, had responded but indifferently and within narrow limits to the steadily growing unofficial pressure.

There were, it is true, a number of treaties by which nations undertook to regulate their future conduct in specific directions, such as, the Slave-Trade Treaty, in 1890; the establishment of the International Bureau of Weights and Measures, in 1875; the Convention for the International Protection of Industrial Property, in 1883; for the Protection of Submarine Cables, in 1884; for the Exchange of Official Documents, in 1886; for the Publication of Customs Tariffs, in 1890; the agreement made at Saint Petersburg for the Prohibition of the Use of Explosive Bullets, in 1868; and the Geneva Convention relating to the Treatment of the Wounded of Armies in the Field, in 1864. But mere agreements by which nations stipulate as to their future conduct do not of themselves make international law. They are binding only as contracts generally are binding. It is true also that the results of private formulation and discussion of rules of international law, well known to the foreign offices of the world, produced an effect upon the conduct of nations tending to bring about that usage which in the long course of time would ultimately be capable of proof as amounting to a confirmation.

There were also during the same period a few exceptional instances of a new departure in the way of making international law by substituting a formal governmental declaration of the law for the proof of conduct in specific instances necessary to establish confirmation by long usage.

The difficulties experienced in the Crimean War led the negotiators of the Treaty of Peace in 1856 to embody in the Declaration of Paris a statement of four rules affecting captures at sea, three of which received general adherence. The requirements of a great volunteer army, not very familiar with the history and customs of warfare, in 1863, led to the formulation by Doctor Francis Lieber of his famous instructions for the government of the armies of the United States in the field — a code of one hundred and fifty-seven articles, which was approved by President Lincoln as "General Order No. 100 of 1863." This codification produced among the European publicists of that day an impression which time has not weakened. Its intrinsic merit and its practical application on a large scale, although by a single government, gave it a distinction and authority in the opinions of mankind which it has never lost.

When Great Britain and the United States were about to submit the Alabama claims to arbitration in 1871 they agreed so far as they could upon the law regarding the rights and duties of neutrals which should govern the arbitrators,

FUNCTION OF PRIVATE CODIFICATION 67

and formulated their agreement in the three rules of the Treaty of Washington. The success of the Geneva arbitration and the great impression produced by that illustration of the practicability of peaceable judicial settlement gave great credit to the steps by which the result was attained; but of course the agreement of two nations did not make the three rules of the treaty international law any more than President Lincoln's approval of Doctor Lieber's code made that international law.

The year 1899 found two bodies of actors in the field of international law development — the private persons who had been discussing and formulating and codifying on the one hand, and the governments, who alone had power to make law, on the other hand, quite separate and distinct; the codifiers apparently pure theorists engaged in academic discussion; the governments apparently stolid and indifferent to all but the specific difficulties with which they were called upon to deal from day to day. Then a very great event was brought about. It was unpremeditated, unintended, and unforeseen. The Czar of Russia, by his note of August 12–24, 1898, inspired by a noble humanitarian sentiment, had called an international conference for the specific purpose of considering the limitation of armaments. In that note Count Mouravieff said:

> To put an end to these incessant armaments and to seek the means of warding off the calamities which are threatening the whole world, — such is the supreme duty which is today imposed on all States.
>
> Filled with this idea, His Majesty has been pleased to order me to propose to all the Governments whose representatives are accredited to the Imperial Court, the meeting of a conference which would have to occupy itself with this grave problem.

The powers assented to the Russian proposal, but before the conference met it had become evident that there was no possibility whatever of securing an agreement upon any plan to accomplish the purpose for which the conference was called. If public failure was to be avoided it was necessary to find something for the conference to do, and for the conference to do something quite apart from its original purpose. What the conference did was to bridge the chasm between individual opinion and government action; between the codifiers of international law and the makers of international law. Then was inaugurated for the first time an institution through which instructed, deliberate, and mature opinion might find the method and machinery for its direct and effective development into law through the concerted action in prescribed and orderly procedure, of the law-making powers constituting the community of nations. The Second Hague Conference in 1907, in its broader and progressive results and its provision for still a third conference, made certain the continued life of the institution. In these great assemblies the work of the codifiers bore fruit. Lieber's epoch-making code of rules for the conduct of armies in the field became law. The three rules of the Treaty of Washington became law. Much of the painstaking and public-spirited work of the Institute of International Law, and notably that contained in its codification of the laws of war on land, adopted at its meeting of 1880, became law. The patient thought which had evoked from the wilderness of precedent and philosophical discussion, and had tested and codified and formulated in systematic statement the rules that ought to govern nations, had prepared material, directed thought, and created opinion which made it possible for The Hague conferences to act. The instructed thought of the world, the sentiment of the world in favor of effective law, the belief of the world in the possibility of effective law, had been led to such a condition that the atmosphere of the conferences discouraged factious opposition, gave heart to the friends of progressive development, and disappointed the cynical disbelief of hide-bound reactionaries.

FUNCTION OF PRIVATE CODIFICATION   69

The success of The Hague conferences was possible because in the fullness of time the world was ready for them; and the world was made ready by the voluntary service of a multitude of private, unofficial workers in the field of international law working out just conclusions by scientific methods in practical form and urging upon the attention of mankind the need and the possibility of extending the control over nations of universally accepted law. While mankind has looked with approval upon the specific results attained by the two Hague conferences, it does not yet appreciate the tremendous significance of the institution which has been created, or fully discern the fact that a new era in the law of nations has been inaugurated; and very few men appreciate the great part which has been played by the unofficial international lawyer in this great movement of civilization.

The final act of the Second Hague Conference declared:

Finally, the Conference recommends to the powers the assembling of a Third Peace Conference, which might be held within a period corresponding to that which has elapsed since the preceding conference, at a date to be fixed by common agreement between the powers, and it calls their attention to the necessity of preparing the programme of this Third Conference a sufficient time in advance to ensure its deliberations being conducted with the necessary authority and expedition.

In order to attain this object the Conference considers that it would be very desirable that, some two years before the probable date of the meeting, a preparatory committee should be charged by the governments with the task of collecting the various proposals to be submitted to the conference, of ascertaining what subjects are ripe for embodiment in an international regulation, and of preparing a programme which the governments should decide upon in sufficient time to enable it to be carefully examined by the countries interested. This committee should further be intrusted with the task of proposing a system of organization and procedure for the conference itself.

Here lies the pressing duty of the international lawyer. What subjects shall be " ripe for embodiment in international regulation " when the next great law-making council of the nations convenes; where lies the greatest need; in what direction are the lines of least resistance; upon what subject is general opinion most nearly ready for crystallization. That some subject shall be ready with opinions sufficiently matured to make it possible for a conference within the short space of a few months to reach effective conclusions is vital to the continuance of the progress in which we are all so deeply interested. Now, as heretofore, the work of preparation must be done chiefly upon private and unofficial initiative. Codifiers must draft and systematize and clarify. Associations must discuss and obviate objections, and reconcile the philosophical and the practical, and work out conclusions and educate opinion. Industry, learning, accurate thought, knowledge of practical affairs and breadth of view must prepare the definite expression of what has been found to be just and reasonable, so that there may be that formal acceptance which shall make it international law.

The necessity of this development of international law to the movement for international judicial settlement is well illustrated by the Conference of London. The convention of the Second Hague Conference for the establishment of an international Prize Court marks the furthest point to which the movement for the judicial settlement of international disputes has gone. It establishes a regular court of justice composed of judges appointed to the Court and paid a fixed compensation as distinguished from arbitrators selected for a particular case, with compulsory jurisdiction in cases of prize either by appeal from or a rehearing notwithstanding the decisions of national tribunals.

It provides that if there be a treaty between the parties, the treaty provisions shall govern, but that, " in the absence of such provisions the Court shall apply the rules of international law. If no generally recognized rule exists, the Court shall give judgment in accordance with the general principles of justice and equity."

FUNCTION OF PRIVATE CODIFICATION 71

When Great Britain came to consider the ratification of this convention it seemed to her government that there were so many important questions coming within the jurisdiction of the Court upon which no generally recognized rule existed and that there was so much doubt as to how the Court would apply the general principles of justice and equity that the interest of her naval power and vast commerce, required some further agreement as to the law which the Court was to administer. Accordingly a new conference of the principal naval powers was called by Great Britain and met in London in 1908.

The conference was attended by the representatives of Germany, the United States, Austria-Hungary, Spain, France, Great Britain, Italy, Japan, the Netherlands and Russia. After months of discussion it adopted a declaration concerning the laws of naval war, in seventy-one articles, classified in nine chapters, concerning blockade in time of war, contraband, unneutral service, destruction of neutral prizes, transfer to a neutral flag, enemy character, convoy, resistance to search, and compensation. The declaration settled many questions discussion upon which had been historic. The operative provision was in these words:

> The signatory powers are agreed that the rules contained in the following chapters correspond in substance with the generally recognized principles of international law.

The declaration concluded with an invitation for the adherence of other powers. How universal the confirmation of the declaration may be or what modification, if any, it may require before it becomes final is not yet certain. But the procedure of the conference is a model for international declaratory legislation. Its success is proof of the practicability of effective codification and its origin is evidence that a complete system for the judicial settlement of international disputes will require the codification of international law.

It is cause for satisfaction that this Association has undertaken and is proceeding in so practical a way to do its share in this great work of preparation. It is to be hoped that we may work usefully in the spirit of those Americans who played such an honorable part in the beginning of this great movement by which, in the last half-century, the development of international law has been carried so far.

THE REAL SIGNIFICANCE OF THE DECLARATION OF LONDON

PRESIDENTIAL ADDRESS AT THE SIXTH ANNUAL MEETING OF THE AMERICAN SOCIETY OF INTERNATIONAL LAW WASHINGTON, APRIL 25, 1912

The arguments for the establishment of an international prize court are set forth in the following address, in which are also stated the reasons for the meeting of the Naval Conference of London, December 2, 1908, participated in by ten leading maritime powers. The document called the Declaration of London was adopted by this conference February 26, 1909.

Through Mr. Root's intervention as senator, the Declaration of London was advised and consented to by the United States Senate on April 24, 1912. The legislation necessary to carry it into effect was passed by the British House of Commons, but was rejected by the House of Lords on December 15, 1911. This failure, and the failure of Great Britain to ratify the Declaration, prevented that country from fixing a date for the deposit of ratifications at London, as contemplated by Article 67 of the Declaration.

The provisions of the Declaration were incorporated in the German Prize Ordinance of September 30, 1909, and issued on August 3, 1914; and in the French *Instructions sur l'application du droit international en cas de guerre* of December 19, 1912.

Upon the outbreak of the war in 1914, the United States suggested to the belligerent powers that the Declaration of London should be observed as a rule of conduct during the continuance of the war. This proposition did not meet with the approval of all the belligerents, and was withdrawn. The Declaration of London cannot therefore be considered as international law, although its moral effect has been considerable.

THE principal achievement of The Hague Conference of 1907 was the Convention for an International Prize Court. That Convention provided for a real and permanent court composed of judges who were to be appointed by the contracting powers for terms of six years, were required to be "judges of known proficiency in questions of international maritime law and of the highest moral reputation," and were to be paid a stated compensation from a fund contributed by all the powers.

Jurisdiction was conferred upon the court to review on appeal all judgments of national prize courts. By a subsequent agreement, for the purpose of avoiding difficulties presented by the constitutions of some of the signatory powers, an alternative procedure was authorized under which the new court might pass upon the question involved in the case of prize *de novo*, and notwithstanding any judgment of the national prize court, instead of passing upon it by way of appeal from that judgment. Article 7 of the Convention provides:

If a question of law to be decided is covered by a treaty in force between the belligerent captor and a power which is itself or whose subject or citizen is a party to the proceedings, the court is governed by the provisions of the said treaty.

In the absence of such provisions the court shall apply the rule of international law. If no generally recognized rule exists the court shall give judgment in accordance with the general principles of justice and equity.

In estimating the value of such an agreement among the civilized powers it is worth while even for a student of international law to recall the wide range and critical importance of the questions to be included within the jurisdiction of the new court.

When war breaks out between two considerable maritime powers the commerce of the whole world is immediately affected. Each belligerent nation undertakes, so far as it can, to cripple its enemy both by direct military and naval operations and by cutting off supplies, interfering with sources of income, and generally weakening the enemy's national power to maintain an army and navy.

The liability of enemy merchant ships to capture tends to throw the commerce formerly carried on by the belligerent nations into the hands of neutrals while the necessary policy of each belligerent urges it to circumscribe and prevent so far as it can the neutral commerce with the other belligerent. Blockades and searches and seizures for carrying contraband goods are familiar methods of giving effect to this policy. Added to this is the necessity of constant watchfulness by belligerents to prevent neutral vessels from rendering direct service to the enemy's forces, such as the transportation of officers and troops or messengers, or the transmission of intelligence. In this way belligerents fall into an attitude of suspicion toward neutral vessels and unfriendliness toward neutral commerce, and the peaceable commerce of the world falls into an attitude of resenting what it regards as unwarranted interference. The most striking illustration of this tendency is to be found in the tremendous conflicts of the Napoleonic wars, when Pitt and Napoleon waged war not merely with armies and navies but with British Orders in Council and Continental Decrees. The Prussian Decree which began the series at the instance of Napoleon, on March 28, 1806, declared the coast of the North Sea closed against Great Britain. On April 8, 1806, Great Britain retaliated for that Decree by the first Order in Council, which declared the blockade of the Ems, the Weser, the Elbe, and the Trave. On May 16, 1806, came the second Order in Council declaring a blockade of the whole coast of the Continent from the Elbe to Brest. On October 14, 1806, Napoleon retaliated with the famous Berlin Decree, which prohibited all commerce with England. On January 7, 1807, another British Order in Council declared all neutral trading with France, or from port to port with any possession of France, or with any of the allies of France anywhere, to be ground for condemnation. On December 17, 1807, Napoleon's Milan Decree declared a sentence of outlawry upon England and all English ships. It was impossible that such a process should not involve all Europe in a universal war; and an aftermath of England's enforcement of her policy upon the neutral shipping of the United States was the War of 1812. The Civil War in the United States gave rise to a multitude of controversies between the United States and Great Britain, arising on one side from the seizure by the United States of numerous vessels charged with directly or indirectly attempting to violate the blockade of the southern coast, or with carrying contraband, and arising on the other side from the fitting out of Confederate cruisers in the neutral ports of Great Britain. The negotiations which led to the settlement of both classes of these claims by arbitration under the Treaty of Washington involved no slight strain upon the temper and good sense of both nations, and the result was reached against most violent protest on the part of many who preferred war to concession. In the recent war between Russia and Japan a feeling of strong resentment was created in England by Russia's course in sinking the British merchantmen, the *Knight Commander*, the *Saint Kilda*, the *Hipsang*, and the *Allenton*, and in the capture of the *Malacca* by Russian vessels which had passed the Dardanelles and the Suez Canal as merchantmen and then converted themselves into cruisers.

There is no more fruitful source of international controversy, of international resentment and dislike, than in the great multitude of questions relating to the rights and wrongs of neutrals and of belligerents in a war between maritime powers. The tendency always is for the war to spread through these controversies and exasperated feelings, and the adjudication of questions by national prize courts naturally fails to allay the irritation. Provision for the international judicial determination of such questions is adapted not only to preserve the substantial rights of neutral commerce and of belligerents, but also to prevent the spread of war much as municipal ordinances are framed to check the spread of fire, and sanitary regulations to prevent the communication of infectious disease. Considered by itself, the concurrence of the major part of the civilized world in the project of this convention was an event of the first importance in the development of international peace.

When Great Britain, however, came to consider the ratification of the Prize Court Convention she found herself confronted by practical considerations arising from her insular position, her dependence upon foreign food supplies, the wide extension of her colonial empire, her enormous merchant marine, and the relation between the effectiveness of her great navy and her national existence. The effect of these considerations upon the Government of Great Britain is best stated in the words of a communication which that Government addressed on February 27, 1908, to the other principal maritime powers. In that communication Sir Edward Grey said:

> Article 7 of the convention provides that, in the absence of treaty stipulations applicable to the case, the Court is to decide the appeals that come before it, in accordance with the rules of international law, or if no generally recognized rules exist, in accordance with the general principles of justice and equity.
>
> The discussions which took place at The Hague during the recent conference showed that on various questions connected with maritime war divergent views and practices prevailed among the nations of the world. Upon some of these subjects an agreement was reached, but on others it was not found possible within the period for which the conference assembled, to arrive at an understanding. The impression was gained that the establishment of the International Prize Court would not meet with general acceptance so long as vagueness and uncertainty exist as to the principles which the Court, in dealing with appeals brought before it, would apply to questions of far-reaching importance affecting naval policy and practice.
>
> His Majesty's Government therefore propose that another conference should assemble during the autumn of the present year, with the object of arriving at an agreement as to what are the generally recognized principles of international law, within the meaning of paragraph 2 of article 7 of the convention, as to those matters wherein the practice of nations has varied, and of then formulating the rules which, in the absence of special treaty provisions applicable to a particular case, the Court should observe in dealing with appeals brought before it for decision.

That is to say, the realization of the International Prize Court must be postponed until an agreement can be reached upon the rules of law and the principles of justice and equity which the Court is to apply to international controversies. No dissent from this view appears to have been expressed and pursuant to the British invitation, Austria-Hungary, France, Germany, Italy, Japan, Russia, Spain, the Netherlands, and the United States, sent their delegates to the proposed conference in London. The conference met on December 4, 1908, and continued to February 26, 1909.

The task of the conference was delicate and difficult. The Declaration of Paris in 1856 had, it is true, furnished four rules as a point of departure:

(1) Privateering is and remains abolished.
(2) The neutral flag covers enemy's merchandise with the exception of contraband of war.
(3) Neutral merchandise, with the exception of contraband of war, is not capturable under the enemy's flag.
(4) Blockades, in order to be obligatory, must be effective; that is to say, maintained by a force sufficient to really prevent access to the coast of the enemy.

But the half-century which had elapsed since the Declaration of Paris had shown that these rules left uncovered a great field of controversy and that they had themselves given rise to numerous questions for which they afforded no solution. The divergent views upon these subjects of controversy had become intrenched in many traditional ideas of different nations as to the requirements of their national interests either as possible belligerents or possible neutrals, and these ideas made concessions difficult, so difficult that at the Second Hague Conference it had been found quite impracticable to reach any conclusions upon questions of this character having real importance.

The members of the London Conference addressed themselves to their work with ability, knowledge, and good

DECLARATION OF LONDON

temper, and they agreed upon a code of rules which they called a "Declaration concerning the Laws of Naval War", and which is known as the Declaration of London. The first chapter of the Declaration, containing twenty-one articles, deals with the law of blockade in time of war. The second chapter covers the law of contraband, in twenty-three articles. The third chapter contains three articles upon the law of unneutral service. The fourth chapter, seven articles, on the destruction of neutral prizes. The fifth chapter, two articles, on transfer of flag. The sixth chapter, four articles, on enemy character. The seventh chapter, two articles regarding convoy. The eighth chapter, one article concerning resistance to search. The ninth chapter, an article upon compensation. Then follow seven final articles. The preamble of the Declaration declares the Powers (naming them) —

Considering the invitation which the British Government has given to various Powers to meet in conference in order to determine together as to what are the generally recognized rules of international law within the meaning of Article 7 of the Convention of October 18, 1907, relative to the establishment of an International Prize Court;

Recognizing all the advantages which in the unfortunate event of a naval war an agreement as to the said rules would present, both as regards peaceful commerce, and as regards the belligerents and as regards their political relations with neutral Governments;

Considering that the general principles of international law are often in their practical application the subject of divergent procedure;

Animated by the desire to insure henceforward a greater uniformity in this respect;

Hoping that a work so important to the common welfare will meet with general approval:

Have appointed as their Plenipotentiaries, that is to say: (names of plenipotentiaries)

Who, after having communicated their full powers, found in good and due form, have agreed to make the present Declaration: —

PRELIMINARY PROVISION

The Signatory Powers are agreed in declaring that the rules contained in the following Chapters correspond in substance with the generally recognized principles of international law.

It is interesting to observe that in the rules regarding contraband, the doctrine of continuous voyages, with which the Americans were so much concerned during the Civil War, is applied to absolute contraband but not to conditional contraband; that the great extension of the list of contraband articles, which, in the war between Russia and Japan, caused such general dissatisfaction among neutrals and threatened to nullify the doctrine that free ships make free goods, has been checked by a definite list of articles which are not under any circumstances to be considered contraband, and by carefully framed provisions requiring affirmative proof that goods are destined for the use of the armed forces or a government department of the enemy as a condition upon the right to seize conditional contraband. It is also interesting that the question so much discussed at the time of the *Trent* affair between England and the United States has been disposed of by the provision of Article 47 that " any individual embodied in the armed forces of the enemy who is found on board a neutral merchant vessel may be made a prisoner of war even though there may be no ground for the capture of the vessel."

This by implication excludes civil agents such as Mason and Slidell from capture but approves the method followed by Captain Wilkes in taking persons assumed to be liable to capture from the vessel and releasing the vessel.

It is not, however, my purpose to discuss the specific provisions of these rules.

The Declaration was accompanied by a very lucid and illuminating report prepared by M. Renault, which was presented to the Conference upon behalf of the Drafting Committee and which, under Continental usage, is to be treated as an authoritative explanation of the text. The report says of the Declaration:

The body of rules contained in the Declaration, which is the result of the deliberations of the Naval Conference, and which is to be entitled Declaration concerning the Laws of Naval War, answers well to the desire expressed by the British Government in its invitation of February, 1908. The questions of the programme are all settled except two, concerning which explanations will be given later. The solutions have been deduced from the various views or different practices and correspond to what may be called the *media sententia*. They do not always harmonize absolutely with the views peculiar to each country, but they do not shock the essential ideas of any. They should not be examined separately, but as a whole, otherwise one runs the risk of the most serious misunderstandings. In fact, if one considers one or more isolated rules either from the belligerent or the neutral point of view, he may find the interests with which he is especially concerned have been disregarded by the adoption of these rules, but the rules have their other side. The work is one of compromise and a mutual concession. Is it, as a whole, a good work?

We confidently hope that those who study it seriously will answer affirmatively. The Declaration substitutes uniformity and certainty for the diversity and the obscurity from which international relations have too long suffered. The Conference has tried to reconcile in an equitable and practical way the rights of belligerents and those of neutral commerce; it is made up of Powers placed in very unlike conditions, from the political, economic, and geographical points of view. There is on this account reason to suppose that the rules on which these Powers are in accord take sufficient account of the different interests involved, and hence may be accepted without disadvantage by all the others.

Two questions proposed by Great Britain to the Conference remain unanswered: one, relating to the transformation of merchant vessels into warships on the high seas, and the other, the question whether the nationality or the domicile of the owner should be adopted in determining whether property is enemy property. Upon these questions the divergence of views remains unsettled. But throughout the great field of controversy in this branch of international law all existing differences have been settled by fair agreement upon just and reasonable rules.

Professor Westlake said, in the *Nineteenth Century*, for March, 1910:

That the ten greatest naval powers of the world should have met in conference on the laws of naval war as affecting neutrals, and that after careful consideration they should have agreed upon a code so comprehensive as that contained in the Declaration of London, would alone suffice to make the year nineteen hundred and nine memorable to all who are interested in the improvement of international relations. It remains for the year nineteen hundred and ten to make that code binding on the parties by ratification, after which the natural course of events will speedily make it the binding code of the world.

It appeared to many of us, indeed, when the agreement was reached and the Conference dissolved, that a great thing had been done and that the way had been cleared to carry into effect the Prize Court Convention and to establish upon a permanent basis the judicial settlement of this class of international controversies through the application of an accepted code of law.

Unfortunately, that belief has not been justified. An excited controversy immediately arose regarding the effect of the rules contained in the Declaration of London upon the interests of Great Britain. One set of objectors declared that the rules sacrificed the interests of Great Britain as a belligerent. Another set asserted that the rules destroyed the interests of Great Britain as a neutral. Both could not be true, yet each set of objectors continued strenuously to oppose the Declaration upon its own grounds.

An examination of the arguments on both sides in Great Britain leads to the conclusion that Mr. Norman Bentwich sums up the controversy fairly when he says, in the *Fortnightly Review:*

Great Britain should now be in a position to ratify The Hague Prize Court Convention, when at least she has made the necessary changes in her national prize law. She has come out very well indeed from the international bargaining: she had most to lose by the previous uncertainty; she has gained most by the settlement. At Paris, in 1856, she gave up one of her most powerful belligerent rights — the right to capture enemy property in neutral ships. Now in London she has not given up a single established belligerent right of value, her sole concession being on the question of convoy which is more apparent than real; and, on the other hand, she has gained a number of safe-guards for her neutral commerce, and a number of limitations of the alleged belligerent rights of other powers. There is indeed a naval school which is bitterly hostile to the ratification of the Declaration, on the ground that by it England gives up certain national claims of long standing and concedes certain rights against which she has long struggled. But the claims we give up have not been effectively exercised by us, the rights we concede have regularly been practised against us.

Nevertheless the Prize Court Bill, introduced in Parliament to give effect to the Convention and the Declaration, passed the House of Commons but was rejected by the House of Lords, and so the matter stands.

This is unfortunate not merely because the rules of law contained in the Declaration are wise and just and would be beneficial to the world, but because the most promising forward movement toward the peaceable settlement of international disputes is frustrated by the kind of treatment which, if persisted in, must apparently prevent all forward movement in the same line. The Prize Court Convention is representative of the general movement for judicial settlement. The Declaration of London is representative of the agreement upon the rules of international law which is essential to the establishment of the practice of judicial settlement in all other branches of international controversy.

For some time past there has been a growing impression among men familiar with international affairs that the obstacles to the development of any real system for the submission of international disputes to impartial decision are to be found not so much in the unwillingness of nations to submit their disputes to such a decision, but in the lack of adequate machinery through which such decisions may be secured. The tendency of arbitrations in which representatives of the disputing countries are joined with eminent publicists from other countries for the determination of international controversies is not to decide questions of fact and law, but it is to negotiate a settlement. Arbitrators as a rule act as diplomatists under the diplomatic sense of honorable obligation rather than as judges under the judicial sense of honorable obligation. Their tendency is to do what they think is wise and for the best interests of all concerned and to get the controversy disposed of in some way without too much ill feeling upon either side. In this process the frequent failure of international law to furnish any certain or undisputed guide for action affords free opportunity for the personal predilections of the arbitrator, often colored or determined by the prevailing opinions in the country from which he comes; and these opinions are often quite unlike those which prevail among the people of either of the disputing countries. It often happens, therefore, that the selection of the arbitrators is the most critical and decisive step in the arbitration. It is very difficult to apply to such a proceeding the analogy of a judicial proceeding under municipal law for the trial and decision of cases between private litigants. It may well be that countries are unwilling to have their interests disposed of in that way, although they would be perfectly ready to submit their cases to the decision of judges acting under the judicial sense of responsibility. Many of us are convinced that the true line of development for the peaceable settlement of international controversies is to be found in the establishment of a real international court which shall hear and determine questions instead of negotiating a settlement of them. This question was much discussed in The Hague Conference of 1907, which approved and recommended to the Powers the adoption of a draft convention for the creation of a Judicial Arbitral Court to be composed of judges appointed for fixed periods with stated compensation and chosen from persons " fulfilling the conditions qualifying them in their respective countries to occupy high legal posts,

DECLARATION OF LONDON

or to be jurists of recognized competence in matters of international law." The procedure, powers, and jurisdiction of the court were all provided for and the draft convention as approved by the Conference was defective only in not determining how the judges should be appointed. The determination upon this matter was prevented by difference of opinion between the larger and the smaller powers represented in the Conference. The provision for a general judicial court with jurisdiction to hear and determine all matters of international dispute was thus carried within one step of the completeness which was reached in the convention for the International Prize Court. The Prize Court thus became the advance guard of the proposed judicial system, the experiment upon which the success of the whole plainly depends. President Roosevelt, in his message to Congress of December 3, 1907, said truly:

Not only will the International Prize Court be the means of protecting the interest of neutrals, but it is in itself a step toward the creation of the most general court for the hearing of international controversies, to which reference has just been made. The organization and action of such a Prize Court cannot fail to accustom the different countries to the submission of international questions to the decision of an international tribunal, and we may confidently expect the results of such submission to bring about a general agreement upon the enlargement of the practice.

The relations between the project for the **Prize Court** and the project for the general **Judicial Arbitral Court** are so manifest that the United States has already proposed to the other Powers an enlargement of the jurisdiction of the Prize Court so that any question between the signatory Powers can be heard and determined by the judges of the Prize Court. This was done by instructions to the delegates of the United States at the London Conference, dated February 6, 1909, by an identic circular note to the Powers represented at that Conference dated March 5, 1909, and by a formal communication from the Department of State to the Powers, dated October 18, 1909. The form given to the proposal in the last mentioned communication from the American State Department was that there should be —

<blockquote>a further agreement that the International Court of Prize established by the Convention signed at The Hague, October 18, 1907, and the judges thereof shall be competent to entertain and decide any case of arbitration presented to it by a signatory of the International Court of Prize, and that when sitting as a Court of Arbitral Justice the said International Court of Prize shall conduct its proceedings in accordance with the draft convention for the establishment of a Court of Arbitral Justice, approved and recommended by the Second Hague Peace Conference, on October 18, 1907.</blockquote>

I am advised that this proposal was favorably received and that action to give it effect in some practicable form only awaits the ratification of the Prize Court Convention. This line of advance also is thus blocked by the failure to confirm the Declaration of London.

This review of the origin and nature of the Declaration of London and of the attendant conditions exhibits the true significance of the Declaration. It is not merely a code of useful rules. It is necessary to the existence of the International Prize Court and therefore to the existence of any Judicial Arbitral Court. It is the one indispensable forward step without which no practical progress can now be made in the further development of a system of peaceable settlement of international disputes. It is to be hoped that a fuller realization of its far-reaching importance will soon lead to its acceptance. I cannot avoid the conviction that a broad-minded and statesmanlike treatment of this constructive measure for practical progress in international relations, is of greater value than merely benevolent but academic declarations in favor of peace which are to be found in general treaties of arbitration and in diplomatic correspondence and in public speeches.

Indeed the whole practice of making general treaties of arbitration cannot fail to be discredited by the failure, if there is to be a failure, of the Prize Court Convention, for the cynical are sure to question the sincerity of general treaties of arbitration covering the whole field of international relations between nations which refuse to assent to this convention covering but a small part of the same field.

FRANCIS LIEBER

PRESIDENTIAL ADDRESS AT THE SEVENTH ANNUAL MEETING
OF THE AMERICAN SOCIETY OF INTERNATIONAL LAW
WASHINGTON, APRIL 24, 1913

THIS year, 1913, is the fiftieth anniversary of a very important event in the history of international law — the adoption and enforcement by the American Government of the code of rules governing the conduct of armies in the field, which is known to the American army as General Orders No. 100, of 1863. It happens that without any intention to create a coincidence the seventh annual meeting of the American Society of International Law is appointed and we are met here, exactly fifty years after the twenty-fourth day of April, 1863, when President Lincoln promulgated that famous order. It seems appropriate for this Society at this time to celebrate the event by paying honor to Francis Lieber, the author of the instructions embodied in the order.

In the early stages of the American Civil War both parties put into the field immense armies, commanded for the most part by volunteer officers drawn from the ordinary occupations of civil life and quite ignorant of the laws and usages of war. The sources of information were to be found only in scattered text-books and treatises, most of them in foreign languages, few of them readily accessible, and requiring the painstaking and diligent labor of the student to search out rules which were at the best subject to doubt and dispute. It was manifest that the officers of the Union and Confederate armies had neither time nor opportunity to enter upon an extended study of the international laws of war, and that unless some one indicated to these uninstructed and untrained combatants what was and what was not permissible in warfare, the conflict would be waged without those restraints upon the savage side of human nature, by which modern civilization has somewhat mitigated and confined the barbarous cruelties of war. Fortunately, General Halleck, who was put in chief command of the Union army in July, 1862, was an accomplished student of international law. He had already published an excellent book on that subject. While the duties of commanding general during an active conflict left him no time for research and codification himself, he knew what ought to be done and how it ought to be done; and he called Francis Lieber, then a professor in Columbia College, and already a publicist distinguished upon both sides of the Atlantic, to the assistance of the Government. The first service which Lieber rendered was the preparation in 1862 of a statement or essay upon *Guerilla Parties Considered with Reference to the Laws and Usages of War.* One cannot read this paper now, with its definite and lucid statements based upon grounds of reason and supported by historical reference, without feeling that it must have been a real satisfaction to the burdened and harassed Union authorities at Washington to have such a guide in dealing with the multitude of cases continually arising in that debatable land which intervenes between disciplined and responsible warfare on the one hand and simple robbery and murder on the other.

On the seventeenth of December, 1862, by order of Secretary Stanton, a board was created " to propose amendments or changes in the rules and articles of war and a code of regulations for the government of armies in the field as authorized by the laws and usages of war," and this board was made up of Francis Lieber, LL.D., and four volunteer officers, Generals Hitchcock, Cadwalader, Hartsuff and Martindale. That part of the board's work which consisted of preparing the code of regulations appears to have been committed to Dr. Lieber. The nature of the field upon which he entered and the spirit in which he did his work are indicated by Lieber's letter transmitting the result to General Halleck, on February 20, 1863:

> Here is the project of the code I was charged with drawing up. I am going to send fifty copies to General Hitchcock for distribution, and I earnestly ask for suggestions and amendments. I am going to send for that purpose a copy to General Scott, and another to Honorable Horace Binney. . . . I have earnestly endeavored to treat of these grave topics conscientiously and comprehensively; and you, well-read in the literature of this branch of international law, know that nothing of the kind exists in any language. I had no guide, no ground-work, no text-book. I can assure you, as a friend, that no counselor of Justinian sat down to his task of the Digest with a deeper feeling of the gravity of his labor, than filled my breast in the laying down for the first time such a code, where nearly everything was floating. Usage, history, reason, and conscientiousness, a sincere love of truth, justice and civilization have been my guides; but of course the whole must be still very imperfect. . . .

Lieber's estimate of the work and of the occasion for it is shown in a letter from him to General Halleck of May 20, 1863:

> I have the copy of General Orders 100 which you sent me. The generals of the board have added some valuable parts; but there have also been a few things omitted, which I regret. As the order now stands, I think that No. 100 will do honor to our country. It will be adopted as a basis for similar works by the English, French, and Germans. It is a contribution by the United States to the stock of common civilization. I feel almost sad in closing this business. Let me hope it will not put a stop to our correspondence. I regret that your name is not visibly connected with this Code. *You* do not regret it, because you are void of ambition, — to a faulty degree, as it seems to me . . . I believe it is now time for you to issue a *strong* order, directing attention to those paragraphs in the Code which prohibit devastation, demolition of private property, etc. I know by letters from the West and the South, written by men on our side, that the wanton destruction of property by our men is alarming. It does incalculable injury. It demoralizes our troops; it annihilates wealth irrecoverably, and makes a return to a state of peace more and more difficult. Your order, though impressive and even sharp, might be written with reference to the Code, and pointing out the disastrous consequences of reckless devastation, in such a manner as not to furnish our reckless enemy with new arguments for his savagery.

The instructions comprise one hundred and fifty-seven articles. The scope of the work can be indicated briefly by stating the titles of the ten sections in which the articles are grouped:

Martial Law; Military Jurisdiction; Military Necessity; Retaliation.
Public and Private Property of the Enemy; Protection of Prisoners, and especially Women; of Religion, the Arts and Sciences — Punishment of Crimes Against the Inhabitants of Hostile Countries.
Deserters; Prisoners of War; Hostages; Booty on the Battlefield.
Partisans; Armed Enemies not Belonging to Hostile Armies; Scouts; Armed Prowlers; War Rebels.
Safe Conduct; Spies; War Traitors; Captured Messengers; Abuse of the Flag of Truce.
Exchange of Prisoners; Flags of Truce; Flags of Protection.
The Parole.
Armistice — Capitulation.
Assassination.
Insurrection; Civil War; Rebellion.

The provisions on these subjects give evidence of great learning and careful consideration. They cover the entire historical field of questions which had arisen and the possibilities of questions likely to arise, calling for instruction and direction. The definitions are clear, the injunctions and prohibitions distinct and unambiguous, and, while the instrument was a practical presentation of what the laws and usages of war were, and not a technical discussion of what the writer thought they ought to be, in all its parts may be discerned an instinctive selection of the best and most humane practice and an assertion of the control of morals to the limit permitted by the dreadful business in which the rules were to be applied.

These instructions directed the action of the Union officers and controlled the conduct of the Union forces during that great war which ended in the triumph of the armies on which their limitations were imposed. No one can say how far it was due to the instructions, but in honoring the memory of

Francis Lieber we should not forget that after the surrender and the triumph came reconciliation, friendship, the restoration of a united country, and, beyond all human experience, even within the lifetime of the generation which had waged the conflict, freedom from the bitterness of spirit that time cannot soften.

Although the instructions were prepared for use in a civil war, a great part of them were of general application, and they were adopted by the German Government for the conduct of its armies in the field in the war of 1870 with France. It is interesting that this work of a simple private citizen should become the law controlling the mightiest forces of both the country of his adoption and the country of his birth. The sanction of two powerful governments for these rules and their successful employment in two of the greatest wars of modern times gave to them an authority never before acquired by any codification or statement of any considerable number of rules intended for international application. The prediction of Lieber that General Orders No. 100 would do honor to our country, that it would be adopted as a basis for similar works by the English, French, and Germans, and that it would be a contribution by the United States to the stock of common civilization, was justified. In the Brussels Conference of 1874, convened at the instance of the Emperor of Russia for the purpose of codifying the laws and customs of war, the Russian delegate, Baron Jomini, as president of the conference, declared that the project of an international convention then presented had its origin in the rules of President Lincoln. The convention agreed upon at Brussels was not ratified, but in 1880 the Institute of International Law made the work of the Brussels Conference and the work of Lieber, which so far as it was of general application was incorporated in that convention, the basis of a manual of the laws of war upon land; and finally, in The Hague Conferences of 1899 and 1907, the conventions with respect to the laws and customs of war on land gave the adherence of the whole civilized world in substance and effect to those international rules which President Lincoln made binding upon the American armies fifty years ago. Writing of Lieber's work, Sheldon Amos says in his book on *Political and Legal Remedies for War:*

> The instructions were, in fact, the first attempt to make a comprehensive survey of all the exigencies to which a war of invasion is likely to give rise; and it is said on good authority that, with one exception (that of concealing in an occupied district arms or provisions for the enemy), no case presented itself during the Franco-German War of 1870 which had not been provided for in the American instructions.

Frederic de Martens, after describing the way in which Lieber's work came to be done, says:

> So it is to the United States of North America and to President Lincoln that belongs the honor of having taken the initiative in defining with precision the customs and laws of war. This first official attempt to codify the customs of war and to collect in a code the rules binding upon military forces has notably contributed to impress the character of humanity upon the conduct of the northern states in the course of that war.

Bluntschli says, in his article on *Lieber's Service to Political Science and International Law:*

> The Instructions for the Government of Armies of the United States in the Field were drawn up by Lieber at the instance of President Lincoln, and formed the first codification of International Articles of War. This was a deed of great moment in the history of international law and civilization. Throughout this work also we see the stamp of Lieber's peculiar genius. His legal injunctions rest upon the foundation of moral precepts. The former are not always sharply distinguished from moral injunctions, but nevertheless, through a union with the same, are ennobled and exalted. Everywhere reigns in this body of law the spirit of humanity, which spirit recognizes as fellow-beings, with lawful rights, our very enemies, and which forbids our visiting upon them unnecessary injury, cruelty, or destruction. But at the same time, our legislator remains fully aware that, in time of war, it is absolutely necessary to provide for the safety of armies and for the successful conduct of a campaign; that, to those engaged in it, the harshest measures and most reckless exactions cannot be denied; and that

tender-hearted sentimentality is here all the more out of place, because the greater the energy employed in carrying on the war, the sooner will it be brought to an end, and the normal condition of peace restored.

Then follows a very interesting statement by Bluntschli which points out a consequence of the instructions not the least in value to the student of international law and to the development of that science upon which the hoped-for peace of the world so largely depends. It appears that Bluntschli found in Lieber's work the inspiration of his celebrated codification of international law, for he says:

> These instructions prepared by Lieber, prompted me to draw up, after his model, first, the laws of war, and then, in general, the law of nations, in the form of a code, or law book, which should express the present state of the legal consciousness of civilized peoples.

Professor Ernest Nys sums up the far-reaching effect of Lieber's codification by the statement:

> The ideas of the American publicist have penetrated not only the scientific world through the works of Bluntschli, but by the work of the Conference of Brussels, in 1874, and The Hague in 1899 and 1907, they have penetrated international politics.

When we recall the frightful cruelties upon combatants, upon prisoners, upon citizens, the overturning of all human rights to life and liberty and property, the fiendish malignity of oppression by brutal force, which have characterized the history of war, we cannot fail to set a high estimate upon the service of the man who gave form and direction and effectiveness to the civilizing movement by which man at his best, through the concurrence of nations, imposes the restraint of rules of right conduct, upon man at his worst, in the extreme exercise of force.

Let me say something about the man himself. He was born in Berlin on March 18, 1800. His childhood was passed in those distressful times when the declaration of the rights of man and the great upheaval of the French Revolution had inspired throughout the continent of Europe a conception of popular liberty and awakened a strong desire to attain it, while the people of Prussia were held in the strictest subjection to an autocratic government of inveterate and uncompromising traditions. In the meantime foreign conquest, with the object lessons of Jena and Friedland and the Confederation of the Rhine, threatened the destruction of national independence; and love of country urged Germans to the support of a government which the love of liberty urged them to condemn. It was one of the rare periods in which political ideas force themselves into the thought and feeling of every intelligent life, and, alongside with the struggle for subsistence, the average man finds himself driven by a sense of necessity into a struggle for liberty, opportunity, peace, order, security for life and property — things which in ordinary times he vaguely assumes to come by nature like the air he breathes. So the early ideas of the child were filled with deep impressions of the public life of the time. He remembered the entry of Napoleon into Berlin after Jena. He remembered the humiliation of the peace of Tilsit. He remembered Schill, the defender of Colberg, and Stein, and Scharnhorst. He was a disciple of Dr. Jahn, the manual-trainer of German patriotism. At fifteen, after the escape from Elba, he enlisted in the Colberg regiment and fought under Blücher at Waterloo. He was seriously wounded in the Battle of Namur and had the strange and vital discipline of lying long on the battlefield in expectation of death. He was a member of patriotic societies and was arrested in his nineteenth year, and imprisoned four months on suspicion of dangerous political designs. He was excluded from membership in the German universities, except Jena, where he received his degree of Doctor of Philosophy in 1820. At twenty-one he made his way to Greece with a company of other young Germans, inspired, by a generous enthusiasm for liberty, to an unavailing attempt to aid in the Greek War of Independence. Returning penniless from Greece he found his way to Rome, became a tutor in the family of Barthold Georg Niebuhr, then Prussian Ambassador, and there he won the confidence and lifelong friendship of that great historian whose influence in familiar intercourse both increased the learning and calmed and sobered the judgment of the impetuous youth. Returning to Prussia, he was again arrested and imprisoned for nearly a year upon charges of disaffection to the government. Released through the intercession of Niebuhr, he went to England, and after a year's hard struggle there, he came, in 1827, to the United States and to Boston. Seeking employment he found it in taking charge of the Boston Gymnasium. Through Niebuhr's good offices he became the American correspondent of a group of German newspapers. He devised a plan for the publication of an encyclopedia, and for this he secured a distinguished list of contributors and associates. He became its editor, and in 1829 the publication of the *Encyclopædia Americana* was begun. It was a distinct success. Lieber's connection with it not only forced him to a broad and accurate knowledge of American life, but brought him in contact with a great range of leaders of American thought and opinion, and this association gave him an intimate knowledge of American social conditions and public affairs. Bancroft, and Hilliard, and Everett, and Story, and Nicholas Biddle, and Charles Sumner were among his friends. In June, 1835, he was made Professor of History and Political Economy in South Carolina College, and for twenty-two years he held that chair, until, in 1857, he was called to Columbia College to be Professor of Modern History, Political Science, International Law, Civil and Common Law. His connection with Columbia and his residence in New York continued until his death in October, 1872. In the meantime, to the service as adviser to the Government, which I have already described, he added the classification and arrangement of the Confederate archives in the office of the War Department, and long served as umpire under the Mexican Claims Commission of July 4, 1868.

Lieber himself has said that his life had been made up of many geological layers. The transition from his adventurous youth to the life of an American college professor did indeed carry him from igneous to sedimentary conditions. Under the new conditions, however, his surpassing energy and capacity for application found exercise in authorship. His work on *Political Ethics*, published in 1838, and that on *Civil Liberty and Self Government*, published in 1853, gave him high rank among writers upon the philosophy of government. Judge Story said of the former:

> It contains by far the fullest and most correct development of the true theory of what constitutes the state that I have ever seen. It abounds with profound views of government which are illustrated with various learning. To me many of the thoughts are new, and striking as they are new. I do not hesitate to say that it constitutes one of the best theoretical treatises on the true nature and objects of government which has been produced in modern times, containing much for instruction, much for admonition, and much for deep meditation, addressing itself to the wise and virtuous of all countries.

And in an introduction to the latter work, Theodore Dwight Woolsey said:

> It would be a grateful task to speak at length here of the service Doctor Lieber rendered to political science in this country. . . . He was indeed the founder of this science in this country in so far as by his method, his fulness of historical illustration, his noble, ethical feeling, his sound practical judgment, which was of the English rather than of the German type, he secured readers among the first men of the land, influenced political thought more than any one of his contemporaries in the United States, and made I think, a lasting impression on many students who were forming themselves for the work of life.

By a great variety of miscellaneous essays, addresses, and magazine articles on subjects of education, penology, history, biography, constitutional, and international law, he exercised a powerful influence upon the development of American thought. By voluminous correspondence with many foremost Americans who were engaged in public affairs he made his influence felt upon the solution of specific questions in the conduct of government. A correspondence of many years with Charles Sumner is especially rich in matter of this description.

The philosophical habit of the German, the practical habit of the Englishman, the freedom from traditional limitations upon thought of the American, the breadth of view of his cosmopolitan experience, the intensity of his enthusiasm at once for liberty and for order, and the strength of his genuine sympathy for all mankind combined to set him in advance of his time in his views upon international law and his proposals for its development. We find him writing to Sumner on December 27, 1861, after the Trent Affair — more than fifty years ago:

> This would be a fair occasion to propose a congress of all maritime nations, European and American, to settle some more canons of the law of nations than were settled at the Peace of Paris, — canons chiefly or exclusively relating to the rights and duties of belligerents and neutrals on the sea; for there lies the chief difficulty. The sea belongs to all; hence the difficulty of the sea police, because there all are equals. I mean no codification of international law; I mean that such a congress, avowedly convened for such a purpose, should take some more canons out of the cloudy realm of precedents than the Peace of Paris did almost incidentally. Suppose Russia, Austria, and other nations (naming them) could be induced to send, each power, two jurists (with naval advisers if they chose), does any one, who knows how swelling civilization courses in our history, doubt that their debates and resolutions would remain useless, — even though the whole should lead, this time, to no more than an experiment? All those ideas that are now great and large blessings of our race, having wrought themselves into constitutions or law systems, belonged once to Utopia.

On April 16, 1866, he writes to Bluntschli in Heidelberg:

> Your intention to write a brief code on the Rights of Nations, in the middle of the nineteenth century, is a noble and daring one. For a long

time it was a favorite project of mine that four or five of the most distinguished jurists should hold a congress in order to decide on several important but still unsettled questions of national equity, and perhaps draw up a code. First I proposed that it should be an official congress under the government, and corresponded with Senator Sumner on the subject. But after a while it became clear to me that it would be much better if a private congress were established, whose work would stand as an authority by its excellence, truthfulness, justice, and superiority in every respect.

June 18, 1866, to his wife:

Have you read the noble declaration of Prussia, that she will not capture enemies' property at sea during war ? Such things warm one like a glass of Burgundy. . . .

December 15, 1866, to Andrew D. White:

I fancy sometimes — but only fancy — how fine a thing it would be for one of the Peabodies, or some such gold vessel, to give, say twenty-five thousand dollars gold, for the holding of a private — i. e., not diplomatic, although international — congress of some eight or ten jurists, to concentrate international authority and combined weight on certain great points, on which we have now only individual authorities. I have spoken about this years ago to Mr. Field.

On June 11, 1868, to Sumner:

What an advance it would be — though requiring nearly twenty-two centuries — from the time when Thucydides said that private property was not acknowledged at sea as on land, to the middle of the nineteenth century, when private property — even of the enemy — should be declared to be protected, even floating without defence, on the wide sea. . . . I say that civilization would hardly have made or be able to make a greater stride in our century, than by the United States and North Germany agreeing on the great principle and thus inducing others to follow.

On May 7, 1869, to Judge Thayer:

The strength, authority, and grandeur of the law of nations rests on, and consists in, the very fact that reason, justice, equity, speak through men 'greater than he who takes a city' — single men, plain Grotius; and that nations, and even Congresses of Vienna, cannot avoid hearing, acknowledging, and quoting them. But it has ever been, and is still, a favorite idea of mine that there should be a congress of from five to ten acknowledged jurists to settle a dozen or two of important yet unsettled points — a private and boldly self-appointed congress, whose whole authority should rest on the inherent truth and energy of their own *proclama-*

On April 10, 1872 to General Dufour, honorary president of the International Committee of Geneva:

One of far the most effectual and beneficent things that, at this very juncture, could be done for the promotion of the intercourse of nations in peace or war (and there is *intercourse* in war, since man cannot meet man without intercourse) — one of the most promising things in matters of internationalism, would be the meeting of the most prominent jurists of the law of nations, of our Cis-Caucasian race — one from each country in their individual and not in any public capacity — to settle among themselves certain great questions of the law of nations as yet unsettled, such as neutrality, or the aid of barbarians, or the duration of the claims of obligations, of citizenship. I mean *settle* as Grotius *settled*, — by the strength of the great argument of justice. A code of proclamation, as it were, of such a body, would soon acquire far greater authority than the book of the greatest single jurist. I hope such a meeting may be brought about in 1874.

On May 26, 1872, to Von Holtzendorff:

In 1846, in one of my writings, I recalled the fact that under Adrian, professors were appointed to lecture in different places, and Polemon of Laodicea instructed in oratory at Rome, Laodicea, Smyrna, and Alexandria. The traveling professor had a free passage on the emperor's ships, or on the vessels laden with grain. In our days of steamboats and railroads the traveling professor should be reinstated. Why could not the same person teach in New York and in Strasburg ?

You will perceive that here was a proposal of the exchange professorship, which we are putting in practice forty years after. Here was another proposal which was realized by the formation of the Institute of International Law. Of this Professor Bluntschli says:

Lieber had great influence, I may add, in founding the *Institut de Droit International*, which was started in Ghent, in 1873, and forms a permanent alliance of leading international jurists from all civilized nations, for the purpose of working harmoniously together, and thus serving as an organ for the legal consciousness of the civilized world. Lieber was the first to propose and to encourage the idea of professional jurists of all nations thus coming together for consultation, and seeking to establish a common understanding. From this impulse proceeded Rolin-Jaequemyns' circular letter, drawn up in Ghent, calling together a number of men eminent for their learning. This latter proposal to found a *permanent academy for International Law* met with general acceptance, but this was merely a further development of the original idea of Lieber, which was at the bottom of the whole scheme.

Here also was the proposal for a meeting of official representatives which was the precursor of the conferences at The Hague. It is interesting to observe that while Lieber considered the unofficial meeting to be an alternative for the official one, both have been realized, and in practice the work of the unofficial members of the Institute of International Law has made possible the success of the official conferences at The Hague, by preparing their work beforehand and agreeing upon conclusions which the official conferences could accept.

The important characteristic which marshaled all Lieber's forces for leadership of opinion and gave his work its chief and permanent value was an elevation of spirit, a pervading moral quality which was refined by adversity and trial throughout the formative period of his life; and this quality was well expressed by two maxims which he made his guides. He says, in writing to Judge Thayer:

> From early times I observed that in the French Revolution people had always clamored for rights and never thought of duty; that more or less this is the case in all periods of agitation, and almost universally so in our own times and in our country . . . *right* and *duty*; both together, and all is well; right alone, despotism, — duty alone, slavery.

And, writing to Sumner, he says:

> Let me now give you what I consider my chief law maxim: *Nullum jus sine officio, nullum officium sine jure,* — forgotten by despot and *Rouge* (they want nothing but rights), forgotten by the slave who thinks he has nothing but duty or obligation.

And this he condensed into the maxim: "*Droit oblige.*"

The other maxim he kept displayed on the walls of his lecture room: "*Patria Cara: Carior Libertas: Veritas Carissima.*" And these maxims he exemplified in his life and in his service to mankind.

He was no dry student delving for knowledge he could not use; but a living soul instinct with human sympathy and love of liberty and justice, seizing eagerly the weapons of learning to strike blows in the struggle for nobler and happier life among men. He was no vapid theorist who 'argued about it and about, but evermore came out by the same door where in he went,' but a sagacious, practical man among men, dealing with human nature as it was, with all its weakness and folly and error, all its nobility and power; and seeking to shape the human material upon which he wrought to its best uses according to its real capacity and strength.

It was a wonderful career. It was a great thing to be the author of the *Instructions*. It was a great thing to give the impetus which produced the *Institut de Droit International* and made possible the success of the Hague Conferences. It was a great thing to be the man he was and to live a long life, loving learning and law, and liberty, and country, and kind, and blessed by consciousness of distinguished service to them all. It stirs the imagination that the boy who lay wounded on the battlefield of Namur for his country's sake and who languished in prison for liberty's sake and who left his native land that he might be free, should build his life into the structure of American self-government and leave a name honored by scholars and patriots the world over.

If our Society, at once national and international, were about to choose a patron saint, and the roll were to be called, my voice for one would answer " Francis Lieber."

THE REAL MONROE DOCTRINE

PRESIDENTIAL ADDRESS AT THE EIGHTH ANNUAL MEETING
OF THE AMERICAN SOCIETY OF INTERNATIONAL LAW
WASHINGTON, APRIL 22, 1914

I ASK your attention for a few minutes to some observations upon the Monroe Doctrine. If I am justified in taking your time it will be not because I say anything novel, but because there is occasion for restating well-settled matters which seem to have been overlooked in some recent writings on the subject.

We are all familiar with President Monroe's famous message of December 2, 1823:

The occasion has been judged proper for asserting as a principle in which the rights and interests of the United States are involved, that the American Continents, by the free and independent condition which they have assumed and maintain, are henceforth not to be considered as subjects for future colonization by any European Powers. . . .

In the wars of the European Powers in matters relating to themselves we have never taken any part, nor does it comport with our policy to do so. It is only when our rights are invaded or seriously menaced that we resent injuries or make preparation for our defense. With the movements in this hemisphere we are of necessity more immediately connected and by causes which must be obvious to all enlightened and impartial observers.

We owe it, therefore, to candor, and to the amicable relations existing between the United States and those Powers, to declare that we should consider any attempt on their part to extend their system to any portion of this hemisphere as dangerous to our peace and safety. With the existing colonies or dependencies of any European Power we have not interfered and shall not interfere. But with the governments who have declared their independence and maintained it, and whose independence we have on great consideration and on just principles, acknowledged, we could not view any interposition for the purpose of oppressing them, or controlling in any other manner, their destiny, by any European Power, in any other light than as the manifestation of an unfriendly disposition toward the United States. In the war between these new governments and Spain we declared our neutrality at the time of their recognition, and to this we have adhered and shall continue to adhere, provided no change shall occur which, in the judgment of the competent authorities of this government, shall make a corresponding change on the part of the United States indispensable to their security. . . .

It is impossible that the allied Powers should extend their political system to any portion of either continent without endangering our peace and happiness; nor can any one believe that our southern brethren, if left to themselves, would adopt it of their own accord. It is equally impossible, therefore, that we should behold such interposition, in any form, with indifference.

The occasion for these declarations is a familiar story — the revolt of the Spanish provinces in America which Spain, unaided, was plainly unable to reduce to their former condition of dependence; the reaction against liberalism in Europe which followed the downfall of Napoleon and the restoration of the Bourbons to the throne of France; the formation of the Holy Alliance; the agreement of its members at the Conferences of Aix-la-Chapelle and Laybach and Verona for the insurance of monarchy against revolution; the restoration of Ferdinand the Seventh to the throne of Spain by the armed power of France pursuant to this agreement; the purpose of the Alliance to follow the restoration of monarchy in Spain by the restoration of that monarchy's control over its colonies in the New World; the claims both of Russia and of Great Britain to rights of colonization on the northwest coast; the proposals of Mr. Canning to Richard Rush for a joint declaration of principles by England and the United States adverse to the interference of any other European Power in the contest between Spain and her former colonies; the serious question raised by this proposal as to the effect of a joint declaration upon the American policy of avoiding entangling alliances.

The form and phrasing of President Monroe's message were adapted to meet these conditions. The statements made were intended to carry specific information to the members of the Holy Alliance that an attempt by any of them to coerce the new states of South America would be not a simple expedition against weak and disunited colonies, but the much more difficult and expensive task of dealing with the formidable maritime power of the United States as well as the opposition of England, and they were intended to carry to Russia and incidentally to England the idea that rights to territory in the New World must thenceforth rest upon then existing titles, and that the United States would dispute any attempt to create rights to territory by future occupation.

It is undoubtedly true that the specific occasions for the declaration of Monroe no longer exist. The Holy Alliance long ago disappeared. The nations of Europe no longer contemplate the vindication of monarchical principles in the territory of the New World. France, the most active of the Allies, is herself a republic. No nation longer asserts the right of colonization in America. The general establishment of diplomatic relations between the Powers of Europe and the American republics, if not already universal, became so when, pursuant to the formal assent of the Powers, all the American republics were received into the Second Conference at The Hague and joined in the conventions there made, upon the footing of equal sovereignty, entitled to have their territory and independence respected under that law of nations which formerly existed for Europe alone.

The declaration, however, did more than deal with the specific occasion which called it forth. It was intended to declare a general principle for the future, and this is plain not merely from the generality of the terms used but from the discussions out of which they arose and from the understanding of the men who took part in the making and of their successors.

When Jefferson was consulted by President Monroe before the message was sent he replied:

> The question presented by the letters you have sent me is the most momentous which has ever been offered to my contemplation since that of independence. That made us a nation; this sets our compass and points the course which we are to steer through the ocean of time opening on us. And never could we embark upon it under circumstances more auspicious. Our first and fundamental maxim should be, never to entangle ourselves in the broils of Europe; our second, never to suffer Europe to intermeddle with cis-atlantic affairs.

Three years later Daniel Webster declared that the doctrine involved the honor of the country. He said in the House of Representatives:

> I look upon it as a part of its treasures of reputation; and, for one, I intend to guard it. . . . I will neither help to erase it or tear it out; nor shall it be, by any act of mine, blurred or blotted. It did honor to the sagacity of the government, and will not diminish that honor.

Mr. Cleveland said in his message of December 17, 1895:

> The doctrine upon which we stand is strong and sound because its enforcement is important to our peace and safety as a nation, and is essential to the integrity of our free institutions and the tranquil maintenance of our distinctive form of government. It was intended to apply to every stage of our national life and cannot become obsolete while our republic endures.

As the particular occasions which called it forth have slipped back into history, the declaration itself, instead of being handed over to the historian, has grown continually a more vital and insistent rule of conduct for each succeeding generation of Americans. Never for a moment have the responsible and instructed statesmen in charge of the foreign affairs of the United States failed to consider themselves bound to insist upon its policy. Never once has the public opinion of the people of the United States failed to support every just application of it as new occasion has arisen. Almost every President and Secretary of State has restated the doctrine with vigor and emphasis in the discussion of the diplomatic affairs of his day. The governments of Europe have gradually come to realize that the existence of the policy which Monroe declared is a stubborn and continuing fact to be recognized in their controversies with American countries. We have seen Spain, France, England, Germany, with admirable good sense and good temper, explaining beforehand to the United States that they intended no permanent occupation of territory, in the controversy with Mexico forty years after the declaration, and in the controversy with Venezuela eighty years after. In 1903 the Duke of Devonshire declared " Great Britain accepts the Monroe Doctrine unreservedly." Mr. Hay coupled the Monroe Doctrine and the Golden Rule as cardinal guides of American diplomacy. Twice within very recent years the whole treaty-making power of the United States has given its formal approval to the policy by the reservations in the signature and in the ratification of the arbitration conventions of The Hague Conferences, expressed in these words by the Senate resolution agreeing to ratification of the convention of 1907:

Nothing contained in this convention shall be so construed as to require the United States of America to depart from its traditional policy of not intruding upon, interfering with, or entangling itself in the political questions of policy or internal administration of any foreign state, nor shall anything contained in the said convention be construed to imply a relinquishment by the United States of its traditional attitude towards purely American questions.

It seems fair to assume that a policy with such a history as this has some continuing and substantial reason underlying it; that it is not outworn or meaningless or a purely formal relic of the past, and it seems worth while to consider carefully what the doctrine is and what it is not.

No one ever pretended that Mr. Monroe was declaring a rule of international law or that the doctrine which he declared has become international law. It is a declaration of the United States that certain acts would be injurious to the peace and safety of the United States and that the United States would regard them as unfriendly. The declaration does not say what the course of the United States will be in case such acts are done. That is left to be determined in each particular instance. Mr. Calhoun said, in the Senate debate on the Yucatan Bill, in 1848:

> Whether you will resist or not and the measure of your resistance — whether it shall be by negotiation, remonstrance, or some intermediate measure, or by a resort to arms; all this must be determined and decided on the merits of the question itself. This is the only wise course. . . . There are cases of interposition where I would resort to the hazard of war with all its calamities. Am I asked for one? I will answer. I designate the case of Cuba.

In particular instances indeed the course which the United States would follow has been very distinctly declared, as when Mr. Seward said, in 1865:

> It has been the President's purpose that France should be respectfully informed upon two points; namely, first, that the United States earnestly desire to continue and to cultivate sincere friendship with France. Secondly, that this policy would be brought in imminent jeopardy unless France could deem it consistent with her honor to desist from the prosecution of armed intervention in Mexico to overthrow the domestic republican government existing there and to establish upon its ruins the foreign monarchy which has been attempted to be inaugurated in the capital of that country.

So Secretary Buchanan said, in 1848:

> The highest and first duty of every independent nation is to provide for its own safety; and acting upon this principle, we should be compelled to resist the acquisition of Cuba by any powerful maritime state, with all means which Providence has placed at our command.

And Secretary Clayton said, in 1849:

> The news of the cession of Cuba to any foreign Power would in the United States be the instant signal for war. No foreign Power would attempt to take it that did not expect a hostile collision with us as an inevitable consequence.

The doctrine is not international law but it rests upon the right of self-protection and that right is recognized by international law. The right is a necessary corollary of independent sovereignty. It is well understood that the exercise of the right of self-protection may and frequently does extend in its effect beyond the limits of the territorial jurisdiction of the state exercising it. The strongest example probably would be the mobilization of an army by another Power immediately across the frontier. Every act done by the other Power may be within its own territory. Yet the country threatened by the state of facts is justified in protecting itself by immediate war. The most common exercise of the right of self-protection outside of a state's own territory and in time of peace is the interposition of objection to the occupation of territory, of points of strategic military or maritime advantage, or to indirect accomplishment of this effect by dynastic arrangement. For example, the objection of England in 1911 to the occupation of a naval station by Germany on the Atlantic coast of Morocco; the objection of the European Powers generally to the vast force of Russia extending its territory to the Mediterranean; the revision of the Treaty of San Stefano by the Treaty of Berlin; the establishment of buffer states; the objection to the succession of a German prince to the throne of Spain; the many forms of the Eastern question; the centuries of struggle to preserve the balance of power in Europe; all depend upon the very same principle which underlies the Monroe Doctrine; that is to say, upon the right of every sovereign state to protect itself by preventing a condition of affairs in which it will be too late to protect itself. Of course each state must judge for itself when a threatened act will create such a situation. If any state objects to a threatened act and the reasonableness of its objection is not assented to, the efficacy of the objection will depend upon the power behind it.

It is doubtless true that in the adherence of the American people to the original declaration there was a great element of sentiment and of sympathy for the people of South America who were struggling for freedom, and it has been a source of great satisfaction to the United States that the course which it took in 1823 concurrently with the action of Great Britain played so great a part in assuring the right of self-government to the countries of South America. Yet it is to be observed that in reference to the South American governments, as in all other respects, the international right upon which the declaration expressly rests is not sentiment or sympathy or a claim to dictate what kind of government any other country shall have, but the safety of the United States. It is because the new governments cannot be overthrown by the allied Powers " without endangering our peace and happiness ", that " the United States cannot behold such interposition in any form with indifference."

We frequently see statements that the doctrine has been changed or enlarged; that there is a new or different doctrine since Monroe's time. They are mistaken. There has been no change. One apparent extension of the statement of Monroe was made by President Polk in his messages of 1845 and 1848, when he included the acquisition of territory by a European Power through cession as dangerous to the safety of the United States. It was really but stating a corollary to the doctrine of 1823 and asserting the same right of self-protection against the other American states as well as against Europe.

This corollary has been so long and uniformly agreed to by the Government and the people of the United States that it may fairly be regarded as being now a part of the doctrine.

But, all assertions to the contrary notwithstanding, there has been no other change or enlargement of the Monroe Doctrine since it was first promulgated. It must be remembered that not everything said or written by Secretaries of State or even by Presidents constitutes a national policy or can enlarge or modify or diminish a national policy. It is the substance of the thing to which the nation holds, and that is and always has been that the safety of the United States demands that American territory shall remain American.

The Monroe Doctrine does not assert or imply or involve any right on the part of the United States to impair or control the independent sovereignty of any American state. In the lives of nations as of individuals, there are many rights unquestioned and universally conceded. The assertion of any particular right must be considered, not as excluding all others but as coincident with all others which are not inconsistent. The fundamental principle of international law is the principle of independent sovereignty. Upon that all other rules of international law rest. That is the chief and necessary protection of the weak against the power of the strong. Observance of that is the necessary condition to the peace and order of the civilized world. By the declaration of that principle the common judgment of civilization awards to the smallest and weakest state the liberty to control its own affairs without interference from any other Power, however great.

The Monroe Doctrine does not infringe upon that right. It asserts the right. The declaration of Monroe was that the rights and interests of the United States were involved in maintaining a condition, and the condition to be maintained was the independence of all the American countries. It is " the free and independent condition which they have assumed and maintained " which is declared to render them not subject to future colonization. It is " the governments who have declared their independence and maintained it and whose independence we have on great consideration and on just principles acknowledged " that are not to be interfered with. When Mr. Canning's proposals for a joint declaration were under consideration by the Cabinet in the month before the famous message was sent, John Quincy Adams, who played the major part in forming the policy, declared the basis of it in these words:

> Considering the South Americans as independent nations, they themselves and no other nation had the right to dispose of their condition. We have no right to dispose of them either alone or in conjunction with other nations. Neither have any other nations the right of disposing of them without their consent.

In the most critical and momentous application of the doctrine Mr. Seward wrote to the French Minister:

> France need not for a moment delay her promised withdrawal of military forces from Mexico and her putting the principle of non-intervention into full and complete practice in regard to Mexico through any apprehension that the United States will prove unfaithful to the principles and policy in that respect which on their behalf it has been my duty to maintain in this now very lengthened correspondence. The practice of this government from its beginning is a guarantee to all nations of the respect of the American people for the free sovereignty of the people in every other state. We received the instruction from Washington. We applied it sternly in our early intercourse even with France. The same principle and practice have been uniformly inculcated by all our statesmen, interpreted by all our jurists, maintained by all our Congresses, and acquiesced in without practical dissent on all occasions by the American people. It is in reality the chief element of foreign intercourse in our history.

In his message to Congress of December 3, 1906, President Roosevelt said:

> In many parts of South America there has been much misunderstanding of the attitude and purposes of the United States toward the other American republics. An idea had become prevalent that our assertion of the Monroe Doctrine implied or carried with it an assumption of superiority and of a right to exercise some kind of protectorate over the countries to whose territory that doctrine applies. Nothing could be farther from the truth.

He quoted the words of the Secretary of State then in office to the recent Pan-American Conference at Rio Janeiro:

We deem the independence and equal rights of the smallest and weakest member of the family of nations entitled to as much respect as those of the greatest empire and we deem the observance of that respect the chief guaranty of the weak against the oppression of the strong. We neither claim nor desire any rights or privileges or powers that we do not freely concede to every American republic.

And the President then proceeded to say of these statements:

They have my hearty approval, as I am sure they will have yours, and I cannot be wrong in the conviction that they correctly represent the sentiments of the whole American people. I cannot better characterize the true attitude of the United States in its assertion of the Monroe Doctrine than in the words of the distinguished former Minister of Foreign Affairs of Argentina, Doctor Drago . . . " the traditional policy of the United States without accentuating superiority or seeking preponderance condemned the oppression of the nations of this part of the world and the control of their destinies by the great Powers of Europe."

Curiously enough, many incidents and consequences of that independent condition itself which the United States asserted in the Monroe Doctrine have been regarded in some quarters as infringements upon independence resulting from the Monroe Doctrine. Just as the personal rights of each individual free citizen in the state are limited by the equal rights of every other free individual in the same state, so the sovereign rights of each independent state are limited by the equal sovereign rights of every other independent state. These limitations are not impairments of independent sovereignty. They are the necessary conditions to the existence of independent sovereignty. If the Monroe Doctrine had never been declared or thought of, the sovereign rights of each American republic would have been limited by the equal sovereign rights of every other American republic, including the United States. The United States would have had a right to demand from every other American state observance of treaty obligations and of the rules of international law. It would have had the right to insist upon due protection for the lives and property of its citizens within the territory of every other American state, and upon the treatment of its citizens in that territory according to the rules of international law. The United States would have had the right as against every other American state to object to acts which the United States might deem injurious to its peace and safety just as it had the right to object to such acts as against any European Power and just as all European and American Powers have the right to object to such acts as against each other. All these rights which the United States would have had as against other American states it has now. They are not in the slightest degree affected by the Monroe Doctrine. They exist now just as they would have existed if there had been no Monroe Doctrine. They are neither greater nor less because of that doctrine. They are not rights of superiority, they are rights of equality. They are the rights which all equal independent states have as against each other. And they cover the whole range of peace and war.

It happens, however, that the United States is very much bigger and more powerful than most of the other American republics. And when a very great and powerful state makes demands upon a very small and weak state it is difficult to avoid a feeling that there is an assumption of superior authority involved in the assertion of superior power, even though the demand be based solely upon the right of equal against equal. An examination of the various controversies which the United States has had with other American Powers will disclose the fact that in every case the rights asserted were rights not of superiority but of equality. Of course it cannot be claimed that great and powerful states shall forego their just rights against smaller and less powerful states. The responsibilities of sovereignty attach to the weak as well as to the strong, and a claim to exemption from those responsibilities would imply not equality but inferiority. The most that can be said concerning a question between a powerful state and a weak one is that the great state ought to be especially considerate and gentle in the assertion and maintenance of its position; ought always to base its acts not upon a superiority of force, but upon reason and law; and ought to assert no rights against a small state because of its weakness which it would not assert against a great state notwithstanding its power. But in all this the Monroe Doctrine is not concerned at all.

The scope of the doctrine is strictly limited. It concerns itself only with the occupation of territory in the New World to the subversion or exclusion of a pre-existing American government. It has not otherwise any relation to the affairs of either American or European states. In good conduct or bad, observance of rights or violations of them, agreement or controversy, injury or reprisal, coercion or war, the United States finds no warrant in the Monroe Doctrine for interference. So Secretary Cass wrote, in 1858:

> With respect to the causes of war between Spain and Mexico, the United States have no concern, and do not undertake to judge them. Nor do they claim to interpose in any hostilities which may take place. Their policy of observation and interference is limited to the permanent subjugation of any portion of the territory of Mexico, or of any other American state, to any European Power whatever.

And Mr. Seward wrote, in 1861, concerning the allied operation against Mexico:

> As the undersigned has heretofore had the honor to inform each of the plenipotentiaries now addressed, the President does not feel at liberty to question, and does not question, that the sovereigns represented have undoubted right to decide for themselves the fact whether they have sustained grievances, and to resort to war against Mexico for the redress thereof, and have a right also to levy the war severally or jointly.

So when Germany, Great Britain and Italy united to compel by naval force a response to their demands on the part of Venezuela and the German Government advised the United States that it proposed to take coercive measures to enforce its claims for damages and for money against Venezuela, adding, " We declare especially that under no circumstances do we consider in our proceedings the acquisition or permanent occupation of Venezuelan territory," Mr. Hay replied that the Government of the United States, although it

regretted that European Powers should use force against Central and South American countries, could not object to their taking steps to obtain redress for injuries suffered by their subjects, provided that no acquisition of territory was contemplated.

Quite independent of the Monroe Doctrine, however, there is a rule of conduct among nations under which each nation is deemed bound to render the good offices of friendship to the others when they are in trouble. The rule has been crystallized in the provisions of The Hague Convention for the Pacific Settlement of International Disputes. Under the head of " The Maintenance of General Peace " in that convention substantially all the Powers of the world have agreed:

With a view to obviating as far as possible recourse to force in the relations between states, the contracting Powers agree to use their best efforts to ensure the pacific settlement of international differences.

In case of serious disagreement or dispute, before an appeal to arms, the contracting Powers agree to have recourse, as far as circumstances allow, to the good offices or mediation of one or more friendly Powers.

Independently of this recourse, the contracting Powers deem it expedient and desirable that one or more Powers, strangers to the dispute, should, on their own initiative and as far as circumstances may allow, offer their good offices or mediation to the states at variance. . . . The exercise of this right can never be regarded by either of the parties in dispute as an unfriendly act.

The part of the mediator consists in reconciling the opposing claims and appeasing the feelings of resentment which may have arisen between the states at variance.

The United States has frequently performed this duty in controversies between American republics among themselves and between American republics and European states. So in the controversy last referred to, the United States used its good offices to bring about a series of arbitrations which superseded the resort to force determined upon by the allied Powers against Venezuela. It did this upon the request of Venezuela. It did it in the performance of no duty and the exercise of no right whatever except the duty and the right of friendship between equal sovereign states. The Monroe Doctrine has nothing whatever to do with acts of this description; yet many times censorious critics, unfamiliar with the facts and uninstructed in the customs and rules of action of the international world, have accused the United States in such cases of playing the rôle of school master, of assuming the superiority of guardianship, of aiming at a protectorate.

As the Monroe Doctrine neither asserts nor involves any right of control by the United States over any American nation, it imposes upon the United States no duty towards European Powers to exercise such a control. It does not call upon the United States to collect debts or coerce conduct or redress wrongs or revenge injuries. If matters ever come to a point where in any American country the United States intervenes by force to prevent or end an occupation of territory to the subversion or exclusion of an American government, doubtless new rights and obligations will arise as a result of the acts done in the course of the intervention. Unless such a situation shall have arisen there can be no duty on the part of the United States beyond the exercise of good offices as between equal and independent nations.

There are indeed special reasons why the United States should perform that duty of equal friendship to the full limit of international custom and international ethics as declared in The Hague Convention, whenever occasion arises in controversy between American and European Powers. There is a motive for that in the special sympathy and friendship for the gradually developing republics of the south which the American people have always felt since the days of Monroe and John Quincy Adams and Richard Rush and Henry Clay. There is a motive in the strong desire of our government that no controversy between a European and an American state shall ever come to the point where the United States may be obliged to assert by force the rule of national safety declared by Monroe. And there is a motive in the proper desire of the United States that no friendly nation of Europe or America shall be injured or hindered in the prosecution of its rights in any way or to any extent that can possibly be avoided because that nation respects the rule of safety which Mr. Monroe declared and we maintain. None of these reasons for the exercise of the good offices of equality justifies nor do all of them together justify the United States in infringing upon the independence or ignoring the equal rights of the smallest American state.

Nor has the United States ever in any instance during the period of almost a century which has elapsed, made the Monroe Doctrine or the motives which lead us to support it, the ground or excuse for overstepping the limits which the rights of equal sovereignty set between equal sovereign states.

Since the Monroe Doctrine is a declaration based upon this nation's right of self-protection, it cannot be transmuted into a joint or common declaration by American states or any number of them. If Chile or Argentina or Brazil were to contribute the weight of its influence toward a similar end, the right upon which that nation would rest its declaration would be its own safety, not the safety of the United States. Chile would declare what was necessary for the safety of Chile. Argentina would declare what was necessary for the safety of Argentina. Brazil, what was necessary for the safety of Brazil. Each nation would act for itself and in its own right and it would be impossible to go beyond that except by more or less offensive and defensive alliances. Of course such alliances are not to be considered.

It is plain that the building of the Panama Canal greatly accentuates the practical necessity of the Monroe Doctrine as it applies to all the territory surrounding the Caribbean or near the Bay of Panama. The plainest lessons of history and the universal judgment of all responsible students of the subject concur in teaching that the potential command of the route to and from the Canal must rest with the United States and that the vital interests of the nation forbid that such command shall pass into other hands. Certainly no nation which has acquiesced in the British occupation of Egypt will dispute this proposition. Undoubtedly as one passes to the south and the distance from the Caribbean increases, the necessity of maintaining the rule of Monroe becomes less immediate and apparent. But who is competent to draw the line? Who will say, "To this point the rule of Monroe should apply; beyond this point, it should not"? Who will say that a new national force created beyond any line that he can draw will stay beyond it and will not in the long course of time extend itself indefinitely?

The danger to be apprehended from the immediate proximity of hostile forces was not the sole consideration leading to the declaration. The need to separate the influences determining the development and relation of states in the New World from the influences operating in Europe played an even greater part. The familiar paragraphs of Washington's Farewell Address upon this subject were not rhetoric. They were intensely practical rules of conduct for the future guidance of the country.

> Europe has a set of primary interests, which to us have none, or a very remote, relation. Hence, she must be engaged in frequent controversies, the causes of which are essentially foreign to our concerns. Hence, therefore, it must be unwise in us to implicate ourselves, by artificial ties, in the ordinary vicissitudes of her politics, or the ordinary combinations and collisions of her friendships or enmities. Our detached and distant situation invites and enables us to pursue a different course.

It was the same instinct which led Jefferson, in the letter to Monroe already quoted, to say:

> Our first and fundamental maxim should be, never to entangle ourselves in the broils of Europe; our second, never to suffer Europe to intermeddle with cis-atlantic affairs.

The concurrence of Washington and Hamilton and Jefferson in the declaration of this principle of action entitles it to great respect. They recalled the long period during which every war waged in Europe between European Powers and arising from European causes of quarrel was waged also in the New World. English and French and Spanish and Dutch killed and harried each other in America, not because of quarrels between the settlers in America but because of quarrels between the European Powers having dominion over them. Separation of influences as absolute and complete as possible was the remedy which the wisest of Americans agreed upon. It was one of the primary purposes of Monroe's declaration to insist upon this separation, and to accomplish it he drew the line at the water's edge. The problem of national protection in the distant future is one not to be solved by the first impressions of the casual observer, but only by profound study of the forces which, in the long life of nations, work out results. In this case the results of such a study by the best men of the formative period of the United States are supported by the instincts of the American democracy holding steadily in one direction for almost a century. The problem has not changed essentially. If the declaration of Monroe was right when the message was sent, it is right now. South America is no more distant today than it was then. The tremendous armaments and international jealousies of Europe afford little assurance to those who think we may now abandon the separatist policy of Washington. That South American states have become too strong for colonization or occupation is cause for satisfaction. That Europe has no purpose or wish to colonize American territory is most gratifying. These facts may make it improbable that it will be necessary to apply the Monroe Doctrine in the southern parts of South America; but they furnish no reason whatever for retracting or denying or abandoning a declaration of public policy, just and reasonable when it was made, and which, if occasion for its application shall arise in the future, will still be just and reasonable.

A false conception of what the Monroe Doctrine is, of what it demands and what it justifies, of its scope and of its limits, has invaded the public press and affected public opinion within the past few years. Grandiose schemes of national expansion invoke the Monroe Doctrine. Interested motives to compel Central or South American countries to do or refrain from doing something by which individual Americans may profit invoke the Monroe Doctrine. Clamors for national glory from minds too shallow to grasp at the same time a sense of national duty invoke the Monroe Doctrine. The intolerance which demands that control over the conduct and the opinions of other peoples which is the essence of tyranny invokes the Monroe Doctrine. Thoughtless people who see no difference between lawful right and physical power assume that the Monroe Doctrine is a warrant for interference in the internal affairs of all weaker nations in the New World. Against this supposititious doctrine, many protests both in the United States and in South America have been made, and justly made. To the real Monroe Doctrine these protests have no application.

CONFERENCE OF TEACHERS OF INTERNATIONAL LAW

A conference of teachers of international law was held at the city of Washington, April 23-25, 1914, under the auspices of the American Society of International Law, " in order to consider what measures, if any, could properly be taken to arouse a greater interest in international law where taught in American institutions of learning; to secure its introduction in American institutions of learning where it is not taught; to call attention to its importance to lawyers in the practice of their profession; and to suggest the advisability of a knowledge of its principles for admission to the bar; and to show, finally, the necessity of an understanding of the subject by the public at large, which in a democracy such as ours determines in the ultimate resort the foreign policy of the United States."

The Conference unanimously adopted a series of resolutions and these resolutions, in so far as they are of a general nature, were approved on January 8, 1916, by the Second Pan-American Scientific Congress, and form articles 23-32 of its Final Act.

For the proceedings and the text of resolutions of the Teachers' Conference, see *Proceedings of the American Society of International Law* (1914), pp. 250-324.

For the recommendations of the Second Pan-American Scientific Congress, see its Final Act and interpretative commentary thereon by James Brown Scott (1916), pp. 92-110.

As president of the Society, Mr. Root called the Conference together, and made the following opening remarks:

IT gives me very great pleasure to welcome you to participation in this, the Conference of Teachers of International Law and Related Subjects, held in connection with the Eighth Annual Meeting of the American Society of International Law, and to express the grateful appreciation of the officers and members of the Society to the instructors in international law who have left their customary duties, to come here for the purpose of taking part in this conference.

The invitation which led to this meeting had its origin in a resolution which was offered by that honored and admired leader in American education, Mr. Andrew D. White, at a meeting of the Trustees of the Carnegie Endowment for International Peace. One of the divisions of work established under that trust is the Division of International Law, of which Dr. James Brown Scott is the head; and Mr. White, responding to the double impulse of his old enthusiasm as a teacher and organizer of education and as a diplomatist, as the representative of his country at the court of Germany, and as the first delegate of his country to the First Hague Conference, offered this resolution:

Resolved: That the Executive Committee be directed to propose and carry out, subject to the approval of this Board, a plan for the propagation, development, maintenance and increase of sound, progressive and fruitful ideas on the subject of arbitration and international law and history as connected with arbitration, especially through addresses or courses of lectures delivered before the leading universities, colleges and law schools of the United States, and to report on the same at the next regular meeting of the Board, or, should the Committee think best, at a special meeting to be called for that purpose.

In taking the first steps in compliance with this resolution, the Executive Committee found it desirable to ascertain, as a basis of action, what was already being done in the United States along the lines indicated by the resolution; and, accordingly, an inquiry was set on foot and prosecuted, in which was developed the state of education upon this subject in all the leading colleges and universities and law schools of the country, and a very full report was made upon that subject.

The consideration of the facts developed by that report led to the conclusion that the program, the method of procedure, the scope of enterprise and activity in the spirit of Mr. White's resolution, were something that no individual and no committee organized for any other purpose, as was the Executive Committee of the Peace Endowment, could properly handle, could adequately deal with; and, accordingly, the suggestion was made that the American Society of International Law, which deals specifically with the subject-matter of the resolution, should take it up, and that the men who know best what is needed and how that shall be done and can be done, should come together and confer upon the subject. So you see that the initial impulse which brings you here is a source which must be respected by every American educator, and has a purpose which is certified to by the highest ability and the broadest experience.

I will detain you from the practical work which lies before you in organizing the conference, by only a single suggestion. The putting of instruction in international law in American educational institutions on a broader basis, giving it a wider scope and greater efficiency, is not a mere matter of book learning. It is not a mere matter of science. It is a matter of patriotic duty.

More and more, as the years follow one another with the swiftness of our modern life, democracy is coming to its own. More and more the people, the men on the farms and in the shops, the men with the pick and shovel in their hands, are assuming the direction of the operations of government, both internal and external. More and more they are directly responsible for the operations of government. Presidents and Congresses more and more look for immediate response from constituencies upon the most difficult and intricate questions in the foreign relations of the country, questions the right solution of which requires broad knowledge, which cannot be solved by the impressions of the moment, which cannot be solved by emotional response to oratory.

I think no one can study the movement of the times without realizing that the democracy of the world — for it is not alone in this country — is realizing its rights in advance of its realization of its duties. And that way lies disaster. That way lies hideous wrong. That way lies the exercise of the mighty powers of modern democracies to destroy themselves, to destroy the vitality of the principles upon which they depend. And there is no duty more incumbent today upon the men whose good fortune has made it possible for them to acquire a broader knowledge upon the subjects with which democracy deals, than to become themselves leaders of opinion and teachers of their people. Unless the popular will responds to the instructed and competent leadership of opinion upon the vital questions of our foreign relations, the worst impulses of democracy will control. At the bottom of wise and just action lies an understanding of national rights and national duties. Half the wars of history have come because of mistaken opinions as to national rights and national obligations, have come from the unthinking assumption that all the right is on the side of one's own country, all the duty on the side of some other country. Now I say the thing most necessary for the good of our country in the foreign relations which are growing every year more and more intricate and critical, is that there shall be intelligent leadership of opinion as to national rights and national obligations; and nobody can bring that about as the educators of America can bring it about. It is in the hope that you will be able to organize, to give direction and wise guidance to a systematic movement to accomplish this good service for our country, that I take the deepest interest in this conference, and bid you God-speed in your labors.

THE HAGUE PEACE CONFERENCES

ADDRESS IN OPENING THE NATIONAL ARBITRATION AND
PEACE CONGRESS, IN THE CITY OF NEW YORK,
APRIL 15, 1907

IN submitting the Hague Conventions of 1907 to the Senate, Mr. Root, as Secretary of State, said:

Let me go beyond the limits of the customary formal letter of transmittal and say that I think the work of the Second Hague Conference, which is mainly embodied in these Conventions, presents the greatest advance ever made at any single time toward the reasonable and peaceful regulation of international conduct, unless it be the advance made at The Hague Conference of 1899.

The most valuable result of the Conference of 1899 was that it made the work of the Conference of 1907 possible. The achievements of the Conferences justify the belief that the world has entered upon an orderly process through which, step by step, in successive Conferences, each taking the work of its predecessor as its point of departure, there may be continual progress toward making the practice of civilized nations conform to their peaceful professions.

At a later date, Mr. Root furnished a prefatory note to Scott's *Texts of the Peace Conferences at the Hague*, from which the following paragraph is quoted as further illustrating his views as to the importance of the international conference and the process by which it accomplishes its results:

The question about each international conference is not merely what it has accomplished, but also what it has begun, and what it has moved forward. Not only the conventions signed and ratified, but the steps taken toward conclusions which may not reach practical and effective form for many years to come, are of value. Some of the resolutions adopted by the last conference do not seem to amount to very much by themselves, but each one marks on some line of progress the farthest point to which the world is yet willing to go. They are like cable ends buoyed in mid-ocean, to be picked up hereafter by some other steamer, spliced, and continued to shore. The greater the reform proposed, the longer must be the process required to bring many nations differing widely in their laws, customs, traditions, interests, prejudices, into agreement. Each necessary step in the process is as useful as the final act which crowns the work and is received with public celebration.

In order fully to appreciate Mr. Root's deep interest in The Hague Conferences and the importance he attached to them as an agency in the development of international law and in reaching agreements upon international conduct, the reader is referred to Mr. Root's instructions, as Secretary of State, to the American delegates to the Second Hague Peace Conference. These instructions will be found in the collection of state papers in this series.

IN every country which has reached a high stage of civilization may be seen the working of two distinct and apparently inconsistent motives or principles of national conduct. On the one hand, there is the narrowly and immediately utilitarian motive, and there is the competitive attitude fashioned upon the habits of self-preservation and self-assertion enjoined by the necessities of the struggle for existence. With this motive each country pursues specific national advantages meeting in a hard, dry, business-like way, without sympathy or sentiment, the facts of a world in which there is much selfishness and greed, in which every nation is primarily looking out for itself, and in which there is ordinarily some aggressor ready to take advantage of the over-trusting and defenseless.

On the other hand, there is the ethical, altruistic, humane impulse that presses forward constantly toward ideals. Its possessors, loving liberty and justice and peace, long to make all men free and safe and secure in their rights; their eyes are fixed upon the ultimate goal toward which civilization tends; they are striving that better things shall replace the cynicism and selfishness and cruelty which have always so widely characterized mankind; they assert principles and set up standards of action, which they call upon mankind to adopt, and mankind too often gives theoretical assent but denies practical conformity.

In every man's nature there are manifestations or traces of each of these impulses; and in every nation there are many citizens in whom one, and many in whom the other, impulse strongly predominates. As circumstances bring one class of motives or another into control of national conduct in different fields of national action, strangely variant and inconsistent national action results. The same nation may be seen hard and practical, and at another time, or perhaps in another field at the same time, exhibiting the highest degree of unselfishness and humanity. Under the predominance of one motive, national power has been built up; administration has been made effective; commerce has been extended; material wealth, the matrix of civilization, has been created and protected; the citizens of each country have been secured against aggression from without; and, in the slow process of centuries, the code of practical rules convenient and necessary to the peaceable intercourse of nations has been elaborated. Under the predominance of the other motive, the conception of individual charity and humanity, which found its highest expression in the Christian revelation, has slowly impressed itself upon the conception of national duty and responsibility. In its development the idea of national conscience and national ethics has been forced into the international system, which formerly acknowledged the undisputed sway of selfishness and cruelty, long condemned as immoral in the relations between individuals.

It is natural that the hard and practical motive shall be uppermost in the men engaged in the conduct of government; they are endowed with limited and definite powers and charged with specific trusts for the benefit of their own people; their duties are to protect and advance the interests of their own country, and those duties relate, in the main, to the material interest of their countrymen; their specific powers are given to them for that specific purpose; they have no warrant of attorney to express or give effect to the benevolent or humanitarian impulses of their constituents; under constitutional government, as a rule, such expression is not committed by law to public officers, but is reserved to the people. In the discharge of their international duties governmental officers have to deal with a world of selfish competition and ever-present possibility of aggression and injury, which compel them to think first and chiefly of the interest of their own country as a lawyer argues the case of his own client. They are constrained by the rules of conduct between nations which the experience of centuries has shown to be necessary to the peace of the world. Among the first of these is, that the government of each nation shall attend to its own business and respect the sovereignty and refrain from interfering with the internal affairs of every other nation. This rule is the chief protection of the liberty of small and weak nations against the aggression of the strong. To break it down whenever the officers of one government disapprove the conduct of another government within its own jurisdiction, would be to break down the barriers which civilization has erected for the protection of the weak, with results as fatal as if the executive were allowed to make orders and the judge to issue decrees according to their own kindly impulses, without regard to the limitations of law.

It is natural that the altruistic and humanitarian view, broader and less immediately practical, shall be taken by students and thinkers, by teachers and philosophers, by men who, not burdened by the necessity of putting theories into practice, are at liberty to look upon the world as it ought to be and to urge mankind on toward acceptance of their ideals. These men are masters of their own power; they have a warrant from all whom their eloquence, their persuasion, their reasoning, or the inherent soundness of their ideas bring into agreement with them, to press their views upon the world and insist upon conformity. In every civilized land their numbers, their power, and their following have increased, most of all in lands where freedom is most perfect and justice most pure, until the voices of the few visionaries, long ago crying in the wilderness, have become the sound of a multitude; and a public opinion of the world, insisting upon righteousness and peace among nations as among individuals, is beginning to be perceived and to affect the national purposes which governments represent.

It is inevitable that the men who are directed by these two widely differing impulses should sometimes be impatient of each other. The humanitarian is repelled by the hardness of the practical man, who seems unsympathetic in his failure to act upon views that are certainly sound in the abstract and which ought to be accepted by all the world. The practical administrator is distressed by the urgency of the theorist, who, ignorant of real conditions, urges him to a course of action which he knows cannot possibly be taken, or, if it were taken under existing conditions, would result only in evil. One tends to think lightly of the other as an impracticable theorist, and in return is condemned by the other as unfeeling and cynical. Both judgments are probably often, to some extent, true, but both are generally, and to a much greater extent, wrong. Each class plays its necessary part in the great work of advancing civilization. It cannot be doubted that the supreme results for humanity are secured by the combination, the union, the blending of the two impulses, to the end that national selfishness may be most broadly intelligent and humanitarian idealism most effectively practical.

Your invitation to take part in the opening of this Peace Congress has come to me as an occasion to declare the alliance and sympathy of the American Government with that other power — the sentiment of humanity — which in all lands, and most strongly in our generation, without fleets or armies or titles or dignities or compulsion of force, is leading mankind continually to a nobler life. The American people are practical, material, strenuous in business, eager for wealth, energetic in production and venturous in commerce, insistent upon their rights, proud of their country, jealous of its power and its prestige; but there is a strain of idealism in the American nature which saves our nation from the grossness of sordid materialism and makes it responsive to every appeal in behalf of liberty and righteousness, of peace with justice, and of human brotherhood the world over. No American Government could truly represent its people if it did not sympathize heartily with the purposes which this Congress meets to promote, and the American Government of today does sympathize heartily with those purposes. In behalf of the Government I give you the kindly and appreciative greeting of the people of the United States and welcome you as spiritual kindred of those Americans of great heart and clear intelligence who in times past, striving for ordered liberty and the peace of justice in this land, have conferred inestimable benefits upon all mankind, and whose memory and example are our most precious possessions.

He is mistaken who depreciates the value of such a meeting as this, or regards its discussions as merely academic, because its members have not the power themselves to give effect to their resolutions. The open, public declaration of a principle in such a way as to carry evidence that it has the support of a great body of men entitled to respect has a wonderfully compelling effect upon mankind. The adoption of a new standard of human action is never the result of force or the threat of force; it is always the result of a moral process, and to the initiation and continuance of that process public assertion and advocacy of the principle are essential. When that process has been worked out and the multitude of men whom governments represent have reached the point of genuine and not perfunctory acceptance of the new standard, governments conform themselves to it.

THE HAGUE PEACE CONFERENCES   135

It is a common saying that the world is ruled by force — that the ultimate sanction for the rules of right conduct between nations is the possibility of war. That is less than a half truth. There was a time when the official intercourse between nations which we call diplomacy consisted chiefly of bargaining and largely of cheating in the bargain. Diplomacy now consists chiefly in making national conduct conform or appear to conform to the rules which codify, embody, and apply certain moral standards evolved and accepted in the slow development of civilization. The continual and unceasing process of diplomatic intercourse by which these standards are pressed upon the government of every nation, backed by the tremendous power of the opinion of the civilized world, enforced by the desire for the good opinion and apprehension of the disfavor of mankind, forms a strong external restraint upon national conduct; and these standards have been created by the evolution of moral as opposed to physical forces.

The value of declaring a principle may be illustrated by the effect of the arbitration convention agreed upon in the International Peace Conference at The Hague in 1899. That convention did little more than to declare principles; it provided machinery by which there might be arbitration, but it bound nobody to arbitrate, or to mediate, or to accept mediation. The machinery provided has been but little used; the arbitrations at The Hague have been few and not of the first order of importance; yet no one can for a moment question the enormous impetus given to the principle of arbitration of international controversies in lieu of war by that open and public declaration that such controversies ought to be arbitrated.

The thoughts of all men who hope for the peace of the world are now turned toward the Second Peace Conference so soon to meet at The Hague. It is cheering to note the difference between the attitude of the world toward this Conference about to meet and the way in which the world looked upon the First Conference at The Hague eight years ago. The generous impulse and noble sentiment of the Emperor of Russia which dictated the call for that Conference, supported by his great power and commanding position, compelled respect, or the appearance of respect, from all the great Powers; yet it is safe to say that the prevailing sentiment among the Powers as to the practical value of the Conference was one of polite incredulity, and that the delegates whom he had called together met amid an almost universal belief that nothing would or could be accomplished. The primary object of the call for the First Conference — the accomplishment of the great design which Henry IV of France conceived three centuries ago for the limitation of armaments in Europe — failed for the time; yet the Conference accomplished other things of the highest value to humanity, and it demonstrated for the first time in the world's history the potent and epoch-making fact that a congress of the world's powers convened, not to deal with some concrete question demanding immediate solution, but convened to consider and discuss the application of the general and fundamental principles of justice and humanity under all circumstances and to all international questions, can be made a practical and effective agency in the government of the world; it developed a new method and a new power for the betterment of international conduct, far superior to the ordinary rules of diplomatic intercourse, far broader in its scope, far nobler in its purpose. Upon the eve of the Second Conference, whose very possibility demonstrates the success and approves the wisdom of the first, it seems to me that all men who love their fellow-men and who hope for the rule of righteousness and peace on earth should feel a deep sentiment of gratitude toward that sovereign whose noble character led him to call together the First Conference and an equally deep sympathy with him in the hard and difficult task in which he is now engaged of establishing constitutional government in his own dominions.

The Second Conference is about to meet amid universal recognition that it is of practical significance. It commands respect; its possibilities are the object of solicitude; the resolutions which it may reach are anticipated as of probable potency in the affairs of nations; it is not regarded as an occasion for mere academic discussion, but it finds its place among the agencies by which the world is governed. I cannot doubt that it will accomplish much for the benefit of mankind; that in many things it will bring the practice of nations into closer conformity with those great principles of conduct to which nations have accorded such ready assent in theory but such reluctant compliance when their particular interests are involved.

The First Conference relegated to a future conference the consideration of three broad, general questions affecting the conduct of nations toward each other: first, the rights and duties of neutrals; second, the inviolability of private property in naval warfare; and, third, the bombardment of towns, villages, and ports by a naval force. It is understood that all these subjects shall be considered at the Second Conference.

The First Conference also adopted two resolutions relating to naval and military armament. The first was:

> The Conference is of opinion that the restriction of military charges, which are at present a heavy burden on the world, is extremely desirable for the increase of the material and moral welfare of mankind.

The second was:

> The Conference expresses the wish that the governments, taking into consideration the proposals made at the Conference, may examine the possibility of an agreement as to the limitation of armed forces by land and sea and of war budgets.

The Government of the United States has been of the opinion that the subject-matter of these resolutions ought to be further considered and discussed in the Second Conference; that the subject is in the nature of unfinished business and cannot be ignored, but must be dealt with; that there ought to be at least an earnest effort to reach, or to make progress toward reaching, some agreement under which the enormous expenditure of money and the enormous withdrawal of men from productive industry for warlike purposes may be reduced or arrested or retarded. We have not been unmindful of the fact that the question is one which primarily and in its present stage concerns Europe rather than America; that the conditions which have led to the great armaments of the present day are mainly European conditions, and that it would ill become us to be forward or dogmatic in a matter which is so much more vital to the nations of Europe than to ourselves. It sometimes happens, however, that a state having little or no special material interest in a proposal can, for that very reason, advance the proposal with the more advantage and the less prejudice. The American Government accordingly, at an early stage of the discussion regarding the program, reserved the right to present this subject for the consideration of the Conference. Several European Powers have also given notice of their intention to present the subject. It may be that the discussion will not bring the Second Conference to any definite and practical conclusion; certainly no such conclusion can be effective unless it meet with practically universal assent, for there can be no effective agreement which binds some of the Great Powers and leaves others free. There are serious difficulties in formulating any definite proposal which would not be objectionable to some of the Powers, and upon the question whether any specific proposal is unfair and injurious to its interests each Power must be, and is entitled to be, its own judge.

THE HAGUE PEACE CONFERENCES 139

Nevertheless, the effort can be made; it may fail in this Conference, as it failed in the first, but even if it fails one more step will have been taken toward ultimate success. Long-continued and persistent effort is always necessary to bring mankind into conformity with great ideals; every great advance that civilization has made on its road from savagery has been upon stepping-stones of failure, and a good fight bravely lost for a sound principle is always a victory.

The Government of the United States has also considered that the Second Hague Conference might well agree in putting some limitation upon the use of force for the collection of ordinary contract debts due by one government to the citizens of another.

It has long been the established policy of the United States not to use its army and navy for the collection of such debts. We have not considered the use of force for such a purpose consistent with that respect for the independent sovereignty of other members of the family of nations which is the most important principle of international law and the chief protection of weak nations against oppression. It seems to us that the practice is injurious in its general effect upon relations of nations and upon the welfare of weak and disordered states, whose development ought to be encouraged in the interests of civilization, and that it offers frequent temptation to bullying and oppression and to unnecessary and unjustifiable warfare. It may be that the non-payment of public debts may be accompanied by such circumstances of fraud and wrongdoing or violation of treaties as to justify the use of force as a last resort; but we hope to see an international consideration of the subject which shall discriminate between such cases and the simple non-performance of a contract with a private person, and to see a resolution in favor of reliance exclusively upon peaceful means in cases of the latter class. It may well be that the principle of arbitration can be so extended in its application that the class of adventurers who have long been in the habit of trading upon the necessities of weak and distressed governments may be required to submit their often exorbitant and unconscionable demands to an impartial tribunal, before which both parties may be heard both as to the validity and the amount of their claims and the time and manner of payment to which they are entitled. The record of the cases which have been submitted to arbitration during recent years shows that the total awards of the arbitral tribunals have amounted to a very small percentage of the demands submitted. It is difficult to resist the inference that the claims of private citizens who seek the good offices of their own governments to obtain payment from other countries generally need investigation by fair tribunals rather than immediate and peremptory enforcement.

In the general field of arbitration we are surely justified in hoping for a substantial advance both as to scope and effectiveness. It has seemed to me that the great obstacle to the universal adoption of arbitration is not the unwillingness of civilized nations to submit their disputes to the decision of an impartial tribunal; it is rather an apprehension that the tribunal selected will not be impartial. In a dispatch to Sir Julian Pauncefote dated March 5, 1896, Lord Salisbury stated the difficulty. He said that —

> If the matter in controversy is important, so that defeat is a serious blow to the credit or the power of the litigant who is worsted, that interest becomes a more or less keen partisanship. According to their sympathies, men wish for the victory of one side or another. Such conflicting sympathies interfere most formidably with the choice of an impartial arbitrator. It would be too invidious to specify the various forms of bias by which, in any important controversy between two great powers, the other members of the commonwealth of nations are visibly affected. In the existing condition of international sentiment each great power could point to nations whose admission to any jury by whom its interests were to be tried it would be bound to challenge; and in a litigation between two great

powers the rival challenges would pretty well exhaust the catalogue of the nations from which competent and suitable arbiters could be drawn. It would be easy, but scarcely decorous, to illustrate this statement by examples. They will occur to anyone's mind who attempts to construct a panel of nations capable of providing competent arbitrators, and will consider how many of them would command equal confidence from any two litigating powers.

This is the difficulty which stands in the way of unrestricted arbitration. By whatever plan the tribunal is selected, the end of it must be that issues in which the litigant states are most deeply interested will be decided by the vote of one man, and that man a foreigner. He has no jury to find his facts; he has no court of appeal to correct his law; and he is sure to be credited, justly or not, with a leaning to one litigant or the other.

The feeling which Lord Salisbury so well expressed is, I think, the great stumbling-block in the way of arbitration. The essential fact which supports that feeling is that arbitrators too often act diplomatically rather than judicially; they consider themselves as belonging to diplomacy rather than to jurisprudence; they measure their responsibility and their duty by the traditions, the sentiments, and the sense of honorable obligation which have grown up in centuries of diplomatic intercourse, rather than by the traditions, the sentiments, and the sense of honorable obligation which characterize the judicial departments of civilized nations. Instead of the sense of responsibility for impartial judgment which weighs upon the judicial officers of every civilized country, and which is enforced by the honor and self-respect of every upright judge, an international arbitration is often regarded as an occasion for diplomatic adjustment. Granting that the diplomats who are engaged in an arbitration have the purest motives; that they act in accordance with the policy they deem to be best for the nations concerned in the controversy; assuming that they thrust aside entirely in their consideration any interests which their own countries may have in the controversy or in securing the favor or averting the displeasure of the parties before them — nevertheless it remains that in such an arbitration the litigant nations find that questions of policy, and not simple questions of fact and law, are submitted to alien determination, and an appreciable part of that sovereignty which it is the function of every nation to exercise for itself in determining its own policy is transferred to the arbitrators.

An illustration of this view is to be found in the fact that one of the features of the extraordinary advance made by the nations of South America in the arts of peace is the development of arbitration for the settlement of disputes, and especially boundary disputes, to a greater degree than in any other part of the world. This has been facilitated by the almost complete detachment of South American politics from the national politics of Europe; so that it has been easy for the South American states to find arbitrators who neither knew nor cared for any political question in South America, and who, therefore, have been able to determine the questions before them with sole reference to the merits of the question, as a trained and upright judge decides a case submitted to his court.

What we need for the further development of arbitration is the substitution of judicial action for diplomatic action, the substitution of judicial sense of responsibility for diplomatic sense of responsibility. We need for arbitrators, not distinguished public men concerned in all the international questions of the day, but judges who will be interested only in the question appearing upon the record before them. Plainly, this end is to be attained by the establishment of a court of permanent judges, who will have no other occupation and no other interest but the exercise of the judicial faculty under the sanction of that high sense of responsibility which has made the courts of justice in the civilized nations of the world the exponents of all that is best and noblest in modern civilization.

THE HAGUE PEACE CONFERENCES 143

Let me add a few words of warning concerning your anticipations of what the Second Peace Conference is to do. Do not expect too much from it.

It is an essential characteristic of such a conference that it shall deal, not with matters upon which the nations differ, but with matters upon which the nations agree. Immaterial differences may be smoothed away; misunderstandings may be explained; consideration and discussion along lines that do not run counter to any immediate and specific interest may work out methods of applying general principles in such a way as to prevent future differences; progress may be made toward agreement upon matters which are not yet ripe for complete adjustment; but the moment an attempt is made to give such a conference any coercive effect, the moment any number of nations endeavor to use the conference for the purpose of compelling any other nation to do what it deems inconsistent with its interests, that moment the conference fails.

Such a conference is an agency of peace; not the peace of conquest, but the peace of agreement; not enforced agreement, but willing and cheerful agreement. So far as the nations can go together in such an agreement the conference can go, and no farther.

Many lovers of their kind, certain that the principles which they see so clearly ought to be accepted of all men, are unmindful of the many differences which divide the nations in the competition for trade and wealth, for honor and prestige; unmindful that the selfishness and greed and willingness to do injustice which have marked all human history still exist in the world; unmindful that because of these the instinct of self-protection engenders distrust and suspicion among the nations; and they will be sadly disappointed because The Hague Conference of 1907 does not realize their dreams and usher in the parliament of man — the federation of the world. But let them take heart. A forward step will be taken; an advance will be made toward the reign of peace and justice and righteousness among men, and that advance will go just so far as the character of the great mass of civilized men permits. There lies the true measure of possibility and the true origin of reforming force. Arbitrations and mediations, treaties and conventions, peace resolutions, declarations of principle, speeches and writings, are as naught unless they truly represent and find a response in the hearts and minds of the multitude of the men who make up the nations of the earth, whose desires and impulses determine the issues of peace and war. The end toward which this assemblage strives — the peace of the world — will be attained just as rapidly as the millions of the earth's peoples learn to love peace and abhor war; to love justice and hate wrongdoing; to be considerate in judgment and kindly in feeling toward aliens as toward their own friends and neighbors; and to desire that their own countries shall regard the rights of others rather than be grasping and overreaching. The path to universal peace is not through reason or intellectual appreciation, but through the development of peace-loving and peace-keeping character among men; and that this development, slow though it be as measured by our short lives, is proceeding with steady and unremitting advance from generation to generation no student of history can question. The greatest benefit of the Peace Conference of 1907 will be, as was that of the Peace Conference of 1899, in the fact of the conference itself; in its powerful influence moulding the characters of men; in the spectacle of all the great powers of the earth meeting in the name of peace, and exalting, as worthy of honor and desire, national self-control and considerate judgment and willingness to do justice.

THE IMPORTANCE OF JUDICIAL SETTLEMENT

OPENING ADDRESS AT THE INTERNATIONAL CONFERENCE OF THE AMERICAN SOCIETY FOR JUDICIAL SETTLEMENT OF INTERNATIONAL DISPUTES, WASHINGTON, D.C. DECEMBER 15, 1910

In introducing the speaker the presiding officer, James Brown Scott, said:

For centuries it was the plan of the philosopher and the hope of the philanthropist that some means might be found by which international conflicts should be settled peacefully without a resort to arms, and the dreamers of dreams, philosophers and philanthropists, proposed that the questions at issue between nations should be settled either in conference, in diplomatic assemblies or by temporary tribunals of arbitration created for the express purpose. That which the dreamers of dreams have dreamed, and the philosophers have planned, that which the philanthropists saw before them as if in a vision, took definite form and shape in the year 1907, when our accomplished Secretary of State, the Honorable Elihu Root, instructed the American delegation to the Second Hague Peace Conference to propose a permanent court to be composed of judges who should act under a sense of judicial responsibility, and which court should represent the various judicial systems of the world. Pursuant to these instructions the delegation, under the leadership of the Honorable Joseph H. Choate, introduced such a proposition, and after weeks of discussion and debate the Conference adopted a draft convention consisting of thirty-five articles for the organization, the jurisdiction and the procedure of a permanent court of arbitral justice, leaving it, however, to the nations to constitute the court, through diplomatic channels, when an agreement should be reached upon the appointment of the judges.

WE all of us agree, and a very large part of the world agrees, that there ought to be an end to war, that it is brutal, wasteful and stupid. We have been talking about it for a great many years. The volume of sound has swelled and grown into a great chorus of universal acclaim for the principles of peace with justice.

But all great movements have a definite development. They pass from stage to stage. The declaration of principles in the beginning is but the first step, and the method of development is from the general to the particular, from the theoretical to the practical, from the proposal to the accomplishment.

Now, the movement for peace, for the settlement of the disputes of mankind by peaceful means, is, it seems to me, passing from one stage to another in these wonderful years in which we live. Having accumulated enough momentum, by means of the missionary work that has been done, by means of the propaganda which has been prosecuted, we are beginning now to pass into the stage of careful, thoughtful, definite, certain inquiry into the specific causes of war and the specific remedies to be applied. So only can progress be made towards a practical conclusion.

The organization of this Society is one of the great steps forward in this second stage of development of the worldwide peace movement.

The causes of war may be roughly, and of course superficially and generally distributed into three categories. First, there are the real differences between nations as to their respective rights. One nation claims territory and another claims the same territory. One nation claims the right to trade in a particular way, at a particular place, and another nation claims an exclusive right. There are a myriad ways in which nations may come into dispute regarding real rights, each nation believing that its side of the controversy is based upon justice.

A second category is what I might call that of policy. The policy of a country may be to push its trade, to acquire territory, to obtain a dominant influence, to insist upon a certain course of action by other countries for its own protection asserting that a different course of conduct would be dangerous to its safety. All those questions of policy, however, are to a considerable degree, and very frequently, dependent upon the determination of certain facts and the decision of certain questions of international law.

JUDICIAL SETTLEMENT

A third category of causes of war may be described as being matters of feeling. Deep and bitter feeling is often awakened between peoples of different countries. We have got away from the time when the pique or whim of an individual monarch might plunge his subjects into a bloody and devastating war, but we remain in the time when great masses of people in different countries may become indignant over some slight or insult, or a course of conduct which they deem to be injurious and unfair. These matters of feeling, which are the most dangerous of all causes of war because they make the peoples of two different countries want to fight, — these matters of feeling ordinarily depend in the beginning upon different views regarding the specific rights of the two countries.

Now, as to the first kind of causes of war, the real controversies about rights, it is plain that they ought to be decided, and that all war based upon them may easily be obviated by having them decided, in accordance with the rules of right reason.

As to the two other classes of reasons for war, it is plain that the little beginnings out of which they arise, the excuses upon which they depend, may also be disposed of if taken in time, and disposed of by reason and kindly consideration. So that while it does not cover the whole ground, while it does not by any means solve the whole question, yet at the bottom of all the attempts practically to dispose of the causes of war, lies the peaceable decision of questions of fact and law in accordance with the rules of justice.

Now we have been for a good many years more and more seeking to accomplish that by means of arbitration, and the machinery for arbitration has been carefully devised and agreed upon by the nations of the earth at the two successive Hague conferences, so that it is comparatively easy for nations to have recourse to that method of settling their disputes.

But there are some difficulties about arbitration, practical difficulties in the way of settling questions. I have said many times and in many places that I do not think the difficulty that stands in the way of arbitration today is an unwillingness on the part of the civilized nations of the earth to submit their disputes to impartial decision. I think the difficulty is a doubt on the part of civilized nations as to getting an impartial decision. And that doubt arises from some characteristics of arbitral tribunals which are very difficult to avoid.

In the first place, these tribunals are ordinarily made up by selecting publicists, men of public affairs, great civil servants, members of the foreign offices, men trained to diplomacy; and the inevitable tendency is, and the result often has been, in the majority of cases has been, that the arbitral tribunal simply substitutes itself for the negotiators of the two parties, and negotiates a settlement. Well, that is quite a different thing from submitting your views of right and wrong, your views of the facts and the law on which you base your claims to right, to the decision of a tribunal, of a court. It is merely handing over your interests to somebody to negotiate for you; and there is a very widespread reluctance to do that in regard to many cases; and the nearer the question at issue approaches the verge of the field of policy, the stronger the objection to doing that.

Another difficulty is that the arbitral tribunals, of course being made up largely of members from other countries, the real decision ordinarily being made by arbiters who come from other countries and not from the countries concerned, questions have to be presented to men trained under different systems of law, with different ways of thinking and of looking at matters. There is a very wide difference between the way in which a civil lawyer and a common-law lawyer will approach a subject, and it is sometimes pretty hard for them to understand each other even though they speak the same language, while if they speak different languages it is still more difficult.

Another difficulty is that a large part of the rules of international law are still quite vague and undetermined, and upon many of them, and especially upon those out of which controversy is most likely to arise, different countries take different views as to what the law is and ought to be. And no one can tell how one of these extemporized tribunals, picked at haphazard, or upon the best information the negotiators of two countries can get, — no one can tell what views they are going to take about questions of international law, or how they are going to approach subjects and deal with them.

Now, it has seemed to me very clear that in view of these practical difficulties standing in the way of our present system of arbitration, the next step by which the system of peaceable settlement of international disputes can be advanced, the pathway along which it can be pressed forward to universal acceptance and use, is to substitute for the kind of arbitration we have now, in which the arbitrators proceed according to their ideas of diplomatic obligation, real courts where judges, acting under the sanctity of the judicial oath, pass upon the rights of countries, as judges pass upon the rights of individuals, in accordance with the facts as found and the law as established. With such tribunals, which are continuous, and composed of judges who make it their life business, you will soon develop a bench composed of men who have become familiar with the ways in which the people of every country do their business and do their thinking, and you will have a gradual growth of definite rules, of fixed interpretation, and of established precedents, according to which you may know your case will be decided. It is with that view that I have felt grateful to the gentlemen who have been giving their time and efforts to the organization and establishment of this Society. I am sure that it is a step along the scientific and practical method of putting into operation all the principles that we have been preaching and listening to for so many years. It is practical, and I believe it will be effective.

There is a great deal of work for the Society to do. Our people here in the United States are probably more ready to assent to such a view as this than the people of any other country in the world, because we have been long accustomed to the existence of a great tribunal, a part of whose duty it is to sit in judgment upon the question whether the governments of the sovereign states and the government of our own nation, in their acts, conform to the great principles of justice and right conduct embodied in our Constitution. That arrangement, of embodying the eternal principles of justice in a written instrument, investing a court with the power to declare all acts of congresses, and legislatures, and presidents and governors, void and of no effect when they fail to conform to those principles, is, it seems to me, the greatest contribution of America to the political science of the world. We are accustomed to seeing the actions of the men who hold the power, the actions of the legislative bodies that hold the purse strings, submitted to the adjudication of the court which has no power to enforce its decrees, except the confidence of the whole people behind it. We are accustomed to that, and it seems natural to us that nations, however great, and rulers, however powerful, should go before a court and submit the question whether their actions and their views accord with the principles of justice. But it does not seem so to most of the world. It is rather a new idea, and it will take time and argument and exposition to bring the world in general to the acceptance of that view. And upon that long journey this Society has entered. A prosperous voyage to it, and a safe arrival!

I have said that the time has come for practical dealing with specific causes and specific remedies. Do not understand me as believing that this is to be substituted for the continuous and unwearied assertion and reassertion of the great principles upon which the movement for peace and justice must depend in all parts and in every phase. For, however great may be the material wealth and power of these great nations, after all, what rules the world, the one thing that is eternal and all-powerful, is the intangible and the sentimental.

To the first meeting of the American Society for Judicial Settlement of International Disputes, Mr. Root sent a letter, from which the following is an extract:

I beg to say to your guests that I sympathize very strongly with their object and believe that the proposed organization is adapted to render a great public service. I assume that the new organization is to have a definite, specific object which may be indicated by emphasizing the word "judicial" in its title to indicate a distinction between that kind of settlement of international disputes and the ordinary arbitration as it has been understood in the past and is generally understood now.

I assume that you are going to urge that disputes between nations shall be settled by judges acting under the judicial sense of honorable obligation, with a judicial idea of impartiality, rather than by diplomats acting under the diplomatic ideas of honorable obligation and feeling bound to negotiate a settlement rather than to pass without fear or favor upon questions of fact and law.

It seems to me that such a change in the fundamental idea of what an arbitration should be is essential to any very great further extension of the idea of arbitration. I have been much surprised, however, to see how many people there are of ability and force who do not agree with this idea at all, particularly people on the other side of the Atlantic. The extraordinary scope of judicial power in this country has accustomed us to see the operations of government and questions arising between sovereign states submitted to judges who apply the test of conformity to established principles and rules of conduct embodied in our constitutions.

It seems natural and proper to us that the conduct of government affecting substantial rights, and not depending upon questions of policy, should be passed upon by the courts when occasion arises. It is easy, therefore, for Americans to grasp the idea that the same method of settlement should be applied to questions growing out of the conduct of nations and not involving questions of policy.

In countries, however, where the courts exercise no such power, the idea is quite a new one to most people, and, if it is to prevail, there must be a process of education. Such a process will naturally receive its chief impulse in the United States, and I hope your new society will give such an impulse with vigor and accurate direction.

NOBEL PEACE PRIZE ADDRESS

REQUIRED BY THE STATUTES OF THE NOBEL FOUNDATION UPON THE AWARD OF THE PEACE PRIZE FOR THE YEAR 1912

The Swedish scientist, Alfred Nobel, inventor of dynamite, died December 10, 1896, and established by his will a fund of approximately nine million dollars, the interest of which should every year be distributed to those who had contributed most to " the good of humanity." The interest thus provided for was to be divided into five equal shares and distributed " one to the person who in the domain of physics has made the most important discovery or invention, one to the person who has made the most important chemical discovery or invention, one to the person who has made the most important discovery in the domain of medicine or physiology, one to the person who in literature has provided the most excellent work of an idealistic tendency, and *one to the person who has worked most or best for the fraternization of nations, and the abolition or reduction of standing armies, and the calling and propagating of peace congresses.*"

The fund became available in the year 1901, and the individual prize, amounting to about $40,000, is awarded annually on the anniversary of Mr. Nobel's death.

The Nobel Peace Prize for 1912, reserved, in conformity with article 5 of the statutes, for the year 1913, was conferred upon Elihu Root. The committee made its decisions known to the public on December 10, 1913, the anniversary of Mr. Nobel's death, in the hall of the Nobel Institute at Christiania. Mr. Lövland, president of the committee, presided at the ceremony. The secretary of the committee, Mr. Moe, delivered an address on Mr. Root's political career, from which the following is an extract:

In August, 1899, he [Mr. Root] was appointed Secretary of War by President McKinley and remained in office during Mr. Roosevelt's administration until February, 1904. Upon the death of Secretary of State John Hay, in July, 1905, Mr. Root succeeded to that office and directed the foreign affairs of the United States up to the expiration of Mr. Roosevelt's term, in March, 1909. It was his task, as Secretary of War, to lay the bases of the plan for the reorganization of Cuba and the Philippines in their relation to the United States after the Spanish-American war.

As Secretary of State, he made a notable journey to South America, during which he visited the Third Pan-American Congress at Rio de Janeiro. In 1907, he visited Mexico. The object of these visits was to remove the long-standing distrust of their Anglo-Saxon sister on the part of the Latin Republics, and to further the efforts made in the interest of Pan-Americanism. In 1908 there was founded at Washington the Pan-American Bureau, under the direction of the Secretary of State of the United States, in coöperation with the Ministers of the American Republics accredited to Washington. Mr. Root took the initiative in calling a Central American Peace Congress at Washington in 1907. The following year a permanent court for the Central American states was created at Cartago, Costa Rica.

The most difficult task that fell to Mr. Root as Secretary of State was the settlement of the dispute between the United States and Japan on the question of Japanese immigrants in California, in 1906–07. It is impossible to give here the history of this great question, which assumed a threatening aspect in the winter of 1907. It will suffice to say that the peaceful settlement of the dispute, clinched by the action of the Congress at Washington in passing the immigration act of March 19, 1907, followed by the identic note of November, 1908, was due to the efforts of Mr. Root.

Long alone among American statesmen in his stand on the question, he vigorously attacked the act of August, 1912, providing for the free passage of American coastwise vessels through the Panama Canal. His eloquent speech in the Senate on January 21, 1913, was distributed among the friends of peace throughout the entire world. Since his retirement Mr. Root has been recognized as the leader of the peace movement in the United States. He is President of the American Society of International Law and of the great Carnegie Endowment for International Peace.[1]

In accordance with the statutes of the Nobel Foundation, the laureate of the Peace Prize is required to deliver an address in person at Christiania, Norway. The date for the delivery of Mr. Root's address was set for September 8, 1914, but delivery was prevented by the outbreak of the European war.

The address prepared by Mr. Root for that occasion is here printed exactly as it was prepared for delivery before the outbreak of the war, without the change of a word or syllable.

THE humanitarian purpose of Alfred Nobel in establishing the peace prize which bears his name was doubtless not merely to reward those who should promote peace among nations, but to stimulate thought upon the means and methods best adapted, under the changing conditions of future years, to approach and ultimately attain the end he so much desired.

The apparent simplicity of the subject is misleading. Recognition of the horrors of war and the blessings of peace, acceptance of the dogma " War is wrong and to keep the peace a duty," are so universal that upon the surface it seems only necessary to state a few incontrovertible truths and to press them upon the attention of mankind, in order to have war end and peace reign perpetually.

[1] Translated from *Les Prix Nobel en 1913*, Stockholm (1914), pp. 64–65.

Yet the continual recurrence of war and the universally increasing preparations for war based upon expectation of it among nations all of whom declare themselves in favor of peace, indicate that intellectual acceptance of peace doctrine is not sufficient to control conduct, and that a general feeling in favor of peace, however sincere, does not furnish a strong enough motive to withstand the passions which lead to war when a cause of quarrel has arisen. The methods of peace propaganda which aim at establishing peace doctrine by argument and by creating a feeling favorable to peace in general, seem to fall short of reaching the springs of human action and of dealing with the causes of the conduct which they seek to modify. It is much like treating the symptoms of disease instead of ascertaining and dealing with the cause of the symptoms. The mere assemblage of peace-loving people to interchange convincing reasons for their common faith; mere exhortation and argument to the public in favor of peace in general fall short of the mark.

They are useful, they serve to strengthen the faith of the participants, they tend very gradually to create a new standard of conduct, just as exhortations to be good and demonstrations that honesty is the best policy have a certain utility by way of suggestion. But they do not, as a rule, reach or extirpate or modify the causes of war.

Occasionally some man with exceptional power of statement or of feeling, and possessed by the true missionary spirit, will deliver a message to the world, putting old truths in such a way as to bite into the consciousness of civilized peoples and move mankind forward a little, with a gain never to be altogether lost. But the mere repetition of the obvious by good people of average intelligence, while not without utility and not by any means to be despised as an agency for peace, nevertheless is subject to the drawback that the unregenerate world grows weary of iteration and reacts in the wrong direction. The limitation upon this mode of promoting peace lies in the fact that it consists in an appeal to the civilized side of man, while war is the product of forces proceeding from man's original savage nature. To deal with the true causes of war one must begin by recognizing as of prime relevancy to the solution of the problem the familiar fact that civilization is a partial, incomplete, and, to a great extent, superficial modification of barbarism. The point of departure of the process to which we wish to contribute is the fact that war is the natural reaction of human nature in the savage state, while peace is the result of acquired characteristics. War was forced upon mankind in his original civil and social condition. The law of the survival of the fittest led inevitably to the survival and predominance of the men who were effective in war and who loved it because they were effective. War was the avenue to all that mankind desired. Food, wives, a place in the sun, freedom from restraint and oppression, wealth of comfort, wealth of luxury, respect, honor, power, control over others, were sought and attained by fighting. Nobody knows through how many thousand of years fighting men have made a place for themselves while the weak and peaceable have gone to the wall. Love of fighting was bred in the blood of the race, because those who did not love fighting were not suited to their environment and perished. Grotius himself sets war first in the title of his great work, *De Jure Belli ac Pacis*, as if, in his mind, war was the general and usual condition with which he was to deal, and peace the occasional and incidental field of international relation. And indeed the work itself deals chiefly with war, and only incidentally with peaceful relations.

In attempting to bring mankind to a condition of permanent peace in which war will be regarded as criminal conduct, just as civilized communities have been brought to a condition of permanent order, broken only by criminals who war against society, we have to deal with innate ideas, impulses and habits, which became a part of the cave man's nature by necessity from the conditions under which he lived; and these ideas and impulses still survive more or less dormant under the veneer of civilization, ready to be excited to action by events often of the most trifling character. As Lord Bacon says " Nature is often hidden, sometimes overcome, seldom extinguished." To eradicate or modify or curb the tendencies which thus survive among civilized men is not a matter of intellectual conviction or training. It is a matter primarily of development of character and the shifting of standards of conduct — a long, slow process in which advance is to be measured, not by days and years but by generations and centuries in the life of nations.

The attractive idea that we can now have a parliament of man with authority to control the conduct of nations by legislation or an international police force with power to enforce national conformity to rules of right conduct is a counsel of perfection. The world is not ready for any such thing, and it cannot be made ready except by the practical surrender of the independence of nations, which lies at the basis of the present social organization of the civilized world. Such a system would mean that each nation was liable to be lawfully controlled and coerced by a majority of alien powers. That majority alone could determine when and for what causes and to what ends the control and coercion should be exercised. Human nature must have come much nearer perfection than it is now, or will be in many generations, to exclude from such a control prejudice, selfishness, ambition and injustice. An attempt to prevent war in this way would breed war, for it would destroy local self-government and drive nations to war for liberty. There is no nation in the world which would seriously consider a proposal so shocking to the national pride and patriotism of its people.

To help in the most practical and efficient way towards making peace permanent, it is needful to inquire with some analysis what are the specific motives and impulses, the proximate causes which, under the present conditions of the civilized world, urge nations to the point where the war passion seizes upon them. And then we should inquire what are the influences which naturally tend or may be made to tend towards checking the impulse, destroying the motive, preventing the proximate cause, before passion has become supreme and it is too late.

It is to be observed that every case of war averted is a gain in general, for it helps to form a habit of peace, and community habits long continued become standards of conduct. The life of the community conforms to an expectation of their continuance, and there comes to be an instinctive opposition to any departure from them.

The first and most obvious cause for international controversy which suggests itself is in the field of international rights and obligations. Claims of right and insistence upon obligations may depend upon treaty stipulations or upon the rules of international law or upon the sense of natural justice applied to the circumstances of a particular case, or upon disputed facts. Upon all these there are continually arising controversies as to what are the true facts; what is the rule of international law applicable to the case; what is the true interpretation of the treaty; what is just and fair under the circumstances. This category does not by any means cover the entire field out of which causes of war arise, but no one should underestimate its importance. Small differences often grow into great quarrels, and honest differences of opinion frequently produce controversies in which national *amour propre* is involved and national honor, dignity and prestige are supposed to be at stake. Rival claimants to an almost worthless strip of land along a disputed boundary, a few poor fishermen contesting each others' rights to set nets in disputed waters, may break into violence which will set whole nations aflame with partisanship upon either side. Reparation demanded for injury to a citizen or an insult to a flag in foreign territory may symbolize in the feeling of a great people their national right to independence, to respect, and to an equal place in the community of nations. The people of a country, wholly mistaken as to their national rights, honestly ignorant of their international obligations, may become possessed of a real sense of injustice, of deep resentment, and of a sincere belief that the supreme sacrifice of war is demanded by love of country, its liberty and independence, when in fact their belief has no just foundation whatever.

In this field the greatest advance is being made towards reducing and preventing in a practical and effective way the causes of war, and this advance is proceeding along several different lines. First, by providing for the peaceable settlement of such controversies by submission to an impartial tribunal. Up to this time that provision has taken the form of arbitration, with which we are all familiar. There have been occasional international arbitrations from very early times, but arbitration as a system, a recognized and customary method of diplomatic procedure rather than an exceptional expedient, had its origin in The Hague Conference of 1899. It is interesting to recall the rather contemptuous reception accorded to the Convention for the Pacific Settlement of International Disputes concluded at that conference, and to the Permanent Court at The Hague which it created. The convention was not obligatory. No power was bound to comply with it. The cynicism with which the practical diplomatist naturally regards the idealist pronounced it a dead letter. But the convention expressed, and, by expressing, established, a new standard of international conduct which practical idealism had long been gradually approaching, for which thoughtful men and women in all civilized lands had been vaguely groping, which the more advanced nations welcomed and the more backward nations were ashamed to reject. Let me quote the recitals with which the delegates prefaced their work:

Animated by a strong desire to concert for the maintenance of the general peace;

Resolved to second by their best efforts the friendly settlement of international disputes;

Recognizing the solidarity which unites the members of the society of civilized nations;

Desirous of extending the empire of law, and of strengthening the appreciation of international justice;

Convinced that the permanent institution of a Court of Arbitration, accessible to all, in the midst of the independent Powers, will contribute effectively to this result;

Having regard to the advantages attending the general and regular organization of arbitral procedure;

Sharing the opinion of the august initiator of the International Peace Conference that it is expedient to record in an international agreement the principles of equity and right, on which are based the security of states and the welfare of peoples, etc.

These declarations, although enforced by no binding stipulation, nevertheless have become principles of action in international affairs, because, through the progress of civilization and the influence of many generations of devoted spirits in the cause of humanity, the world had become ready for the setting up of the standard. The convention would have been a dead letter if the world had not been made ready for it, and, because the world was ready, conformity to the standard year by year has become more universal and complete. Since this convention, which was binding upon no state, one hundred and thirteen obligatory general treaties of arbitration have been made between powers who have taken part in The Hague Conferences, and sixteen international controversies have been heard and decided, or are pending before that tribunal according to the last report of the Administrative Council of the Court.

Quite apart from the statistics of cases actually heard or pending, it is impossible to estimate the effect produced by the existence of this court, for the fact that there is a court to which appeal may be made always leads to the settlement of far more controversies than are brought to judgment. Nor can we estimate the value of having this system a part of the common stock of knowledge of civilized men, so that, when an international controversy arises, the first reaction is, not to consider war but to consider peaceful litigation.

Plainly, the next advance to be urged along this line is to pass on from an arbitral tribunal, the members of which are specifically selected from the general list of the court for each case, and whose service is but an incident in the career of a diplomatist or a publicist, to a permanent court composed of judges who devote their entire time to the performance of judicial duties and proceed in accordance with a sense of judicial obligation, not to adjust or compromise differences, but to decide upon rights in accordance with the facts and the law.

Long steps in this direction were made in the Second Hague Conference by the convention for the establishment of a permanent international prize court and by the formulation and adoption of a draft convention relative to the creation of a general judicial arbitration court. This draft convention lacked nothing of completion except an agreement upon the method by which the judges were to be selected. Towards the creation of such a court the best efforts of those who wish to promote peace should be directed.

The second line of advance in this same field of international controversy is in pressing forward the development of international law and the agreement of nations upon its rules. Lord Mansfield described the law of nations as "founded upon justice, equity, convenience, the reason of the thing, and confirmed by long usage." There are multitudes of events liable to occur frequently in the intercourse of nations, regarding which there has never been any agreement as to what is just, equitable, or convenient, and, as to many of the classes of controversy, different views are held by different nations, so that in a large part of the field with which an arbitral tribunal or international court should deal there is really no law to be applied. Where there is no law, a submission to arbitration or to judicial decision is an appeal, not to the rule of law but to the unknown opinions or predilections of the men who happen to be selected to decide. The development of the peaceable settlement of international disputes by the decision of impartial tribunals waits therefore upon the further development of international law by a more complete establishment of known and accepted rules for the government of international conduct.

In this direction also great progress has been made within recent years. The ordinary process of reaching rules of international law through the universal assent of nations, expressed as particular cases arise from time to time in the ordinary course of international affairs, is so slow that, instead of making progress towards a comprehensive law of nations by such a method, the progress of the law has been outstripped by the changes of condition in international affairs, so that the law has been growing less and less adequate to settle the questions continually arising. The Declaration of Paris, in 1856, by a few simple rules dealing, not with particular cases, but looking to the future through an agreement of the powers signing the convention, was a new departure in the method of forming international law. That method has developed into the action of the two Hague Conferences of 1899 and 1907, which were really law-making bodies, establishing, by the unanimous vote of the powers, rules of conduct for the future, covering extensive portions of the field of international conduct. The action of The Hague Conferences would have been impossible if it had not been for the long continued and devoted labors of the *Institut de Droit International*, which, in its annual meetings for forty years, has brought together the leaders of thought in the science of the law of nations in all the countries of the civilized world to discuss unofficially, with a free and full expression of personal opinion, the unsettled problems as to what the law is and ought to be. The conclusions of that body furnished to the successive Hague Conferences the matured results of years of well directed labor and bore the same relation to the deliberations of the conferences as the report of a committee of a legislative body in furnishing the basis for deliberation and action. Their work should be encouraged and their example should be followed.

Further Hague Conferences should be insisted upon. They should be made to recur at regular periods without requiring the special initiative of any country. The process of formulating and securing agreement upon rules of international law should be pressed forward in every direction.

There is a third line of progress, little, if any, less important than the two already mentioned, and that is, the instruction of students and of the great bodies of the people of civilized countries in the knowledge of international law. Under the modern development of constitutional governments, with varying degrees of extension of suffrage, more and more the people who cast the ballots determine the issues of peace and war. No government now embarks in war without the assurance of popular support. It is not uncommon in modern times to see governments straining every nerve to keep the peace, and the people whom they represent, with patriotic enthusiasm and resentment over real or fancied wrongs urging them forward to war. Nothing is more important in the preservation of peace than to secure among the great mass of the people living under constitutional government a just conception of the rights which their nation has against others and of the duties their nation owes to others. The popular tendency is to listen approvingly to the most extreme statements and claims of politicians and orators who seek popularity by declaring their own country right in everything and other countries wrong in everything. Honest people, mistakenly believing in the justice of their cause, are led to support injustice. To meet this tendency there should be not merely definite standards of law to be applied to international relations, but there should be general public understanding of what those standards are. Of course it is not possible that all the people of any country can become familiar with international law, but there may be such knowledge and leadership of opinion in every country on the part of the most intelligent and best educated men that in every community mistaken conceptions can be corrected and a true view of rights and obligations inculcated. To attain this end much has been done and much is in contemplation. Societies of international law have been formed in many countries for the discussion of international questions and the publication and distribution of the results. Many journals of international law have been established and are rapidly increasing their circulation and influence. More and more colleges and universities are establishing chairs and giving instruction in international law to their students. A further step is about to be taken at The Hague by the establishment there of an international school of international law to which scholars from all over the civilized world will come and in which the great masters of the science have undertaken to give instruction. There can be no better augury for the success of the new institution than the fact that it found its origin in the general enthusiasm of Ludwig von Bar of Göttingen, of Otfried Nippold of Frankfort, of Demetrius

Sturdza of Roumania, and of T.M.C. Asser of Holland; and that it has for its president Louis Renault of France. The distinctive feature of this new departure is that it will bring together teachers and students from many countries; so that their intercourse and instruction will tend towards the unification of rules and the establishment of a general standard of law instead of perpetuating the differing and often antagonistic conceptions which obtain within the limits of different nations.

Along all these lines of practical effort for peace in the development of arbitration and judicial decision in the development of a definite system of law determining the rights and obligations of nations, and in the enlightenment of the civilized nations as to what their rights and obligations are, the present generation has rendered a service in the cause of peace surpassing that of many centuries gone before, and in further development along these same lines the present generation has before it a golden opportunity for further service.

There is, however, another class of substantive causes of war which the agencies I have described do not reach directly. This comprises acts done or demanded in pursuance of national policy, and ordinarily either for the enlargement or protection of territory or for trade or industrial advantage. The conduct of a nation under such a policy is often regarded by other nations as unwarranted aggression or as threatening their safety or their rights. Illustrations of this kind of question are to be found in the protean forms of the Eastern question and of the balance of power in Europe, in the assertion of the Monroe Doctrine by the United States; in the position of Germany regarding the settlement of Morocco, before the Conference of Algeciras; in the attitude of Great Britain regarding Agadir, after that conference. It is plain that, under the present organization of civilization in independent nationalities, questions of public policy supposed to be vital cannot be submitted to arbitration, because that would be an abdication of independence and the placing of government *pro tanto* in the hands of others. The independence of a state involves that state's right to determine its own domestic policy and to decide what is essential to its own safety.

It does not follow, however, that we are without opportunity to promote and strengthen specific influences tending to diminish or prevent causes of war of this description. In the first place, when there is a policy of intentional aggression, inspired by a desire to get possession of the territory or the trade of another country, right or wrong, a pretext is always sought. No nation now sets forth to despoil another upon the avowed ground that it desires the spoils. Some ground of justification is always alleged. The wolf always charges the lamb with muddying the stream. The frank and simple days of the Roman proconsul and of the robber baron have passed, and three things have happened: First, there has come to be a public opinion of the world; second, that opinion has set up a new standard of national conduct which condemns unjustified aggression; and third, the public opinion of the world punishes the violation of its standard. It has not been very long since the people of each country were concerned almost exclusively with their own affairs, and, with but few individual exceptions, neither knew nor cared what was going on outside their own boundaries. All that has changed. The spread of popular education; the enormous increase in the production and circulation of newspapers and periodicals and cheap books; the competition of the press, which ranges the world for news; the telegraph, which carries instantly knowledge of all important events everywhere to all parts of the world; the new mobility of mankind, which availing itself of the new means of travel by steamship and railroad, with its new freedom under the recently recognized right of expatriation and the recently established right of free travel, moves to and fro by the million across the boundaries of the nations; the vast extension of international commerce; the recognition of interdependence of the peoples of different nations engendered by this commerce and this intercourse; their dependence upon each other for the supply of their needs and for the profitable disposal of their products, for the preservation of health, for the promotion of morals and for the increase of knowledge and the advance of thought; — all these are creating an international community of knowledge and interest, of thought and feeling. In the hundreds of international associations reported by Senator LaFontaine's *L'Office Central* at Brussels, men of all nations are learning to think internationally about science and morals and hygiene and religion and society and business. Gradually, everything that happens in the world is coming to be of interest everywhere in the world, and, gradually, thoughtful men and women everywhere are sitting in judgment upon the conduct of all nations. Some very crass and indefensible things have been done by nations within the past few years, but no one can read the discussions about those national acts without seeing that the general judgment of mankind has sunk deep into the hearts of the people of the countries responsible; that a great new force is at work in international affairs; that the desire for approval and the fear of condemnation by the contemporary opinion of the civilized world is becoming a powerful influence to control national conduct. True, we are but at the beginning, but it is the beginning of a great new era in which the public opinion of mankind renders judgment, not upon peace and war, for a vast majority of mankind is in favor of war when that is necessary for the preservation of liberty and justice, but upon the just and unjust conduct of nations, as the public opinion of each community passes upon the just and unjust conduct of its individual members. The chief force which makes for peace and order in the community of individuals is not the police officer, with his club, but it is the praise and blame, the honor and shame, which follow observance or violation of the community's standards of right conduct. In the new era that is dawning of the world's public opinion we need not wait for the international policeman, with his artillery, for, when any people feels that its government has done a shameful thing and has brought them into disgrace in the opinion of the world, theirs will be the vengeance and they will inflict the punishment.

Two conclusions from all these considerations are quite obvious: First, that the development and understanding of international law and the habit of submitting international controversies to judicial decision will continually tend to hinder wanton aggression, because it will tend to make it more difficult to find pretexts, excuses, or justification. Second, that quite apart from argument and exhortation concerning war and peace, there is a specific line of effort along which those who seek to promote peace may most usefully proceed; by insisting upon a willingness to do justice among nations, and this, not justice according to the possibly excited and warped opinion of the particular nation, but according to the general public judgment of the civilized world; by condemning injustice on the part of nations as we condemn injustice on the part of individuals; by pressing upon the peoples of the earth a consciousness that if they are arrogant and grasping and overbearing and use their power to oppress and despoil the weak, they will be disgraced in the estimation of mankind. Such an effort is not a denial of the innate impulses of the race, but is an appeal to them. It accords with the line of historic development. The taboo of savage tribes is nothing else. The social penalties of civilized communities are the same thing. The theoretical postulate of all diplomatic discussion between nations is the assumed willingness of every nation to do justice. The line of least resistance in the progress of civilization is to make that theoretical postulate real by the continually increasing force of the world's public opinion.

Yet there are other influences tending in the same direction which may be usefully promoted. The self-interest which so often prompts nations to unjust aggression can no longer safely assume that its apparent profit is real; for a nation which has been built up by the industry and enterprise of its people, which depends upon its products and the marketing of them, upon its commerce and the peaceful intercourse of commerce for its prosperity, the prize of aggression must be rich indeed to counterbalance the injury sustained by the interference of war with both production and commerce. At the same time, freedom of trade regardless of political control is diminishing the comparative value of extension of territory. The old system of exploitation of colonies and the monopolization of their trade for the benefit of the mother country has practically disappeared. The best informed men are coming to understand that, under modern conditions, the prosperity of each nation is enhanced by the prosperity of all other nations; and that the government which acquires political control over new territory may gratify pride and minister to ambition, but can have only a slight effect to advance the welfare of its people.

The support of these statements rests upon the facts of economic science. If they are true, as I am sure we all believe them to be, they should be forced upon the attention of the peoples, not by mere assertion, which avails but little, but by proof drawn from the rich stores of evidence to be found in the history of mankind. For the accomplishment of this purpose a meeting of eminent economists and publicists was held three years ago at Berne. They came from Denmark, Holland, Belgium, Great Britain, France, Germany, Switzerland, Italy, Austria-Hungary, the United States and Japan. For some weeks they devoted themselves to the preparation of a program for systematic, scientific investigation into the historical and economic causes and effects of war. For the three years which have ensued they have been engaged, with ample and competent assistance, in pursuing their investigations. The first installments of their work are ready for publication, and they reconvened last month to review what has been done and to lay down the lines of further work. The results of their labors, when made available, should be eagerly sought by every lover of peace who is competent by tongue or pen to be a teacher of his fellow-men, for we may be confident they will show that while the sacrifice of war may be demanded for justice, for liberty, for national life, yet war is always a sacrifice, and never is a rational mode of promoting material prosperity.

There yet remain certain disposing causes, which, quite apart from real substantive questions in controversy, operate upon national feeling and give injurious effect to trifling or fancied occasions for offense. There is no international controversy so serious that it cannot be settled if both parties really wish to settle it. There are few controversies so trifling that they cannot be made the occasion for war if the parties really wish to fight. Among these disposing causes which create an atmosphere of belligerency are:

Race and local prejudice, breeding dislike and hatred between the peoples of different countries.

Exaggerated national *amour propre*, which causes excessive sensitiveness and excessive resentment of foreign criticism or opposition.

With these go the popular assumption, often arrogant, often ignorant, that the extreme claims of one's country are always right and are to be rigidly insisted upon as a point of national honor. With them go intolerance of temperate discussion, of kindly consideration, and of reasonable concession.

Under these feelings insulting words and conduct towards foreign governments and people become popular, and braggart defiance is deemed patriotic. Under them the ambitious aspirants of domestic politics seek preferment through avenues of military success.

And under them deep and real suspicions of the sinister purpose of other nations readily take possession of a people, who become ready to believe that an attack by their own country is the only recourse to guard effectually against an attack upon their country by others, and that patriotism requires them to outstrip other countries in armament and preparation for war.

Prejudice and passion and suspicion are more dangerous than the incitement of self-interest or the most stubborn adherence to real differences of opinion regarding rights. In private life more quarrels arise, more implacable resentment is caused, more lives are sacrificed, because of insult than because of substantial injury. And it is so with nations.

The remedy is the same. When friends quarrel we try to dissipate their misunderstandings, to soften their mutual feelings, and to bring them together in such a way that their friendship may be renewed. Misunderstanding and prejudice and dislike are, as a rule, the fruits of isolation. There is so much of good in human nature that men grow to like each other upon better acquaintance, and this points to another way in which we may strive to promote the peace of the world. That is, by international conciliation through intercourse, not the formal intercourse of the traveller or the merchant, but the intercourse of real acquaintance, of personal knowledge, of little courtesies and kindly consideration; by the exchange of professors between universities, by the exchange of students between countries; by the visits to other countries on the part of leaders of opinion, to be received in private hospitality and in public conference; by the spreading of correct information through the press; by circulating and attracting attention to expressions of praise and honor rather than the reverse; by giving public credit where credit is due and taking pains to expose and publish our good opinions of other peoples; by coöperation in the multitude of causes which are world-wide in their interest; by urging upon our countrymen the duty of international civility and kindly consideration; and by constant pressure in the right direction in a multitude of ways — a slow process, but one which counts little by little if persisted in.

Each separate act will seem of no effect but all together they will establish and maintain a tendency towards the goal of international knowledge and broad human sympathy. There is a homely English saying, "Leg over leg the dog went to Dover." That states the method of our true progress. We cannot arrive at our goal *per saltum*. Not by invoking an immediate millenium, but by the accumulated effects of a multitude of efforts, each insignificant in itself, but steadily and persistently continued, we must win our way along the road to better knowledge and kindliness among the peoples of the earth which the will of Alfred Nobel describes as " the fraternity of nations."

There are many reasons to believe that progress toward the permanent prevalence of peace may be more rapid in the future than in the past.

Standards of conduct are changing in many ways unfavorable to war.

Civilized man is becoming less cruel. Cruelty to men and to the lower animals as well, which would have passed unnoticed a century ago, now shocks the sensibilities and is regarded as wicked and degrading. The severity of punishments for minor offenses which formerly prevailed now seems to us revolting. The torture of witnesses or of criminals has become unthinkable. Human life is held in much higher esteem and the taking of it, whether in private quarrel or by judicial procedure, is looked upon much more seriously than it was formerly. The social reaction from the theories of the individualistic economists of the last century has brought with it a very wide-spread sense that men have some sort of responsibility to cause affairs to be so ordered in civilized communities that their fellow-men have a chance to live. The Hague Conventions to regulate the conduct of war and the Geneva Conventions to ameliorate its horrors have a significance which goes beyond their professions. They mark the changing attitude of the world towards the subject to which they relate; and they introduce into the business of warfare obligatory considerations of humanity and respect for human rights which tend to destroy the spirit upon which alone the business itself can continue. No one can read those conventions closely without being struck by the similarity of the process of regulation and limitation which they exhibit with the historic process by which private war was ultimately regulated out of existence in the greater part of the civilized world. The growth of modern constitutional government compels for its successful practice the exercise of reason and considerate judgment by the individual citizens who constitute the electorate. The qualities thus evoked in the training schools of domestic affairs are the qualities which make for national self-restraint and peace in international affairs. History is being rewritten, and the progress of popular education is making men familiar with it; and as the world, which worships strength and has most applauded military glory, grows in knowledge, the great commanding figures rising far above the common mass of mere fighters, the men who win the most imperishable fame have come to be the strong, patient, great-hearted ones like Washington, and Lincoln, and William the Silent, and Cavour, whose genius inspired by love of country and their kind urges them to build up and not to destroy. The sweetest incense offered to the memory of the soldier is not to the brutal qualities of war but to the serene courage ennobled by sympathy and courtesy of a Bayard or a Sidney. The hero-worshipper is gradually changing from the savage to the civilized conception of his divinities. Taken all in all the clear and persistent tendencies of a slowly developing civilization justify cheerful hope.

We may well turn from Tripoli and Mexico and the Balkans with the apocryphal exclamation of Galileo, "And still the world moves."

THE ETHICS OF THE PANAMA QUESTION

AN ADDRESS BEFORE THE UNION LEAGUE CLUB OF CHICAGO, FEBRUARY 22, 1904

As Secretary of State, Mr. Root was exceedingly anxious to secure the recognition by Colombia of the independence of Panama, and to restore the friendly relations which had existed between Colombia and the United States but which were unfortunately strained to the breaking-point by the revolution in Panama, and the recognition of its independence by the United States. He, therefore, negotiated a tripartite agreement, consisting of three separate treaties, each of which was to be ratified in order that the tripartite agreement should be binding upon the contracting parties. The agreement entitled "The Ship Canal Treaty", was signed at Washington, January 9, 1909.

The first treaty was between Colombia and the United States, and its ratification was advised and consented to by the Senate on February 24, 1909; the second treaty was between Panama and the United States, and its ratification was advised and consented to by the Senate on March 3, 1909; the third treaty was between Colombia and Panama. The failure of Colombia to ratify these treaties, or any of them, prevented the adjustment of the difficulty between Colombia and the United States during Mr. Root's tenure of office.

The text of the three treaties forming the tripartite agreement is to be found in "Treaties, Conventions, International Acts, Protocols and Agreements between the United States and Other Powers", compiled by Garfield Charles, vol. 3, pp. 235–247, Washington, 1913.

ON November 3, 1903 the people of Panama revolted against the government of Colombia, and proclaimed their independence. On the thirteenth of November the United States recognized the independence of the republic of Panama, by receiving a minister from the new Government, and at the opening of the regular session of Congress in December the President asked the consent of the Senate to a treaty negotiated between our Secretary of State, Mr. Hay, and the minister of Panama, Mr. Varilla, providing for the construction by the United States of a ship canal across the Isthmus, to be kept by us open, neutral, and free upon equal terms for the use of all mankind. After long and exhaustive discussion that treaty is about to be confirmed. In the meantime the Senate by a great majority has approved the recognition of independence by confirming the nomination of William I. Buchanan as minister from the United States to Panama. The revolutionary leaders have submitted their action to the people of Panama, who have, by a popular vote, given it their unanimous approval, and have elected a constitutional convention, framed and adopted a constitution, chosen a president and congress, and established a republican government according to the forms which find their model in the constitutions of our own country. In the meantime, also, many other governments have followed the United States in receiving the new republic into the family of nations. On the eighteenth of November, five days after our recognition, France recognized the republic of Panama; on the twenty-second, China; on the twenty-seventh, Austria; on the thirtieth, Germany; and following them Denmark, Russia, Sweden and Norway, Belgium, Nicaragua, Peru, Cuba, Great Britain, Italy, Switzerland, Costa Rica, Japan, Guatemala, Netherlands, Venezuela, Portugal, in the order named.

The independence of Panama, the grant to the United States of the right to construct the canal across the Isthmus, and the assumption by the United States of the duty to construct the canal and to maintain it for the equal benefit of mankind, are accomplished facts. Nothing can do away with them, unless it be some future war of conquest waged against the liberties of Panama, and at the same time against the rights of the United States held in trust for the commerce of the world.

The conduct of the United States Government in recognizing the independence of Panama, in making the treaty, and in exercising police power over territory traversed by the Panama Railroad and the partly-constructed canal, during the period of the revolution, has been severely criticised by some of our own citizens, who have said, in substance, that in this business our Government has violated the rules of international law, has been grasping and unfair, and has, by the exercise of brute force, trampled down the rights of a weaker nation, in violation of those principles of justice which should control the conduct of nations as of men.

In considering these charges we may well thrust aside as carrying no weight of authority, the expressions of those who while they condemn the conduct of our Government, are in favor of the treaty. They curiously reverse the divine rule, and seem to hate the sinner while they love the sin; and their adverse criticism may fairly be ascribed to the exigencies of the pending presidential campaign. Some of them may be sincere, but upon that question they naturally invite the comment made upon Lady Macbeth, that " she might be a lady, but she did not show it by her conduct."

We need not pay very much heed, either, to that class of temperamental and perennial faultfinders whom we have and always will have with us, as an incident of free institutions, who are against every government of which they do not personally form a part, and in whose eyes everything done by others is wrong. This class of our citizens, with slight changes in personnel, would have condemned any course of conduct by our Government, whatever it was, and their condemnation of the particular course followed merely announces their existence.

Nevertheless, there remain good and sincere men and women who have thought our course to be wrong, and many others, whose character and patriotism entitle them to the highest respect, are troubled in spirit. They would be glad to be sure that our country is not justly chargeable with dishonorable conduct. May the time never come when such men and women are wanting, or are constrained to remain silent, in America. May the time never come when the conscience of America shall cease to apply the rules of upright conduct to national as well as to personal life; when our Government feels absolved from the obligation to answer in that forum for conformity to the rules of right or when material advantage shall be held to excuse injustice. For if such a time ever does come the beginning of the end of our free institutions will have come also.

I wish to present some of the fundamental facts bearing upon the question of right in the Panama business, although they have been stated already better than I can state them, with the hope that they may thus reach the attention of some of the good and sincere citizens who are troubled about the matter.

I am not going to discuss technical rules or precedents or questions whether what was done should have been done a little earlier or a little later, but the broad question whether the thing we have done was just and fair.

It frequently happens in affairs of government that most important rights are created, modified, or practically destroyed by gradual processes, and by the indirect effect of events; and that only an intimate knowledge of the process enables one to realize the change until some practical question arises which requires every one interested to study the subject. If the typical New Zealander, ignorant of our political history, were to read our Constitution and laws, he would suppose that a presidential elector in the United States is entitled to exercise freedom of choice in his vote for President, and he would be quite certain that we were guilty of gross injustice in the treatment which we should certainly accord to an elector who voted for any one but the candidate of his own party. In forming this judgment, he would be misled by the form and appearance of things which he found upon the statute book, and would misjudge a people who were acting in accordance with the substance and reality of things as they knew them to be. In the same way, they are in error who assume that the relations of Colombia to the other nations of the earth as regards the Isthmus of Panama were, in truth, of unqualified sovereignty and right of domestic control according to her own will, governed and protected by the rules of international law, which describe the attributes of complete sovereignty; that the relations of Colombia to the people of Panama were, in truth, those appearing in the written instrument called the Constitution of Colombia; or that the rights and duties of the United States in regard to the Isthmus were confined to the simple duty of aiding Colombia to maintain her control over the Isthmus, and the simple right to ask from Colombia privileges which that country was entitled to grant or withhold at her own pleasure.

The stupendous fact that has dominated the history and must control the future of the Isthmus of Panama is the possibility of communication between the two oceans. It is possible for human hands to pierce the narrow forty miles of solid earth which separate the Caribbean from the Bay of Panama, to realize the dreams of the early navigators, to make the pathway to the Orient they vainly sought, to relieve commerce from the toils and perils of its nine thousand miles of navigation around Cape Horn through stormy seas and along dangerous coasts with its constant burden of wasted effort and shipwreck and loss of life, and to push forward by a mighty impulse that intercommunication between the distant nations of the earth which is doing away with misunderstanding, with race prejudice and bigotry, with ignorance of human rights and opportunity for oppression, and making all the world kin.

Throughout the centuries since Philip II sat upon the throne of Spain, merchants and statesmen and humanitarians and the intelligent masses of the civilized world have looked forward to this consummation with just anticipations of benefit to mankind. No savage tribes who happened to dwell upon the Isthmus would have been permitted to bar this pathway of civilization. By the universal practice and consent of mankind they would have been swept aside without hesitation. No Spanish sovereign could, by discovery or conquest or occupation, preëmpt for himself the exclusive use of this little spot upon the surface of the earth dedicated by nature to the use of all mankind. No civil society organized upon the ruins of Spanish dominion could justly arrogate to itself over this tract of land sovereignty unqualified by the world's easement and all the rights necessary to make that easement effective. The formal rules of international law are but declarations of what is just and right in the generality of cases. But where the application of such a general rule would impair the just rights or imperil the existence of neighboring states or would unduly threaten the peace of a continent or would injuriously affect the general interests of mankind, it has always been the practice of civilized nations to deny the application of the formal rule and compel conformity to the principles of justice upon which all rules depend. The Danubian principalities and Greece and Crete, and Egypt, the passage of the Dardanelles, and the neutralization of the Black Sea are familiar examples of limitations in derogation of those general rules of international law which describe the sovereignty of nations.

The Monroe Doctrine itself, upon which we stand so firmly, is an assertion of our right for our own interest to interfere with the action of every other nation in those parts of this hemisphere where others are sovereign and where we have no sovereignty or claim of sovereignty, and to say if you do thus and so, even by the consent of the sovereign, we shall regard it as an unfriendly act because it will affect us injuriously. It is said that the Monroe Doctrine is not a rule of international law. It is not a rule at all. It is an assertion of a right under the universal rule that all sovereignty is held subject to limitations in its exercise arising from the just interests of other nations.

By the rules of right and justice universally recognized among men and which are the law of nations, the sovereignty of Colombia over the Isthmus of Panama was qualified and limited by the right of the other civilized nations of the earth to have the canal constructed across the Isthmus and to have it maintained for their free and unobstructed passage.

Colombia and her predecessor, New Granada, have not failed at times to recognize their position. In 1846 New Granada, through her secretary of foreign relations, Mr. Mallarino, applied to the Government of the United States to enter into a treaty which should protect that country against the seizure of the Isthmus by other foreign powers. In effect, she acknowledged the right of way and asked the United States to become the trustee of that right which qualified her sovereignty, to maintain it for the equal benefit of all nations, and at the same time to protect her against its exercise by them in such a manner as to destroy her sovereignty altogether. After describing acts which he conceived to be undue encroachments by Great Britain in South America, Mallarino said:

> And if the usurpation of the Isthmus in its channelizable portion should be added to these encroachments, the empire of American commerce in its strictly useful or mercantile sense would fall into the hands of the only nation that the United States can consider as a badly disposed rival. It would be perfectly superfluous to mention the political consequences that would be entailed upon America. This dominion or ascendancy would be equally ruinous to the commerce of the United States and to the nationality of the Spanish-American republics, most direful for the causes of democracy in the New World, and a constant cause of disturbance of the public peace in this our continent.

From these facts and general considerations may be inferred the urgent necessity in which the United States are of interposing their moral influence, and even their material strength, between the weakness of the new republics and the ambitious views of the commercial nations of Europe. . . . This end is simply and naturally to be obtained by stipulating in favor of the United States a total repeal of the differential duties as a compensation for the obligation they imposed upon themselves of guaranteeing the legitimate and complete or integral possession of those portions of territory that the universal mercantile interests require to be free and open to all nations. . . . When a treaty containing such a stipulation shall exist between New Granada and the United States and it could be completed and perfected by a subsequent and supplementary convention, in which the transit of the interoceanic passage should be arranged and its permanent neutrality confirmed, half the plans of Great Britain would of themselves fail and it would no longer be possible for her to encroach upon the Isthmus.

He said he assumed that the United States would in the proposed treaty —

guarantee to New Granada the Isthmus or at least as much of it as was required for the construction of a canal or railroad upon the most favorable route; and moreover that it was important that this guaranty should appear in the treaty as a condition for the right of way and the abolition of the discriminating differential duties, otherwise New Granada would be obliged to grant the same privileges unconditionally to England.

And he appealed to the declaration of the Monroe Doctrine, reiterated by President Polk to the Congress of 1845–46, as the basis of his request.

Upon this appeal, the treaty of December 12, 1846, between the United States and New Granada, was made and signed in behalf of Colombia by the secretary, Mallarino, whose words I have quoted. The thirty-fifth article of the treaty contained the following provision:

The Government of New Granada guarantees to the Government of the United States that the right of way or transit across the Isthmus of Panama upon any modes of communication that now exist, or that may be hereafter constructed, shall be open and free to the Government and citizens of the United States. . . . And in order to secure to themselves the tranquil and constant enjoyment of these advantages, and as an especial compensation for the said advantages and for the favors they have acquired by the fourth, fifth, and sixth articles of this treaty, the United States guarantee positively and efficaciously to New Granada by the present stipulation the perfect neutrality of the before-mentioned Isthmus with the view that the free transit from the one to the other sea may not be interrupted or embarrassed in any future time while this treaty exists, and in consequence the United States also guarantee in the same manner the rights of sovereignty and property which New Granada has and possesses over the said territory.

In transmitting this treaty to the Senate on February 10, 1847, President Polk made these observations:

1. The treaty does not propose to guarantee a territory to a foreign nation in which the United States will have no common interest with that nation. On the contrary, we are more deeply and directly interested in the subject of this guaranty than New Granada herself or any other country.

2. The guaranty does not extend to the territories of New Granada generally, but is confined to the single province of the Isthmus of Panama, where we shall acquire, by the treaty, a common and coextensive right of passage with herself.

3. It will constitute no alliance for any political object, but for a purely commercial purpose in which all the navigating nations of the world have a common interest.

You will perceive that in this transaction New Granada recognized the subordination of her sovereignty to the world's easement of passage by railroad or by canal, and, apprehending that other nations might seek to exercise that right through the destruction of her sovereignty and the appropriation of her territory, she procured the United States to assume the responsibility of protecting her against such treatment. The United States assumed that burden and by way of consideration —

First. The United States received an express grant of the right of way which President Polk described as constituting a " common and coextensive right of passage with New Granada herself," and as making the United States " more deeply and directly interested in the subject of this guaranty than New Granada herself or any other country."

Second. The United States received a grant of power and assumed a duty herself to keep the transit free and uninterrupted and unembarrassed, and to keep the territory of the transit neutral.

The duties assumed by the United States to maintain neutrality and free passage were undertaken for the benefit of all the world. The right to maintain free passage was, however, not merely for the general benefit, but was specifically declared to be " in order to secure to themselves (the United States) the tranquil and constant enjoyment " of the right of way. The United States assumed the burden of protecting New Granada against an unjust exercise of the world's right of passage. She assumed the correlative duty of safeguarding the just exercise of the world's right of passage, and she acquired for herself a specific grant of the right of way and the power to exercise for her own benefit in that territory the functions of sovereignty which were necessary for the peaceable enjoyment of the interest thus acquired by her.

Both countries have agreed in the construction that this treaty imposed upon the United States no duty toward Colombia to help her put down domestic insurrection. With that form of assault upon the sovereignty of Colombia the United States has had no concern, except when it tended to interfere with free transit, and then the action of the United States has been, not in the exercise of a duty toward Colombia, but in protection of her own rights.

Throughout the half-century past since the treaty was made, the United States has been faithful to her obligations. The distinct announcement of her protection and her constantly increasing power have been an adequate barrier against foreign aggression upon the Isthmus. In all the long and monotonous series of revolutions and rebellions in which Colombia from the beginning showed herself wholly incapable of maintaining order, United States sailors and marines have policed the railroad, its terminal cities and its harbors — sometimes by Colombia's request and sometimes without it — prohibiting action sometimes by the forces of the party in power and sometimes by the forces of the party out of power, but always enforcing peace upon the line of transit. In a long and unbroken series of formal binding official declarations by nearly every administration for more than half a century, we have committed our country as a matter of traditional policy to the execution of the trust to protect and control the passage of the Isthmus for the equal uses of all nations.

It will be observed that one effect of the treaty of 1846 was that foreign powers were to be excluded from the opportunity to construct the canal themselves. It followed from this that if private enterprise should fail to build the canal, the United States assumed the obligation to build it herself. We could not play dog in the manger on the Isthmus. We could not refuse to permit the work to be done by any one else competent to do it and refuse the burden ourselves. The obligation of the United States to build the canal and the obligation of Colombia to permit her to build it, both followed necessarily from the relations and obligations assumed by them in the treaty of 1846.

Private enterprise has failed to build the canal. The great French company organized by De Lesseps, after spending and wasting an incredible amount of treasure and after the sacrifice of thousands of lives, has abandoned hope of completing the undertaking. No private company again will grapple with the colossal enterprise. Other nations are excluded from the attempt by the force of our agreement with Colombia. If the canal is to be built, we must build it.

The United States has answered to that obligation. Again upon the request of Colombia, she entered upon the negotiation of the further treaty described by the Granadian secretary, Mallarino, in 1846 as "a subsequent and supplementary convention, in which the transit of the interoceanic passage should be arranged and its permanent neutrality confirmed."

Colombia stood to profit more by the building of that canal than any other nation upon earth. Her territory stretching across the northwestern end of South America was without internal communication or unity. Her principal towns upon her Atlantic and her Pacific coasts were separated by ranges of lofty mountains not traversed by any railroad, and for the most part without roads of any kind. The building of a canal would, for the first time, establish practical and easy communication between her different provinces. The work of construction would bring enormous sums to be expended in her territory, and the operation of the canal would set Colombia upon a great highway of the world's commerce with incalculable opportunities for development and wealth. She had acknowledged the world's right to the canal. She had specifically granted the right of way to the United States. She had induced the United States to assume the moral obligation for its construction by excluding all other nations from the Isthmus for her protection. When she came to settle the terms of this "supplementary convention," the detailed arrangements under which this enormous benefit might be conferred upon mankind, and especially upon herself, she demanded to be paid.

Reluctantly, and with a sense that it was an unjust exaction, the United States agreed to pay ten million dollars down and two hundred and fifty thousand dollars per annum in perpetuity — substantially the entire amount exacted by Colombia. We were not going into the enterprise to make money, but for the common good. We did not expect the revenues of the canal to repay its cost, or to receive any benefit from it, except that which Colombia would share to a higher degree than ourselves. Against the hundreds of mil-

ETHICS OF THE PANAMA QUESTION 187

lions which we were obligating ourselves to expend, Colombia was expected only to permit the use of a small tract of otherwise worthless land already, in substance, devoted to that purpose. We were not seeking a privilege which Colombia was entitled to withhold but settling the method in which the acknowledged right of mankind over a portion of her soil should be exercised, with due regard to her special interests. It was not just that we should pay anything, but it was better to pay than to coerce a weaker nation. The treaty was ratified by the Senate, and forwarded to Bogota. At the same time we arranged that upon the final ratification of the treaty we should pay to the Panama Canal Company, forty million dollars, the entire appraised value of its work upon the canal, in which it had expended nearly two hundred million dollars. The concessions made in the treaty to the Government of Colombia, however, seemed merely to inspire in that Government a belief that there was no limit to the exactions which they could successfully impose. They demanded a further ten million dollars from the Panama Canal Company, and upon its refusal, they rejected the treaty.

This rejection was a substantial refusal to permit the canal to be built. It appears that the refusal contemplated not merely further exactions from us but the spoliation of the canal company. That company's current franchise was limited by its terms to October 31, 1904. There was an extension for six years granted by the President and for which the company had paid five million francs. These patriots proposed to declare the extension void and the franchise ended and to confiscate the forty million dollars worth of property of the company and take from the United States for themselves, in payment for it, the forty million dollars we had agreed to pay the company. The report of the committee on which the Colombian senate acted, contained the following:

> By the thirty-first of October of next year — that is to say, when the next congress shall have met in ordinary session — the extension will have expired, and every privilege with it. In that case, the republic will become the possessor and owner, without any need of a previous judicial decision and without any indemnity, of the canal itself, and of the adjuncts that belong to it, according to the contracts of 1878 and 1900.
>
> When that time arrives the republic, without any impediment, will be able to contract and will be in more clear, more definite, and more advantageous possession, both legally and materially. The authorizations which would then be given by the next congress would be very different from those that would be given by the present one.

By becoming a party to this scheme, we might indeed have looked forward to the time when the appetite of Colombia being satisfied at the expense of the unfortunate stockholders of the French Company, we could proceed with the work; but such a course was too repugnant to the sense of justice that obtains in every civilized community to be for a moment contemplated. We had yielded to the last point, beyond reason and justice, in agreeing to pay for a privilege to which we were already entitled and we could not, with self-respect, submit to be mulcted further. We could negotiate no further. Rejection of the treaty was practically a veto of the canal. Every effort was made to bring Colombia to a realization of what it was that she was doing; the effort was in vain, and on the thirty-first of October, when the Colombian Congress adjourned, the inchoate treaty had expired by limitation.

The questions presented to the United States by this rejection were of the gravest importance. Lewis Cass, Secretary of State, said in 1858:

> The progress of events has rendered the interoceanic route across the narrow portion of Central America vastly important to the commercial world, and especially to the United States, whose possessions extend along the Atlantic and the Pacific coasts, and demand the speediest and easiest modes of communication. While the rights of sovereignty of the States occupying this region should always be respected, we shall expect that these rights be exercised in a spirit befitting the occasion and the wants and circumstances that have arisen. Sovereignty has its duties as well as its

ETHICS OF THE PANAMA QUESTION 189

rights, and none of these local governments, even if administered with more regard to the just demands of other nations than they have been, would be permitted in a spirit of Eastern isolation to close the gates of intercourse on the great highways of the world and justify the act by the pretention that these avenues of trade and travel belong to them and that they choose to shut them, or what is almost equivalent, to encumber them with such unjust relations as would prevent their general use.

The time had apparently come to stand upon this declaration or abandon the canal. The question was, should we submit to be deprived of the canal at the will of Colombia, whose sovereignty was justly subject to the world's right of passage? Should we continue to maintain upon the Isthmus that feeble sovereignty whose existence had depended for half a century upon our protection, in order that it might still bar the way of the world's progress and the exercise of our just rights? Should we prepare to protect that sovereignty in its scheme of spoliation, against the justly indignant protests of France surely coming to the support of the stockholders of the French Canal Company? Or, should we say to Colombia, you have no right to prevent the construction of this canal; you are bound to consent to it upon reasonable terms; by your request we have assumed a position in which we are bound to build it for the use of the nations and in which we are entitled to build it for our own interest; and we shall now proceed to build it with due regard for your interests, whether you agree upon the terms and conditions or not.

I think that Secretary Cass answered the question forty-five years ago. In Europe a concert of the Powers would have made short work of the question. In Central America they would have made short work of it but for the Monroe Doctrine, to which New Granada appealed, and the protection which we guaranteed to her under the treaty of 1846. By the assertion of that doctrine and the engagements of that treaty we took the responsibility upon ourselves alone, to do for civilization what otherwise all the maritime powers would have united in requiring; it was for us alone to act; and I have no question that our right and duty were to build the canal, with or without the consent of Colombia.

These were the conditions existing when the revolution of the third of November happened. To an understanding of that revolution a knowledge of the character and history of Panama is essential. Some uninformed persons have assumed that it was merely a number of individual citizens of Colombia living in the neighborhood of the proposed canal who combined to take possession of that part of Colombian territory and set up a government of their own. No conception could be more inadequate. The sovereign state of Panama was an organized civil society possessed of a territory extending over four hundred miles in length from Costa Rica on the west to the mainland of South America on the east. It had a population of over three hundred thousand the greater part of whom lived in the western part of the country, toward Costa Rica, and farthest removed from South America. Between the inhabited part of this territory and the inhabited part of Colombia, stretched hundreds of miles of tropical forest so dense as to be impassable by the ordinary traveler, so that there was no communication by land between the two countries. The only intercourse was by long sea voyages, as if Panama were a distant island; and the journey from the Isthmus to the capital of Colombia was longer in time than from the Isthmus to Washington.

Panama was not an original part of Colombia, or of New Granada, but obtained its own independence from Spain and established its own government in November, 1821, and thereafter voluntarily entered the Granadian Confederation. When that confederation was broken up into Venezuela, Ecuador, and New Granada in 1832, Panama remained with

New Granada, and so continued until the year 1840, when she again became independent and remained a separate sovereignty until 1842. She then returned to New Granada and remained a part of that country until 1855, when by amendment to the constitution these provisions went into effect:

ARTICLE 1. The territory which comprises the provinces of the Isthmus of Panama, to wit, Panama, Ezuero, Veraguas, and Chiriqui, form a sovereign, federal integral part of New Granada under the name of the State of Panama.

ART. 3. The State of Panama is subject to that of New Granada in the matters which are here mentioned:
1. All matters concerning foreign relations;
2. Organization and service of the regular army and of the marines;
3. Federal finances;
4. Naturalization of foreigners;
5. Official weights, balances, and measures.

ART. 4. In all other matters of legislation and administration, the State of Panama shall legislate freely in the manner it considers proper in accordance with the rules of practice of its own constitution.

Since that time, now nearly fifty years ago, the state of Panama has never voluntarily surrendered her sovereignty. In 1858, in 1860 and 1861, new confederations were formed in which Panama became a contracting party. In 1863 a new constitution was formed, the first two articles of which were as follows:

ARTICLE 1. The sovereign States of Antioquia, Bolivar, Boyaca, Cauca, Cundinamarca, Magdalena, Panama, Santander, and Tolima, created, respectively, by the acts of February 27, 1855, June 11, 1856, May 13, 1857, June 15 of the same year, April 12, 1861, and September 3 of the same year, unite and confederate forever, consulting their external security and reciprocal aid, and form a free, sovereign, and independent nation under the name of the " United States of Colombia."

ART. 2. The said States engage to aid and defend themselves mutually against all violence that may injure the sovereignty of the Union or that of the States.

This constitution undertook to distribute general and local powers between the federal and the state governments upon the principles followed in the Constitution of the United States. But it provided:

ART. 25. Every act of the National Congress or of the executive power of the United States, which shall violate the rights warranted in the fifteenth article, or attack the sovereignty of the States, shall be liable to abrogation by the vote of the latter expressed by the majority of their respective legislatures.

And it provided that it could be amended only in the following manner:

1. That the amendments be solicited by the majority of the legislatures of the States;
2. That the amendments be discussed and approved in both houses, according to what has been established for the enactment of laws; and
3. That the amendments be ratified by the unanimous votes of the senate of plenipotentiaries, each State having one vote.

It may also be amended by a convention called therefor by the Congress on the application of the whole of the legislatures of the States and composed of an equal number of deputies from each State.

Under this constitution Mr. King, the American minister at Bogota, reported to the Secretary of State at Washington:

The States comprising the Union were vested with absolute and unqualified sovereignty. From them emanated all authority, and without their assent none could be exercised by the Federal functionaries of the nation.

Under that constitution the sovereign state of Panama lived in confederation with the other states of Colombia for twenty-three years, until the year 1886. She never legally lost her rights under that constitution, but she was deprived of them in fact by force in the manner which I shall now describe.

In the year 1885 Rafael Nunez, having been elected President of the Confederation of Colombia under the Constitution of 1863, undertook to govern in disregard of constitutional limitations, and was resisted in many parts of Colombia, including Panama. The resistance was overcome, and when that was accomplished Nunez declared " the

ETHICS OF THE PANAMA QUESTION

constitution of 1863 no longer exists." He put Panama under martial law, not during the civil war, but after its close, and appointed a governor of the state. He also appointed governors for the other states in the confederation. He then directed these governors to appoint delegates to a constitutional convention; and the delegates thus appointed framed what is known as the constitution of 1886. The two delegates appointed to represent Panama in this convention were residents of Bogota. Neither of them had ever resided in Panama, and one of them never had set foot in Panama. The pretended constitution thus framed by the appointees of Nunez was declared to be adopted without compliance with a single one of the requisites prescribed by the constitution of 1863 for its amendment. It robbed the people of Panama of every vestige of self-government. It gave them a governor to be appointed by the president at Bogota, and he, in turn, appointed all the administrative officers of the department. It left to the other states their legislatures, but it took away from Panama its legislature and subjected the Isthmus directly in all things to the legislative authority of the Congress at Bogota. It provided that the president might at any time, in case of civil commotion, declare the public order to be disturbed, and that he should thereupon have authority to issue decrees having the force of legislative enactments. It gave him absolute power over the press and power to imprison or expatriate any citizen at will. It took away the property, the powers, the corporate existence, the civil organization of the state, and placed the property and the lives of its people absolutely under the authority and power of a single dictator in a distant capital with which there was no communication by land, and which it required longer to reach than it did to reach the city of Washington. This pretended constitution was never submitted to the people of Panama for their approval or rejection. It was never consented to by them. Our minister at Bogota, Mr. King, closed his dispatch describing the new instrument with these words:

> No generous mind can contemplate the disasters which have befallen this people, or meditate on the ills that may flow from their reckless experiment of violent political change, without feeling a deep sorrow for the pains endured by a weak and long-suffering race, who mourn the destruction of their chartered rights as the loss of a cherished freedom that must be recovered at the cost of every peril.

In an address made by President Nunez to this convention of his own appointees he indicated clearly the way in which he proposed to make the new constitution effective in Panama. He said:

> To what has been stated is added the necessity of maintaining for some time a strong army which shall serve as a material support to the acclimatization of peace which cannot be produced instantaneously by a system of government little in harmony with the defective habits acquired in so many years of error. The state of Panama alone requires a large and well-paid garrison, in order that acts may not again occur endangering our sovereignty; without such precaution excluding the most certain one, which is the prudent cultivation of our relations with the North American Government, which has just given us clear evidence of its good faith.

The evidence of good faith to which he referred was that our armed forces had just turned the Isthmus over from the control of the troops of Panama to the control of the troops of Nunez; and the meaning was that he intended to hold the people of Panama subject by force of arms and the aid of the United States.

In May, 1886, our consul at Panama reported to the State Department:

> The people of the Isthmus are ground down by excessive taxation, and they fear to acquire property lest they shall not only be robbed by the tax gatherers but also imprisoned to cloak the robbery under a false charge. At the present time the revenue derived from the cities of Panama and Colon and intermediary villages is at the rate of $1,000,000 a year. Not one tenth of this revenue is spent for the benefit of the people. It is used to keep the forces to keep them in subjection.

On December 24, 1886, four months after the promulgation of the constitution, he reported:

Three fourths of the people of this Isthmus desire separation and the independence of the extinguished state of Panama. They feel but little more affection for the Governor at Panama than the Poles did forty years ago for their masters at St. Petersburg. They would revolt if they could get arms and if they felt that the United States would not interfere.

A signed article published in December last in the newspaper *El Relator* of Bogota sums up the story of oppression and spoliation under which the people of Panama have suffered during these recent years. The facts which the writer states appear also spread at large in numerous reports upon the files of our State Department. He says:

When the Isthmus in 1821 had sealed its independence and had incorporated itself spontaneously to great Colombia, undoubtedly it had the conviction that we would not annul its rights and its liberty as a nation; it thought that we would always respect the integrity of its own government. Whether we have betrayed or not the confidence that the Isthmians had in our country, the history of the last twenty years and the work of inequity and spoiling realized in Panama will answer.

We have converted the lords and masters of that territory into pariahs of their native soils. We have cut off their rights and suppressed all their liberties unexpectedly. We have robbed them of the most precious faculty of a free people — that of electing their mandataries; their legislators, their judges.

We have restricted for them the right of suffrage; we have falsified the count of votes; we have made prevalent over the popular will the will of a mercenary soldiery and that of a series of employees entirely strange to the interests of the department; we have taken away from them the right of law-making, and as a compensation we have put them under the iron yoke of exceptional laws; state, provinces, and municipalities have lost entirely the autonomy which they were enjoying formerly. . . .

In towns of a cosmopolitan character on the Isthmus, we did not found any national schools where children could learn our religion, our language, our history, and how to love their country. In the face of the world, we have punished with imprisonment, with expulsion, with fines, and whippings the writers for the innocent expression of their thought. From December, 1884, to October, 1903, the presidents, governors, secretaries, prefects, mayors, chiefs of police, military chiefs, officials, and soldiers, inspectors of police, the police itself, captains and surgeons of harbors, magistrates, judges of all descriptions, state attorneys — everybody came from the high plains of the Andes and from other parts of the republic to impose on the Isthmus the will, the law, or the whims of the more powerful, to sell justice or speculate with the treasury. This series of employees, similar to an octopus with its multiple arms, was sucking the blood of an oppressed people and was devouring what only the Panamans had right to devour. We have made of the Isthmus a real military province, and when this nation of three hundred and fifty thousand souls had men of continental reputation like Justo Arosemana; legislators of the first order and of an irresistible popularity like Pablo Arosemana and like Gil Colunje; men of talent like Ardila; brilliant diplomats like Hurtado; and scientific celebrities of European reputation like Sosa, we leave them aside, we relegate them in contempt and in forgetfulness instead of putting them at the head of the Isthmus, in order to quench the thirst of equity and justice and satisfy the legitimate aspirations of all the Panamans. Such a way of proceeding has wounded the pride, the dignity, and the patriotism of all the intellectual people of the Isthmus, and has provoked and developed the hatred and the anger of the popular mass.

The people of Panama fought to exhaustion in 1885 to prevent the loss of their liberty and they were defeated through the action of the naval forces of the United States. Three times since then they have risen in rebellion against their oppressors.

In 1895 they arose and were suppressed by force; in 1899 they arose again and for three years maintained a war for liberation, which ended in 1902 through the interposition of the United States by armed force. The rising of November, 1903, was the fourth attempt of this people to regain the rights of which they had been deprived by the usurpation of Nunez. The rejection of the canal treaty by the Bogota Congress was the final and overwhelming injury to the interests of Panama; the conclusive evidence of indifference to her welfare and disregard of her wishes; and it also created the opportunity for success in her persistent purpose to regain civil liberty; for it was plain that under the strained relations created by that rejection, the United States naturally would

ETHICS OF THE PANAMA QUESTION

not exercise her authority again upon the Isthmus, as she had exercised it before, to aid the troops of Colombia. She was under no obligation to do so, and she could not do so without aiding in the denial of her own rights and the destruction of her own interests. Upon that the people of Panama relied in their last attempt, and they relied upon it with reason.

In the meantime there had been a curious grafting of usurpation upon usurpation at Bogota. In 1898 M. A. Sanclamente was elected president, and J. M. Maroquin, vice-president, of the republic of Colombia. It is true that there was no freedom of election. Our minister had reported of a preceding election: " None but the soldiers, police, and employees of the Government voted, thus making the victory of the Government complete "; but there was a form of election, and Sanclamente became the only president there was, and Maroquin the vice-president. Article twenty-four of the constitution of 1886 provided:

> The vice-president of the republic shall perform the duties of the executive office during the temporary absence of the president. In case of the permanent absence of the president, the vice-president shall occupy the office of the president during the balance of the time for which he was elected.

On July 31, 1900, the vice-president, Maroquin, executed a *coup d'état* by seizing the person of the president, Sanclamente, and imprisoning him at a place a few miles outside of Bogota. Maroquin thereupon declared himself possessed of the executive power because of the absence of the president. He then issued a decree that public order was disturbed, and, upon that ground, assumed to himself legislative power under another provision of the constitution which I have already cited. Thenceforth, Maroquin, without the aid of any legislative body, ruled as the supreme executive, legislative, civil, and military authority in the so-called republic of Colombia.

The absence of Sanclamente from the capital became permanent by his death in prison in the year 1902. When the people of Panama declared their independence in November last, no Congress had sat in Colombia since the year 1898, except the special Congress called by Maroquin to reject the canal treaty, and which did reject it by a unanimous vote, and adjourned without legislating on any other subject. The constitution of 1886 had taken away from Panama the power of self-government and vested it in Colombia. The *coup d'état* of Maroquin took away from Colombia herself the power of government and vested it in an irresponsible dictator.

The true nature of the government against which Panama rebelled is plainly shown by the proposals to the United States by the Bogota government upon receipt of the first news of the revolution. On the sixth of November the United States minister at Bogota, Mr. Beaupré, telegraphed to Mr. Hay:

> Knowing that the revolution has already commenced in Panama, General Reyes says that if the Government of the United States will land troops to preserve Colombian sovereignty and the transit of the Isthmus, if requested by the chargé d'affaires of Colombia, this Government will declare martial law and by virtue of vested constitutional authority, when public order is disturbed, will approve by decree the ratification of the canal treaty as signed; or, if the Government of the United States prefers, will call an extra session of Congress with new and friendly members next May, to approve the treaty.

On the seventh of November Mr. Beaupré telegraphed to Mr. Hay:

> General Reyes leaves next Monday for Panama invested with full powers. He has telegraphed chiefs of the insurrection that his mission is to the interests of Isthmus. He wishes answer from you before leaving, to the inquiry in my telegram of yesterday, and wishes to know if the American commander will be ordered to coöperate with him and with new Panama government to arrange peace and the approval of Canal Treaty, which will be accepted on condition that the integrity of Colombia be preserved.

He has telegraphed President of Mexico to ask the Government of the United States and all the countries represented at the Pan-American Conference to aid Colombia to preserve her integrity. The question of the approval of the treaty mentioned in my telegram yesterday will be arranged in Panama; he asks that before taking definite action you will await his arrival there, and that the Government of the United States in the meantime preserve the neutrality and transit of the Isthmus, and do not recognize the new Government.

The General Reyes of these dispatches is now the president-elect of Colombia. Upon reading them, who can fail to see that there was no constitutional government in Colombia; that no government of law protected the people of Panama and their interests against the will of an arbitrary and foreign power; that the deliberations and unanimous action of the special Congress at Bogota had been a sham and a pretense; that Panama's rights, that the rights of the United States, that the world's rights to the passage of the Isthmus, had been the subject of disingenuous juggling at the hands of successful adventurers, and not of the fair expression of a free nation's will.

When these dispatches were received the die was not cast on the Isthmus; the United States had not recognized the new republic of Panama; she had assumed no obligations toward the leaders of the new movement or toward their followers; Colombia and Panama then both held out to us the offer of the right and opportunity to build the canal. Colombia said, " We will ratify the treaty — we will ratify it by decree, or we will call a Congress selected for the purpose of ratifying the treaty, as the preceding Congress was selected for the purpose of rejecting it — if you will preserve our integrity." Panama said, " Recognize our independence, and the treaty follows of course, for the building of the canal is our dearest hope." There was no question of interest on the part of the United States; the treaty was secure; the canal was secure; but there was a question of right, a question of justice, a question of national conscience to be dealt with. What was the duty of the United States toward the people of Panama and the dictator at Bogota?

The people of Panama were the real owners of the canal route; it was because their fathers dwelt in the land, because they won their independence from Spain, because they organized a civil society there that it was not to be treated as one of the waste places of the earth. They owned that part of the earth's surface just as much as the state of New York owns the Erie Canal. When the sovereign state of Panama confederated itself with the other states of Colombia under the constitution of 1863, it did not part with its title or its substantial rights, but constituted the Federal Government its trustee for the representation of its rights in all foreign relations, and imposed upon that Government the duty of protecting them. The trustee was faithless to its trust; it repudiated its obligations without the consent of the true owner; it seized by the strong hand of military power the rights which it was bound to protect; Colombia herself broke the bonds of union and destroyed the compact upon which alone depended her right to represent the owner of the soil. The question for the United States was: Shall we take this treaty from the true owner or shall we take it from the faithless trustee, and for that purpose a third time put back the yoke of foreign domination upon the neck of Panama, by the request of that Government which has tried to play toward us the part of the highwayman? There was no provision of our treaty with Colombia which required us to answer to her call, for our guaranty of her sovereignty in that treaty relates solely to foreign aggression. There was no rule of international law which required us to recognize the wrongs of Panama or the justice of her cause, for international law does not concern itself with the internal affairs of states. But I put it to the conscience of the American people who are passing judgment upon the action of their Government, whether the decision of our President and Secretary of State and the Senate was not a righteous decision.

By all the principles of justice among men and among nations that we have learned from our fathers, and that all peoples and all governments should maintain, the revolutionists in Panama were right, the people of Panama were entitled to be free again, the Isthmus was theirs and they were entitled to govern it; and it would have been a shameful thing for the Government of the United States to return them again to servitude.

It is hardly necessary to say now that our Government had no part in devising, fomenting, or bringing about the revolution on the Isthmus of Panama. President Roosevelt said in his message to Congress of January 4, 1904:

> I hesitate to refer to the injurious insinuations which have been made of complicity by this Government in the revolutionary movement in Panama. They are as destitute of foundation as of propriety. The only excuse for my mentioning them is the fear lest unthinking persons might mistake for acquiescence the silence of mere self-respect. I think proper to say, therefore, that no one connected with this Government had any part in preparing, inciting, or encouraging the late revolution on the Isthmus of Panama, and that save from the reports of our naval and military officers, given above, no one connected with this Government had any previous knowledge of the revolution except such as was accessible to any person of ordinary intelligence who read the newspapers and kept up a current acquaintance with public affairs.

The people of the United States, without distinction of party, will give to that statement their unquestioning belief.

All the world knew that there would be a rising by the people of Panama, if the Colombian Congress adjourned without approving the treaty, as it did adjourn on the thirty-first of October. The newspapers of the United States were filled with statements to that effect, and our State and Navy Departments could not fail to be aware of it. They took the same steps they had always taken under similar circumstances to have naval vessels present to keep the transit open and protect American life and property. If any criticism is to be made upon their course, it is that there was too little rather than too much prevision and preparation. There was no naval vessel of the United States at the city of Panama, and there were no armed forces of the United States there when the rising occurred. There was one small vessel at Colon which was able to land a force of forty-two marines and blue-jackets; that was the entire force which the United States had on the Isthmus at the time of the revolution. They were landed at Colon as our troops had many times before been landed, and they were landed under these circumstances: On the morning of November third, the day of the rising at Panama, about four hundred and fifty Colombian troops landed at Colon and their two generals proceeded by rail to the city of Panama, where they were arrested and placed in confinement by the insurgents, who had been joined by all the Colombian troops on the Isthmus except the four hundred and fifty just landed, and who had a force of fifteen hundred men under arms. On the morning of the next day, the fourth of November, the remaining commander of this body of Colombian troops in Colon sent a notice to the American consul that if the officers who had been arrested by the insurgents in Panama the evening before were not released by two o'clock in the afternoon, he would open fire on the town of Colon and kill every United States citizen in the place. There was then no American armed force of any description on the soil of the Isthmus. The *Nashville* was in the harbor. The American consul appealed to the commander of the *Nashville* for protection, and he landed the forty-two marines and blue-jackets. They took possession of the shed of the Panama Railroad Company, a stone building capable of defense, collected there the American men residing in Colon, sent the American women and

ETHICS OF THE PANAMA QUESTION   203

children on board a Panama Railroad steamer and a German steamer which were lying at the dock, and prepared to receive the threatened attack. The building was surrounded by the Colombian troops, and for an hour and a half this little force stood to its arms ready to fire and expecting to receive the threatened and apparently intended attack of ten times their number. Then cooler judgment prevailed with the Colombian officers, and the tension was relieved. On the following day a renewal of the threatening attitude of the Colombian troops led to a reoccupation of the railroad shed and a return of the women and children to the steamers; but again the danger passed without conflict; and on the evening of the second day, the fifth of November, after conferences with the insurgent leaders, in which the American officers took no part, the Colombian troops boarded a Colombian ship and sailed away from the harbor of Colon, leaving no Colombian force on the Isthmus. The commander of the *Nashville* closes his report of these occurrences in these words:

> I beg to assure the Department that I had no part whatever in the negotiations that were carried on between Colonel Torres and the representatives of the provisional government; that I landed an armed force only when the lives of American citizens were threatened, and withdrew this force as soon as there seemed to be no ground for further apprehension of injury to American lives and property; that I relanded an armed force because of the failure of Colonel Torres to carry out his agreement to withdraw and announced intention to return; and that my attitude throughout was strictly neutral as between the two parties, my only purpose being to protect the lives and property of American citizens and to preserve the free and uninterrupted transit of the Isthmus.

Objection has been made that owing to American direction the Panama Railroad Company refused to transport the four hundred and fifty Colombian soldiers to Panama to attack the fifteen hundred insurgents in arms there, and that the officers of the American Government were directed to prevent any troops of either party from making the line of the railroad the theatre of hostilities; but this was no new policy devised or applied for this occasion; and it was impartial as to both parties to the controversy. The insurgents were anxious that the transportation should be given, for they outnumbered the Colombians more than three to one, and when it was refused they asked for transportation for themselves to attack the Colombians in Colon, and that was refused. The year before a communication had been sent to the Commander of the Colombian forces and the commander of the insurgent forces on the Isthmus in these words:

U. S. S. *Cincinnati, September 19, 1902.*

DEAR SIR: — I have the honor to inform you that the United States naval forces are guarding the railway trains and the line of transit across the Isthmus of Panama from sea to sea, and that no persons whatever will be allowed to obstruct, embarrass, or interfere in any manner with the trains or the route of transit. No armed men except forces of the United States will be allowed to come on or use the line.

All of this is without prejudice or any desire to interfere in domestic contentions of the Colombians.

Please acknowledge receipt of this communication.

With assurances of high esteem and consideration, I remain,
   Very respectfully,
             T. C. MCLEAN,
   Commander, United States Navy, Commanding.

The policy embodied in this official notice of 1902 was the same policy followed in November, 1903, and none other; it was the outcome of the experience gained during the long course of warfare and the painful experience of property destroyed and traffic suspended, which showed that if the rights of the United States on the Isthmus of Panama were to be protected they must be protected by the United States itself insisting that its right of way should not be made the field of battle, as it had been in 1885, when Colon was burned with the railroad terminals and wharves, when Panama was captured, track was torn up, cars were broken open, telegraph wires were cut and armored trains were a necessity. The warrant for the execution of that policy is the right of self-protection. The things done by our officers might not have been permissible in the territory of a country of strong and orderly government possessing and exercising the power to prevent lawless violence and to protect the lives and property of citizens and foreigners alike; but action of this character is, according to the universal rules obtaining among civilized nations, not only permissible, but a duty of the highest obligation in countries whose feeble governments exercise imperfect control in their own territory and fail to perform the duties of sovereignty for the protection of life and property. The armed force of American sailors who during the past few weeks have been protecting American life and property in the friendly capital of Korea have not been making war upon that power. The expeditionary force which marched to Peking under Chaffee in the summer of 1900, and carrying the capital of China by assault, rescued the residents of the American legation, was not making war upon that nation, which relies with just confidence upon our constant friendship. In that category of incapacity to protect the rights of others, Colombia has placed herself as to the Isthmus of Panama by the record of the past years. She could not maintain order upon the Isthmus because she did not seek to maintain justice; she could not command respect for her laws because she had abandoned the rule of law and submitted to the control of an arbitrary dictator. The right of self-protection for American interests rested upon these facts emphasized and enforced by the grant of power in the treaty of 1846, and by Colombia's own appeals to the American Government to intervene for the maintenance of order.

It was not the neutral force of forty-two marines and bluejackets, or anything that the American Government or American officers said or did, that led the four hundred and fifty Colombians to retire from Colon; it was the fact that they found themselves alone among a hostile and unanimous people with an overwhelming insurgent force in arms against them which left no alternative but capture or retreat. The recognition of independence and the treaty with Panama are the real grounds of Colombia's complaint, and upon the justice of those acts America stands, fairly, openly, with full disclosure of every step taken and every object sought.

Upon the firm foundation of that righteous action, with the willing authority of the lawful owners of the soil, we will dig the canal, not for selfish reasons, not for greed of gain, but for the world's commerce, benefiting Colombia most of all. We shall not get back the money we spend upon the canal any more than we shall get back the money we have expended to make Cuba a free and independent republic, or the money we have expended to set the people of the Philippines on the path of ordered liberty and competency for self-government. But we shall promote our commerce, we shall unite our Atlantic and Pacific coasts, we shall render inestimable service to mankind, and we shall grow in greatness and honor and in the strength that comes from difficult tasks accomplished and from the exercise of the power that strives in the nature of a great constructive people.

THE OBLIGATIONS OF THE UNITED STATES AS TO PANAMA CANAL TOLLS

ADDRESS IN THE SENATE OF THE UNITED STATES
JANUARY 21, 1913

Chapter 390 of the laws of 1912, entitled "An Act to provide for the opening, maintenance, protection, and operation of the Panama Canal, and the sanitation and government of the Canal Zone," passed the Senate, August 9, 1912, and became a law August 24, 1912. When the bill was before the Senate for final action, Mr. Root moved to strike out the line in Section 5 providing that "no tolls shall be levied upon vessels engaged in the coastwise trade of the United States." This amendment was rejected without roll call, and the bill passed as originally reported: yeas, 47; nays, 15; not voting, 32.

On December 11, 1912, Sir Edward Grey, Principal Secretary for Foreign Affairs of Great Britain, formally protested to the United States against this provision of the Panama law, as a violation of the terms of the Hay-Pauncefote Treaty between Great Britain and the United States signed November 18, 1901, and proclaimed February 22, 1902.

On January 14, 1913, Mr. Root introduced Senate Bill No. 8114, being in identical terms with his motion above referred to. On the same date he announced his intention to speak upon the subject on January 21.

On March 5, 1914, President Wilson delivered a message to Congress in person in which he said:

I have come to ask you for the repeal of that provision of the Panama Canal Act of August 24, 1912, which exempts vessels engaged in the coastwise trade of the United States from payment of tolls and to urge upon you the justice, the wisdom, and the large policy of such a repeal with the utmost earnestness of which I am capable.

In my own judgment, very fully considered and maturely formed, that exemption constitutes a mistaken economic policy from every point of view, and is, moreover, in plain contravention of the treaty with Great Britain concerning the canal concluded on November 18, 1901. But I have not come to urge upon you my personal views. I have come to state to you a fact and a situation. Whatever may be our own differences of opinion concerning this much-debated measure, its meaning is not debated outside the United States. Everywhere else the language of the treaty is given but one interpretation, and that interpretation precludes the exemption I am asking you to repeal. We consented to the treaty; its language we accepted, if we did not originate; and we are too big, too powerful, too self-respecting a nation to interpret with too strained or refined a reading the words of our own promises just because we have power enough to give us leave to read them as we please. The large thing to do is the only thing that we can afford to do, a voluntary withdrawal from a position everywhere questioned and misunderstood. We ought to reverse our action without raising the question whether we were right or wrong, and so once more deserve our reputation for generosity and for the redemption of every obligation without quibble or hesitation. I ask this of you in support of the foreign policy of the Administration.

The repealing bill was debated at length in both Houses of Congress and on May 21, 1914, Mr. Root delivered his address entitled: "Panama Canal Tolls: Speech in Reply," which is printed immediately following the address below.

Mr. T. W. Sims, of Tennessee, had meanwhile introduced in the House of Representatives a bill to repeal the clause exempting American coastwise shipping from the payment of tolls on the Panama Canal, which passed the House, March 31, 1914, and passed the Senate, June 11, 1914, by the following vote: yeas, 50; nays, 35; not voting, 10. It was approved June 15, 1914.

This repealing act is Public 1131, Sixty-third Congress, Second session.

MR. PRESIDENT, in the late days of last summer, after nearly nine months of continuous session, Congress enacted, in the bill to provide for the administration of the Panama Canal, a provision making a discrimination between the tolls to be charged upon foreign vessels and the tolls to be charged upon American vessels engaged in coastwise trade. We all must realize, as we look back, that when that provision was adopted the members of both Houses were much exhausted; our minds were not working with their full vigor; we were weary physically and mentally. Such discussion as there was was to empty seats. In neither House of Congress, during the period that this provision was under discussion, could there be found more than a scant dozen or two of members. The provision has been the cause of great regret to a multitude of our fellow-citizens, whose good opinion we all desire and whose leadership of opinion in the country makes their approval of the course of our Congress an important element in maintaining that confidence in government which is so essential to its success. The provision has caused a painful impression throughout the world that the United States has departed from its often-announced rule of equality of opportunity in the use of the Panama Canal, and is seeking a special advantage for itself in what is believed to be a violation of the obligations of a treaty. Mr. President, that opinion of the civilized world is something which we may not lightly disregard. "A decent respect to the opinions of mankind" was one of the motives stated for the people of these colonies in the great Declaration of American Independence.

The effect of the provision has thus been doubly unfortunate, and I ask the Senate to listen to me while I endeavor to state the situation in which we find ourselves; to state the case which is made against the action that we have taken, in order that I may present to the Senate the question whether we should not either submit to an impartial tribunal the question whether we are right, so that if we are right, we may be vindicated in the eyes of all the world; or whether we should not, by a repeal of the provision, retire from the position which we have taken.

In the year 1850, Mr. President, there were two great powers in possession of the North American Continent to the north of the Rio Grande. The United States had but just come to its full stature. By the Webster-Ashburton Treaty of 1842 our northeastern boundary had been settled, leaving to Great Britain that tremendous stretch of seacoast including Nova Scotia, New Brunswick, Newfoundland, Labrador, and the shores of the Gulf of St. Lawrence, now forming the Province of Quebec. In 1846 the Oregon boundary had been settled, assuring to the United States a title to that vast region which now constitutes the states of Washington, Oregon, and Idaho. In 1848 the treaty of Guadalupe-Hidalgo had given to us that great empire wrested from Mexico as a result of the Mexican War, which now spreads along the coast of the Pacific as the state of California and the great region between California and Texas.

Inspired by the manifest requirements of this new empire, the United States turned its attention to the possibility of realizing the dream of centuries and connecting its two coasts — its old coast upon the Atlantic and its new coast upon the

Pacific — by a ship canal through the Isthmus; but when it turned its attention in that direction it found the other empire holding the place of advantage. Great Britain had also her coast upon the Atlantic and her coast upon the Pacific, to be joined by a canal. Further than that, Great Britain was a Caribbean power. She had Bermuda and the Bahamas; she had Jamaica and Trinidad; she had the Windward Islands and the Leeward Islands; she had British Guiana and British Honduras; she had, moreover, a protectorate over the Mosquito Coast, a great stretch of territory upon the eastern shore of Central America which included the river San Juan and the valley and harbor of San Juan de Nicaragua, or Greytown. All men's minds then were concentrated upon the Nicaragua Canal route, as they were until after the treaty of 1901 was made.

And thus when the United States turned its attention toward joining these two coasts by a canal through the Isthmus it found Great Britain in possession of the eastern end of the route which men generally believed would be the most available route for the canal. Accordingly, the United States sought a treaty with Great Britain by which Great Britain should renounce the advantage which she had and admit the United States to equal participation with her in the control and the protection of a canal across the Isthmus. From that came the Clayton-Bulwer Treaty.

Let me repeat that this treaty was sought not by England but by the United States. Mr. Clayton, who was Secretary of State at the time, sent our minister to France, Mr. Rives, to London for the purpose of urging upon Lord Palmerston the making of the treaty. The treaty was made by Great Britain as a concession to the urgent demands of the United States.

I should have said, in speaking about the urgency with which the United States sought the Clayton-Bulwer Treaty,

PANAMA CANAL TOLLS 211

that there were two treaties made with Nicaragua, one by Mr. Heis and one by Mr. Squire, both representatives of the United States. Each gave, so far as Nicaragua could, great powers to the United States in regard to the construction of a canal, but they were made without authorization from the United States, and they were not approved by the Government of the United States and were never sent to the Senate. Mr. Clayton, however, held those treaties in abeyance as a means of inducing Great Britain to enter into the Clayton-Bulwer Treaty. He held them practically as a whip over the British negotiators, and having accomplished the purpose they were thrown into the waste basket.

By that treaty Great Britain agreed with the United States that neither Government should " ever obtain or maintain for itself any exclusive control over the ship canal "; that neither would " make use of any protection " which either afforded to a canal " or any alliance which either " might have " with any State or people for the purpose of erecting or maintaining any fortifications, or of occupying, fortifying, or colonizing Nicaragua, Costa Rica, the Mosquito Coast, or any part of Central America, or of assuming or exercising dominion over the same," and that neither would " take advantage of any intimacy, or use any alliance, connection or influence that either " might " possess with any State or Government through whose territory the said canal may pass, for the purpose of acquiring or holding, directly or indirectly, for the citizens or subjects of the one, any rights or advantages in regard to commerce or navigation through the said canal which shall not be offered on the same terms to the citizens or subjects of the other."

You will observe, Mr. President, that under these provisions the United States gave up nothing that it then had. Its obligations were entirely looking to the future; and Great Britain gave up its rights under the protectorate over the

Mosquito Coast, gave up its rights to what was supposed to be the eastern terminus of the canal. And, let me say without recurring to it again, under this treaty, after much discussion which ensued as to the meaning of its terms, Great Britain did surrender her rights to the Mosquito Coast, so that the position of the United States and Great Britain became a position of absolute equality. Under this treaty also both parties agreed that each should " enter into treaty stipulations with such of the Central American States as they " might " deem advisable for the purpose " — I now quote the words of the treaty — " for the purpose of more effectually carrying out the great design of this convention, namely, that of constructing and maintaining the said canal as a ship communication between the two oceans for the benefit of mankind, on equal terms to all, and of protecting the same."

That declaration, Mr. President, is the corner stone of the rights of the United States upon the Isthmus of Panama, rights having their origin in a solemn declaration that there should be constructed and maintained a ship canal " between the two oceans for the benefit of mankind, on equal terms to all."

In the eighth article of that treaty the parties agreed:

The Governments of the United States and Great Britain having not only desired, in entering into this convention, to accomplish a particular object, but also to establish a general principle, they hereby agree to extend their protection, by treaty stipulations, to any other practicable communications, whether by canal or railway, across the isthmus which connects North and South America, and especially to the interoceanic communications, should the same prove to be practicable, whether by canal or railway, which are now proposed to be established by the way of Tehuantepec or Panama. In granting, however, their joint protection to any such canals or railways as are by this article specified, it is always understood by the United States and Great Britain that the parties constructing or owning the same shall impose no other charges or conditions of traffic thereupon than the aforesaid Governments shall approve of as just and equitable; and that the same canals or railways, being open to the citizens and subjects of the United States and Great Britain on equal terms, shall also be open on like terms to the citizens and subjects of every other State which is willing to grant thereto such protection as the United States and Great Britain engage to afford.

There, Mr. President, is the explicit agreement for equality of treatment of the citizens of the United States and of the citizens of Great Britain in any canal, wherever it may be constructed, across the Isthmus. That was the fundamental principle embodied in the treaty of 1850. And we are not without an authoritative construction as to the scope and requirements of an agreement of that description, because we have another treaty with Great Britain — a treaty which formed one of the great landmarks in the diplomatic history of the world, and one of the great steps in the progress of civilization—the Treaty of Washington of 1871, under which the Alabama Claims were submitted to arbitration. Under that treaty there were provisions for the use of the American canals along the waterway of the Great Lakes, and the Canadian canals along the same line of communication, upon equal terms to the citizens of the two countries.

Some years after the treaty, Canada undertook to do something quite similar to what we have undertaken to do in this law about the Panama Canal. It provided that while nominally a toll of twenty cents a ton should be charged upon the merchandise both of Canada and of the United States there should be a rebate of eighteen cents for all merchandise which went to Montreal or beyond, leaving a toll of but two cents a ton for that merchandise. The United States objected; and I beg your indulgence while I read from the message of President Cleveland upon that subject, sent to the Congress, August 23, 1888. He says:

> By Article 27 of the Treaty of 1871 provision was made to secure to the citizens of the United States the use of the Welland, St. Lawrence, and other canals in the Dominion of Canada on terms of equality with the inhabitants of the Dominion, and also to secure to the subjects of Great Britain the use of the St. Clair Flats Canal on terms of equality with the inhabitants of the United States.

The equality with the inhabitants of the Dominion which we were promised in the use of the canals of Canada did not secure to us freedom from tolls in their navigation, but we had a right to expect that we, being Americans and interested in American commerce, would be no more burdened in regard to the same than Canadians engaged in their own trade; and the whole spirit of the concession made was, or should have been, that merchandise and property transported to an American market through these canals should not be enhanced in its cost by tolls many times higher than such as were carried to an adjoining Canadian market. All our citizens, producers and consumers as well as vessel owners, were to enjoy the equality promised.

And yet evidence has for some time been before the Congress, furnished by the Secretary of the Treasury, showing that while the tolls charged in the first instance are the same to all, such vessels and cargoes as are destined to certain Canadian ports —

their coastwise trade —

are allowed a refund of nearly the entire tolls, while those bound for American ports are not allowed any such advantage.

To promise equality and then in practice make it conditional upon our vessels doing Canadian business instead of their own, is to fulfill a promise with the shadow of performance.

Upon the representations of the United States embodying that view, Canada retired from the position which she had taken, rescinded the provision for differential tolls, and put American trade going to American markets on the same basis of tolls as Canadian trade going to Canadian markets. She did not base her action upon any idea that there was no competition between trade to American ports and trade to Canadian ports, but she recognized the law of equality in good faith and honor; and to this day that law is being accorded to us and by each great nation to the other.

I have said, Mr. President, that the Clayton-Bulwer Treaty was sought by us. In seeking it, we declared to Great Britain what it was that we sought. I ask the Senate to listen to the declaration that we made to induce Great Britain to enter into that treaty, — to listen to it because it is the declaration by which we are in honor bound as truly as if it were signed and sealed.

Here I will read from the report made to the Senate on April 5, 1900, by Senator Cushman K. Davis, then chairman of the Committee on Foreign Relations. So you will perceive that this is no new matter to the Senate of the United States, and that I am not proceeding upon my own authority in thinking it worthy of your attention.

Mr. Rives was instructed to say and did say to Lord Palmerston, in urging upon him the making of the Clayton-Bulwer Treaty, this:

> The United States sought no exclusive privilege or preferential right of any kind in regard to the proposed communication, and their sincere wish, if it should be found practicable, was to see it dedicated to the common use of all nations on the most liberal terms and a footing of perfect equality for all.
>
> That the United States would not, if they could, obtain any exclusive right or privilege in a great highway which naturally belonged to all mankind.

That, sir, was the spirit of the Clayton-Bulwer convention. That was what the United States asked Great Britain to agree upon. That self-denying declaration underlay and permeated and found expression in the terms of the Clayton-Bulwer convention. And upon that representation, Great Britain in that convention relinquished her coign of vantage which she herself had for the benefit of her great North American empire for the control of the canal across the Isthmus.

Mr. CUMMINS. Mr. President —

The PRESIDENT pro tempore. Does the Senator from New York yield to the Senator from Iowa?

Mr. ROOT. I do, but —

Mr. CUMMINS. I will ask the Senator from New York whether he prefers that there shall be no interruptions? If he does, I shall not ask any question.

Mr. ROOT. Mr. President, I should prefer it, because what I have to say involves establishing the relation between a considerable number of acts and instruments, and interruptions naturally would destroy the continuity of my statement.

Mr. CUMMINS. The question I was about to ask was purely a historic one.

Mr. ROOT. I shall be very glad to answer the Senator.

Mr. CUMMINS. The Senator has stated that at the time of the Clayton-Bulwer Treaty we were excluded from the Mosquito Coast by the protectorate exercised by Great Britain over that coast. My question is this: Had we not at that time a treaty with New Granada that gave us equal or greater rights upon the Isthmus of Panama than were claimed even by Great Britain over the Mosquito Coast?

Mr. ROOT. Mr. President, we had the treaty of 1846 with New Granada, under which we undertook to protect any railway or canal across the Isthmus. But that did not apply to the Nicaragua route, which was then supposed to be the most available route for a canal.

Mr. CUMMINS. I quite agree with the Senator about that. I only wanted it to appear in the course of the argument that we were then under no disability so far as concerned building a canal across the Isthmus of Panama.

Mr. ROOT. We were under a disability so far as concerned building a canal by the Nicaragua route, which was regarded as the available route until the discussion in the Senate after 1901, in which Senator Spooner and Senator Hanna practically changed the judgment of the Senate with regard to what was the proper route to take. And in the treaty of 1850, so anxious were we to secure freedom from the claims of Great Britain on the eastern end of the Nicaragua route that, as I have read, we agreed that the same contract should apply not merely to the Nicaragua route but to the whole of the Isthmus. So that from that time on the whole Isthmus was impressed by the same obligations which were impressed upon the Nicaragua route, and whatever rights we had under our treaty of 1846 with New Granada, we were thenceforth bound to exercise with due regard and subordination to the provisions of the Clayton-Bulwer Treaty.

Mr. President, after the lapse of some thirty years, during the early part of which we were strenuously insisting upon the observance by Great Britain of her obligations under the Clayton-Bulwer Treaty and during the latter part of which we were beginning to be restive under our obligations by reason of that treaty, we undertook to secure a modification of it from Great Britain. In the course of that undertaking, there was much discussion and some difference of opinion as to the continued obligations of the treaty. But I think that was finally put at rest by the decision of Secretary Olney in the memorandum upon the subject made by him in the year 1896. In that memorandum he said:

> Under these circumstances, upon every principle which governs the relation to each other, either of nations or of individuals, the United States is completely estopped from denying that the treaty is in full force and vigor.
>
> If changed conditions now make stipulations, which were once deemed advantageous, either inapplicable or injurious, the true remedy is not in ingenious attempts to deny the existence of the treaty or to explain away its provisions, but in a direct and straightforward application to Great Britain for a reconsideration of the whole matter.

We did apply to Great Britain for a reconsideration of the whole matter, and the result of the application was the Hay-Pauncefote Treaty. That treaty came before the Senate in two forms: first, in the form of an instrument signed on February 5, 1900, which was amended by the Senate; and, second, in the form of an instrument signed on November 18, 1901, which contained the greater part of the provisions of the earlier instrument, but somewhat modified or varied the amendments which had been made by the Senate to that earlier instrument.

It is really but one process by which the paper sent to the Senate in February, 1900, passed through a course of amendment; first, at the hands of the Senate, and then at the hands of the negotiators between Great Britain and the United States, with the subsequent approval of the Senate. In both the first form and the last of this treaty, the preamble provides for preserving the provisions of article eight of the Clayton-Bulwer Treaty. Both forms provide for the construction of the canal under the auspices of the United States alone, instead of its construction under the auspices of both countries.

Both forms of that treaty provide that the canal might be —

constructed under the auspices of the Government of the United States, either directly at its own cost or by gift or loan of money to individuals or corporations or through subscription to or purchase of stock or shares —

that being substituted for the provisions of the Clayton-Bulwer Treaty under which both countries were to be patrons of the enterprise.

Under both forms it was further provided that —

Subject to the provisions of the present convention, the said Government —

the United States —

shall have and enjoy all the rights incident to such construction, as well as the exclusive right of providing for the regulation and management of the canal.

That provision, however, for the exclusive patronage of the United States was subject to the initial provision that the modification or change from the Clayton-Bulwer Treaty was to be for the construction of such canal under the auspices of the Government of the United States, without impairing the general principle of neutralization established in article eight of that convention.

Then the treaty as it was finally agreed to provides that the United States " adopt, as the basis of such neutralization of such ship canal," the following rules, substantially as embodied in the convention " of Constantinople, signed October 28, 1888," for the free navigation of the Suez Maritime Canal; that is to say:

First. The canal shall be free and open . . . to the vessels of commerce and of war of all nations " observing these rules on terms of entire equality, so that there shall be no discrimination against any nation or its citizens or subjects in respect to the conditions or charges of traffic, or otherwise." Such conditions and charges of traffic shall be just and equitable.

Then follow rules relating to blockade and vessels of war, the embarkation and disembarkation of troops, and the extension of the provisions to the waters adjacent to the canal.

Now, Mr. President, that rule must, of course, be read in connection with the provision for the preservation of the principle of neutralization established in article eight of the Clayton-Bulwer convention.

Let me take your minds back again to article eight of the Clayton-Bulwer convention, consistently with which we are bound to construe the rule established by the Hay-Pauncefote convention. The principle of neutralization provided for by the eighth article is neutralization upon terms of absolute equality both between the United States and Great Britain and between the United States and all other powers.

It is always understood —

says the eighth article —

by the United States and Great Britain that the parties constructing or owning the same —

that is, the canal —

shall impose no other charges or conditions of traffic thereupon than the aforesaid Governments shall approve of as just and equitable, and that the same canals or railways, being open to the citizens and subjects of the

United States and Great Britain on equal terms, shall also be open on like terms to the citizens and subjects of every other State which is willing to grant thereto such protection as the United States and Great Britain engage to afford.

Now, we are not at liberty to put any construction upon the Hay-Pauncefote Treaty which violates that controlling declaration of absolute equality between the citizens and subjects of Great Britain and the United States.

Mr. President, when the Hay-Pauncefote convention was ratified by the Senate, it was in full view of this controlling principle, in accordance with which their act must be construed; for Senator Davis, in his report from the Committee on Foreign Relations, to which I have already referred —

Mr. McCumber. On the treaty in its first form.

Mr. Root. Yes; the report on the treaty in its first form. Mr. Davis said, after referring to the Suez convention of 1888:

> The United States cannot take an attitude of opposition to the principles of the great act of October 28, 1888, without discrediting the official declarations of our Government for fifty years on the neutrality of an isthmian canal and its equal use by all nations without discrimination.
>
> To set up the selfish motive of gain by establishing a monopoly of a highway that must derive its income from the patronage of all maritime countries would be unworthy of the United States if we owned the country through which the canal is to be built.
>
> But the location of the canal belongs to other governments, from whom we must obtain any right to construct a canal on their territory, and it is not unreasonable, if the question was new and was not involved in a subsisting treaty with Great Britain, that she should question the right of even Nicaragua and Costa Rica to grant to our ships of commerce and of war extraordinary privileges of transit through the canal.

I shall revert to that principle declared by Senator Davis. I continue the quotation:

> It is not reasonable to suppose that Nicaragua and Costa Rica would grant to the United States the exclusive control of a canal through those States on terms less generous to the other maritime nations than those prescribed in the great act of October 28, 1888, or if we could compel

them to give us such advantages over other nations it would not be creditable to our country to accept them.

That our Government or our people will furnish the money to build the canal presents the single question whether it is profitable to do so. If the canal, as property, is worth more than its cost, we are not called on to divide the profits with other nations. If it is worth less and we are compelled by national necessities to build the canal, we have no right to call on other nations to make up the loss to us. In any view, it is a venture that we will enter upon if it is to our interest, and if it is otherwise we will withdraw from its further consideration.

The Suez Canal makes no discrimination in its tolls in favor of its stockholders, and, taking its profits or the half of them as our basis of calculation, we will never find it necessary to differentiate our rates of toll in favor of our own people in order to secure a very great profit on the investment.

Mr. President, in view of that declaration of principle, in the face of that declaration, the United States cannot afford to take a position at variance with the rule of universal equality established in the Suez Canal convention — equality as to every stockholder and all non-stockholders, equality as to every nation whether in possession or out of possession. In the face of that declaration, the United States cannot afford to take any other position than upon the rule of universal equality of the Suez Canal convention, and upon the further declaration that the country owning the territory through which this canal was to be built would not and ought not to give any special advantage or preference to the United States as compared with all the other nations of the earth. In view of that report, the Senate rejected the amendment which was offered by Senator Bard, of California, providing for preference to the coastwise trade of the United States. This is the amendment which was proposed:

The United States reserves the right in the regulation and management of the canal to discriminate in respect of the charges of traffic in favor of vessels of its own citizens engaged in the coastwise trade.

I say, the Senate rejected that amendment upon this report, which declared the rule of universal equality without any preference or discrimination in favor of the United States as being the meaning of the treaty and the necessary meaning of the treaty.

There was still more before the Senate, there was still more before the country, to fix the meaning of the treaty. I have read the representations that were made, the solemn declarations made by the United States to Great Britain establishing the rule of absolute equality without discrimination in favor of the United States or its citizens, to induce Great Britain to enter into the Clayton-Bulwer Treaty.

Now let me read the declaration made to Great Britain to induce her to modify the Clayton-Bulwer Treaty and give up her right to joint control of the canal and put in our hands the sole power to construct it or patronize it or control it.

Mr. Blaine said in his instructions to Mr. Lowell on June 24, 1881, directing Mr. Lowell to propose to Great Britain the modification of the Clayton-Bulwer Treaty — I read his words:

> The United States recognizes a proper guarantee of neutrality as essential to the construction and successful operation of any highway across the Isthmus of Panama, and in the last generation every step was taken by this Government that it deemed requisite in the premises. The necessity was foreseen and abundantly provided for long in advance of any possible call for the actual exercise of power. . . . Nor, *in time of peace, does the United States seek to have any exclusive privileges accorded to American ships in respect to precedence or tolls through an interoceanic canal any more than it has sought like privileges for American goods in transit over the Panama Railway, under the exclusive control of an American corporation.* The extent of the privileges of American citizens and ships is measureable under the treaty of 1846 by those of Colombian citizens and ships. *It would be our earnest desire and expectation to see the world's peaceful commerce enjoy the same just, liberal, and rational treatment.*

Secretary Cass had already said to Great Britain in 1857:

> The United States, as I have before had occasion to assure your Lordship, *demand no exclusive privileges in these passages,* but will always exert their influence *to secure their free and unrestricted benefits, both in peace and war, to the commerce of the world.*

Mr. President, it was upon that declaration, upon that self-denying declaration, upon that solemn assurance, that the United States sought not and would not have any preference for her own citizens over the subjects and citizens of other countries, that Great Britain abandoned her rights under the Clayton-Bulwer Treaty and entered into the Hay-Pauncefote Treaty, with the clause continuing the principles of clause eight, which embodied these same declarations, and the clause establishing the rule of equality, taken from the Suez Canal convention. We are not at liberty to give any other construction to the Hay-Pauncefote Treaty than the construction which is consistent with that declaration.

Mr. President, these declarations, made specifically and directly to secure the making of these treaties, do not stand alone. For a longer period than the oldest Senator has lived, the United States has been from time to time making open and public declarations of her disinterestedness, her altruism, her purposes for the benefit of mankind, her freedom from desire or willingness to secure special and peculiar advantage in respect of transit across the Isthmus. In 1826, Mr. Clay, then Secretary of State in the Cabinet of John Quincy Adams, said, in his instructions to the delegates to the Panama Congress of that year:

> If a canal across the Isthmus be opened so as to admit of the passage of sea vessels from ocean to ocean, the benefit of it ought not to be exclusively appropriated to any one nation, but should be extended to all parts of the globe upon the payment of a just compensation for reasonable tolls.

Mr. Cleveland, in his annual message of 1885, said:

> The lapse of years has abundantly confirmed the wisdom and foresight of those earlier administrations which, long before the conditions of maritime intercourse were changed and enlarged by the progress of the age, proclaimed the vital need of interoceanic transit across the American Isthmus and consecrated it in advance to the common use of mankind by their positive declarations and through the formal obligations of treaties. Toward such realization the efforts of my administration will be

applied, ever bearing in mind the principles on which it must rest and which were declared in no uncertain tones by Mr. Cass, who, while Secretary of State in 1858, announced that " What the United States want in Central America next to the happiness of its people is the security and neutrality of the interoceanic routes which lead through it."

By public declarations, by the solemn asseverations of our treaties with Colombia in 1846, with Great Britain in 1850, our treaties with Nicaragua, our treaty with Great Britain in 1901, our treaty with Panama in 1903, we have presented to the world the most unequivocal guaranty of disinterested action for the common benefit of mankind and not for our selfish advantage.

In the message which was sent to Congress by President Roosevelt on January 4, 1904, explaining the course of this Government regarding the revolution in Panama and the making of the treaty by which we acquired all the title that we have upon the Isthmus, President Roosevelt said:

If ever a Government could be said to have received a mandate from civilization to effect an object the accomplishment of which was demanded in the interest of mankind, the United States holds that position with regard to the interoceanic canal.

Mr. President, there has been much discussion for many years among authorities upon international law, as to whether artificial canals for the convenience of commerce did not partake of the character of natural passageways to such a degree that, by the rules of international law, equality must be observed in the treatment of mankind by the nation which has possession and control. Many very high authorities have asserted that that rule applies to the Panama Canal even without a treaty. We base our title upon the right of mankind in the Isthmus, treaty or no treaty. We have long asserted, beginning with Secretary Cass, that the nations of Central America had no right to debar the world from its right of passage across the Isthmus. Upon that view, in the words which I have quoted from President Roosevelt's message to Congress, we base the justice of our entire action upon the Isthmus which resulted in our having the Canal Zone. We could not have taken it for our selfish interest; we could not have taken it for the purpose of securing an advantage to the people of the United States over the other peoples of the world. It was only because civilization had its rights to passage across the Isthmus, and because we made ourselves the mandatory of civilization to assert those rights, that we are entitled to be there at all. On the principles which underlie our action and upon all the declarations that we have made for more than half a century, as well as upon the express and positive stipulations of our treaties, we are forbidden to say we have taken the custody of the Canal Zone to give ourselves any right of preference over the other civilized nations of the world, beyond those rights which go to the owner of a canal to have the tolls that are charged for passage.

Well, Mr. President, asserting that we were acting for the common benefit of mankind, willing to accept no preferential right of our own, just as we asserted it to secure the Clayton-Bulwer Treaty, just as we asserted it to secure the Hay-Pauncefote Treaty, when we had recognized the republic of Panama, we made a treaty with her on November 18, 1903. I ask your attention now to the provisions of that treaty. In that treaty both Panama and the United States recognize the fact that the United States was acting, not for its own special and selfish interest, but in the interest of mankind.

The suggestion has been made that we are relieved from the obligations of our treaties with Great Britain because the Canal Zone is our territory. It is said that, because it has become ours, we are entitled to build the canal on our own territory and do what we please with it. Nothing can be further from the fact. It is not our territory, except in trust. Article two of the treaty with Panama provides:

The republic of Panama grants to the United States in perpetuity the use, occupation, and control of a zone of land and land under water for the construction, maintenance, operation, sanitation, and protection of said canal —

and for no other purpose —

of the width of ten miles extending to the distance of five miles on each side of the center line of the route of the canal to be constructed. . . .

The republic of Panama further grants to the United States in perpetuity the use, occupation, and control of any other lands and waters outside of the zone above described which may be necessary and convenient for the construction, maintenance, operation, sanitation, and protection of the said canal or of any auxiliary canals or other works necessary and convenient for the construction, maintenance, operation, sanitation, and protection of the said enterprise.

Article three provides:

The republic of Panama grants to the United States all the rights, power, and authority within the zone mentioned and described in article 2 of this agreement —

from which I have just read —

and within the limits of all auxiliary lands and waters mentioned and described in said article 2 which the United States would possess and exercise if it were the sovereign of the territory within which said lands and waters are located to the entire exclusion of the exercise by the republic of Panama of any such sovereign rights, power, or authority.

Article five provides:

The republic of Panama grants to the United States in perpetuity a monopoly for the construction, maintenance, and operation of any system of communication by means of canal or railroad across its territory between the Caribbean Sea and the Pacific Ocean.

I now read from article eighteen:

The canal, when constructed, and the entrances thereto shall be neutral in perpetuity, and shall be opened upon the terms provided for by section 1 of article 3 of, and in conformity with all the stipulations of, the treaty entered into by the Governments of the United States and Great Britain on November 18, 1901.

So, Mr. President, far from our being relieved of the obligations of the treaty with Great Britain by reason of the title that we have obtained to the Canal Zone, we have taken that title impressed with a solemn trust. We have taken it for no purpose except the construction and maintenance of a canal in accordance with all the stipulations of our treaty with Great Britain. We cannot be false to those stipulations without adding to the breach of contract a breach of the trust which we have assumed, according to our own declarations, for the benefit of mankind, as the mandatory of civilization.

In anticipation of the plainly-to-be-foreseen contingency of our having to acquire some kind of title in order to construct the canal, the Hay-Pauncefote Treaty provided expressly in article four:

> It is agreed that no change of territorial sovereignty or of international relations of the country or countries traversed by the beforementioned canal shall affect the general principle of neutralization or the obligation of the high contracting parties under the present treaty.

So you will see that the treaty with Great Britain expressly provides that its obligations shall continue, no matter what title we get to the Canal Zone; and the treaty by which we get the title expressly impresses upon it as a trust the obligations of the treaty with Great Britain. How idle it is to say that because the Canal Zone is ours, we can do with it what we please!

There is another suggestion made regarding the obligations of this treaty, and that is that matters relating to the coasting trade are matters of special domestic concern, and that nobody else has any right to say anything about them. We did not think so when we were dealing with the Canadian canals. But that may not be conclusive as to rights under this treaty. Let us examine it for a moment.

It is rather poverty of language than a genius for definition which leads us to call a voyage from New York to San Francisco, passing along countries thousands of miles away from our territory, " coasting trade," or to call a voyage from New York to Manila, on the other side of the world, " coasting trade." When we use the term " coasting trade," what we really mean is that under our navigation laws a voyage which begins and ends at an American port has certain privileges and immunities and rights, and it is necessarily in that sense that the term is used in this statute. It must be construed in accordance with our statutes.

Sir, I do not for a moment dispute that ordinary coasting trade is a special kind of trade that is entitled to be treated differently from trade to or from distant foreign points. It is ordinarily neighborhood trade, from port to port, by which the people of a country carry on their intercommunication, often by small vessels, poor vessels, carrying cargoes of slight value. It would be quite impracticable to impose upon trade of that kind the same kind of burdens which great oceangoing steamers, trading to the farthest parts of the earth, can well bear. We make that distinction. Indeed, Great Britain herself makes it, although Great Britain admits all the world to her coasting trade. But it is by quite a different basis of classification — that is, the statutory basis — that we call a voyage from the eastern coast of the United States to the Orient a coasting voyage, because it begins and ends in an American port.

This is a special, peculiar kind of trade which passes through the Panama Canal. You may call it " coasting trade," but it is unlike any other coasting trade. It is special and peculiar to itself.

Grant that we are entitled to fix a different rate of tolls for that class of trade from that which would be fixed for other classes of trade. Ah, yes; but Great Britain has her coasting trade through the canal under the same definition, and Mexico has her coasting trade, and Germany has her coasting trade, and Colombia has her coasting trade, in the same sense that we have. You are not at liberty to discriminate in fixing tolls between a voyage from Portland, Maine, to Portland, Oregon, by an American ship, and a voyage from Halifax to Victoria in a British ship, or a voyage from Vera Cruz to Acapulco in a Mexican ship, because when you do so you discriminate, not between coasting trade and other trade, but between American ships and British ships, Mexican ships, or Colombian ships. That is a violation of the rule of equality which we have solemnly adopted, and asserted and reasserted, and to which we are bound by every consideration of honor and good faith. Whatever this treaty means, it means for that kind of trade as well as for any other kind of trade.

The suggestion has been made, also, that we should not consider that the provision in this treaty about equality as to tolls really means what it says, because it is not to be supposed that the United States would give up the right to defend itself, to protect its own territory, to land its own troops, and to send through the canal as it pleases its own ships of war. That is disposed of by the considerations which were presented to the Senate in the Davis report, to which I have already referred, in regard to the Suez convention.

The Suez convention, from which these rules of the Hay-Pauncefote Treaty were taken almost — though not quite — textually, contained other provisions which reserved to Turkey and to Egypt, as sovereigns of the territory through which the canal passed — Egypt as the sovereign and Turkey as the suzerain over Egypt — all of the rights that pertained to sovereigns for the protection of their own territory. As when the Hay-Pauncefote Treaty was made neither party to the treaty had any title to the region which would be traversed by the canal, no such clauses could be introduced. But, as was pointed out, the rules which were taken from the Suez Canal for the control of the canal management would necessarily be subject to these rights of sovereignty which were still to be secured from the countries owning the territory. That is recognized by the British Government in the note which has been sent to us and has been laid before the Senate, or is in the possession of the Senate, from the British foreign office.

In Sir Edward Grey's note of November 14, 1912, he says what I am about to read. This is an explicit disclaimer of any contention that the provisions of the Hay-Pauncefote Treaty exclude us from the same rights of protection of territory which Nicaragua or Colombia or Panama would have had as sovereigns, and which we succeed to, *pro tanto*, by virtue of the Panama Canal treaty.

Sir Edward Grey says:

I notice that in the course of the debate in the Senate on the Panama Canal bill the argument was used by one of the speakers that the third, fourth, and fifth rules embodied in article 3 of the treaty show that the words "all nations" cannot include the United States, because, if the United States were at war, it is impossible to believe that it could be intended to be debarred by the treaty from using its own territory for revictualling its warships or landing troops.

The same point may strike others who read nothing but the text of the Hay-Pauncefote Treaty itself, and I think it is therefore worth while that I should briefly show that this argument is not well founded.

I read this not as an argument but because it is a formal, official disclaimer which is binding.

Sir Edward Grey proceeds:

The Hay-Pauncefote Treaty of 1901 aimed at carrying out the principle of the neutralization of the Panama Canal by subjecting it to the same régime as the Suez Canal. Rules 3, 4, and 5 of article 3 of the treaty are taken almost textually from articles 4, 5, and 6 of the Suez Canal Convention of 1888.

At the date of the signature of the Hay-Pauncefote Treaty the territory on which the Isthmian Canal was to be constructed did not belong to the United States, consequently there was no need to insert in the draft treaty provisions corresponding to those in articles 10 and 13 of the Suez Canal Convention, which preserve the sovereign rights of Turkey and of Egypt, and stipulate that articles 4 and 5 shall not affect the right of Turkey, as the local sovereign, and of Egypt, within the measure of her autonomy, to take such measures as may be necessary for securing the defense of Egypt and the maintenance of public order, and, in the case of Turkey, the defense of her possessions on the Red Sea.

Now that the United States has become the practical sovereign of the canal, His Majesty's Government do not question its title to exercise belligerent rights for its protection.

Mr. President, Great Britain has asserted the construction of the Hay-Pauncefote Treaty of 1901, the arguments for which I have been stating to the Senate. I realize, sir, that I may be wrong. I have often been wrong. I realize that the gentlemen who have taken a different view regarding the meaning of this treaty may be right. I do not think so. But their ability and fairness of mind would make it idle for me not to entertain the possibility that they are right and I am wrong. Yet, Mr. President, the question whether they are right and I am wrong depends upon the interpretation of the treaty. It depends upon the interpretation of the treaty in the light of all the declarations that have been made by the parties to it, in the light of the nature of the subject-matter with which it deals.

Gentlemen say the question of imposing tolls or not imposing tolls upon our coastwise commerce, is a matter of our concern. Ah! we have made a treaty about it. If the interpretation of the treaty is as England claims, then it is not a matter of our concern; it is a matter of treaty rights and duties. But, sir, it is not a question as to our rights to remit tolls to our commerce. It is a question whether we can impose tolls upon British commerce when we have remitted them from our own. That is the question. Nobody disputes our rights to allow our own ships to go through the canal without paying tolls. What is disputed is our right to charge tolls against other ships when we do not charge them against our own. That is, pure and simple, a question of international right and duty, and depends upon the interpretation of the treaty.

Sir, we have another treaty, made between the United States and Great Britain on April 4, 1908, in which the two nations have agreed as follows:

> Differences which may arise of a legal nature or relating to the interpretation of treaties existing between the two contracting parties and which it may not have been possible to settle by diplomacy, shall be referred to the Permanent Court of Arbitration established at The Hague by the convention of July 29, 1899, provided, nevertheless, that they do not affect the vital interests, the independence, or the honor of the two contracting states, and do not concern the interests of third parties.

Of course, the question of the rate of tolls on the Panama Canal does not affect any nation's vital interests. It does not affect the independence or the honor of either of these contracting states. We have a difference relating to the interpretation of this treaty, and that is all there is to it. We are bound, by this treaty of arbitration, not to stand with arrogant assertion upon our own Government's opinion as to the interpretation of the treaty, not to require that Great Britain shall suffer what she deems injustice by violation of the treaty, or else go to war. We are bound to say, " We keep the faith of our treaty of arbitration, and we will submit the question as to what this treaty means to an impartial tribunal of arbitration."

Mr. President, if we stand in the position of arrogant refusal to submit the questions arising upon the interpretation of this treaty to arbitration, we shall not only violate our solemn obligation, but we shall be false to all the principles that we have asserted to the world, and that we have urged upon mankind. We have been the apostle of arbitration. We have been urging it upon the other civilized nations. Presidents, secretaries of state, ambassadors, and ministers — aye, Congresses, the Senate and the House, all branches of our Government have committed the United States to the principle of arbitration irrevocably, unequivocally, and we have urged it in season and out of season on the rest of mankind.

Sir, I cannot detain the Senate by more than beginning upon the expressions that have come from our Government upon this subject, but I will ask your indulgence while I call your attention to a few selected from the others.

On June 9, 1874, the Senate Committee on Foreign Relations reported and the Senate adopted this resolution:

Resolved, That the United States having at heart the cause of peace everywhere, and hoping to help its permanent establishment between nations, hereby recommend the adoption of arbitration as a great and practical method for the determination of international difference, to be maintained sincerely and in good faith, so that war may cease to be regarded as a proper form of trial between nations.

On June 17, 1874, the Committee on Foreign Affairs of the House adopted this resolution:

WHEREAS, War is at all times destructive of the material interests of a people, demoralizing in its tendencies, and at variance with an enlightened public sentiment; and whereas, *differences between nations should in the interests of humanity and fraternity be adjusted, if possible, by international arbitration:* therefore,

Resolved, That the people of the United States being devoted to the policy of peace with all mankind, enjoining its blessings and hoping for its permanence and its universal adoption, hereby through their representatives in Congress recommend such arbitration as a rational substitute for war; and they further recommend to the treaty-making power of the Government to provide, if practicable, that hereafter in treaties made between the United States and foreign powers war shall not be declared by either of the contracting parties against the other until efforts shall have been made to adjust all alleged cause of difference by impartial arbitration.

On the same June 17, 1874, the Senate adopted this resolution:

Resolved, etc., That the President of the United States is hereby authorized and requested to negotiate with all civilized powers who may be willing to enter into such negotiations for the establishment of an international system whereby matters in dispute between different Governments agreeing thereto may be adjusted by arbitration, and, if possible, without recourse to war.

On June 14, 1888, and again on February 14, 1890, the Senate and the House adopted a concurrent resolution in the words which I now read:

> *Resolved by the Senate (the House of Representatives concurring)*, That the President be, and is hereby, requested to invite, from time to time, as fit occasions may arise, negotiations with any Government with which the United States has, or may have, diplomatic relations, to the end that any differences or disputes arising between the two Governments which cannot be adjusted by diplomatic agency may be referred to arbitration and be peaceably adjusted by such means.

This was concurred in by the House on April 3, 1890.

Mr. President, in pursuance of those declarations by both Houses of Congress, the Presidents and the Secretaries of State and the diplomatic agents of the United States, doing their bounden duty, have been urging arbitration upon the people of the world. Our representatives in The Hague Conference of 1899, and in The Hague Conference of 1907, and in the Pan-American Conference in Washington, and in the Pan-American Conference in Mexico, and in the Pan-American Conference in Rio de Janeiro, were instructed to urge and did urge and pledge the United States in the most unequivocal and urgent terms to support the principle of arbitration upon all questions capable of being submitted to a tribunal for a decision.

Under those instructions, Mr. Hay addressed the people of the entire civilized world with the request to come into treaties of arbitration with the United States. Here was his letter. After quoting from the resolutions and from expressions by the President he said:

> Moved by these views, the President has charged me to instruct you to ascertain whether the Government to which you are accredited, which he has reason to believe is equally desirous of advancing the principle of international arbitration, is willing to conclude with the Government of the United States an arbitration treaty of like tenor to the arrangement concluded between France and Great Britain on October 14, 1903.

PANAMA CANAL TOLLS 235

That was the origin of this treaty. The treaties made by Mr. Hay were not satisfactory to the Senate because of the question about the participation of the Senate in the make-up of the special agreement of submission. Mr. Hay's successor modified that on conference with the Committee on Foreign Relations of the Senate, and secured the assent of the other countries of the world to the treaty with that modification. We have made twenty-five of these treaties of arbitration, covering the greater part of the world, under the direction of the Senate of the United States and the House of Representatives of the United States and in accordance with the traditional policy of the United States, holding up to the world the principle of peaceful arbitration.

One of these treaties is here, and under it Great Britain is demanding that the question as to what the true interpretation of our treaty about the canal is, shall be submitted to decision and not be made the subject of war or of submission to what she deems injustice to avoid war.

In response to the last resolution which I have read, the concurrent resolution passed by the Senate and the House requesting the President to enter into the negotiations which resulted in these treaties of arbitration, the British House of Commons passed a resolution accepting the overture. On July 16, 1893, the House of Commons adopted this resolution:

Resolved, That this House has learnt with satisfaction that both Houses of the United States Congress have, by resolution, requested the President to invite from time to time, as fit occasions may arise, negotiations with any government with which the United States have or may have diplomatic relations, to the end that any differences or disputes arising between the two governments which cannot be adjusted by diplomatic agency may be referred to arbitration and peaceably adjusted by such means, and that this House, cordially sympathizing with the purpose in view, expresses the hope that Her Majesty's Government will lend their ready coöperation to the Government of the United States upon the basis of the foregoing resolution.

Her Majesty's Government did, and thence came this treaty.

Mr. President, what revolting hypocrisy we convict ourselves of, if after all this, the first time there comes up a question in which we have an interest, the first time there comes up a question of difference about the meaning of a treaty as to which we fear we may be beaten in an arbitration, we refuse to keep our agreement! Where will be our self-respect if we do that? Where will be that respect to which a great nation is entitled from the other nations of the earth?

I have read from what Congress has said. Let me read something from President Grant's annual message of December 4, 1871. He is commenting upon the arbitration provisions of the treaty of 1871, in which Great Britain submitted to arbitration our claims against her, known as the Alabama Claims, in which Great Britain submitted those claims where she stood possibly to lose but not possibly to gain anything, and submitted them against the most earnest and violent protest of many of her own citizens. President Grant said:

> The year has been an eventful one in witnessing two great nations speaking one language and having one lineage, settling by peaceful arbitration disputes of long standing and liable at any time to bring those nations into costly and bloody conflict. An example has been set which, if successful in its final issue, may be followed by other civilized nations and finally be the means of returning to productive industry millions of men now maintained to settle the disputes of nations by the bayonet and by broadside.

Under the authority of these resolutions, our delegates in the first Pan-American Conference at Washington secured the adoption of this resolution April 18, 1890:

> ARTICLE 1. The republics of North, Central, and South America hereby adopt arbitration as a principle of American international law for the settlement of the differences, disputes, or controversies that may arise between two or more of them.

And this:

> The International American Conference resolves that this conference, having recommended arbitration for the settlement of disputes among the

republics of America, begs leave to express the wish that controversies between them and the nations of Europe may be settled in the same friendly manner.

It is further recommended that the Government of each nation herein represented communicate this wish to all friendly powers.

Upon that Mr. Blaine, that most vigorous and virile American, in his address as the presiding officer of that first Pan-American Conference in Washington said:

If, in this closing hour, the Conference had but one deed to celebrate we should dare call the world's attention to the deliberate, confident, solemn dedication of two great continents to peace and to the prosperity which has peace for its foundation. We hold up this new Magna Charta, which abolishes war and substitutes arbitration between the American republics, as the first and great fruit of the International American Conference. That noblest of Americans, the aged poet and philanthropist, Whittier, is the first to send his salutation and his benediction, declaring, " If in the spirit of peace the American conference agrees upon a rule of arbitration which shall make war in this hemisphere well-nigh impossible, its sessions will prove one of the most important events in the history of the world."

President Arthur in his annual message of December 4, 1882, said, in discussing the proposition for a Pan-American Conference:

I am unwilling to dismiss this subject without assuring you of my support of any measure the wisdom of Congress may devise for the promotion of peace on this continent and throughout the world, and I trust the time is nigh when, with the universal assent of civilized peoples, all international differences shall be determined without resort to arms by the benignant processes of arbitration.

President Harrison in his message of December 3, 1889, said concerning the Pan-American Conference:

But while the commercial results which it is hoped will follow this Conference are worthy of pursuit and of the great interests they have excited, it is believed that the crowning benefit will be found in the better securities which may be devised for the maintenance of peace among all American nations and the settlement of all contentions by methods that a Christian civilization can approve.

President Cleveland, in his message of December 4, 1893, said, concerning the resolution of the British Parliament of July 16, 1893, which I have already read, and commenting on the concurrent resolution of February 14 and April 18, 1890:

It affords me signal pleasure to lay this parliamentary resolution before the Congress and to express my sincere gratification that the sentiment of two great kindred nations is thus authoritatively manifested in favor of the rational and peaceable settlement of international quarrels by honorable resort to arbitration.

President McKinley, in his message of December 6, 1897, said:

International arbitration cannot be omitted from the list of subjects claiming our consideration. Events have only served to strengthen the general views on this question expressed in my inaugural address. The best sentiment of the civilized world is moving toward the settlement of differences between nations without resorting to the horrors of war. Treaties embodying these humane principles on broad lines without in any way imperiling our interests or our honor shall have my constant encouragement.

President Roosevelt, in his message of December 3, 1905, said:

I earnestly hope that the Conference —

the second Hague Conference —

may be able to devise some way to make arbitration between nations the customary way of settling international disputes in all save a few classes of cases, which should themselves be sharply defined and rigidly limited as the present governmental and social development of the world will permit. If possible, there should be a general arbitration treaty negotiated among all nations represented at the Conference.

O Mr. President, are we Pharisees ? Have we been insincere and false ? Have we been pretending in all these long years of resolution and declaration and proposal and urgency for arbitration ? Are we ready now to admit that our country, that its Congresses and its Presidents, have all been guilty of false pretense, of humbug, of talking to the galleries, of fine words to secure applause, and that the instant we have an interest we are ready to falsify every declaration, every promise, and every principle? But we must do that if we arrogantly insist that we alone will determine upon the interpretation of this treaty and will refuse to abide by the agreement of our treaty of arbitration.

Mr. President, what is all this for? Is the game worth the candle? Is it worth while to put ourselves in a position and to remain in a position, to maintain which we may be driven to repudiate our principles, our professions, and our agreements for the purpose of conferring a money benefit — not very great, not very important, but a money benefit — at the expense of the Treasury of the United States, upon the most highly and absolutely protected special industry in the United States? Is it worth while? We refuse to help our foreign shipping, which is in competition with the lower wages and the lower standard of living of foreign countries, and we are proposing to do this for a part of our coastwise shipping which has now by law the absolute protection of a statutory monopoly and which needs no help.

Mr. President, there is but one alternative consistent with self-respect. We must arbitrate the interpretation of this treaty or we must retire from the position we have taken.

O Senators, consider for a moment what it is that we are doing. We all love our country; we are all proud of its history; we are all full of hope and courage for its future; we love its good name; we desire for it that power among the nations of the earth which will enable it to accomplish still greater things for civilization than it has accomplished in its noble past. Shall we make ourselves in the minds of the world like unto the man who in his own community is marked as astute and cunning to get out of his obligations? Shall we make ourselves like unto the man who is known to be false to his agreements; false to his pledged word? Shall we have it understood the whole world over that " you must look out

for the United States or she will get the advantage of you ";
that we are clever and cunning to get the better of the other
party to an agreement, and that at the end —

Mr. BRANDEGEE. " Slippery " would be a better word.

Mr. ROOT. Yes; I thank the Senator for the suggestion —
" slippery." Shall we in our generation add to those claims
to honor and respect that our fathers have established for our
country good cause that we shall be considered slippery?

It is worth while, Mr. President, to be a citizen of a great
country, but size alone is not enough to make a country great.
A country must be great in its ideals; it must be great-
hearted; it must be noble; it must despise and reject all
smallness and meanness; it must be faithful to its word; it
must keep the faith of treaties; it must be faithful to its
mission of civilization in order that it shall be truly great.
It is because we believe that of our country that we are proud,
aye, that the alien with the first step of his foot upon our soil
is proud to be a part of this great democracy.

Let us put aside the idea of small, petty advantage; let us
treat this situation and these obligations in our relation to
this canal in that large way which befits a great nation.

Mr. President, how sad it would be if we were to dim the
splendor of that great achievement by drawing across it the
mark of petty selfishness; if we were to diminish and reduce
for generations to come the power and influence of this free
republic for the uplifting and the progress of mankind by
destroying the respect of mankind for us! How sad it would
be if you and I, Senators, were to make ourselves responsible
for destroying that bright and inspiring ideal which has
**enabled free America to lead the world in progress toward
liberty and justice!**

PANAMA CANAL TOLLS

SPEECH IN REPLY IN THE SENATE OF THE UNITED STATES
MAY 21, 1914

The Senate, as in Committee of the Whole, had under consideration the bill (H. R. 14385) to amend section 5 of an act to provide for the opening, maintenance, protection, and operation of the Panama Canal and the sanitation of the Canal Zone, approved August 24, 1912.

MR. PRESIDENT, some time ago I taxed the patience of the Senate by rather extended remarks upon the duty of the United States in regard to tolls upon the Panama Canal; and what I have to say now upon that subject is rather in the way of reply to arguments which have been made, views which have been expressed, and opinions which have been made manifest by various Senators in the course of the long debate which has intervened.

I wish, before proceeding, to express my very great satisfaction with the character of the debate in this Chamber upon this subject. The excitement and fervor of a false patriotism, the insolence and rancor which ill befit the consideration of a serious international subject by a great people, but which have been injected into the popular discussion of this question in some quarters, have found but little response among the members of the Senate of the United States. The question which is before us has been debated with a sense of responsibility and dignity. Senators have argued the question as lawyers and legislators upon its merits. I address myself to a reply to some of the arguments which have been made with a sense of serene satisfaction in dealing with a question which rests in the minds of my colleagues upon considerations of right reason and just regard for national obligations and national rights.

Let me try, sir, to state the question; and to state the question, I must state the situation as it is presented. The bill which is before the Senate proposes to repeal certain clauses of the Panama Canal Act passed August 24, 1912. That act was designed to provide for the opening, maintenance, protection, and operation of the canal, and it conferred authority upon the President in respect of establishing tolls for the use of the canal and imposed certain limitations upon him. Section five of the act authorized the President to prescribe and from time to time change the tolls; it provided " that no tolls, when prescribed as above, shall be changed " without six months' notice; it provided that no tolls shall be levied upon vessels engaged in the coastwise trade of the United States. Further, the act provided:

> When based upon net registered tonnage for ships of commerce, the tolls shall not exceed $1.25 per net registered ton, nor be less, other than for vessels of the United States and its citizens, than the estimated proportionate cost of the actual maintenance and operation of the canal.

Then it goes on to say:

> Nor be less than the equivalent of seventy-five cents per net registered ton.

So that the President is authorized to impose tolls not exceeding $1.25 per net registered ton, except for vessels of the United States and its citizens, and not less than seventy-five cents per net registered ton, and is prohibited from imposing any tolls upon vessels engaged in the coastwise trade of the United States. He is required to impose tolls of at least seventy-five cents per net registered ton upon all foreign vessels. He is authorized to impose no tolls upon any American vessel, and is required to impose no tolls upon American vessels engaged in the coastwise trade.

The President has issued a proclamation imposing tolls of $1.20 per net registered ton upon vessels loaded, a smaller amount upon vessels in ballast, and no tolls upon vessels engaged in American coastwise trade. A question has been raised by Great Britain as to the conformity of that action with a treaty made between the United States and Great Britain in 1901, known as the Hay-Pauncefote Treaty. It is claimed that that treaty requires that there shall be no discrimination between the tolls imposed upon foreign vessels and the tolls imposed upon vessels owned by citizens of the United States.

The first thing which we naturally do when such a question is presented is to inquire: What is our title ? What are the rights that we have ?

Until very recently the Isthmus of Panama was not the property of the United States, and we had no rights there except certain rights derived from an old treaty with New Granada, made in 1846, by which New Granada gave to the United States certain privileges in any lines of communication which might be constructed, either railroad or canal, but gave the United States no right to construct a canal and no property rights whatever.

How did we get the canal upon which we are proposing to exact tolls ? It was under a treaty made with the republic of Panama, sometimes called the Hay-Bunau-Varilla Treaty. It was signed at Washington on November 18, 1903. Under that treaty with Panama, the owner of the Isthmus, by article two —

granted to the United States in perpetuity the use, occupation, and control of a zone of land and land under water, for the construction, maintenance, operation, sanitation, and protection of said canal, of the width of ten miles —

and so forth. By article three it granted to the United States all the rights, power, and authority which the United States would possess and exercise if it were the sovereign of the territory, to the exclusion of Panama. In article eighteen it provided that —

The canal, when constructed, and the entrances thereto, shall be neutral in perpetuity and shall be opened upon the terms provided for by section 1 of article 3 of, and in conformity with all the stipulations of, the treaty entered into by the Governments of the United States and Great Britain on November 18, 1901.

That treaty with Panama is the basis of our rights. That treaty lies at the foundation of any question that can be raised as to what we do with the canal which we are constructing, because it is by that treaty, and by that treaty alone, that we get our title. By that treaty the grant of property and jurisdiction upon which we have proceeded, upon which we hold the canal, is subject to the provision that the canal, when constructed, and the entrances thereto, shall be neutral in perpetuity, and shall be opened upon the terms provided for by the treaty between the United States and Great Britain of November 18, 1901.

So the treaty with Great Britain which is referred to here is carried into our title as a limitation upon it.

Let us turn to the treaty with Great Britain which is referred to by Panama in this grant. That treaty was signed at Washington November 18, 1901. It recites that a convention was considered expedient by the United States and Great Britain —

to facilitate the construction of a ship canal to connect the Atlantic and Pacific Oceans, by whatever route may be considered expedient, and to that end to remove any objection which may arise out of the convention of April 19, 1850, commonly called the Clayton-Bulwer Treaty . . . without impairing the " general principle " of neutralization established in article 8 of that convention.

It proceeds to say:

The canal may be constructed under the auspices of the Government of the United States, either directly at its own cost, or by gift or loan of money to individuals or corporations, or through subscription to or purchase of stock or shares, and that, subject to the provisions of the present treaty, the said Government shall have and enjoy all the rights incident to such construction, as well as the exclusive right of providing for the regulation and management of the canal.

It then proceeds with article three:

The United States adopts as the basis of the neutralization of such ship canal the following rules, substantially as embodied in the Convention of Constantinople, signed October 28, 1888, for the free navigation of the Suez Canal; that is to say:
1. The canal shall be free and open to the vessels of commerce and of war of all nations observing these rules on terms of entire equality, so that there shall be no discrimination against any such nation, or its citizens or subjects, in respect of the conditions or charges of traffic or otherwise. Such conditions and charges of traffic shall be just and equitable.

Rule 1, which I have just read, is the section 1 of article 3 of the treaty with Great Britain, which is specified in the eighteenth article of our grant of title from Panama as being especially and peculiarly and signally incumbent upon us to observe. " The canal," says the treaty with Panama, " when constructed, and the entrances thereto, shall be neutral in perpetuity and shall be opened upon the terms provided for by section 1 of article 3 " of the treaty with Great Britain.

I have now read section 1 of article 3. There follows, then, in article 3, a series of provisions relating specifically to the kind of neutrality which shall be imposed. They are in substance these:

First. There shall be no blockade of the canal or act of war in it or in its terminal waters.

Second. There shall be no delay in transit in time of war by a belligerent.

Third. No troops or supplies in time of war shall be landed or taken on by vessels in the canal.

Fourth. Belligerent ships shall remain but twenty-four hours in the terminal waters.

Fifth. A war vessel of one belligerent shall not leave the canal within twenty-four hours after the vessel of another belligerent has left.

All of those are covered by the general provision of the article in the treaty with Panama in these words:

And in conformity with all the stipulations of the treaty entered into by the Governments of the United States and Great Britain.

Under these provisions, first, of the Panama treaty, and, second, of the treaty with Great Britain, which is incorporated into the grant of title to us, one question, and one question only, is raised. That is: What is the measure of the tolls that we are at liberty to charge a ship belonging to a British or German or French citizen passing through the canal?

It is quite natural to say that this is a question of the exemption of our ships. It is not a question of the exemption of our ships. No one doubts our right to pass our ships through the canal free, or for any tolls that we choose to impose and that they are able and willing to pay. The question is whether we are bound to take our treatment of the ships belonging to American citizens as the measure of the treatment that we accord to ships belonging to the citizens of other countries.

We have the canal at the Sault, through which pass a greater tonnage and a greater traffic than we can anticipate for the Panama Canal for generations. We charge no tolls to American vessels — that is to say, vessels owned by American citizens — passing through the canal at the Sault; and by treaty we grant to the citizens of Great Britain and Canada the same treatment we accord to our own citizens and their vessels. We have agreed that the measure that we mete to our own citizens shall be the measure we mete to the citizens of Canada. There is no question there about our rights with our own, and there is no question here about our rights with our own.

Nor, Mr. President, is there any question here about the absolute and complete control of the canal by the United States. There is no question, there can be no question, about it. Political control, military control, administrative control, all are ours. The only question is, What standard are we bound to apply in making a charge to the citizens of another country for the use of the canal for passing the ships through? The treaty itself is quite clear. It says:

> Subject to the provisions of the present treaty, the said Government shall have and enjoy all the rights incident to such construction, as well as the exclusive right of providing for the regulation and management of the canal.

We occupy a variety of relations to that business. We are the practical sovereign of the territory, and we have all the rights of sovereignty in respect of the territory. We are the owner of the canal just as a canal company would be the owner if it had constructed it under a charter, just as the Panama Railroad Company owns the Panama Railroad. We shall be the owner of many ships that pass through the canal. We owe protection to many citizens of the United States who will own ships that pass through the canal.

Those four different relations of the United States to this business stand each by itself, and the rights and obligations of each may be clearly ascertained and stated. Sometimes a dual quality will effect an extinguishment of rights and obligations, as, for instance, if the United States as the owner of a ship sends its ship through a canal and is also the owner of the canal, the obligation as owner of the ship to the owner of the canal will be offset; but for any clear conception of what the rights and obligations are, we must consider each character in which the United States stands by itself.

It would be impossible to state more distinctly the precise relation that we have in regard to the control of the canal than Mr. Choate stated it in his letter of October 2, 1901, to Mr. Hay, when the treaty was agreed upon. He said:

> I am sure that in this whole matter, since the receipt by him of your new draft, Lord Lansdowne has been most considerate and more than

generous. He has shown an earnest desire to bring to an amicable settlement, honorable alike to both parties, this long and important controversy between the two nations. In substance, he abrogates the Clayton-Bulwer Treaty, gives us an American canal — ours to build as and where we like, to own, control, and govern — on the sole condition of its being always neutral and free for the passage of the ships of all nations on equal terms, except that if we get into a war with any nation we can shut its ships out and take care of ourselves.

Nor is there any question here about ships owned by the United States. There is much confusion in discussing this subject, arising from the use of the term " ships of the United States " or " American ships." The Senator from Mississippi [Mr. Williams] called attention to that the other day very pointedly. There are ships owned by the United States. When the United States acquires the other character of owner of the canal, of course there can be no question about tolls on those ships; but ships owned by citizens of the United States are quite a different thing. Citizens of the United States are not the United States. They are separate and distinct entities. We tax them, we regulate them, we fine them, we impose charges upon them. If they acquire property from the United States, they pay for it, and if the United States acquires property from them, it pays for it. They are entirely separate and distinct individuals from the United States. The question here is about charges that shall be made by the United States to two different classes of separate and distinct individuals, both classes being the owners of ships, one class being citizens of the United States and the other class being citizens of some other country.

The words of this Hay-Pauncefote Treaty, Mr. President, are framed to cover both a canal company and the United States. Observe that article 2 of the Hay-Pauncefote Treaty says:

It is agreed that the canal may be constructed under the auspices of the Government of the United States, either directly at its own cost or by gift or loan of money to individuals or corporations, or through subscription to or purchase of stock or shares, and that, subject to the provisions of the present treaty, the said Government shall have and enjoy —

and so forth.

Now, there is a variety of contingencies to which the words of this treaty are addressed, and you must construe the words as they would apply to a canal company in which the Government of the United States had become a stockholder, as it is of the Panama Railroad Company today, or the bonds of which the United States has guaranteed, as it guaranteed the bonds of the Pacific railroad companies. The fact that the United States has stepped in and itself taken the character of a canal company makes no difference whatever in the meaning and force and interpretation and application of these words. The treaty remains the same, the meaning of it the same. The acquisition of additional and different rights by the United States may arise merely to modify the effect of the application of the treaty.

Nor, Mr. President, is there any question here about the right of the United States to subsidize its own ships. That is as clear and as unquestionable as its right to appropriate money to put up a public building in the city of Washington. It does not rest upon our assertion, for Sir Edward Grey, the secretary of state for foreign affairs of Great Britain, in his memorandum handed to our Secretary of State on December 9, 1912, says, commenting upon President Taft's memorandum accompanying the signature to the bill —

The President argues upon the assumption that it is the intention of His Majesty's Government to place upon the Hay-Pauncefote Treaty an interpretation which would prevent the United States from granting subsidies to their own shipping passing through the canal, and which would place them at a disadvantage as compared with other nations. This is not the case. His Majesty's Government regard equality of all nations as the fundamental principle underlying the treaty of 1901 in the same way that it was the basis of the Suez Canal convention of 1888, and they do not seek to deprive the United States of any liberty which is open either to themselves or to any other nation; nor do they find either in the letter or in the spirit of the Hay-Pauncefote Treaty any surrender by either of the contracting powers of the right to encourage its shipping or its commerce by such subsidies as it may deem expedient.

I take the line to be at the point where title to the money vests in the United States. If the construction which I feel forced to give to this treaty is a sound one, we are not at liberty to produce the result of a subsidy to American ships by relieving them of tolls which we impose upon other ships. We are not at liberty to produce the effect of a subsidy in that way; but the instant that the money paid for tolls becomes the property of the United States, becomes a part of the general fund of the United States, the United States has absolute and uncontrollable authority in the disposition of that money. All lawyers are familiar with the distinction between accomplishing an unlawful object in a lawful way and accomplishing a lawful object in an unlawful way. To subsidize American ships is lawful. However we may differ about the policy, we have the power; we have the right; but if the construction I give to this treaty is the correct one, we have excluded ourselves by solemn covenant from accomplishing that lawful result in this particular way; and if it be true that we have excluded ourselves from doing it in this particular way, it is no answer to say the same result could be accomplished in another way. In my view it is no concern of ours why Great Britain chooses to insist upon our keeping the covenant and not to produce the effect of a subsidy in that particular way. If this construction of the treaty is right, she has a right to say, "You shall not do that thing in that way"; and if we made the covenant, it is none of our affairs why she chooses to say it.

Now, upon what conflict of reasons rests the decision of the question whether we are bound to regulate the tolls upon foreign shipping by the tolls on American shipping? The underlying question has been stated quite frequently as being whether the words " all nations " in rule 1 of article 3 include the United States or not. Rule 1 reads:

> The canal shall be free and open to the vessels of commerce and war of all nations observing these rules on terms of entire equality.

I say that very often the subject has been discussed upon the assumption that the answer to the practical question raised depends upon whether the term " all nations " includes the United States or not. That does not get to the foundation upon which the reasoning should rest. The fundamental question is, What kind of equality did the makers of this treaty intend? Says the treaty:

> The canal shall be free and open to all vessels of commerce and war of all nations observing these rules on terms of entire equality.

When a French or a German ship sails into that canal and has imposed upon it a toll, and says, " this toll is unequal because the vessel that passed here immediately before me was allowed to go with a lower rate of toll," can that be said, if the vessel before was an American ship —

Mr. WILLIAMS. The ship of an American citizen.

Mr. ROOT. The ship of an American citizen; or can it be said only if it was the ship of some foreign power? What is the " entire equality " contemplated by rule 1 of article 3 of this treaty? Is it entire so that it assures equality in comparison with all ships engaged in the same trade similarly situated, the same kind of trade, or is it partial, so as to be equality in comparison only with certain ships engaged in the same kind of trade and not applying to other ships engaged in the same kind of trade, to wit, not applying to ships which are owned by American citizens? The rule proceeds:

> So that there shall be no discrimination against any such nation or its citizens or subjects in respect of the conditions or charges of traffic or otherwise.

Is the kind of equality that is assured such that there will be no discrimination, or that there will be no discrimination except against the ships of other nations and in favor of ships belonging to American citizens?

Now, let us examine the question in the light of the circumstances which surrounded the making of this treaty and the conditions under which it was made. Treaties cannot be usefully interpreted with the microscope and the dissecting knife, as if they were criminal indictments. Treaties are steps in the life and the development of great nations. Public policies enter into them; public policies certified by public documents and authentic expressions of public officers. Long contests between the representatives of nations enter into the choice and arrangement of the words of a treaty. If you would be sure of what a treaty means, if there be any doubt, if there are two interpretations suggested, learn out of what conflicting public policies the words of the treaty had their birth; what arguments were made for one side or the other, what concessions were yielded in the making of a treaty. Always, with rare exceptions, the birth and development of every important clause may be traced by the authentic records of the negotiators and of the countries which are reconciling their differences. So it is the universal rule in all diplomatic correspondence regarding international rights, in all courts of arbitration, that far more weight is given to records of negotiations, to the expressions of the negotiators, to the history of the provisions than is customary in regard to private contracts or criminal indictments.

This question as to the kind of equality that the makers of this treaty intended to give, divides itself very clearly and distinctly into a question between two perfectly well-known expedients of treaty making; one is the favored-nation provision, with which we are all very familiar in commercial treaties, and the other is the provision according to citizens of another country rights measured by the rights of the nationals or citizens of the contracting country. The most-favored-nation provision has its most common expression in the provision regarding tariff duties, a provision that no higher duties shall be charged upon goods imported from one foreign country than upon goods imported from other foreign countries. That is the common " most-favored-nation clause."

The other has its probably most common provision in the laws relating to the treatment of vessels in the ports of a contracting country, assuring to them that no higher tolls or charges, harbor dues or light dues, or dues of that description shall be charged against them than against the vessels of the country in which the port is situated.

This question here is between those two. I cannot better illustrate the two kinds I have mentioned than by referring to the treaty with the Argentine Republic in 1853, a typical treaty of friendship, commerce, and navigation. Before I read from it, I will state what is an almost universal custom among civilized nations in regard to the use of these two standards of comparison for the purpose of assuring one or another kind of equality. It is the practically universal custom, where the citizens of another country bear the same relation to a particular anticipated transaction or course of business, that the citizens of the contracting country bear, in treaties of peace and friendship and amity, to accord to citizens of the other country equality measured by the treatment of the citizens of the contracting country; and, in general, it is only when the citizens of the other country bear a different relation to the anticipated transaction or course of business, that recourse is had to the favored-nation clause, as where the people of one country are exporting goods and the people of the contracting country are importing goods. Plainly you cannot give to the exporter the same treatment you give to the importer; they are two different classes.

Let me illustrate that by referring to the Argentine treaty:

ARTICLE 2. There shall be between all the territories of the United States and all the territories of the Argentine Confederation a reciprocal freedom of commerce. The citizens of the two countries, respectively, shall have liberty, freely and securely, to come with their ships and cargoes to all places, ports, and rivers in the territories of either, to which other foreigners, or the ships or cargoes of any other foreign nation or state, are, or may be, permitted to come.

. . . .

ARTICLE 3. The two high contracting parties agree that any favor, exemption, privilege, or immunity, whatever, in matters of commerce and navigation, which either of them has actually granted, or may hereafter grant, to the citizens or subjects of any other government, nation, or state, shall extend, in identity of cases and circumstances, to the citizens of the other contracting party.

. . . .

ARTICLE 4. No higher or other duties shall be imposed on the importation into the territories of either of the two contracting parties of any article of the growth, produce, or manufacture of the territories of the other contracting party than are, or shall be, payable on the like article of any other foreign country.

Those are favored-nation clauses. Article 5 provides:

No other or higher duties or charges, on account of tonnage, light, or harbor dues, pilotage, salvage in case of average or shipwreck, or any other local charges, shall be imposed in the ports of the two contracting parties on the vessels of the other than those payable in the same ports on its own vessels.

There is the higher type of equality, because the ships coming into an American port have the same relation to that port, whether they belong to an Argentine citizen or to an American.

ARTICLE 6

The same duties shall be paid, and the same drawbacks and bounties allowed, upon the importation or exportation, of any article into or from the territories of the United States or into or from the territories of the Argentine Confederation whether such importation or exportation be made in vessels of the United States or in vessels of the Argentine Confederation.

ARTICLE 8

All merchants, commanders of ships, and others, citizens of the United States, shall have full liberty in all the territories of the Argentine Confederation to manage their own affairs themselves or to commit them to the management of whomsoever they please as broker, factor, agent, or interpreter; nor shall they be obliged to employ any other persons in those capacities than those employed by citizens of the Argentine Confederation. . . .

ARTICLE 9

In whatever relates to the police of the ports, the lading and unlading of ships, the safety of the merchandise, goods and effects, and to the acquiring and disposing of property of every sort and denomination, either by sale, donation, exchange, testament, or in any other manner whatsoever, as also to the administration of justice, the citizens of the two contracting parties shall reciprocally enjoy the same privileges, liberties, and rights as native citizens.

And so on through a great number of other provisions. In brief, a careful examination shows this to be a fact: that it is the universal rule, with rare exceptions, that wherever the rights of the citizens of a contracting country can be made the standard of equality for the citizens of another country they are made so, and that recourse is not had to the most-favored-nation clause, except where that higher degree of equality is impossible because the citizens of the two countries occupy different relations to the business that is contemplated.

So we have the question between these two kinds of equality clearly drawn and resting upon long experience of nations, a subject fully understood by the negotiators of this treaty upon both sides.

We know now that the negotiators of this treaty, the men who made it, all understood that the larger equality was intended by its terms. Of course, what the negotiator of a treaty says cannot be effective to overthrow a treaty; but I think we must all start, in considering this question, with the assumption that the words are capable of two constructions. I think no one can deny that, in view of the differences of opinion which have been expressed here regarding their meaning. So here are words capable of two constructions, a broad construction and a narrow construction, but the fact that all the makers of the treaty intended that the words they used should have the larger effect, is certainly very persuasive toward the conclusion that those words should receive the larger effect. Not only the American negotiators but the British negotiators as well so understood it. Whenever we seek to impose upon these words a narrower construction for our own interests than the makers of the treaty understood them to have, we should remember the fundamental rule of morals that a promisor is bound to keep a promise in the sense in which he had reason to believe the promisee understood it was made.

Let us look at the understanding of the negotiators. Mr. Choate writes this in a letter to Honorable Henry White, dated April 14, 1914:

> As I telegraphed to you last night, on receipt of your telegram of yesterday, I wrote to the chairman of the committee, Senator O'Gorman, inclosing to him, by the express permission of the Secretary of State, a copy of my letters to Secretary Hay between August 3, and October 12, 1901, the same that you have. To my mind they establish beyond question the intent of the parties engaged in the negotiation, that the treaty should mean exactly what it says, and excludes the possibility of any exemption of any kind of vessels of the United States. Equality between Great Britain and the United States is the constant theme, and especially in my last letter of October 2, 1901, where I speak of Lord Lansdowne's part in the matter, and say, "He has shown an earnest desire to bring to an amicable settlement, honorable alike to both parties, this long and important controversy between the two nations. In substance, he abrogates the Clayton-Bulwer Treaty, gives us an American canal, ours to build as and where we like, to own, control, and govern, on the sole condition of its being always neutral and free for the passage of the ships of all nations on equal terms, except that if we get into a war with any nation we can shut its ships out and take care of ourselves."
>
> This was the summing-up of our whole two months' negotiation.

Mr. Henry White's understanding of it is shown in the testimony before the Committee on Interoceanic Canals, April 14, 1914. He says:

PANAMA CANAL TOLLS 257

During the entire period of those negotiations and in all of my conversations with Lord Salisbury or with any one else on either side of the Atlantic I never heard the subject of our coastwise traffic mentioned. It was always assumed by those carrying on the negotiations — it certainly was by me in my interview with Lord Salisbury — that he meant that our ships should be considered, or rather that the United States should be considered, as included in the term "all nations."

Senator SIMMONS. And our coastwise ships?

Mr. WHITE. All ships.

The CHAIRMAN. You are stating now what your understanding is, not what the language was?

Mr. WHITE. No; my understanding. The language was "ships of all nations on equal terms." That was the language used by Lord Salisbury, which I cabled the same day to Mr. Hay. Mr. Hay had asked Lord Salisbury to remove such obstacles in the Clayton-Bulwer Treaty as stood in the way of our building the canal, and his reply was that he had no doubt these obstacles would eventually be removed, provided the ships of all nations should go through the canal on equal terms.

Senator SIMMONS. Do I understand you to say you had suggestions from any direction that our coastwise ships were to be treated differently?

Mr. WHITE. Never from beginning to end.

We know from many sources what Mr. Hay's views were. The Senator from Connecticut [Mr. McLean] has read to you a statement of them, authentic, made about the time of the treaty, at the time the treaty with Panama was under consideration. Here is what Mr. Hay says:

"All means all. The treaty was not so long that we could not have made room for the word 'other' if we had understood that it belonged there. 'All nations' means all nations, and the United States is certainly a nation."

"That was the understanding between yourself and Lord Pauncefote when you and he made the treaty?" I pursued.

"It certainly was," he replied. "It was the understanding of both Governments, and I have no doubt that the Senate realized that in ratifying the second treaty without such an amendment it was committing us to the principle of giving all friendly nations equal privileges in the canal with ourselves. That is our golden rule."

I cannot pass from this subject without also calling attention to the language used by President Roosevelt in his message to the Senate, upon which the Panama treaty was ratified. President Roosevelt said in this message of January 4, 1904, laying before Congress the Panama treaty:

The proper position for the United States to assume in reference to this canal, and therefore to the Governments of the Isthmus, had been clearly set forth by Secretary Cass in 1858. In my annual message I have already quoted what Secretary Cass said; but I repeat the quotation here, because the principle it states is fundamental:

" While the rights of sovereignty of the states occupying this region (Central America) should always be respected, we shall expect that these rights be exercised in a spirit befitting the occasion and the wants and circumstances that have arisen. Sovereignty has its duties as well as its rights, and none of these local governments, even if administered with more regard to the just demands of other nations than they have been, would be permitted in a spirit of Eastern isolation to close the gates of intercourse on the great highways of the world and justify the act by the pretension that these avenues of trade and travel belong to them and that they choose to shut them, or, what is almost equivalent, to encumber them with such unjust relations as would prevent their general use."

The principle thus enunciated by Secretary Cass was sound then and it is sound now. The United States has taken the position that no other Government is to build the canal. In 1889, when France proposed to come to the aid of the French Panama Company by guaranteeing their bonds, the Senate of the United States in executive session, with only some three votes dissenting, passed a resolution, as follows:

" That the Government of the United States will look with serious concern and disapproval upon any connection of any European Government with the construction or control of any ship canal across the Isthmus of Darien or across Central America, and must regard any such connection or control as injurious to the just rights and interests of the United States and as a menace to their welfare."

Under the Hay-Pauncefote Treaty it was explicitly provided that the United States should control, police, and protect the canal which was to be built, keeping it open for the vessels of all nations on equal terms. The United States thus assumed the position of guarantor of the canal and of its peaceful use by all the world.

Who were these men ? Certainly, any one who finds in this treaty now a meaning different from that which they thought their words carried, should consider many times the steps by which he reaches his conclusion.

Mr. Choate, the head of the American bar, clear, able, with penetrating intelligence, with vast experience in the use of words and the construction of treaties, of statutes, of contracts, unquestionable in the virile strength and loyalty of his Americanism. When he thought that the words he used had a particular meaning, we may well think twice before we say that they have not that meaning.

Henry White, one of the few diplomats trained from their youth up in the American service.

John Hay, the pride of our generation in American diplomacy. John Hay, that sensitive soul who could produce the American types of the Pike County ballads, and the charm, the felicity of whose phrases makes them jewels in the history of American literature. John Hay, who received the spirit, the motive, the characteristics of his Americanism as the young secretary and the confidential and intimate friend of Lincoln.

Theodore Roosevelt, with his swift, incisive mind and his high courage.

All these — the chargé d'affaires who opened the negotiations with Lord Salisbury, the ambassador who carried on the negotiations, the Secretary of State who supervised and authorized the negotiations, the President who authorized, as one of the first acts of his presidency, the signature to the treaty and laid it before the Senate — all these understood that they were making a treaty with the largest equality, and with no trifling, narrow, " favored nation " provision.

Indeed, sir, the " favored nation " clause is of but little value. If the standard of equality be not the standard of the treatment of ships owned by American citizens, and be nothing but the " favored nation " standard — that is, equality as between foreigners — it is of but very little value. That equality would be practically compelled by the usages of civilization without any treaty at all. No nation could ever maintain a practice of charging for the use of a canal connecting two oceans a different rate of tolls as against Germans or French or English or Italians. It never has been done anywhere in the world. It never will be done unless civilization goes back from the level which it has now reached. But the other, the larger, equality is of value; for the treatment of the citizens of the country which owns the canal, the treatment they will submit to, the treatment that it is safe to accord to them before election, is a safe and a sound, substantial guaranty of the treatment the citizens of other nations will receive; so that is of value.

Mr. President, of course what these negotiators all thought they were doing by the use of these words is not conclusive. It is persuasive, but not conclusive. Let us ascertain why they thought so, if we can.

The first reason why it seems to me they could not possibly have meant anything else than they say they meant, is that for three-quarters of a century the United States had been declaring to the world that she sought to procure the making of the canal across the Isthmus as a public-service work, a public calling, a public utility, with all the nations the public to be served. I say, for three-quarters of a century the United States had been making that declaration as to her relation to this work; yes, always without one varying note, until we got the title and control of the canal; and then for the first time is heard the demand that American owners of ships shall receive better treatment in tolls than the ships of other owners.

Now, let me call attention to some of the declarations. You have read them all; they are not new in this debate; but I beg you to consider them as a whole and consider the position in which we stand with reference to them as a series unbroken and unvarying. In 1826, Henry Clay, Secretary of State, said:

If a canal across the Isthmus be opened so as to admit of the passage of sea vessels from ocean to ocean, the benefits of it ought not to be exclusively appropriated to any one nation, but should be extended to all parts of the globe upon the payment of a just compensation or **reasonable tolls.**

In a resolution of the Senate in 1835:

The construction of a ship canal across the Isthmus which connects North and South America, and of securing forever by such stipulations the free and equal right of navigating such canal to all such nations —

is recommended as the subject of negotiation, " free and equal right to all such nations."

In a resolution of the House in 1839:

For the purpose of ascertaining the practicability of effecting a communication between the Atlantic and Pacific Oceans by the construction of a ship canal across the Isthmus and of securing forever, by suitable treaty stipulations, the free and equal right of navigating such canal to all nations —

is recommended.

In the overtures by the United States to Great Britain which resulted in the making of the Clayton-Bulwer Treaty Mr. Rives said to Lord Palmerston in 1849:

That the United States sought no exclusive privilege or preferential right of any kind in regard to the proposed communication, and their sincere wish, if it should be found practical, was to see it dedicated to the common use of all nations on the most liberal terms and a footing of perfect equality for all.

That the United States would not if they could obtain any exclusive right or privilege in a great highway which naturally belongs to all mankind.

In the Clayton-Bulwer Treaty of 1859, article 6, we find

And the contracting parties —

the United States and Great Britain —

likewise agree that each shall enter into treaty stipulations with such of the Central American states as they may deem advisable, for the purpose of more effectually carrying out the great design of this convention, namely, that of constructing and maintaining the said canal as a ship communication between the two oceans for the benefit of mankind, on equal terms to all, and of protecting the same.

In 1858, Secretary Cass, in the utterance which I have just read from the January 4, 1904, message of President Roosevelt.

In 1881, Secretary Blaine. Mr. President, this utterance is of special significance, because it was the first serious overture to Great Britain to bring about that abrogation of the Clayton-Bulwer Treaty and the substitution of a canal under the sole auspices of the United States, which has been realized in the Hay-Pauncefote Treaty. Mr. Blaine, on June 24, 1881, writes to the American minister to open negotiations with Great Britain for obviating the objections in the Clayton-Bulwer Treaty. He says:

> There has never been the slightest doubt on the part of the United States as to the purpose or extent of the obligation then assumed —

that is, in the Colombian treaty of 1846 —

> by which it became surety alike for the free transit of the world's commerce over whatever land-way or water-way might be opened from sea to sea, and for the protection of the territorial rights of Colombia from aggression or interference of any kind.

He then proceeds to say that the President deems it due to frankness to suggest a new arrangement with Great Britain. He says:

> Nor, in time of peace, does the United States seek to have any exclusive privileges accorded to American ships in respect to precedence or tolls through an interoceanic canal any more than it has sought like privileges for American goods in transit over the Panama Railway, under the exclusive control of an American corporation. The extent of the privileges of American citizens and ships is measurable under the treaty of 1846 by those of Colombian citizens and ships. It would be our earnest desire and expectation to see the world's peaceful commerce enjoy the same just, liberal, and rational treatment.

In the following letter of November 19, 1881, he lays down the policy of the United States almost exactly as it was worked out by the negotiators in the Hay-Pauncefote Treaty now in existence. He lays it down to Great Britain, and this utterance of Secretary Blaine was the main expression of American policy which Mr. Hay, Mr. White, Mr. Choate, and Mr. Roosevelt found before them to follow in making this treaty. Let me read it:

> In assuming as a necessity the political control of whatever canal or canals may be constructed across the Isthmus, the United States will act in entire harmony with the Governments within whose territory the canals shall be located. Between the United States and the other American republics there can be no hostility, no jealousy, no rivalry, no distrust. This Government entertains no design in connection with this project for its own advantage which is not also for the equal or greater advantage of the country to be directly and immediately affected. Nor does the United States seek any exclusive or narrow commercial advantage. It frankly agrees and will by public proclamation declare at the proper time, in conjunction with the republic on whose soil the canal may be located, that the same rights and privileges, the same tolls and obligations for the use of the canal, shall apply with absolute impartiality to the merchant marine of every nation on the globe. And equally in time of peace the harmless use of the canal shall be freely granted to the war vessels of other nations. In time of war, aside from the defensive use to be made of it by the country in which it is constructed and by the United States, the canal shall be impartially closed against the war vessels of all belligerents.
>
> It is the desire and determination of the United States that the canal shall be used only for the development and increase of peaceful commerce among all the nations, and shall not be considered a strategic point in warfare which may tempt the aggression of belligerents or be seized under the compulsions of military necessity by any of the great powers that may have contests in which the United States has no stake and will take no part.

Mr. Blaine went out of office; other interests arose — the Venezuelan controversy with Great Britain, the progress of construction by the De Lesseps Company, which seemed for a time to bid fair to produce a canal across the Isthmus of Panama, the Spanish War, all intervened, and these negotiations languished and were intermitted until Mr. Hay, in 1898, reopened the subject with this declaration of Mr. Blaine still standing, declaring what the United States would do if England would give to her the same sole control which she did give in the Hay-Pauncefote Treaty. How could the negotiators intend anything else in the words they used than that same large equality which the United States had thus already offered formally and solemnly?

In 1885, in his message of December 8, Mr. Cleveland says to Congress:

> Whatever highway may be constructed across the barrier dividing the two greatest maritime areas of the world must be for the world's benefit — a trust for mankind, to be removed from the chance of domination by any single power, nor become a point of invitation for hostilities or a prize for warlike ambition.

In 1898, Mr. Hay, in reopening the negotiations which Mr. Blaine had begun, instructs Mr. White to say:

> The President thinks it is more judicious to approach the British Government in a frank and friendly spirit of mutual accommodation, and to ask whether it may not be possible to secure such modification of the provisions of the Clayton-Bulwer Treaty as to admit such action by the Government of the United States as may render possible the accomplishment of a work which will be for the benefit of the entire civilized world. The President hopes he may take it for granted that the British Government not only have no wish to prevent the accomplishment of this great work, but that they feel a lively interest in it and appreciate the fact that the benefits of its successful achievement will be to the advantage not only of England and America but of all commercial nations.

We know that the answer to that by Lord Salisbury was that he would be favorable to such a modification of the treaty relations, provided that the vessels of all nations could use the canal on terms of equality.

In the year 1900, when the first Hay-Pauncefote Treaty came before the Senate, the report of the Committee on Foreign Relations, commonly spoken of as the Davis report, a very able, very thorough, very careful consideration of the whole subject, says:

> It is not reasonable to suppose that Nicaragua and Costa Rica would grant to the United States the exclusive control of a canal through those States on terms less generous to the other maritime nations than those prescribed in the great act of October 28, 1888;

referring to the Suez Canal convention —

or if we could compel them to give us such advantages over other nations it would not be creditable to our country to accept them.

That our Government or our people will furnish the money to build the canal presents the single question whether it is profitable to do so. If the canal, as property, is worth more than its cost, we are not called on to divide the profits with other nations. If it is worth less and we are compelled by national necessities to build the canal, we have no right to call on other nations to make up the loss to us. In any view, it is a venture that we will enter upon if it is to our interest, and if it is otherwise we will withdraw from its further consideration.

The Suez Canal makes no discrimination in its tolls in favor of its stockholders; and, taking its profits or the half of them as our basis of calculation, we will never find it necessary to differentiate our rates of toll in favor of our own people in order to secure a very great profit on the investment.

In 1904, in the message of President Roosevelt from which I have already read, submitting the Hay-Pauncefote Treaty to the Senate, is the last authoritative and unmistakable declaration of the public service for all the world which the United States undertook in building the Panama Canal.

Now, Mr. President, the common law of England and America, the public policy especially of America at the very time this treaty was being negotiated, enforced with unsparing rigor the duty of equal charges and equal service by all public utilities to all the public which they were to serve, and in the face of this long series of public declarations by the Government of the United States committing itself to that relation, the relation of the builder and operator of a public utility for all the world, the makers of this treaty could not honorably have used words with any other meaning than the meaning of the large equality which they say they meant these words should have.

There is another reason. The kind of equality which the negotiators intended — that is, an equality in which the treatment of American citizens is made the standard for the treatment of foreign citizens — had during all the history of the Isthmian Canal efforts been the standard sought for in negotiations and treaties. That kind of equality was the standard adopted by the public policy of the United States for all similar enterprises. It was customary; it was uniform; it was natural for negotiators of a treaty relating to a canal. Let me illustrate that by referring to the initial treaty on this subject, the treaty of New Granada of 1846. When the American negotiators making that treaty dealt with the subject of a railroad and canal, what kind of equality did they stipulate for ? Why, this:

> The Government of New Granada guarantees to the Government of the United States that the right of way or transit across the Isthmus of Panama upon any modes of communication that now exist, or that may be hereafter constructed, shall be open and free to the Government and citizens of the United States, and for the transportation of any articles of produce, manufactures, or merchandise of lawful commerce belonging to the citizens of the United States; that no other tolls or charges shall be levied or collected upon the citizens of the United States or their said merchandise thus passing over any road or canal that may be made by the Government of New Granada or by the authority of the same than is, under like circumstances, levied upon and collected from the Granadian citizens.

The message of President Polk transmitting this New Granada treaty of 1846 to Congress dwells especially upon the assurance to citizens of the United States of equal charges and equal facilities in the use of railroad and canal with citizens of New Granada.

I go back again to the Clayton-Bulwer Treaty of 1850. There is no doubt about the kind of equality which the negotiators considered it to be valuable to get, useful to get, natural to get.

Article 1 of that treaty provides that neither Government shall undertake any control or make any fortifications, make any effort " for the purpose of acquiring or holding, directly or indirectly, for the citizens or subjects of the one, any rights or advantage in regard to commerce or navigation through the said canal which shall not be offered on the same terms to the citizens or subjects of the other."

Article 5 provides that protection may be withdrawn if the company which builds the canal shall make " unfair discriminations in favor of the commerce of one of the contracting parties over the commerce of the other."

Article 6 uses as interchangeable terms the expression " on equal terms to all," and these provisions for measuring the rights of the citizens of one country by the rights accorded to the citizens of the other. They are used interchangeably.

Article 8 provides that —

> It is always understood by the United States and Great Britain that the parties constructing or owning the canal shall impose no other charges or conditions of traffic thereupon than the aforesaid Governments shall approve of as just and equitable, and that the same canals or railways, being open to the citizens and subjects of the United States and Great Britain on equal terms, shall also be open on like terms to the citizens and subjects of every other state.

You will perceive, sir, that the terms on which citizens of other countries were to be allowed to come in were not terms of the most-favored nations as among themselves. They were on like terms with those which existed between Great Britain and the United States; that is to say, each other country which came in and adhered to this Clayton-Bulwer Treaty was to have the rights of its citizens measured by the rights accorded to the citizens of the United States and to the citizens of Great Britain.

In our treaty with Great Britain in 1854, the reciprocity treaty of 1854 —

> It is agreed that the citizens and inhabitants of the United States shall have the right to navigate the River St. Lawrence, and the canals in Canada used as the means of communicating between the Great Lakes and the Atlantic Ocean, with their vessels, boats, and crafts, as fully and freely as the subjects of Her Britannic Majesty, subject only to the same

tolls and other assessments as now are, or may hereafter be, exacted of Her Majesty's said subjects. . . .

It is further agreed that British subjects shall have the right freely to navigate Lake Michigan with their vessels, boats, and crafts so long as the privilege of navigating the River St. Lawrence, secured to American citizens by the above clause of the present article, shall continue; and the Government of the United States further engages to urge upon the State governments to secure to the subjects of Her Britannic Majesty the use of the several State canals on terms of equality with the inhabitants of the United States.

We made a treaty with Nicaragua in 1867, under which, then expecting the canal to be through Nicaraguan territory, it was provided that —

The republic of Nicaragua hereby grants to the United States, and to their citizens and property, the right of transit between the Atlantic and Pacific Oceans through the territory of that republic, on any route of communication, natural or artificial, whether by land or by water, which may now or hereafter exist or be constructed under the authority of Nicaragua, to be used and enjoyed in the same manner and upon equal terms by both republics and their respective citizens.

That treaty further provided:

And no higher or other charges or tolls shall be imposed on the conveyance or transit of persons and property of citizens or subjects of the United States, or of any other country, across the said routes of communication, than are or may be imposed on the persons and property of citizens of Nicaragua.

In 1868, Mr. Seward made a treaty with Colombia, which was never ratified, in which the provision originally proposed by the United States was:

That the tariff of tolls and freights shall be on the basis of perfect equality for both nations and for all other nations who shall be at peace both with the United States of America and the United States of Colombia.

Colombia wished that provision to apply to both times of war and of peace; and accordingly it was modified and came into the completed treaty, which was submitted to the Senate in this form:

The Government of the United States of America shall establish a tariff of tolls and freights for the said canal on a basis of perfect equality for all nations, whether in time of peace or war.

In 1870, another treaty was made with Colombia, in which the provision was that the United States was to establish, just as it does here in the Hay-Pauncefote Treaty, a tariff of charges on merchant vessels and vessels of war upon the basis of perfect equality at all times among all nations, with no other distinctions than are contained in the preceding article.

In the preceding article the distinction is that the parties to the treaty — that is, Colombia and the United States — reserve to themselves the right of passing ships of war, troops, and munitions of war through the canal at all times free of charge of any description.

In 1871, in the great Treaty of Washington of that year, we enlarged the stipulation regarding the use of American and Canadian canals, and the United States stipulated definitely that —

The subjects of Her Britannic Majesty shall enjoy the use of the St. Clair Flats Canal on terms of equality with the inhabitants of the United States.

We have heard much discussion here of the controversy which arose between the United States and Great Britain over the application of that paragraph of the Treaty of Washington giving equality to citizens of the two countries in the use both of American and Canadian canals. Several times the discussion has run into an attack upon the Canadian treatment of the subject, into a declaration that Canada did not yield gracefully or easily; that Canada did not yield until measures of retaliation were proposed. That is quite irrelevant to the bearing of this treaty and the discussion upon the question that is before us and upon the treatment of this subject by the makers of this treaty.

What position did we take ? What was the attitude of the United States toward the subject of equality between the United States and Canada under this treaty stipulating for equality ? That is the important question — not whether Great Britain was right or wrong; not whether Canada did right or wrong; not whether they were willing or unwilling; but what did the United States say and what position could the United States take consistently upon this subject of the equal use of the canals ?

We are not left entirely to the treatment of canals for a guide as to the public policy of the United States. When this treaty was negotiated it had long been the general public policy of the United States to accord to all other nations in all ports and waters of the United States rights in respect of service and of charges, measured by the service and the charges to American citizens. The act of Congress of June 26, 1884, as amended June 19, 1886, reads:

Provided, That the President of the United States shall suspend the collection of so much of the duty herein imposed on vessels entered from any foreign port as may be in excess of the tonnage and lighthouse dues or other equivalent tax or taxes imposed in said port on American vessels by the Government of the foreign country in which such port is situated, and shall, upon the passage of this act, and from time to time thereafter, as often as it may become necessary by reason of changes in the laws of the foreign countries above mentioned, indicate, by proclamation, the ports to which such suspension shall apply, and the rate or rates of tonnage duty, if any, to be collected under such suspension: *Provided further*, That such proclamation shall exclude from the benefits of the suspension herein authorized the vessels of any foreign country in whose ports the fees or dues of any kind or nature imposed on vessels of the United States or the import or export duties on their cargoes are in excess of the fees, dues, or duties imposed on the vessels of the country in which such port is situated, or on the cargoes of such vessels.

I say that was the public policy of the United States regarding all ports and waters of the United States, and it was a policy toward all the world. A controversy arose about it. Canada claimed that we imposed excessive charges upon her vessels, and we claimed that she imposed excessive charges upon ours. A correspondence ensued, and on February 18, 1896, Mr. Olney, then Secretary of State, wrote to Sir Julian Pauncefote as follows:

> The understanding of the Government of the United States in the matter of the uniform treatment of foreign and domestic vessels is that charges on foreign vessels in the ports of the United States should be no higher than those imposed on vessels of the United States in the ports of this country, and that the charges imposed on American vessels in foreign ports should be no higher than the charges imposed on the vessels native to those ports. This is the practice of this Government, and it is in accord with nearly all of its treaties of commerce and navigation with foreign powers.
>
> The fact cited in the Canadian minute that the charges of this Government on lake ports are larger than those imposed by the Dominion authorities will, upon more mature reflection, I am confident, be regarded as irrelevant, since those charges are imposed equally on American and foreign vessels.

On the ninth of June of the same year Sir Julian Pauncefote replied to Mr. Olney as follows:

> SIR: With reference to my note of the twenty-first of February last, and to previous correspondence respecting the alleged discrimination against United States vessels in Canadian ports on the Great Lakes, I have the honor to inform you that the Governor-General of Canada has approved a minute of his privy council, recommending the revocation of the regulations complained of and the abolition of all fees hitherto exacted from vessels navigating inland waters when entering or clearing above Montreal.

That Sir Julian Pauncefote was the Lord Pauncefote who, with Mr. Hay and Mr. White, negotiated the Hay-Pauncefote Treaty. We are asked to believe that starting with the Clayton-Bulwer convention, which gave to Great Britain unquestioned assurance of the larger and more valuable equality of her vessels with the vessels of American citizens, in a negotiation with a country which in all its history had insisted regarding all canals that the measure of equality should be the measure of service and of charges to its national citizens, in negotiating with a country which had just compelled him to yield that equality of treatment as a measure of general public policy, he abandoned the vantage ground of the Clayton-Bulwer Treaty and gave up that basis of equality without one word in the negotiation, without discussion, without its being asked, without its being mentioned, without his knowing it, without the other negotiators' knowing it. But that is not all.

It was not merely the immemorial policy of the United States and Great Britain regarding all canals; it was not merely the general public policy of the United States and Great Britain regarding all ports and waters, but it was the policy of the United States regarding trade the world over, and the champion and protagonist of that policy was John Hay. At the very time that he was negotiating the Hay-Pauncefote Treaty he was appealing to the justice of all the nations of the world for the " open door " in China; he was appealing to them in the interest of the world's commerce, in the interest of civilization to accord in all their possessions in China, what ? Favored-nation treatment ? Oh, no; the same treatment that they accorded to their own citizens. Let me ask you to attend for a moment to things that John Hay wrote regarding this great design, the accomplishment of which will ever stand in the history of diplomacy as one of the proudest contributions of America to the progress of civilization. On September 6, 1899, he wrote to Mr. Choate in London:

> The Government of Her Britannic Majesty has declared that its policy and its very traditions precluded it from using any privileges which might be granted it in China as a weapon for excluding commercial rivals, and that freedom of trade for Great Britain in that Empire meant freedom of trade for all the world alike. While conceding by formal agreements, first with Germany and then with Russia, the possession of " spheres of influence or interest " in China, in which they are to enjoy special rights and privileges, more especially in respect of railroads and mining enter-

prises, Her Britannic Majesty's Government has therefore sought to maintain at the same time what is called the " open-door policy " to insure to the commerce of the world in China equality of treatment within said " spheres " for commerce and navigation.

He wrote to Ambassador White in Germany, September sixth, the same date:

> Earnestly desirous to remove any cause of irritation and to insure at the same time to the commerce of all nations in China the undoubted benefits which should accrue from a formal recognition by the various powers claiming " spheres of interest " that they shall enjoy perfect equality of treatment for their commerce and navigation within such " spheres " the Government of the United States would be pleased to see His German Majesty's Government give formal assurances and lend its coöperation in securing like assurances from the other interested powers that each within its respective sphere of whatever influence. . . .
>
> Third. That it will levy no higher harbor dues on vessels of another nationality frequenting any port in such " sphere " than shall be levied on vessels of its own nationality, and no higher railroad charges over lines built, controlled, or operated within its " sphere " on merchandise belonging to citizens or subjects of other nationalities transported through such " sphere " than shall be levied on similar merchandise belonging to its own nationals transported over equal distances.

So he wrote to all of the great nations of the world an appeal for equal treatment, an appeal for a specific stipulation to secure the equal treatment that no higher charges should be imposed upon the citizens of any other country in the ports and waters possessed by those great powers in China or for freight or passage over the railroads built and controlled by them than were imposed upon their own citizens. To that appeal all the great powers of the world responded in affirmance; and on March 20, 1900, Mr. Hay was able to issue his circular of instructions to all the ambassadors and ministers of the United States announcing the universal assent of the world to that great principle of equality — equality measured by the rights of the citizens of the nation granting it in all the empire of China; yet we are asked to believe that John Hay denied, abjured, repudiated that policy of civilization in regard to the Panama Canal at the very moment that, through the same agents, he was enforcing the policy upon the same countries; and that he did it without knowing it.

But, Mr. President, we are not left to inferences which must be drawn from the circumstances that I have mentioned or from declarations of public policy or from the uniform course and custom of treaty-making regarding canals and regarding public waters and transportation. There is positive, and it appears to me conclusive, affirmative evidence that the negotiators did effectively proceed in making this treaty in accordance with the honorable obligation of their country as the builder and maintainer of a public utility, as the champion of equal commercial rights the world over.

We begin the consideration of the express provisions leading to the conclusion that the larger equality was intended with the communication of the Hay-Pauncefote Treaty to the Senate. Of course, we are all familiar with the terms of the preamble preserving the general principle of article 8 of the Clayton-Bulwer Treaty. Let me read them again, however, for convenience of reference:

> The United States of America and His Majesty Edward the Seventh, of the United Kingdom of Great Britain and Ireland, and of the British dominions beyond the seas, King, and Emperor of India, being desirous to facilitate the construction of a ship canal to connect the Atlantic and Pacific Oceans, by whatever route may be considered expedient, and to that end to remove any objection which may arise out of the convention of April 19, 1850, commonly called the Clayton-Bulwer Treaty, to the construction of such canal under the auspices of the Government of the United States, without impairing the " general principle " of neutralization established in article 8 of that convention, have for that purpose appointed as their plenipotentiaries. . . .

Now we are told that the language of a treaty or of a contract or of a statute cannot be changed by the preamble; but what is the purpose of a preamble? The purpose is to afford a guide to the interpretation of the terms of the treaty or of the statute. When you start with the third article of the Hay-Pauncefote Treaty and have a debate as to its interpretation you turn to the preamble and you find there a guide intended by the makers of the treaty to enable you to reach the right interpretation upon the terms of the third article. But, still further than that, the idea of not impairing the general principle of neutralization is carried into the treaty itself, for in article 4 —

> It is agreed that no change of territorial sovereignty or of international relations of the country or countries traversed by the before-mentioned canal shall affect the general principle of neutralization or the obligation of the high contracting parties under the present treaty.

That is, repeating in the fourth article as being a part of the treaty itself the words of the preamble that the obstacles of the Clayton-Bulwer Treaty are to be removed without impairing the general principle of neutralization established in article 8 of that convention.

This preamble, sir, which refers to the general principle of neutralization in the Clayton-Bulwer Treaty and which manifestly is designed to preserve in the Hay-Pauncefote Treaty something of the Clayton-Bulwer Treaty, has been treated in discussion as being a matter of not very much importance. Not so the view of the negotiators of the treaty. Not so the view of anybody connected with our Government at the time the treaty was made, for you will perceive, in the first place, that in the letters of transmittal of the treaty special pains are taken to have it understood that this treaty preserves unimpaired something which is called the general principle of neutralization.

Mr. Hay, in transmitting the Hay-Pauncefote Treaty to the President, writes:

> I submit for your consideration . . . a convention . . . to remove any objection which may arise out of the . . . Clayton-Bulwer Treaty . . . without impairing the " general principle " of neutralization established in article 8 of that convention.

President Roosevelt, in transmitting the treaty to the Senate, says:

I transmit, for the advice and consent of the Senate to its ratification, a convention signed November 18, 1901, . . . to remove any objection which may arise out of the convention of April 19, 1850, . . . to the construction of such canal under the auspices of the Government of the United States without impairing the " general principle " of neutralization established in article 8 of that convention.

That feature of the Hay-Pauncefote Treaty is dwelt upon and made extraordinarily prominent, and there is a manifest feeling that the Senate ought not to lose sight of it in considering whether it shall advise the ratification of the treaty.

We are not left to that, however. When the treaty negotiations were nearly completed, Mr. Hay wrote to Lord Pauncefote September 2, 1901, regarding the last treaty as compared with the first Hay-Pauncefote Treaty, which failed of ratification. He said:

I considered the adoption by the Senate without change of the preamble of our former treaty —

that is, the first Hay-Pauncefote Treaty —

by which it was declared that the general principle of neutralization established in article 8 of the Clayton-Bulwer convention was not impaired thereby, a fortunate circumstance, as it enabled us in passing a new draft to retain the important utterance in the preamble in the same form to which the Senate had already given its assent.

Not only did Mr. Hay regard that as important, but the British negotiators regarded it as highly important. On September 25, 1901, Mr. Choate wrote to Mr. Hay as follows:

On Monday, the twenty-third, I had an interview with Lord Pauncefote and tried, as I had before, to persuade him that it was neither wise nor necessary to mar your article 4 by the addition proposed in my cable to you. But he thought, as he did before, and more strongly than he did before, that with the addition Parliament and the British press and public could be made to accept the treaty, but that without it they could not.

Referring to article 4 as it now appears in print —

He thought it very necessary that they should be able to say very emphatically that although they had abrogated the Clayton-Bulwer Treaty they had preserved the principle of it.

What was that principle ? We have to turn to the Clayton-Bulwer Treaty again. The principle of neutralization in the eighth article of the Clayton-Bulwer Treaty is to be preserved unimpaired, according to the Hay-Pauncefote Treaty; and it is regarded by the negotiators upon both sides as a matter of great importance. Special attention is called to it when the treaty is submitted to the Senate. Now, let me go over again the provisions of the Clayton-Bulwer Treaty.

In the first article there is an agreement not to take advantage of any alliance or any connection of either Government on the Isthmus —

for the purpose of acquiring or holding, directly or indirectly, for the citizens or subjects of the one any rights or advantages in regard to commerce or navigation through the said canal which shall not be offered on the same terms to the citizens or subjects of the other.

No discriminations are to be made in favor of the commerce of the one against the commerce of the other. The great design of the convention is said to be, in article 6 —

That of constructing and maintaining the said canal as a ship communication between the two oceans for the benefit of mankind, on equal terms to all, and of protecting the same.

In the eighth article it is provided:

The Governments of the United States and Great Britain having not only desired, in entering into this convention, to accomplish a particular object, but also to es*ablish a general principle, they hereby agree to extend their protection, by treaty stipulations, to any other practicable communications, whether by canal or railway, across the isthmus which connects North and South America, and especially to the interoceanic communications, should the same prove to be practicable, whether by canal or railway, which are now proposed to be established by the way of Tehuantepec or Panama. In granting, however, their joint protection to any such canals or railways as are by this article specified, it is always understood by the United States and Great Britain that the parties constructing or owning the same shall impose no other charges or conditions of traffic thereupon than the aforesaid Governments shall approve of as just and equitable; and that the same canals or railways, being open to the citizens and subjects of the United States and Great Britain on equal terms, shall also be open on like terms to the citizens and subjects of every other state which is willing to grant thereto such protection as the United States and Great Britain engage to afford.

What is the principle of neutralization contained in that article ? The negotiators understood that there was such a principle in that article, for they say:

Without impairing the " general principle of neutralization established in article 8 " of that convention.

The only two things in article 8 are the equality of service and of charge between the vessels of the United States and those of Great Britain and the extension of that to other countries that come in and the obligation of protection. The great object of the negotiation of the Hay-Pauncefote Treaty was to take over to the United States alone the duty and the right of protection. That was the difference between the Hay-Pauncefote Treaty and the Clayton-Bulwer Treaty — that Great Britain was to surrender the right of protection, to be relieved from the duty of protection and no other countries were to be permitted to come in and exercise the right of protection. The United States was to put itself on the platform that Blaine laid down in 1881, as the sole protector of the canal. What, then, was there to be preserved unimpaired in the eighth article of the Clayton-Bulwer Treaty ? Nothing except the basis of equality; equality between the United States and Great Britain, equality measured by the treatment of the nationals of one country for the nationals of the other. Nothing else was left to be preserved unimpaired.

Observe that the term used by the preamble and by the fourth article of the Hay-Pauncefote Treaty, is not "neutrality," but "neutralization." They are both well-understood and well-defined terms. By all writers upon international law, in all the literature of international law, the distinction is well understood. Neutralization is the contractual arrangement which produces neutrality. The end to be attained is neutrality. The means by which it is obtained is neutralization.

Now, let us go back to the Clayton-Bulwer Treaty. The only thing in the eighth article that was not expressly and intentionally destroyed was the equality stipulated in the eighth article, stipulated in the fifth article and the sixth article and the first article, and carried into the eighth article by reference. That equality was the principle upon which this canal was to be made neutral. There is no other meaning that you can find for it, and that is what was to be preserved unimpaired.

There is no need of speculating about it. Fortunately, we are told by the negotiators themselves what they meant. I read from a letter of Mr. Choate to Mr. Hay, dated August 20, 1901, when this negotiation had far progressed and this second treaty was in form, and there was nothing at all left to be discussed which affected the subject. When I read these words, I want you to remember that you must construe the equality provision of the Hay-Pauncefote Treaty as being the very equality established in the eighth article of the Clayton-Bulwer Treaty, unless you can find some other meaning in the minds of the makers of this treaty.

Now let me read what Mr. Choate said:

As article 8 stands in the C.-B. treaty —

the Clayton-Bulwer Treaty —

it undoubtedly contemplates further treaty stipulations — not "these" treaty stipulations, in case any other interoceanic route, either by land or by water, should "prove to be practicable," and it proceeds to state what the general principle to be applied is to be, viz.: no other charges or conditions of traffic thereon "than are just and equitable," and that said "canals or railways" being open to the subjects and citizens of Great Britain and the United States on equal terms shall also be open on like terms to the subjects and citizens of other states, which I believe to be the real general principle of neutralization (if you choose to call it so) intended to be asserted by this eighth article of the C.-B. Treaty.

That is from Mr. Choate to Mr. Hay. That is from the man who put those words into the Hay-Pauncefote Treaty for us to the man who authorized the signing of the Hay-Pauncefote Treaty for us, and that is what he meant. That is what he said over his official signature he meant by preserving unimpaired in the Hay-Pauncefote Treaty the general principle of neutralization established in the eighth article of the Clayton-Bulwer Treaty; and no power of reasoning or of sophistry can justify the American Government in putting upon the Hay-Pauncefote Treaty any other meaning than the meaning there declared.

The negotiators on the other side thought the same thing about it. Mr. Choate, on September twenty-first, reports to Mr. Hay a conversation he had had with Lord Pauncefote. He says:

He again insisted, as Lord Lansdowne had insisted, that they must have something to satisfy Parliament and the British public that in giving up the Clayton-Bulwer Treaty they had retained and reasserted the "general principle" of it, that the canal should be technically neutral and should be free to all nations on terms of equality, and especially that in the contingency supposed, of the territory on both sides of the canal becoming ours, the canal, its neutrality, its being free and open to all nations on equal terms should not be thereby affected.

There you perceive that Lord Pauncefote's paraphrase of the terms of the eighth section of the Clayton-Bulwer Treaty is —

should be free to all nations on terms of equality.

It is the provision for equality in the Clayton-Bulwer Treaty which he regarded as the general principle established in the eighth article.

Let me read it again:

They must have something to satisfy Parliament and the British public that in giving up the Clayton-Bulwer Treaty they had retained and reasserted the " general principle " of it, that the canal should be technically neutral and should be free to all nations on terms of equality.

What that equality was, you find in the eighth article of the Clayton-Bulwer Treaty.

Mr. Hay, in his letter to Senator Cullom at the time the treaty was under consideration by the Senate, says:

He (the President) not only was willing but earnestly desired that the " general principle " of neutralization referred to in the preamble of this treaty and in the eighth article of the Clayton-Bulwer Treaty should be perpetually applied to this canal. This, in fact, had always been insisted upon by the United States.

There was no change in policy.

He recognized the entire justice and propriety of the demand of Great Britain that if she was asked to surrender the material interest secured by the first article of that treaty, which might result at some indefinite future time in a change of sovereignty in the territory traversed by the canal, the " general principle " of neutralization as applied to the canal should be absolutely secured.

Whatever else the Hay-Pauncefote Treaty means, it means to secure absolutely the general principle of neutralization contained in the eighth article of the Clayton-Bulwer Treaty, which was, according to the understanding of the makers of the Hay-Pauncefote Treaty, the absolute equality of the ships, the citizens and the subjects of all nations with the ships and the citizens of the United States and of Great Britain; and we are not at liberty to spell out any different meaning of the Hay-Pauncefote Treaty.

In the face of these declarations we are asked to find a meaning of this treaty which ascribes to Great Britain the intent to abandon everything there was in the eighth article of the Clayton-Bulwer Treaty. We are asked, in the face of Mr. Choate's declarations to Mr. Hay, and Mr. Hay's to the

President and to the Senate, to ascribe to this treaty an intention to take away from Great Britain everything there was left of equality in the eighth article of the Clayton-Bulwer Treaty; and we are asked to suppose that that was done without its being mentioned in the negotiations, without one word, without our asking it of Great Britain or Great Britain's offering it to us, without its being discussed, without its being proposed or broached in any way.

As the Senator from North Dakota [Mr. McCumber] suggests to me, Great Britain could have surrendered much more easily. All she need have done was to say: " We consent to the abrogation of the Clayton-Bulwer Treaty."

That, however, is not the only thing. The third article of the Hay-Pauncefote Treaty provides:

> The United States adopts, as the basis of the neutralization of such ship canal, the following rules, substantially as embodied in the convention of Constantinople, signed October 28, 1888, for the free navigation of the Suez Canal; that is to say —

Rules 1 to 6 are then enumerated:

> 1. The canal shall be free and open to the vessels of commerce and of war of all nations observing these rules, on terms of entire equality, so that there shall be no discrimination against any such nation, or its citizens or subjects, in respect of the conditions or charges of traffic or otherwise. Such conditions and charges of traffic shall be just and equitable.

That is declared by the treaty to be substantially as embodied in the convention of Constantinople regarding the Suez Canal. Turn to the convention of Constantinople, and see what guide you find there to determine what was the scope and character of the equality provided in this first rule, which is said to be substantially as provided in the Treaty of Constantinople.

The Treaty of Constantinople was made, not before title to the canal was obtained, as in the case of our Hay-Pauncefote Treaty, but after the title was obtained. The company that built the Suez Canal had already gotten their grant from the territorial sovereign when this convention was made. Our Hay-Pauncefote Treaty was made before the grant was obtained from the territorial sovereign.

Mr. WILLIAMS. As a matter of information, was that after Disraeli bought a majority of the stock in the Suez Canal?

Mr. ROOT. I am not certain.

Mr. WILLIAMS. It was bought prior to that, was it not?

Mr. ROOT. I am not positive.

Mr. WILLIAMS. The date of the treaty was 1888?

Mr. ROOT. October 28, 1888.

Mr. WILLIAMS. That was after Disraeli bought the stock.

Mr. ROOT. It must have been afterwards. This convention provides that Great Britain, Austria-Hungary, Spain, and so forth —

> Wishing to establish by a conventional act a definite system destined to guarantee at all times and for all the powers the free use of the Suez Maritime Canal, and thus to complete the system under which the navigation of this canal has been placed by the firman of His Imperial Majesty, the Sultan, dated February 22, 1866 (2 Zilkadé, 1282), and sanctioning the concessions of His Highness the Khedive, have named as their plenipotentiaries; that is to say —

The firman of the Sultan sanctioning the concession of the Khedive under date of February 22, 1866, referred to in this paragraph, provides for a great variety of circumstances and conditions relating to the construction and operation of the canal, and in article 17 it provides:

> The dues are to be levied without exception or favor upon all vessels under like conditions.

So that was a fundamental basis under which the Suez Canal was to be operated, and to which this convention was to apply. The convention then proceeds:

> The Suez Maritime Canal shall always be free and open, in time of war as in time of peace, to every vessel of commerce or of war, without distinction of flag.

Article 12:

> The high contracting parties, by application of the principle of equality as regards the free use of the canal, a principle which forms one of the bases of the present treaty, agree that none of them shall endeavor to obtain with respect to the canal territorial or commercial advantages or privileges in any international arrangements which may be concluded. Moreover, the rights of Turkey as the territorial power are reserved.

There, sir, you have the Suez Canal convention declaring the principle of equality as one of the bases of its convention, a convention made to regulate the operation of the canal under a concession by the Khedive and a firman by the Sultan, which prescribes that equal tolls shall be exacted of all vessels under like conditions.

Mr. WILLIAMS. And after Great Britain had become the owner.

Mr. ROOT. This convention which makes that declaration of absolute and universal equality of tolls a basis of its agreement was made, as the Senator from Mississippi suggests, after Great Britain had become the chief owner and arbiter of the canal. Now, I come back to the Hay-Pauncefote Treaty. Article 3:

> The United States adopts as the basis —

they use the very term of the twelfth article of the Suez convention, which makes equality one of the bases of its convention. They use the very words of the twelfth article.

> The United States adopts as the basis of the neutralization of such ship canal the following rules, substantially as embodied in the convention of Constantinople, etc.:
>
> 1. The canal shall be free and open to the vessels of commerce and of war of all nations observing these rules on terms of entire equality.

An "entire equality" substantially as embodied in the Suez convention. You are bound to say that the equality was substantially the same. When these negotiators at that very instant were appealing to the Suez convention, and declaring the treaty they were making was substantially the same in the rule of equality which it prescribed, when they were declaring that what they were doing was substantially like what the Suez convention did — you are not at liberty to say that at that very instant they meant something entirely different. If you do that, you say they were dishonest, they were disingenuous, they were deceiving Great Britain.

Ah, Mr. President, the worst thing about it is that our Government has said from generation to generation it was going to treat all the world alike in whatever it did about this canal; that the makers of our treaty declared that they were preserving unimpaired the equality established in the eighth article of the Clayton-Bulwer Treaty; that the makers of our treaty declared that the provision for equality was substantially the same as that in the Suez treaty; that that was the uniform, the unvarying attitude of the United States in every step which we took to acquire title to the Canal Zone, and to get the unrestricted right to own and operate the canal; and not until after we got it, not until after we were secure, did any American ever broach the idea that we were to use the canal for selfish advantage commercially; that to the political control, to the military control, to the power of ownership and regulation and management, we were to add a discrimination against all the rest of the world for the purpose of enabling our merchant ships to outdo them in competition.

Mr. WILLIAMS. Will the Senator pardon me for a suggestion?

Mr. ROOT. Certainly.

Mr. WILLIAMS. We not only waited until after we acquired title but we waited until after we concluded that possibly the operation of the canal would be unprofitable, before we made this claim.

Mr. ROOT. I am obliged to the Senator for his suggestion.

Now, what are the arguments for the narrower construction? It is said that in this first rule the words "observing these rules" limit the words "all nations," so that they cannot be held to include the United States. You cannot give that construction to those words, if there is any construction that can be given to them consistent with the declarations that I have been recounting here. Is it a necessary construction? Certainly not. In the first place, when you look at the history of the words "observing these rules" you see that they were put into the clause for an entirely different purpose. They were not put there for the purpose of excluding the United States. The reason why they were put there appears in full, and with great distinctness and beyond any doubt, in the correspondence and the record of the negotiations.

The original Hay-Pauncefote Treaty contained a clause providing that other nations should be invited to adhere, to come in and become parties to the contract. Our negotiators insisted, in negotiating the second treaty, that that should go out. Indeed, the Senate had stricken it out in its amendment of the first treaty. When Great Britain assented to that she said that that done by itself, leaving the provision that the canal should be free and open to the vessels of all nations upon terms of entire equality, would operate against her in time of war, because the rules from 2 to 5 in the third article of the treaty, which described the conditions and requirements of neutrality of the canal, would be binding upon her, since she was a party to the treaty, and they would not be binding upon any other country; and so other countries, being entirely free from all the limitations of these neutrality provisions, would have an advantage over her and she would be subject to a burden. Accordingly she put into this first clause "all nations agreeing to observe these rules." But Mr. Choate and Mr. Hay said, "No, we will have no nations agreeing at all; that would let them into a contract relation with the United States regarding the canal, and that we will not have. Strike out 'agreeing' and put it 'all nations observing these rules,' because then any country which does not wish to observe the neutrality provisions and rules 2 to 5 or 2 to 6, will be excluded from the use of the canal and Great Britain will not be placed at a disadvantage in time of war." That was the sole reason for putting in those words, and it appears, I say, in full.

Now we are asked to give an entirely different meaning and effect to the introduction of those words, a meaning and effect which the negotiations show never entered the minds of the negotiators upon either side.

It appears very clearly, by the enumeration of the changes in the treaty when it was sent to the Senate, that the introduction of the words " observing these rules " was not understood by the makers of the treaty as producing any change whatever in the meaning of the first article except the limitation that I have referred to; for Mr. Hay, in the memorandum which came with the treaty, states the changes from the first form of the Hay-Pauncefote Treaty, which did not contain the words " observing these rules," but was for all nations, not limited to nations observing these rules. He says they were as follows:

First. In the new draft of treaty the provision superseding the Clayton-Bulwer Treaty as a whole.

Second. By a change in the first line of article 3, instead of the United States and Great Britain jointly adopting as the basis of the neutralization of the canal, the rules of neutrality prescribed for its use as was provided by the former treaty, the United States now alone adopts them.

Third. The omission of the words " in time of war as in time of peace " from clause 1, of article 3.

Fourth. The striking out of the provision by which other powers were to be invited to come in and adhere to the treaty.

Fifth. The change from the former treaty in the omission of the provision in clause 7 of article 3, which prohibited the fortification of the canal, and the transfer to clause 2 of the remaining provision of clause 7, that the United States shall be at liberty to maintain such military police along the canal as may be necessary to protect it against lawlessness and disorder.

Sixth. The omission of the words " in time of war as in time of peace," and dispensing with the necessity of the Davis amendment, giving express authority to the United States to protect itself in time of war.

That is the enumeration of the changes that were made, and you will find no place there for any change made by the introduction of the words " observing these rules." It appears affirmatively otherwise that the negotiators did not consider that they were making any change, for Mr. Choate says in his final account of the second treaty, which I have already read to you, for a different purpose —

> It gives us an American canal, on the sole condition of its being always neutral and free for the passage of the ships of all nations on equal terms.

That is his statement of what this treaty meant. The clause which provided that the treaty was to be for all nations observing these rules on terms of entire equality Mr. Choate translates as being on the sole condition of its being always neutral and free for the ships of all the nations on equal terms; and Mr. Hay, in his account to the Senate of the terms of this final treaty written to Mr. Cullom, says:

> While omitting to invite other nations to adhere to the treaty when ratified, and so to acquire contract rights in the canal, it was thought that the provision that the canal should be free and open to all nations on terms of entire equality would practically meet the objection.

He says, further, that Lord Pauncefote was requested " to reach a conclusion which should be satisfactory to the United States, if this could be done without departing from the great principle of neutrality, including the use of the canal by all nations on equal terms."

And he says it was believed that the declaration that it should be free and open to all nations of the world on terms of entire equality would practically meet the force of the objection which had been made.

I refer you again to the message of President Roosevelt, transmitting this treaty to the Senate, in which he describes it as a treaty which assures the right to the free passage of the canal to all the nations of the world on equal terms.

Mr. SUTHERLAND. Does the Senator from New York think that President Roosevelt intended by that language to exclude the United States from the power to exempt its own coastwise ships?

Mr. ROOT. No; I do not think he had that in mind at all. I think that he had in mind then the subject which I am now discussing. It has nothing to do with the coastwise ships. The subject which I am now discussing is the question what was the rule of equality declared in the third article of the Hay-Pauncefote Treaty. The question whether coastwise vessels furnished an exception to that rule is an entirely different question, which I shall come to presently.

I am certain there is no other conclusion that can be reached, and that President Roosevelt in that message intended to declare that this treaty established the broad rule of equality for all nations. He did not stumble over the words " observing these rules." He said:

> Under the Hay-Pauncefote Treaty it was explicitly provided that the United States should control and protect the canal which was to be built, keeping it open for the vessels of all nations on equal terms.

That is what he understood the treaty meant. But it is said that the broad construction cannot be given, because the United States is not to observe these rules. Nothing could be further from the truth.

I turn again to the words of the Hay-Pauncefote Treaty. Under article 3 there are six rules prescribed. The first is that —

> The canal shall be free and open . . . on terms of entire equality.

We are told that that is not a rule, because it does not relate to neutrality, and that the second, third, fourth, fifth, and sixth paragraphs of article 3 are rules. Well, Mr. President, the treaty says it is a rule. I do not know that any of us should assume to know better than the treaty-makers or assume to know better than the treaty itself. The treaty says:

> The United States adopts as the basis of the neutralization of such ship canal the following rules, substantially as embodied in the convention of Constantinople.

That is to say:

> 1. The canal shall be free and open to the vessels of commerce and of war of all nations observing these rules.

And I ask whether the United States was not to observe this rule?

Mr. SUTHERLAND. How would Great Britain observe that first paragraph?

Mr. ROOT. Perhaps she could not. The rules are to be observed by the countries as they are applicable to those countries. The code of rules may none of them ever have to be observed by any country except the United States, because there may be no country ever under such circumstances as to call one of them into application; but it is quite clear that the first paragraph under the preamble in article 3 is a rule, because the treaty says it is, and that the nation which is primarily charged with the observance of that is the United States, so that the United States must be considered as coming within the description of nations observing these rules. But let us pass to the others:

> 2. The canal shall never be blockaded, nor shall any right of war be exercised nor any act of hostility be committed within it. The United States, however, shall be at liberty to maintain such military police along the canal. . . .

They evidently thought the United States had something to do with that rule or they would not have expressly provided for what they apparently considered an exception to it.

3. Vessels of war of a belligerent shall not revictual nor take any stores.

4. No belligerent shall embark or disembark troops.

5. The provisions of this article shall apply to waters adjacent to the canal, within three marine miles of either end, but a vessel of war of one belligerent shall not depart within twenty-four hours from the departure of a vessel of war of the other belligerent.

Mr. President, all those rules of neutrality, the product of the direct application of the principle of neutralization preserved from the eighth article of the Clayton-Bulwer Treaty, are primarily for the observance of the United States. We are not dealing with an unknown subject here; we are dealing with a subject which has enlisted the attention of publicists and rulers and diplomatists since international law began.

We undertook in the Treaty of Washington to formulate certain rules, and we did formulate certain rules of neutrality, to the observance of which Great Britain and the United States pledged themselves, and for the non-observance of those rules in the past, through the Geneva arbitration, we compelled Great Britain to pay us $15,000,000.

There are two kinds of neutrality — the result of neutralization by a general convention, in which a great number of countries declare certain territory to be neutral and all accept the burden of maintaining the neutrality and observing it; that is one. The other is the neutrality which a territorial sovereign declares in respect of its territory. The leader of the world in neutrality of that description is the United States. It commenced its wise and beneficent treatment of the subject by Washington's neutrality proclamation. When any country declares the neutrality of its territory, as between any two or more belligerents, that country assumes the duty of observing the rules which the law of nations has established for the regulation of neutrality. A part of those rules were codified in the Treaty of Washington in 1871. In that treaty Great Britain and the United States in express terms declare that the high contracting parties agree to observe those rules, that were codified in that treaty. The most enlightened and advanced rules regulating the neutrality of a country under the powers of a single sovereignty were codified here in this Hay-Pauncefote Treaty, and imposed upon the United States, because the change from the first Hay-Pauncefote Treaty to the second treaty changed the character of the neutrality from a neutrality by universal agreement, to a neutrality by the fiat of the sovereign of the territory, the controller of the territory. Those rules have been codified again in the neutrality treaty of the second Hague Conference of 1907; and in that codification there are express provisions, declaring in detail the obligations of the sovereign guaranteeing the neutrality. There is not a rule here, from the second to the fifth, that does not impose duties upon the United States. Where the rule says the canal shall not be blockaded, the duty of observance rests upon Great Britain as a contracting party; it rests upon all other countries that use the canal, because they avail themselves of the privilege; it rests upon the United States, because she has contracted that the canal shall be open; and it will be her duty to stop a blockade if she has the physical power, and if she has not, it will be her duty to exact reparation from any party who violates the rule by blockading the canal.

If ships of war, in time of war, shall loiter in the canal, it is her duty to urge them forward. If a ship stays to the limit of twenty-four hours, it is her duty to give notice and to require it to leave. If a ship undertakes to disembark or to embark men and munitions in time of war, it is the duty of the United States to prevent it. We have time and again in our diplomatic history acknowledged the duty of observance both by the power that guarantees the neutrality of the territory and the duty of the powers that avail themselves of the privilege of using the neutralized territory. We have made amends for violating the territory of a neutral; we have exacted amends of others that have violated our neutral territory; and every rule which is contained in the second article of the Hay-Pauncefote Treaty in regard to neutrality is a rule the observance of which is incumbent upon the United States.

We are told that the United States cannot be supposed to have been laying down rules for herself as a customer; that this article of the Hay-Pauncefote Treaty prescribes rules for the customers of the canal, and that we cannot suppose that the United States expected to be its own customer. Well, that involves confusion of ideas between the vessels of citizens of the United States and vessels of the United States itself, to which I have already adverted. The customers of the canal are not nations in their political capacity. If this canal had been built by a company, as was within the contemplation of the treaty and the words of the treaty, the United States politically would not have been a customer of the canal; but the ships of the citizens of the United States and the owners of those ships would have been customers, the ships of the United States would have been customers, and the ships of all other countries would have been customers. American citizens owning American registered and enrolled ships will be customers of the canal just as much as will be the subjects of other countries.

We are also told that all presumptions are against grants in derogation of sovereignty. There are two things to be said about that: in the first place, when we made this treaty we had no sovereignty. We made no grant in derogation of sovereignty; we made no grant affecting any sovereignty that we had. The observance of this provision is a reservation in favor of the sovereignty of Panama in her grant to us, and the observance of that reservation is one of the stipulations under which we acquired the right to build the canal.

Another thing to be said about that argument is, that no stipulation about the amount of tolls can be in derogation of sovereignty under any circumstances. Fixing tolls is a business transaction. When the United States goes into business as the owner of a railroad or of a canal, the fixing of a charge is not an act of sovereignty; it is an act of business.

Did we derogate from sovereignty when we made our treaty in 1854, our treaty in 1871, and our still more recent treaty of 1909, in which we agreed that the tolls charged upon Canadian or British vessels in all our canals along the boundary should be measured by the tolls charged to American citizens? Have we lost our sovereignty over the Sault Canal? Do we derogate our sovereignty when we agree that we shall charge the same rates in our ports to citizens of other countries that we charge to citizens of our own country? Have we thereby lost our sovereignty over the port of New York or of Boston or of Philadelphia or of Buffalo?

The argument is made that this treaty is no longer binding because there has been a change of sovereignty. There has been much argument made upon the express provision of this treaty, the fourth article, under which it was expressly provided that no change of sovereignty should affect the rights and duties of the parties to the treaty; but the correspondence shows that that fourth article of the treaty was put in for the express purpose of preventing any such argument as has been made here from prevailing. Here is Mr. Choate writing to Mr. Hay about this fourth article. That was proposed by Great Britain. Form was given to it by Mr. Hay. Let me read it again:

> It is agreed that no change of territorial sovereignty or of international relations of the country or countries traversed by the beforementioned canal shall affect the general principle of neutralization or the obligation of the high contracting parties under the present treaty.

Mr. Choate writes:

> The idea "change of sovereignty," of course, relates to the report of an intention on the part of the United ⸺ to acquire a strip of terri-

tory on each side of the canal, and "other change of circumstances" is aimed at the argument in some future epoch against the continuance of this treaty that has often been directed against the continued binding force of the C.-B. Treaty that "change of circumstance" since 1850 has put an end to it.

And Mr. Hay's letter to Senator Cullom, referring to the Lansdowne treatment of the negotiation, says:

> In this connection he referred to the fact that the new treaty contained no stipulation against the acquisition of sovereignty over the territory through which the canal should pass. . . .
>
> It was claimed that if Great Britain were now to be called upon to surrender the interests and the principle thus secured by what remained of the Clayton-Bulwer Treaty, there should be, in view of the character of the treaty now to be concluded and of the "general principle" of neutralization thus reaffirmed in the preamble, some clause inserted agreeing that no change of sovereignty or other change of circumstances in the territory through which the canal is intended to pass shall affect such "general principle" or release the parties, or either of them, from their obligations under this treaty.

Mr. COLT. May I ask the Senator a question for instruction merely? Were any rights of sovereignty reserved to the United States under the Hay-Pauncefote Treaty such as were reserved to Turkey under the Suez convention?

Mr. ROOT. I think I would answer that question in the negative. At the time the Hay-Pauncefote Treaty was made, neither party had sovereignty, and there could be no reservation of any rights of sovereignty. The convention manifestly contemplated that the United States should, either for itself or for a company to be patronized by it, acquire certain rights for the construction of a canal on the Isthmus, either by the way of Nicaragua or of Panama. All questions of sovereignty would necessarily have to be dealt with in the instrument which conferred those rights. In the treaty with Nicaragua, to which I have already referred, the United States acquired rights very far short of sovereignty; in the Hay-Herran Treaty, which was negotiated with Colombia immediately after the Hay-Pauncefote Treaty, and which Colombia refused to ratify, the United States received rights very far short of sovereignty. But in the Panama treaty, for the first time, there was a grant to the United States of what amounted to substantial sovereignty over the Canal Zone, Panama making, however, certain reservations and imposing certain stipulations, among them a stipulation that the canal should always be free and open to ships of all nations upon the terms of the third article and all the terms of the Hay-Pauncefote Treaty.

Mr. COLT. I do not desire to interrupt the Senator. I simply want to suggest that, as it lay in my mind, the provision as to change of sovereignty being inserted in the second Hay-Pauncefote Treaty and our negotiators failing in the conclusion of that treaty to reserve to the United States the same rights of sovereignty of the territorial sovereign which were reserved to Turkey, the territorial sovereign of the Suez Canal, under, I think, the tenth and thirteenth articles of the Suez convention, whether it was not an omission on their part not to reserve to the United States the same sovereign rights reserved in the Suez convention?

Mr. ROOT. Mr. President, it may be that it would have been advisable to put into the Hay-Pauncefote Treaty some clause of that kind; but manifestly the controlling provision must be the provision of the treaty with Panama, because only the sovereign can effectively reserve such rights.

Mr. President, when we are talking about the infringement of sovereignty, and especially when we hear heated denunciations of what is called the surrender of American sovereignty, assertions that we have built the canal on our own territory, with our own money, and can do what we please with it, I cannot forget that four years ago at this time I was representing our country before a great tribunal at The Hague, urging upon that court the rights of the

United States to have observed in good faith by Great Britain the stipulations which she had made in the treaty of 1818, regarding the treatment of our fishermen upon the coasts and in the bays and harbors of Newfoundland. I was urging then that under the treaty of 1818, which provided that American fishermen should have in common with the subjects of His Britannic Majesty the liberty to take fish upon that coast, Great Britain was bound to treat our fishermen in letter and in spirit by the rule of equality and of justice, although it was in her waters, in the unquestioned territory of her oldest colony, that we were claiming to exercise our rights. The result of that arbitration was that, pursuant to the provisions of the award and the agreement between the countries adjusting and giving effect to it, if any law be passed now which the fishermen of the United States regard as unjust and unequal toward them in the exercise of their calling in those British waters, upon the objection of the United States it is suspended in operation and submitted to the arbitration of an impartial international tribunal, to determine whether it shall take effect. Ah, Mr. President, conformity to the obligations of treaties is the highest exercise of sovereignty and not the infringement of sovereignty.

It seems to me, sir, that I have now reached a point where I am justified in leaving the main question, which I have discussed with a feeling that I have, in a poor and halting way, but by the presentation of substantial matter, established the general rule prescribed in the third article of the Hay-Pauncefote Treaty as a rule of real entire equality, of real absence of discrimination, applicable to all the nations of the world, to all ships, to all subjects, and to all citizens.

The question to which we now must pass, is the question whether the statute whose repeal is sought is in conformity with that rule of equality.

It is said that coastwise traffic may be exempted from that rule, and that is claimed on the authority of the case of Olsen against Smith in One hundred and ninety-fifth Supreme Court Reports. In that case the court say:

> Nor is there merit in the contention that as the vessel in question was a British vessel coming from a foreign port, the State laws concerning pilotage are in conflict with the treaty between Great Britain and the United States, providing that " no higher or other duties or charges shall be imposed in any ports of the United States on British vessels than those payable in the same ports by vessels of the United States." Neither the exemption of coastwise steam vessels from pilotage resulting from the law of the United States nor any lawful exemption of coastwise vessels created by the State law concerns vessels in the foreign trade, and therefore any such exemptions do not operate to produce a discrimination against British vessels engaged in foreign trade and in favor of vessels of the United States in such trade. In substance, the proposition but asserts that because by the law of the United States steam vessels in the coastwise trade have been exempt from pilotage regulations, therefore, there is no power to subject vessels in foreign trade to pilotage regulations, even although such regulations apply, without discrimination, to all vessels engaged in such foreign trade, whether domestic or foreign.

It will be perceived that that utterance of the Supreme Court lays down the rule of equality as to trade of the same kind. Now, sir, I do not doubt that coastwise trade, real coastwise trade, is a special kind of trade, standing by itself, quite unlike the great over-seas trade. All countries, as a rule, treat their coastwise trade with special favor; they charge reduced rates for the privileges it has in their ports; and if any such real coastwise trade, any of the trade that has been known to the laws and treaties and navigators and traders time out of mind as coastwise trade, or cabotage, were to pass through the Panama Canal, I should not question the right to treat that in a different way from the great over-seas trade that goes through that canal. But, Mr. President, the real gist of this discrimination is not the discrimination between coastwise trade, properly so called, and other trade. No real coastwise trade will go through that canal.

It is a thousand miles and more away from our coast. The trade that goes through it will be real over-seas trade, carried on by great ships, making long voyages — in its nature the exact antithesis to real coastwise trade.

The trouble with this discrimination is the kind of trade which is included in this statute. The great over-seas trade, the trade from New York to San Francisco; from Portland, Maine, to Seattle; from Philadelphia to Hawaii; from Baltimore to Alaska, in great ships plowing two oceans, great overseas trade, although beginning and ending in American ports, is included by our statute under the term " coastwise " and has the benefit of this discrimination; and other countries have the same kind of trade and will send the same kind of trade through the Suez Canal. The decision of the Supreme Court of the United States was based upon the absence of discrimination between the same kind of trade. Here this discrimination is solely between the same kind of trade. It is a discrimination between a kind of trade carried on in American ships and the same kind of trade carried on in other ships.

Great Britain — Canada — will have the same kind of trade between Halifax and Vancouver. Mexico will have the same kind of trade between Tampico, sometimes Vera Cruz, and Acapulco. Honduras, Nicaragua, Costa Rica, Colombia; Germany between her ports and the Caroline Islands will have just the same kind of trade that we have between our Atlantic ports and Hawaii; England from London to Hong-Kong; Russia from her Baltic ports to her Siberian ports. There is no basis of this discrimination in the kind of trade. The basis of the discrimination is nothing but the flag; and I cannot resist the conclusion, sir, that such discrimination is not in conformity with the rule of equality.

But we are told, sir, that we must not repeal this statute " at the behest of Great Britain." The behest of Great Britain!

What has Great Britain said to us? Let us see. She has said that she considered this statute to be a violation of the contract; and she said, in Mr. Mitchell Innes's note of August 27:

> I am instructed to add at the same time that should there eventually be a difference between the two countries as to the correct interpretation of the Hay-Pauncefote Treaty which cannot be settled by other means, His Majesty's Government would then ask that it should be referred to arbitration in accordance with the provisions of the existing arbitration treaty concluded in 1908.

The same thing was said to Mr. Phillips, who was our chargé in London; and he reports that Sir Edward Grey announced in Parliament that —

> Should there eventually be a difference between the two countries respecting the interpretation of the Hay-Pauncefote Treaty that could not be settled by other means, His Majesty's Government would ask that it be referred to arbitration in accordance with the provisions of the existing arbitration treaty concluded with the United States in 1908.

In the formal note of Sir Edward Grey to our State Department, he concludes:

> His Majesty's Government feel no doubt as to the correctness of their interpretation of the treaties of 1850 and 1901 and as to the validity of the rights they claim under them for British shipping; nor does there seem to them to be any room for doubt that the provisions of the Panama Canal Act as to tolls conflict with the rights secured to their shipping by the treaty. But they recognize that many persons of note in the United States, whose opinions are entitled to great weight, hold that the provisions of the act do not infringe the conventional obligations by which the United States is bound, and under these circumstances they desire to state their perfect readiness to submit the question to arbitration if the Government of the United States would prefer to take this course.

Does that sound like a behest? Is there anything arrogant or insolent about that?

Let me recall to your minds, without going over the long history, what the United States has said and done in respect of arbitration. Let me recall to your minds the resolutions passed by the Senate and by the House calling for the negotiation of treaties of arbitration; the messages of Presidents, in long succession, declaring to Congress the unalterable devotion of the Government of the United States to the principles of arbitration; the multitude of treaties negotiated at the instance and by the request and urgency of the United States pursuant to these resolutions of Congress, and providing for arbitration.

Are we to regard it as arrogant and insolent that a nation with which we have made a treaty regarding the price of a service to be rendered differs from our interpretation of the treaty and proposes arbitration?

Let me recall to you also the Alabama Claims, and the time when we called for arbitration to enforce our demands against Great Britain, and got it, and got judgment for $15,000,000. Let me recall when we called for arbitration of our northwestern boundary, and obtained for ourselves the disputed sovereignty to the island of San Juan, in the Strait of Fuca. Let me recall the time when we wanted arbitration for the rights of our helpless fishermen upon the Newfoundland and the Canadian coasts, and got it, and got protection for them. Let me recall the time when the miners of two countries were standing on either side of the disputed boundary line in Alaska, and in the interest of peace and civilization the two countries arbitrated the Alaska boundary, and we got the territory we claimed. Let me recall to you the Venezuela boundary controversy, when we demanded that Great Britain arbitrate. Let me read to you the language of Secretary Olney to England:

OLNEY TO BAYARD   JULY 20, 1895.

You are instructed, therefore, to present the foregoing views to Lord Salisbury by reading to him this communication (leaving with him a copy, should he so desire), and to reënforce them by such pertinent considerations as will doubtless occur to you. They call for a definite decision upon the point whether Great Britain will consent or will decline to submit the Venezuelan boundary question in its entirety to impartial arbitration.

Those are peremptory words, evincing no doubt of the moral right to demand arbitration.

> It is the earnest hope of the President that the conclusion will be on the side of arbitration, and that Great Britain will add one more to the conspicuous precedents she has already furnished in favor of that wise and just mode of adjusting international disputes. If he is to be disappointed in that hope, however,— a result not to be anticipated and, in his judgment, calculated to greatly embarrass the future relations between this country and Great Britain — it is his wish to be made acquainted with the fact at such early date as will enable him to lay the whole subject before Congress in his next annual message.

He laid it before Congress. You all remember that it was a war message. All the world understood it. He got his arbitration.

Oh, arbitration when we want it, yes; but when another country wants it, "Never, never furl the American flag at the behest of a foreign nation."

Mr. President, the subject that I am now discussing raises sharply the question how the American people want their affairs to be conducted. They have a multitude of relations with other countries. They are doing a business of over four thousand million dollars with other countries. They are travelling all over the world in hundreds of thousands. They are receiving in this country hundreds of thousands of the citizens of other countries. Vast interests of property and of liberty and of life are regulated by the great body of treaties and conventions that we have with other countries. We think ourselves, and rightly think ourselves, leaders in civilization. We are for the amelioration of manners and of conduct which tends to substitute kindly feelings and considerate treatment for the rule of hatred, of strife, and of war.

Do the American people wish their representatives to treat all the other nations that are in conventional relations with us, that are brought in contact with us by travel, by trade, by all the multitudinous intercourse of modern life, upon the theory that any question of right by them is an insult, that any according of a right to them by us is a surrender ? Do they want us to conduct our foreign affairs on the principle of the thoughtless youth who flings up his hat and shouts for the flag, or as just and considerate men transact their own business with each other, as neighbors in a town treat each other, as business men treat their customers and the persons from whom they buy ? Do they want us to be ugly and revengeful and insolent and brutal and boasting, or do they want us to be dignified and calm and considerate and reasonable in our relations with foreign countries ?

I say that the argument that we are called upon to " surrender at the behest of Great Britain " raises the question which I have just described, and which I will not stop to answer, for there can be but one answer and that finds itself in the immediate response of every Senator.

But, Mr. President, why are we here discussing repeal ? Great Britain asked for arbitration. Why are we here discussing repeal ?

Mr. President, Mr. Taft, who was President of the United States when this controversy arose, was in favor of arbitration. He declared for arbitration in a public speech made early in January, 1913. I have not that speech here, but I know that it was before I spoke in the Senate on January 21, 1913, on this subject. Mr. Taft substantially repeated what he then said in a speech at Ottawa on January thirty-first of this year, in which he said:

> Now, we shall doubtless have to arbitrate the matter, unless Congress reverses itself. There are some hot-heads that talk in absurd tones about the right of the United States to manage her own canal and her own property as she likes, no matter what she has agreed to; but that is all froth. Those are the " explosivistas."

President Roosevelt, with all his courageous and combative nature, is in favor of arbitration. President Wilson is devoted to arbitration. Senator Lodge is in favor of arbitration. Senator Sutherland is in favor of arbitration. I refer to them because they have announced it upon the floor in this debate. Why am I discussing the subject here? I am in favor of arbitration.

Will you pardon me if I go back to the first thing that I ever said on this subject? When the Panama Canal bill was up in this body on July 15, 1912, I said:

> It appears quite certain to me, sir, that if we enact the provision which is now before us, making the discrimination against which Great Britain protests, as the other party to this international agreement, the question raised will be one for arbitration under our existing treaty with Great Britain. It will present the simplest, most unquestionable case for the submission to an impartial tribunal of the contending claims of the two parties to the contract. We could not refuse to arbitrate the question. Great Britain could not refuse to arbitrate it. It is the kind of question which our treaty of arbitration expressly requires to be arbitrated, and it is a question which ought to be arbitrated.
>
> Instead of arguing the question, I shall content myself with suggesting to the Senate that any legislation which may be enacted ought to be framed with a view to the fact that this is a matter about which we cannot finally decide. If the judgment of the Senate shall be in favor of the policy of discrimination — and mine is not; I think it is wholly unjustifiable and unnecessary — nevertheless we should exercise our power of legislation with a view to the fact that the question of our right to legislate in such a way as to discriminate is one which may be decided against us by the international tribunal to which we are bound to submit it.

After President Taft had made his public speech in favor of arbitration, I made a speech in the Senate on June 21, 1913, in favor of arbitration. It was an arbitration speech, but I already knew that the obstacles to arbitration which were arising might be insurmountable, and I put the alternative that we must arbitrate or we must withdraw from the position that we refused to arbitrate.

Now, let me answer the question why we are here. I will answer by reading part of the debate in the *Congressional Record* of April ninth. The Senator from Iowa [Mr. Kenyon] had just put into the *Record* the letter of President Roosevelt saying that he considered that the coastwise exemption was permissible under the treaty, but that it was a subject that ought to be arbitrated. He had wound up his letter by this:

But when we have deliberately and solemnly made a promise, then I most emphatically believe that this nation should keep that promise just as an honorable man would do as regards a private promise of the same type. Therefore I believe it to be the bounden duty of this nation to arbitrate the question of the canal tolls under the provisions of our arbitration treaty.

The Senator from Mississippi [Mr. Williams] said:

Mr. President, I agree with the utterances of ex-President Roosevelt to the effect that this is a question which might be very well and ought to be submitted to arbitration; but I wish to ask the question now, Do the followers of ex-President Roosevelt upon this floor believe it?

If it had been thought that this question could be submitted to arbitration, that the Senate would submit it to arbitration, the question never would have been here in its present form. When we were discussing this matter when the Panama Canal Act was passed, the senior Senator from Iowa [Mr. Cummins], the colleague of the Senator who has just had this article read, in his place upon the floor of the Senate said that this was not an arbitrable question. He differed from the ex-President. He thought it was a matter that affected the independence and the vital interests and the honor of the United States. We found, or thought we found, that a good many more than a third of the Senate entertained that idea, and they were not willing to submit the question to arbitration.

I am not one of those who say that the exemption of coastwise shipping from the payment of tolls was a violation of the treaty with Great Britain; but I am one of those who say that the position which the Senate or its members have undoubtedly taken, that they will not submit this question to arbitration, is a violation of another treaty which we have made with about eight or nine powers; a treaty which says that all questions of the interpretation of treaties shall be submitted to arbitration.

Mr. GALLINGER. Mr. President —

The VICE-PRESIDENT. Does the Senator from Mississippi yield to the Senator from New Hampshire?

Mr. WILLIAMS. I yield.

Mr. GALLINGER. I have been a pretty constant attendant upon the sessions of the Senate for a long time, and I do not recall that this question ever was presented to the Senate.

Mr. WILLIAMS. Oh, I did not say it was. There are more ways of finding out what Senators think than by presenting a question to the Senate. Will the Senator say that he believes two thirds of the Senate would submit this question to arbitration, or will he, on the contrary, frankly tell me that he does not believe it?

Mr. GALLINGER. I am always frank when I am dealing with the Senator from Mississippi. He knows that. I will say that I do not think two thirds of the Senate would.

Mr. WILLIAMS. No; I know they would not.

There we are. That is why we are here — all of us who are in favor of arbitration, we who from the beginning declared that this question ought to be determined by an impartial court of arbitration, we who have argued for it. We are here now supporting this repeal bill because, in the judgment of the old and wise and experienced Senators best qualified to judge, it was impossible and is impossible to get a vote of two thirds of the Senate to send the question to arbitration. There were other evidences, but I will not detain you to give them. I could read from the records of the Committee on Interoceanic Canals matter to sustain the same conclusion. A majority of thirty-two of the members of the Senate would be necessary to send this case to arbitration. We are for this repeal first and chiefly because we cannot arbitrate it, and to refuse to arbitrate it would be discredit and dishonor for our country.

Right or wrong, whatever rules or whatever exceptions may justify it, if we decide this in our favor and refuse to arbitrate we are discredited, we are dishonored, we have repudiated our principles.

Now, let any man who votes against this repeal take to himself the responsibility of leading his country into that position. I for one shall not. If every constituent I have were looking with hope for lower freight rates, I would not. If my convictions were so blinded that I saw only the lurid light of red flame when a railroad is mentioned, I would not lead my country into such a position. If I had away back in my childhood learned a tradition of hatred against any other country, I would not lead my own country into such a position as that. I will vote for this repeal because it is the surest and, I believe, the only way to save our country from that most discreditable result.

Mr. President, there is one argument which I have omitted to notice against this repeal. It is the argument that Great Britain alone has protested; that no other country has protested or remonstrated. That is true, so far as I know; but let me call your attention to something that happened in the course of the negotiations. You remember that the Clayton-Bulwer Treaty provided for all other countries coming in and agreeing to share in protection. You remember that the first Hay-Pauncefote Treaty provided that all other countries should be asked to adhere; that is to say, to become parties to the treaty. The Senate struck it out, and in the negotiation of the second Hay-Pauncefote Treaty it was omitted. You remember that Lord Lansdowne wished to have inserted in the treaty a provision limiting the benefits of freedom and equality of the canal to those nations which should agree to observe these rules, and Mr. Hay objected to having the agreement. Here is what Mr. Choate said about it, in giving an account of an interview with Lord Lansdowne:

> Secondly. I told him that I thought his amendment of the first clause of the third article, insisting upon bringing in other nations as parties to the agreement after the Senate had struck out of the Hay-Pauncefote Treaty the article inviting them to come in, would seem counter to the very strong conviction in the Senate, sustained, as I believe, by an equally strong and general popular conviction, that we ought not to accord to other nations any contract rights whatever in the canal which we were to build and own; that none of them, though invited, ever came in or offered to come in under the Clayton-Bulwer Treaty; that at present they had no rights; that they must be content to rely on our national honor to keep the canal open to them, as declared in this treaty with Great Britain.

Mr. Hay reports to the Senate:

This was represented to His Majesty's Government, and it was also insisted on the part of the United States that there was a strong national feeling among the peoples of the United States against giving to foreign powers a contract right to intervene. . . .

That they must rely upon the good faith of the United States in its declaration to Great Britain in the treaty that it adopts the rules and principles of neutralization therein set forth, and that it was not quite correct to speak of the nations other than the United States as being bound by the rules of neutralization set forth in the treaty.

No contract rights are given to these other powers. Our Senate will not permit it; our people will not permit it. France, Germany, Austria-Hungary, Italy, Russia, and all the rest are to have no contract right, but they are to rely on the honor of the United States. They are to have only the good faith of the United States that we will observe the declarations of the treaty. They have made no representation or protest. Oh, no; they cannot. They have no contract rights. They have nothing but our honor; nothing but the good faith of America.

Mr. WILLIAMS. Which can be carried out by no one except ourselves.

Mr. ROOT. Yes. Mr. President, who is the guardian of a nation's honor but her own sons? Do we commit its keeping to England? Oh, no; not to England nor to any other power on earth do we commit the duty of remonstrance against our breach of honor. Our conscience must be our monitor. America must make the demand upon America that her honor and her good faith be kept without stain.

It is no petty question with England about tolls. This is a question whether the United States, put on its honor with the world, is going to make good the public declarations that reach back beyond our lives, whether the honor and good faith of the United States is as good as its bond, whether acute and subtle reasoning is to be applied to the terms of a treaty with England to destroy the just expectations of the world upon more than half a century of American professions, upon which we give no contract right, and there is no security but honor and good faith.

Sir, in the weak and inadequate arguments and appeals that I have made upon this subject I speak not for England. I do not present England's case. I do not care about her case. But I knew something about this treaty. I knew what John Hay thought. I sat next him in the Cabinet of President McKinley while it was negotiated, and of President Roosevelt when it was signed. I was called in with Senator Spooner to help in the framing of the Panama Treaty which makes obedience to this Hay-Pauncefote Treaty a part of the stipulations under which we get our title. I negotiated the treaty with Colombia for the settlement and the removal of the cloud upon the title to the Isthmus of Panama, and carried on the negotiations with England under which she gave her assent to the privileges that were given to Colombia in that treaty. I have had to have a full conception of what this treaty meant for now nearly thirteen years. I know what Mr. Hay felt and what he thought, and, Mr. President, I speak for all the forebears that went before me in America, and for the generations that shall come after me, for the honor and credit of our country, and for that alone. If we do not guard it, who shall?

A settlement? We are told that the speech I made in January, 1913, prevented a settlement. If I could believe that, I would tell it to my children, that they might rejoice after I am gone at that one service rendered to their country. Settle? Compromise? Compromise the honorable obligations of our country? Never. If Great Britain should be so false to the duty she assumed in imposing upon us stipulations as a condition of our having the right to build the canal, if she should be so false to the duty toward mankind which she assumed then, as to commute the obligations that we took upon us for any advantage to herself, I would not consent to give one copper farthing to have her withdraw her demand.

We are right or we are wrong. If the rule of equality which we have prescribed for all the world is infringed by this statute, no negotiations with Great Britain can relieve us of our obligations to arbitrate or withdraw the statute, our obligations to the rest of the world to arbitrate or withdraw the statute, our obligations to ourselves, to our own consciences, our own sense of right and honor.

There is even more than the higher interests of an ordinary nation involved in this question.

It is now some eighty years since De Tocqueville, in his great book, *Democracy in America*, which presented to the world so just and favoring an estimate of our country, wrote these words:

> It is therefore very difficult to ascertain at present what degree of sagacity the American democracy will display in the conduct of the foreign policy of the country, and upon this point its adversaries, as well as its advocates, must suspend their judgment. As for myself, I have no hesitation in avowing my conviction that it is most especially in the conduct of foreign relations that democratic governments appear to me to be decidedly inferior to governments carried on upon different principles.

Mr. President, I have not believed that to be true. I do not believe it to be true. I could not believe it and not despair of the future of our civilization; for more and more the control of all foreign as well as domestic affairs is coming into the hands of democracy. More and more the judgment of the great body of the people determines the actions of secretaries of state and ministers of foreign affairs and foreign ambassadors and ministers. If democracy is incompetent to deal with foreign affairs, more and more the world will return to the chaos of international strife and war.

Our country has taught the world the most valuable lesson of modern history, if not of all history, that a democracy is competent to maintain within its own territory peace and order with justice. Our democracy has set at naught all the dismal forebodings of its enemies and compelled an unwilling assent from the Governments of the world to its entire competency to rule itself. I have believed and I do believe that the power of a developing democracy is competent to the maintenance of international peace and justice, to substitute kindly consideration, the mutual courtesy and forgiveness of international brotherhood for the hatred and strife of monarchical and dynastic rule.

Our democracy has assumed a great duty and asserts a mighty power. I have hoped that all diplomacy would be made better, purer, nobler, placed on a higher plane, because America was a democracy. I believe it has been; I believe that during all our history the right-thinking, the peace-loving, the justice-loving people of America have sweetened and ennobled and elevated the intercourse of nations with each other; and I believe that now is a great opportunity for another step forward in that beneficent and noble purpose for civilization that goes far beyond and rises far above the mere question of tolls or a mere question with England. It is the conduct of our nation in conformity with the highest principles of ethics and the highest dictates of that religion which aims to make the men of all the races of the earth brothers in the end.

Mr. President, the noble American who negotiated this treaty as Secretary of State did his share in his time toward accomplishing the beneficent work of ennobling diplomacy and the relations of states. He did it with purest patriotism and the most unswerving devotion to the interests of his own country; and I cannot but feel that in preventing our country from repudiating the obligation into which he entered to make possible the great work of the canal, we are rendering a service to his memory that must be grateful to his friends. I recall something that he said that is worth remembering when we are dealing with his work and thinking of the spirit in which he wrought. I ask you to listen to it:

> There are many crosses and trials in the life of one who is endeavoring to serve the commonwealth, but there are also two permanent sources of comfort. One is the support and sympathy of honest and reasonable people. The other is the conviction dwelling forever, like a well of living water, in the hearts of all of us who have faith in the country, that all we do, in the fear of God and the love of the land, will somehow be overruled to the public good; and that even our errors and failures cannot greatly check the irresistible onward march of this mighty republic, the consummate evolution of countless ages, called by divine voices to a destiny grander and brighter than we can conceive, and moving always, consciously or unconsciously, along lines of beneficent achievement whose constant aims and ultimate ends are peace and righteousness.

I invoke for the consideration of this obligation of honor and good faith, which he assumed in our behalf and in the name of our country, that nobility and largeness of spirit which he exhibited and illustrated in his life.

THE TREATY OF 1832 WITH RUSSIA

THE RIGHT OF EXPATRIATION

December 19, 1911. — The Senate having under consideration the joint resolution (H.J. Res. 166) providing for the termination of the Treaty of 1832 between the United States and Russia. The joint resolution was approved by the President December 21, 1911.

The first article of the treaty of December 18, 1832, between Russia and the United States, reads as follows:

> There shall be between the territories of the high contracting parties, a reciprocal liberty of commerce and navigation. The inhabitants of their respective states shall mutually have liberty to enter the ports, places, and rivers of the territories of each party, wherever foreign commerce is permitted. They shall be at liberty to sojourn and reside in all parts whatsoever of said territories, in order to attend to their affairs, and they shall enjoy, to that effect, the same security and protection as natives of the country wherein they reside, on condition of their submitting to the laws and ordinances there prevailing, and particularly to the regulations in force concerning commerce.

Article 10 of the treaty provided that certain concessions previously set out in the article " shall not derogate, in any manner, from the force of the laws already published, or which may hereafter be published by His Majesty the Emperor of all the Russias: to prevent the emigration of his subjects."

Difficulties having arisen between the two governments concerning Russian subjects of the Jewish faith who had come to the United States and after acquiring American citizenship, sought to return to Russia, the refusal of the Russian Government to admit such persons and to give them the privileges accorded to other American citizens under this treaty; the insistence of the Russian authorities that there should be noted upon the passports issued to such citizens that the bearers were persons of the Jewish faith, caused great friction between the two countries and led to a joint resolution of Congress, introduced December 4, 1911, in the House, to abrogate the Treaty of 1832. The resolution as passed by both Houses and signed by the President, read as follows:

> WHEREAS, the treaty of commerce and navigation between the United States and Russia, concluded on the eighteenth day of December, eighteen hundred and thirty-two, provides in Article XII thereof that it " shall continue in force until the first day of January, in the year of our Lord eighteen hundred and thirty-nine, and if, one year before that day, one of the high contracting parties shall not have announced to the other, by an official notification, its intention to arrest the operation thereof, this treaty shall remain obligatory one year beyond that day, and so on until the expiration of the year which shall commence after the date of a similar notification "; and
>
> Whereas, on the seventeenth day of December, nineteen hundred and eleven, the President caused to be delivered to the Imperial Russian Government, by the American Ambassador at Saint Petersburg, an official notification

on behalf of the Government of the United States, announcing intention to terminate the operation of this treaty upon the expiration of the year commencing on the first of January, nineteen hundred and twelve; and

Whereas, said treaty is no longer responsive in various respects to the political principles and commercial needs of the two countries; and

Whereas, the constructions placed thereon by the respective contracting parties differ upon matters of fundamental importance and interest to each: Therefore be it

Resolved by the Senate and House of Representatives of the United States of America in Congress assembled, That the notice thus given by the President of the United States to the Government of the Empire of Russia to terminate said treaty in accordance with the terms of the treaty is hereby adopted and ratified.

WERE it not for the references made by the senior Senator from Maryland [Mr. Rayner] in his very eloquent address this morning to some statements made and positions taken by me I should not venture to detain the Senate from a vote on these resolutions by any observations of mine. What the Senator from Maryland referred to was a brief statement which I made in the Committee on Foreign Relations both as to my position and as to the reasons which led to it. Of course, the remarks made in the committee have vanished in thin air and enter into no record; and accordingly the very brief and partial observations of the Senator from Maryland alone remain. I will endeavor to state substantially what I stated in the committee.

I am clearly of the opinion that the United States ought to terminate the Treaty of 1832 with Russia. I do not think, however, that the House resolution which was addressed to that end contains an adequate statement of the reasons why we ought to terminate the treaty, and I do think that the language of that House resolution is in some respects unfortunate.

If the treaty, Mr. President, properly construed, construed as we think it should be construed, would be adequate to meet the needs of our people and would be in conformity to the political principles which we profess, then I should say that instead of abrogating the treaty it would be appropriate

TREATY WITH RUSSIA

to assert our construction and to call upon Russia as a co-signatory with us of The Hague conventions regarding the peaceable settlement of international differences to submit the true construction of the treaty to arbitration; and then, if the decision was against us, we could take whatever course appeared to be wise at that time.

The trouble with taking any such course, however, is that no matter how this treaty is construed, no matter how any real question of difference between us and Russia regarding the construction is resolved, the treaty is and must always remain an unsatisfactory and injurious instrument for us to continue by our assent.

During the eighty years which have elapsed since the making of the treaty, there has been a very momentous change in the attitude of the greater part of the civilized world toward the subject-matter of the treaty, and we have shared in that change.

The treaty in its first article provides that the inhabitants of the respective states shall have liberty to go into each other's territories on condition of their submitting to the laws and ordinances there prevailing, and particularly to the regulations in force concerning commerce; and the tenth article of the treaty concludes with this paragraph:

> But this article shall not derogate in any manner from the force of the laws already published, or which may hereafter be published by His Majesty the Emperor of all the Russias, to prevent the emigration of his subjects.

There is what appears to be and is generally considered to be a clear recognition on the part of the United States of the right of Russia to prohibit the emigration of her subjects.

In 1832, when this treaty was made, the United States equally with Russia maintained the doctrine of indefeasible allegiance. Only shortly before, in the year 1797, the Supreme Court of the United States had asserted that doctrine in the famous Williams case.

Williams was a native American citizen. He had left our country. He had gone to France. He had become naturalized as a French citizen. He had entered into the military or naval forces of France and taken part in conflicts between France and Great Britain. The course that he followed was a course that was forbidden by the laws of the United States to American citizens; and sometime afterwards, returning to this country upon a visit, Williams was arrested, indicted, and tried for a violation of those laws. He pleaded and undertook to prove that he had renounced his allegiance to the United States and had become a French citizen, and that evidence was excluded; and the exclusion was sustained by the Supreme Court of the United States upon the ground that he could not divest himself of his allegiance to his native country and become a citizen of another country.

In 1830, immediately before the negotiation of this treaty, there came up in the Supreme Court of the United States the case of Shank *v.* Dupont, which turned upon the question whether a citizen could divest himself of citizenship and acquire citizenship in another country. The Supreme Court of the United States, Mr. Justice Story delivering the opinion, said:

> The general doctrine is that no persons can, by any act of their own, without the consent of the Government, put off their allegiance and become aliens.

And the case was decided on that ground.

In that same year Mr. Kent, in his *Commentaries*, which were published from 1826 to 1830, declared the general rule maintained by the United States to be the rule of the common law of England of indefeasible allegiance.

So, when this treaty was made and we gave our express recognition of the right of the Emperor of Russia to make laws to prevent the emigration of his subjects, it was a treaty between two powers both of which maintained that no subject or citizen of theirs could ever emigrate to the other country and become a citizen of the other country without the express assent of his native land.

That, sir, was the universal doctrine of the civilized world at that time. We held to that doctrine for many years, until in 1848, James Buchanan — to his eternal credit be it said — as Secretary of State of the United States, first announced the repudiation by the Government of the United States of that theory and declared the inalienable right of man to change his domicile and to change his allegiance at his own will.

There were varying views expressed. After Mr. Buchanan, with views reverting to the old doctrine, came Webster and Everett and Marcy, until Buchanan became President, and then he again asserted his view, and so effectively that it has never been departed from by the United States. It was asserted by Buchanan as President. It was reasoned out by Jeremiah Black as Attorney-General of the United States, in dealing with the Ernst case, that arose regarding the effect of the naturalization here of a citizen of Hanover. In that case, by the action of these great statesmen, to whom sufficient honor has never been given for the firmness and constancy with which they asserted that view — in that case the position of the United States was irrevocably changed, repudiating the view she had taken at the time this treaty was made and repudiating the view under which she gave in this treaty her assent to the right of the Emperor of Russia to prevent the emigration of his subjects.

Of course, sir, this change had come along with a change in conditions. When this treaty was made, the great tide of immigration to this country had not begun. It came first after the famine in Ireland in 1843. It was swelled by a stream from a different source after the political troubles on the Continent in 1848. It was still increased through the continual succession of wars in which Europe was engaged for the quarter of a century beginning with the Crimean War in 1853.

In the meantime, whereas the greatest number of immigrants that ever came to these shores, prior to 1832, was found in the immigration, I think, of 1830, of 27,382, and whereas the first year when the immigration passed a hundred thousand was in 1842, when it reached 104,565, this stream swelled still year after year until hundreds of thousands grew to millions, and a very large part of our people came to be composed either of emigrants or the children of emigrants; and our repudiation of the old doctrine of indefeasible allegiance was a repudiation based upon that clearer view which came from an immediate contact with the living needs of mankind as exhibited by those who came to us from their old homes.

This process, Mr. President, greatly accelerated by the active interest excited in the Warren and Costello cases with Great Britain in 1866, culminated and found its comprehensive and effective declaration on the part of Congress in the statute of July 27, 1868, which has been referred to by both the Senator from Maryland and the Senator from Massachusetts. That statute recites:

> Whereas the right of expatriation is a natural and inherent right of all people.

And then it proceeds to use terms which are pointed directly at and are designed to do away completely with the effect of all the expressions to which I have referred during the period of time in which the United States maintained the doctrine of indefeasible allegiance. It was the clear intention of Congress in passing that statute not to deny that we had ever maintained the doctrine, but to give clear notice that we wiped out the past and took a new departure; for the statute says:

Any declaration, instruction, opinion, order, or decision of any officers of this Government which denies, restricts, impairs, or questions the right of expatriation is hereby declared inconsistent with the fundamental principles of this Government.

That comes very near, Mr. President, the repeal of this treaty which gives assent to the right of the Emperor of all the Russias to prevent by law the emigration of his subjects. It clearly establishes a position on the part of the United States wholly inconsistent with the treaty in that respect.

With this radical change in position, sir, the representatives of the United States in its foreign policy began upon a process which I think has rarely been equaled in the records of any nation — a process most creditable to the good sense and wisdom of the American people and of their representatives, and which, by steady, temperate, and judicious representation and appeal to friendship, to reason, to justice, to the desire for good-fellowship and friendly relations, has, step by step, brought nearly all the governments of the civilized nations of the earth to leave the old position and to stand by the side of the United States in the new.

By the Bancroft treaties of 1868, the year in which this statute was passed, the adhesion of the North German Confederation and substantially all of the states which now make up the German Empire was secured to the doctrine of the right of expatriation and change of allegiance. By the treaty of May 26, 1869, with Sweden and Norway, and of July 20, 1872, with Denmark, the adhesion of the Scandinavian states to the same doctrine of international human freedom was secured. By the treaty of May 13, 1870, Great Britain was brought to abandon the immemorial rule of her common law, whence we derived our doctrine of indefeasible allegiance and to adhere to the new rule. By the treaty of November 16, 1868, Belgium adhered, and by the treaty of September 20, 1870, Austria-Hungary came into the same category.

So you will perceive, Mr. President, that step by step we secured the adoption of the new rule answering to the successive waves of immigration to our shores from different countries. The Irish immigration was set free by the treaty with England; the Scandinavian immigration was set free by the treaties with Sweden and Norway and Denmark; the German immigration was set free by the Bancroft treaties with the German states. The Hungarian immigration was cared for, together with the immigration of Croats and Slavs and other Austrian peoples, by the treaty with Austria-Hungary. France and Italy in their treaties of commerce and navigation with us omitted the last clause as contained in article 10 of the Russian treaty, and in their laws have recognized the right of emigration and naturalization.

The position to which the world was brought by this long course of diplomatic effort and achievement is well stated by a very celebrated Russian publicist, Frederick de Martens, in his recent work entitled *Traité de droit international.* I translate from the French. He says:

> With the exception of Russia, all the civilized contemporaneous states are imbued with the conviction that the right of emigration is one of the inalienable rights pertaining to each citizen, and that every individual is free to change his nationality. This modification has taken place, thanks above all to the profound transformation which has followed in the present century the old political order. Liberty of emigration is the direct consequence of the new social and political order which has for its basis respect for the human personality and for the interests which surround it.

So, Mr. President, the maintenance of this treaty is wholly inconsistent with the solemnly declared principles of the United States. It is a part of an old condition of things long since passed away. It is inconsistent with the view taken by the greater part of the civilized world, and I consider that the first and great reason for ending the treaty is that we may set ourselves right with our own principles and no longer occupy the false position of consenting to that negation of our principles which is involved in the assent to the prevention by the Emperor of Russia of the emigration of his own subjects.

And, Mr. President, no change in construction of the treaty that we can expect, that we can look forward to from diplomacy or from the result of an arbitration, could possibly change this characteristic of the treaty. The time has clearly come — I think the time had come when we passed that statute in 1868, but the time has clearly come now — when consistency and regard for our own principles require us to do what the treaty contemplated — to say that the change of conditions calls upon us to give the notice provided for its termination.

Mr. President, that characteristic of the treaty covers really the great part; it covers the greater part of the field. While it is doubtless true that some native-born Americans have been excluded from Russia when they ought not to have been excluded under the treaty, while it is doubtless true that Russia puts upon the treaty a construction differing from ours as to the nature of the regulations which she is entitled to impose upon American citizens who are Jews, when they come into her territory, still the number of such people is comparatively small, and the great field is the field which affects these millions of new arrivals here who have intimate and direct relations with the country from which they came and from which they are cut off by virtue of the necessary construction of this treaty and by virtue of the severe statutes which the Senator from Maryland has read.

Mr. BAILEY. If it would not interrupt the Senator from New York just now, I should like to ask him how he reconciles the declaration that the right of expatriation is both a natural and a political right, with our Chinese policy. If a Chinaman has a natural and political right to come to this country, then we can have no right to forbid his coming; and wholly independent of the question now under consideration, I would not like to commit myself to the extent of conceding that.

Mr. ROOT. Mr. President, the Senator from Texas has given to the declaration of the right of expatriation a meaning which goes further than I think is warranted.

I have planted myself upon the declaration of the statute of 1868, which I think is the final and authoritative declaration of the policy and the view of this country. The right of expatriation is the right of a man to leave his country and go to another, but it carries no right on his part to force himself into any other country that chooses to reject him.

Mr. BAILEY. But, Mr. President, if the Senator will permit me, the right to leave your own country is a barren one unless you can go into some other country. If every country on the globe would adopt our policy against Chinese immigration, then the Chinaman would have a right to leave his country, but there would be no country to which he could go, and his right would be an utterly barren one.

Mr. ROOT. I think entirely so.

Mr. BAILEY. I can hardly bring myself to think that logically there is a natural right which can be defeated by the action of other people. I will say to the Senator from New York if the Chinese question had been as vital then as it is now, I very seriously doubt if the statute of 1868 would have been quite as broad as it is.

Mr. ROOT. That may be. I am not going to discuss the Chinese question further than to take advantage of the attention called to it by the Senator from Texas, to say that it behooves us to be quite conservative and cautious in the official use of language about this Russian treaty, lest we find ourselves in a moment of enthusiasm or irritation betrayed into an assertion of propositions which will come back to plague us when they are turned the other way.

One very good reason, Mr. President, for giving the notice to terminate this treaty in simple terms and without undertaking to specify reasons is that there are many, I suppose millions, of subjects of Russia of Mongolian birth, whom we would not admit to our country, treaty or no treaty, and we had better not undertake to specify reasons which will involve us in making nice discriminations in regard to the difference between Russia's admitting American citizens there and our admitting Russian subjects here, in advance of thorough and careful consideration of the true meaning and effect of what we say.

There is one other reason, Mr. President, why this treaty is not satisfactory, and that is, it is exceedingly limited in its scope. The construction generally put upon it is, that it applies to entering Russia only for commercial purposes. I do not know that that can be successfully contested. So the treaty itself and all questions regarding the proper enforcement and construction of the treaty cover but a small corner of the real difficulty. The only way to solve the difficulty is to get rid of the treaty and begin anew. In doing that, sir, we will avoid one very serious objection which now exists to our relations with Russia.

When the treaty has been terminated, if no new treaty is made in its place, nobody from the United States will have a right to enter Russia. In that event the effect will not be to admit to Russia the people who have been denied entrance there, but it will be to exclude from Russia all other Americans.

That in some respects would be unfortunate, but, Mr. President, it would be better than the present. It is better that there should not be any discrimination which constitutes two sharply separated classes of our citizens. I would rather have one great body of American citizens who have no right to enter a foreign land than to have two bodies of American citizens one of which has the right under our treaties to enter and the other of which has no right.

So, while I hope that a new treaty will be made, which will give the right of entry to those who have not had it hitherto, and I think it is the duty of our Government to bend every effort toward bringing that about, still, if we must go with no treaty, I shall be better satisfied than to have this treaty of discrimination continued.

Now a word, Mr. President, regarding the terms that we are to use. Of course there is occasion to be more guarded in language between sovereign states, which have over them nobody to control their action, than there is between men, who can be obliged to keep the peace by police officers and the law. The peace of the world rests upon the observance of studied and careful courtesy in the relations between nations.

Mr. President, among men there are more quarrels, there are more assaults, there are more murders brought about by insults, by wounded feelings, and injured honor than there are by the deprivation of property or injury to pecuniary rights. Among nations it is doubly so, because a jealous regard for independence and national honor are the part of patriotism the world over. No one can respect a man who does not resent an insult to his country. No people on earth are quicker to resent it than the people of the United States.

It is difficult for men in one country to realize how their words will be understood and received in another country. You and I are in the habit of thinking alike, talking alike. We are in the same surroundings. We can understand what impulses and feelings move each other. When we are using words which relate to people far away, on the other side of the earth, we can know but little of the weight, stress, and effect which will be produced in those far distant and alien lands. Different conditions may give new and different meanings to the words.

So it is that for the peace of the world, that nations may so conduct their affairs as to enable their people to live in peace and prosperity, it has come to be the universal custom to use especially guarded and courteous terms in diplomatic intercourse. It is not frill and nonsense; it is not fancy or fad; it is the teaching of the universal experience of civilization.

I am most anxious that in adopting a resolution to put an end to this treaty we should do it in accordance with that obligation of courtesy and respect which the peace and dignity of mankind require.

Mr. President, accusations of violations of duty, imputation, insinuations, all controversial matter should be excluded from a resolution like this. If we assert our adherence to a great principle of acknowledged right as a reason for putting an end to this treaty we imply that Russia is opposed to it. We cannot vaunt ourselves, our principles, our virtues, our love of freedom in this resolution, without implying a charge against Russia that she is without them.

Mr. President, were it true, what would be the effect of a charge made expressly or by implication but to begin a controversy? Are we desirous to end this treaty and to secure a better one, or are we desirous to begin a controversy that will end we cannot tell where?

Mr. President, let me say one further thing. If in this resolution we depart from that dignified and courteous treatment which the customs of international intercourse throughout the world require, the sympathy of every civilized people on the face of the earth will be with the nation that has been offended, and the tremendous power of the public opinion of mankind will be behind a refusal of all the efforts of our diplomacy to secure a new arrangement which may benefit our fellow-citizens with whose woes we sympathize so deeply.

It not only will affect us in this particular case, but it will affect the position, the prestige, the good name, and credit of our country in all its foreign relations. It will leave a condition of feeling between us and Russia, our traditional friend, which it would take generations to do away, and it will leave us in all the countries of the world lower in credit and less esteemed than we have been hitherto.

THE MEXICAN RESOLUTION

On April 22, 1914, the President approved the following joint resolution of Congress:

In view of the facts presented by the President of the United States in his address delivered to the Congress in joint session on the twentieth day of April nineteen hundred and fourteen, with regard to certain affronts and indignities committed against the United States in Mexico: Be it

Resolved by the Senate and House of Representatives of the United States of America in Congress assembled, That the President is justified in the employment of the armed forces of the United States to enforce his demand for unequivocal amends for certain affronts and indignities committed against the United States.

Be it further resolved, That the United States disclaims any hostility to the Mexican people or any purpose to make war upon Mexico.

A substitute to the preamble had been proposed by Senator Henry Cabot Lodge of Massachusetts, specifying the violations of American rights in Mexico and the duty of the United States to compel respect for its rights. Mr. Root supported this substitute in the following speech, delivered April 21, 1914:

MR. PRESIDENT, I shall not prolong very much this discussion, for I think that whatever action we take ought to be taken today without further delay. I do wish, however, to state the reasons for supporting the substitute offered by the Senator from Massachusetts [Mr. Lodge] in lieu of the resolution reported by the Committee on Foreign Relations.

The President has asked Congress for its approval of a course which he purposed to follow to compel amends for an insult to the flag of the United States. A resolution has come from the House declaring that the President is justified in the course he proposes and naming General Huerta as the person against whom the present action is understood to be directed. The Committee on Foreign Relations has reported a substitute resolution which omits all reference by name to General Huerta, but so refers to the statements made by the President in his address that in explaining the justification of the course which he proposes, the effect is substantially the same. We are not asked to authorize action; we are asked to justify it.

Mr. President, I have the highest respect — more than respect, I have regard and admiration — for the President of the United States. I have entire confidence in the sincerity of his purpose, in the lofty quality of the ideals which he pursues, and in the genuineness of his adherence to peace.

But we are asked not to express our opinion of the President of the United States, not to express our confidence in him or in his purposes. We are asked in the exercise of our duty as a part of the Government of the United States to declare a specified course of conduct under specified conditions to be justified. It is our duty that we are to perform, our duty as a part of the Government of the United States, our duty to the hundred millions of people of the United States, to the community of nations, to the credit and good name of our country, to the honor and glory that this great democracy has intrusted to our hands as its representatives. This duty we are called upon to perform.

The course which is proposed is the forcible armed compulsion of the people or some of the people of a friendly nation, the armed compulsion of a government which I think we all are agreed is an existing *de facto* government, having in its control the greater part of the territory of Mexico — the armed compulsion of that government to make amends to the United States for an insult to its flag.

What is the justification? We cannot justify, sir, upon confidence which we all have in the President. We must justify upon grounds which commend themselves to our consciences, to our intelligence, to the conscience of the American people, and to the deliberate judgment of the civilized world.

What is the justification? Observe, sir, I do not say that there is no justification. I ask what it is. In the address of the President, in the plain implications and exclusive inferences of the resolution which came from the House, and

THE MEXICAN RESOLUTION

equally in the resolution reported by the committee, the justification is to be found in a single incident. That incident was this: A boat-load of sailors in the uniform of the United States, upon a boat flying the flag of the United States, landed the other day at a wharf in Tampico and were arrested by an officer in charge of a guard, taken through the streets, presently returned to the boat and set free — a very gross offense to the dignity of the United States, an insult which cannot be ignored.

But, sir, immediate amends were made. The action of the officer who made the arrest was disavowed by the government under which he served, the *de facto* government of Mexico, under the *de facto* presidency of General Huerta. It is stated that the officer was in turn arrested and was to be punished. The commandant at Tampico apologized for the act, and promptly upon being advised of the circumstance, the head of the *de facto* government, General Huerta, also apologized. Those amends, which would be all that could be expected from private individuals, were, nevertheless, not satisfactory and not sufficient for the officer in command of the American fleet or squadron at Tampico, and he demanded a formal salute to the American flag.

Mr. President, I agree with the admiral that the amends were not sufficient as coming from the *de facto* government and that there should have been a salute to the American flag, but it appears that there was an interposition by our Government; there were communications between our State Department and our chargé in the City of Mexico, representations to the *de facto* government in Mexico, negotiations and conversations, as to the character of the further amends that should be made. The matter came plainly to be a discussion between the Government of the United States and the *de facto* government of Mexico. Not about the quality of the act that was done; there is no dispute about that. Not about the obligation to make amends; that was done. Not about the obligation to apologize; the apologies were made. But about the form of further amends, how a salute should be fired, what were the proper and customary obligatory incidents in the way of returning such a salute, and the number of guns which should be fired. It is upon that dispute — upon a dispute between these two Governments about the number of guns that are to be fired and about what the proper custom is as to returning the salute when it is fired — it is upon that dispute that this justification is made to rest in the resolution passed by the other House and in the resolution reported by the Committee on Foreign Relations of the Senate.

Mr. President, I feel bound to say that while I would never for a moment fail so far as in me lay in preserving the dignity and honor of the flag of the United States, the dispute to which this incident has come seems to be painfully inadequate to the results which are to be drawn from it. If that is all — if there is nothing else except a question of the number of guns and the form and manner of salute — which stands between the hundred million people of the United States and this poor, harried, and distressed people, it seems to me that the occasion is painfully inadequate to the results that are to follow.

Is that all? We learn tonight that Vera Cruz has fallen, that four American marines lie dead in that city, and that twenty-one lie suffering from wounds. Is there nothing but this dispute about the number of guns and the form and ceremony of a salute to justify the sacrifice of those American lives?

O Mr. President, deeply and sincerely as the President of the United States desires to limit the scope of his action, deeply and sincerely as he desires the maintenance of peace, all history and human experience teach us that once lighted, the fires of war cannot be quenched at will.

It is intervention, technically, but it is war in its essence that we are to vote to justify tonight. How long it will continue, what its results and its incidents will be, no man can state. Men will die, men dear to us will die, because of the action that we are to approve tonight. American homes will be desolate; American women will móurn; American children will go through life fatherless, because of the action that we are to approve tonight; and when those children, grown to manhood, turn back the page to learn in what cause their fathers died, are they to find that it was about a quarrel as to the number of guns and the form and ceremony of a salute, and nothing else?

We are to justify. What is the justification? Is there none but that? We, the representatives of the great peace-loving nation; we, the representatives of the great democracy that prides itself upon demonstrating to the world that democracy can be peaceful and just; we are to justify these acts of war; and is there no justification that we can lay before our countrymen, before the world, before the community of nations, before the judgment seat of history, except our dispute about the number of guns and the form and method of a salute? O Mr. President, how inadequate! How can we justify ourselves if we have no justification but that?

But, sir, that is not all. If it had been all, the President would not have come to the Congress yesterday; if it had been all, we would not be discussing the subject here tonight. Back of the incident, back of the special circumstance which forms the whole of the resolution reported by the committee, there is a great array of facts, a long, dreadful history. Mr. President, if there were nothing else but the incident referred to in the resolution, would the American Government have thought for a moment of treating this poor, weak country in this peremptory way? Such things have happened hundreds of times before. Ignorant subalterns have many and many a time transgressed the limits of propriety, mistaken their duty and their powers, and have done acts which were insults to great governments. It has often occurred in the history of the United States. What have we done? what would we do today if a subordinate officer in a port of England or France or Germany or Italy were to mistake his duty, make an arrest of American sailors, as American sailors have been arrested before, and the act were disavowed by the Government he served and an apology were made, and regret was expressed, and an intention to punish him was expressed — what would we do about the form and method of further amends ? Sir, in the first place, we would settle the facts.

We are now engaged in signing a series of treaties designed to take in all the world, and already a very large number of nations of the world have signed, under which we agree with them that if there be any dispute about any question of fact a commission shall investigate and report, and no action shall be taken for one year, to allow the report to be made. We find here that, while our admiral reported that the American flag was flying on the boat, the Mexican officer reported to General Huerta that no flag was flying. I believe our admiral but can we think it strange that General Huerta believed his officer? If there were nothing else—if this were all—should not that question of fact be determined by peaceful means?

The question of the proper, appropriate, and customary form and method of a salute is a matter of precedent and the usage of nations. It is the universal custom of civilized nations to present in diplomatic communications the precedents, the authorities showing that the custom contended for by one country is the true custom and that the other country is mistaken. In the case that I suppose, of such an incident occurring in a port of France or Germany or England or Italy, sir, we would have presented our facts, investigated the facts, made certain and clear the facts, presented

THE MEXICAN RESOLUTION

the authorities upon precedent and custom, and by peaceable and friendly communication would have reached a result.

If that were all, that is what we would do. If this be all, is this nation of a hundred millions, the richest upon earth, with its mighty power, to treat poor, weak, bankrupt, downtrodden, distressed, despairing Mexico in any less kindly and just a way? If this be all, how can we, in the arrogance of power, justify treating this weak neighbor with a peremptory harshness that we would not think of using toward a powerful nation?

Mr. President, what I have said is what the good people of our country and of the world will think, if we finish our work tonight by the adoption of the resolution reported by the committee. There is no justification for us there. No; by the expression of one thing, the dispute about the salute, we commit ourselves to the exclusion of all other justifications. We commit ourselves to a condemnation that will weigh heavily upon the heart of many a good American who loves his country and her honor, and which as time goes on, and the judgment of the world and of the future is made up, will grow darker and darker.

But, Mr. President, it is not all — it is not all. There is matter of justification; and the Senator from Massachusetts [Mr. Lodge] has sought to lay it before the people of America and of Mexico and of the community of nations by the recital in the substitute resolution which he offers. What is it? It is that lying behind the insult to our flag by this poor, ignorant subordinate are years of violence and anarchy in Mexico. Lying behind it are hundreds of American lives sacrificed, millions of American property destroyed, and thousands of Americans reduced to poverty today through the destruction of their property. Lying behind it is a condition of anarchy in Mexico which makes it impossible to secure, by diplomatic means, protection for American life and property in that country. Lying behind it is a condition of affairs in Mexico which makes that country incapable of performing its international obligations.

The insult to the flag is but a part — the culmination, if you please — of a long series of violations of American rights, a long series of violations of those rights which it is the duty of our country to protect — violations not for the most part of government, but made possible by the weakness of government, because through that country range bands of freebooters and chieftains like the captains of free companies, without control or responsibility. Lying back of this incident is a condition of things in Mexico which absolutely prevents the protection of American life and property except through respect for the American flag, the American uniform, the American Government.

It is that which gives significance to the demand that public respect shall be paid to the flag of the United States. There is our justification. It is a justification lying not in Victoriano Huerta or in his conduct alone, but in the universal condition of affairs in Mexico. The real object to be attained by the course we are asked to approve is not the gratification of personal pride; it is not the satisfaction of an admiral or a Government. It is the preservation of the power of the United States to protect its citizens under those conditions.

If we omit from the resolution that shall be passed tonight all reference to the matters that are enumerated in the substitute, we omit the real object which forms the only justification for action. Without that, sir, upon the showing of the resolution reported by the committee we would be everlastingly wrong. With the facts that are enumerated in the substitute the action of the United States will rest with becoming sense of proportion and national dignity upon adequate foundation and cause.

THE MEXICAN RESOLUTION 335

The Senator from Indiana [Mr. Shively] has observed, in effect, that the substitute resolution thunders in the index. Ah, Mr. President, the capture of Vera Cruz, the death of American citizens, the wounds and sufferings of men who lie there tonight demand something more than formal indictment. The recitals of the substitute resolution are weak in the face of death and wounds and sufferings of Americans in Vera Cruz. No less than the substitute resolution avers can justify us.

The conclusion of the substitute resolution, sir, is the same as that of the other. It justifies the President in the same course of conduct which the committee resolution justifies, but it gives grounds. It gives substantial grounds. It gives grounds creditable to the United States and adequate for the proposed action, instead of leaving this momentous movement of a great naval and military power to rest upon no justification but a dispute with a weak and helpless adversary about the number of guns and the proper ceremonies of a salute.

THE SHIP PURCHASE BILL

On January 4, 1915, the Senate, as in Committee of the Whole, had under consideration the bill (S. 6856) to authorize the United States, acting through a shipping board, to subscribe to the capital stock of a corporation to be organized under the laws of the United States or of a State thereof or of the District of Columbia, to purchase, construct, equip, maintain, and operate merchant vessels in the foreign trade of the United States, and for other purposes.

The President pro tempore. The bill is in Committee of the Whole and open to amendment. Unless there is objection, the committee amendments will be first considered. The Chair hears no objection.

Mr. Root said:

I DO not wish at this time to enter upon a discussion of the merits of this bill, but I do wish to say a very few words regarding the discussion of the bill.

I think it is a bill of vast importance. I have known of no measure laid before the Senate in the past half dozen years which seemed to me weighted with such consequence as is this bill.

There are three major lines of consideration, upon each one of which we must regard this bill as of very great consequence to the people of the country. The first and least is that it proposes to embark the Government of the United States upon a very large expense in a business venture of a kind in which the private enterprise of the United States has uniformly met with loss rather than profit, and it proposes to embark the Government in such a venture practically without limit imposed by the Congress of the United States.

I say that is the least of the reasons why this bill must be regarded as of great importance. A second and more important reason is that it proposes to put the Government of the United States into the foreign trade at a time when that trade necessarily involves frequent, almost constant, questions of critical importance, of great delicacy and difficulty, arising under the law of nations regarding neutral and belligerent rights. It proposes to put the Government of the United States in a position where her good faith will be questioned, where her violation of the law of nations will be asserted, if any situations arise such as have been detailed to us within a few days by the Senator from Montana [Mr. Walsh]. It proposes to create a condition where it will be no mere question of an individual citizen of the United States undertaking and succeeding or failing in carrying contraband to a belligerent, but where the same state of facts will raise the question of the United States violating its neutrality and taking sides with one belligerent or another.

That is the second reason. The third is that this bill proposes a reversal of the policy which has been followed by this Government from the beginning. It proposes to embark the Government of the United States in a business far more extreme than would be the ownership of railroads, far more extreme as an exercise of governmental authority than would be the ownership of telegraph and telephone lines. It proposes to put the Government of the United States in a position where it will step in and remedy the defects, the shortcomings, the failures of individual enterprise by raising money by taxation from all the people in order to carry on the business that individual enterprise has not carried on; and that, sir, means a complete reversal of the policy of the United States. It means a new departure on a line of Government action more important, more fateful in its results than any act which has ever been passed by this Congress since I, since you, Mr. President became a member of this body. It means a repudiation more signal than has ever yet been made of the principles of the great leader of the party which " has the votes " to put this bill through.

Sir, there has been no discussion here since I have been in this body so imperative in its demands upon the members of the Senate as the discussion of this bill. There has been no measure going so deep to the basis of our institutions as this bill. It comes here, sir, under circumstances which are repugnant. There was no hearing before the committee of the House on such a measure as we have before us. There was no hearing before the committee of the Senate. The demand for a hearing was refused, and the bill was reported speedily, peremptorily, with but slight opportunity for discussion; and now, sir, the Senator from Missouri, in advance, with some show of feeling, which I know was evanescent and which, I trust, does not even now continue, has stigmatized all discussion of this bill on the part of the minority as — what were the words ? — " improper and unjustifiable."

The Senator from Florida, with that kindliness and fairness which always characterize him, has told us that there was no disposition to interfere with the debate on this bill, but the Senator from Missouri in advance gives notice to the country that the debate on this bill is to be regarded as obstructive, improper, and unjustifiable. I protest against any such spirit dominating this body, whether it be on the part of those who have the votes or not. May the time be far distant when there is so little spirit of independence, so little courage, so little loyalty to the duty of a minority in this body that such a notice in advance is accepted without just resentment.

Mr. President, the discussion of measures in this body does not consist alone in the making of speeches. We discuss measures with but very few Senators here. There are not twenty in the room at this moment. I counted them a few minutes ago, and there were fourteen. What, then, is the use of discussion ? The use is this, that every speech is going to the country, that every hour passed is calling the attention of the country to the measure. The people of the United States begin to consider, begin to read, begin to discuss, and gradually week by week they form their opinions, and their opinions find their way back here. The process of discussion results ultimately in the reaching of conclusions which are conformable to the will and judgment of the people of the United States. That, sir, is why the long, patient, and sometimes tedious discussion of questions in the Senate of the United States is of vast utility, although we would suppose that it was useless from counting the men who are listening to the speeches which are made.

Now, Mr. President, this bill, fraught with such great consequences, must have and shall have the kind of discussion which brings these grave and serious questions before the people of the United States and which enables them to form their judgments upon the subjects which are involved.

SECOND SPEECH ON THE SHIP PURCHASE BILL

January 25, 1915, the Senate having been in continuous session, with recesses, under the fiction of the legislative day of January 15, Mr. Root spoke again on the Ship Purchase Bill, addressing himself particularly to the pending amendment of Senator Henry Cabot Lodge, of Massachusetts, which was as follows:

Provided, That no vessels shall be purchased under this act which are the property, in whole or in part, or which are in any manner controlled or subsidized by any of the nations now at war, nor shall any vessels be purchased under this act which are the property of any of the subjects or citizens of said belligerent nations.

Mr. Root spoke a third time on this bill on February 9, 1915, addressing himself to the national aspects of the proposed legislation. The Sixty-third Congress adjourned *sine die* on March 4, 1915, without enacting this legislation.

I WISH to address myself this morning to the amendment to the pending ship purchase bill offered by the Senator from Massachusetts [Mr. Lodge]. I may find it necessary hereafter to speak upon another important phase of the proposed legislation, but at present I speak upon that alone.

I wish at the outset to say a few words regarding the discussion of the measure. I hope I am not warped or carried away by feeling or by any partisan considerations, but it does not seem to me that this bill to put the Government of the United States into the business of foreign shipping is receiving the kind of discussion which a measure of great importance and novelty ought to have. It is a very important measure. It is important not merely because it involves the expenditure of a vast sum of money at a time when we have been forced to make up a deficit in our revenues by imposing an extraordinary tax which we call the war-revenue tax, but it is important because it embarks the Government of the United States upon a new departure, based upon a reversal of the principles of government which we have always followed up to this time. No such change of principle and policy was in the contemplation of the people of the United States when the present Administration was put into power by their votes. No such reversal of principle and policy was ever discussed and passed upon by the people of the United States in any election.

Plainly the judgment of the people should be taken, so far as it is possible by the ordinary methods in which a free, self-governing people proceed with the conduct of their Government. Plainly if there be any strength or virtue in our representative government, such a new departure and reversal of principle and policy should have the fullest possible discussion in the great public forum of the Congress of the United States. Is this measure receiving that? It seems to me, sir, that it is not.

The bill in its present form was reported on the sixth of January. During the month before, in December, it had been introduced by the Senator from Missouri [Mr. Stone] and referred to the Committee on Commerce. It was reported by that committee without hearing and without any extended consideration or discussion in the committee.

The bill was brought before the Senate for consideration, if I am not mistaken in my dates, on the fourth day of the present month, and the Senator from Florida presented in a brief and not exhaustive or extensive manner the report in favor of the bill. Upon that day notice was given that discussion of the bill by the minority in the Senate would be regarded as improper and obstructive. Those are substantially the words that were used by the senior Senator from Missouri [Mr. Stone]. Notice was given which stigmatized all discussion of the bill by the minority as obstructive and improper.

Mr. FLETCHER. May I interrupt the Senator?

The VICE-PRESIDENT. Does the Senator from New York yield to the Senator from Florida?

THE SHIP PURCHASE BILL 343

Mr. ROOT. Certainly.

Mr. FLETCHER. May I inquire who gave that notice?

Mr. ROOT. The Senator from Missouri [Mr. Stone] gave that notice.

Mr. FLETCHER. I certainly did not myself, because I stated postively that we would afford ample opportunity for full discussion.

Mr. ROOT. The Senator from Missouri, who introduced the bill, gave the notice, and he accompanied it by the statement that they had the votes to pass the bill. In advance of any discussion, in advance of any consideration, the notice was given that the majority in the Senate had the votes to pass the bill.

Mr. STONE. Mr. President, I was looking for the record of exactly what occurred. I did look that up when the Senator from New York made a statement somewhat similar to the one which he repeats this morning, and I thought later to have the exact facts shown from the record of what was said repeated here. I am not able at this moment to turn to that record, not recalling the exact time when the colloquies occurred; but if the Senator will permit me a few moments, as soon as I can look it up I will be very glad to have the exact facts and everything that was said in consecutive order stated. Now, Mr. President —

Mr. ROOT. Mr. President, it is not my purpose to yield the floor.

Mr. STONE. I am not asking the Senator to yield the floor.

The VICE-PRESIDENT. The Chair would not rule that the Senator from New York had yielded the floor.

Mr. ROOT. I say that because it is commonly reported —

Mr. STONE. But the statement —

Mr. ROOT. That it will be regarded during the progress of this debate as a yielding of the floor by the Senator holding it if he permits any interruption for the purpose of any speech or business whatever — that is the understanding — except the asking of a question.

Mr. STONE. Very well; I will wait until the Senator from New York concludes his address, Mr. President, and then I will produce the *Record*, for I am sure the Senator from New York does not wish to make a misleading statement, although a mistaken one.

Mr. ROOT. Mr. President, I do not wish to do the Senator from Missouri any injustice. Like him, I have not examined to get the precise words which were used. I am stating the effect of what he said upon my mind, the effect upon the mind of all the Senators about me, and upon the minds of all the Senators with whom I have since conversed. The effect was that the Senator from Missouri intended on the fourth of January to give notice that discussion of this ship purchase bill on this side of the aisle would be regarded as improper and obstructive. He accompanied that by the statement: "We have the votes to put the bill through, unless it is prevented from coming to a vote by improper or obstructive tactics." That was but the beginning.

Two days after this notice was given a substitute bill was introduced striking out everything that had been in the measure on the fourth of January and substituting an entirely new measure, with much that was in the old, but a new measure from beginning to end. Since that time we have not been discussing this bill; there has been no discussion of this bill in this representative body. Some of us who have been opposed to the bill have been making speeches about it, but the bill has not been discussed.

I have sat here and counted with wonder from time to time the numbers of the majority who have been present while men eminent for learning and experience and ability and patriotism have been attempting to discuss the bill. I have seen here four Democratic Senators present, three present,

THE SHIP PURCHASE BILL

one present. I marked the presence of but one Democratic Senator in this Chamber by saying to the Senator from New Hampshire [Mr. Gallinger]: "If some one would call Mr. Fletcher out of the Chamber, we might move to adjourn." I say that has been the rule — one, three, four, five, half a dozen Senators present while the Senator from Ohio [Mr. Burton], the senior Senator from Iowa [Mr. Cummins], the junior Senator from Massachusetts [Mr. Weeks], and the senior Senator from Massachusetts [Mr. Lodge], have been trying to perform their duty of discussing this great and novel measure in the Senate of the United States. The men who announced at the beginning that they had the votes to carry the bill have been absent.

The Senator from Mississippi [Mr. Williams], with that genial humor which so often brightens the closing hours of our legislative days, had — I will not say the effrontery, but I will say the disrespect, to tell the Senate that the speeches made by these gentlemen were not worth listening to. He said what was true, that he was not obliged to listen to the Senator from Ohio or to the Senator from Massachusetts or to the Senator from Iowa — that is true — but when having been absent, not having heard one word, he comes into the Senate and says they were not worth listening to, that they were long speeches with nothing in them, he denies the efficacy of the American system of representative government; he discredits the Senate of the United States; for, sirs, there is not now and never has been in our history a group of men whose study and thought and expression upon great public questions have been of greater value to the people of the United States than the Senators whom I have pointed out and who, the Senator from Mississippi says, are not worth listening to.

Why is it, Mr. President, that this course has been followed? Not because the Senators upon the other side really believe that the contributions these Senators have made to the discussion of this bill are not worth listening to, but for a very different reason. It has not been the ordinary fatigue or desire to attend to other business; it has been for a specific purpose. Before I state that purpose, let me add that not only had there been an announcement at the beginning that you had the votes to pass the bill and, subsequent to that, abstention from the meetings of the Senate during our attempts at discussion; not only has there been the open and public declaration that what the ablest men in the minority had to say on this new subject is not worth listening to, but the rules of the Senate have been so used, have been used in such an unusual and extraordinary way as to make any attempt at discussion upon this side of the Chamber most burdensome and difficult.

I am now speaking on the twenty-fifth day of January, but we are proceeding according to the Calendar of Business, from which I read, and according to the order of the majority of the Senate, upon the legislative day of Friday, January 15, 1915. Why is that fiction employed?

Mr. HUGHES. Mr. President —

The VICE-PRESIDENT. Does the Senator from New York yield to the Senator from New Jersey?

Mr. ROOT. I yield so far as I may without losing the floor.

Mr. HUGHES. I merely desire to ask the Senator if that situation does not exist by virtue of unanimous consent entered into in this body?

Mr. ROOT. Mr. President, it does not exist by unanimous consent.

Mr. HUGHES. Well, practically by unanimous consent.

Mr. ROOT. It does not exist practically by unanimous consent. It exists against my open and vigorous objec-

THE SHIP PURCHASE BILL

tion, and it exists because of the voting down of a motion to adjourn made by the junior Senator from Pennsylvania [Mr. Oliver] and the carrying by the majority of a motion for a recess until eleven o'clock, instead of the ordinary adjournment.

Mr. President, why is it that for ten days we have been conducting our business under a fiction, under a false pretense — the pretense that we are in the day of January 15 ? Why, sir, it is in order that we may have from eleven o'clock in the morning until six or seven o'clock in the evening, during which no business can be transacted, except the making of speeches on this bill; that is, eight hours of continuous speaking on this bill with no other business. This fiction of a continuous legislative day cuts out the morning hour; it cuts out the order of business under which petitions and memorials may be presented, under which bills may be introduced, under which reports of committees may be submitted; all business of the Senate is pushed aside by this fiction in order that the opponents of this bill may be turned into the Chamber under the necessity of speaking continuously eight hours every day, and with the threat looming up before us of night sessions also, and speaking to empty benches on the other side.

Mr. President, this bill is being put through by the pressure of physical weakness. It is being put through by means of making it as exhausting as possible for the opponents of the bill to discuss it.

Sir, there are two objects of discussion in a representative body. One is to convince one's colleagues, to produce an effect upon the minds of one's colleagues. That is the deliberation, the consideration of the representative body. That, sir, does not exist in regard to this bill. No one can deny it. There have been discussions behind closed doors, we are told by the newspapers. There have been discussions in the Democratic caucus, amendments offered and adopted, amendments offered and rejected behind closed doors, but no discussion of this great measure in this representative body.

I am not one, sir, who flouts at caucuses. I think there may well come a time in the course of the progress of legislation when a party shall undertake to act as a unit; but, sir, it ought to be after discussion, and not before discussion or as a substitute for discussion. You are substituting secret discussion in your caucus to the exclusion of that discussion and consideration of this great measure which the Constitution, the spirit of our free American Government, demands.

There is another object of discussion, sir, and that is an object which reminds me of the old phrase, so familiar to some of us, " leading in prayer." When we properly discuss a measure of public importance we not only address ourselves to each other, but we are leading, stimulating, inciting the thought and discussion of the people of the whole country; and that, sir, is after all the great, the all-important, the indispensable function of a public legislative body. Once we begin in the Senate to discuss a new measure, as little attention as may seem to be paid to specific utterances, some get into the press; in all the great newspaper offices there are men whose business it is to read the *Record*; public discussion begins; pertinent conversation among citizens begins; in all the places where American voters meet they begin to discuss, and gradually, through the press and through letters, telegrams, and conversations comes back to the body a sense of public judgment.

Mr. President, when has there been proposed to the American Congress a measure which required that kind of discussion more plainly than this novel and important measure? Yet it is denied by the continued pressure of a fictitious legislative day, and long hours, and abstention from discussion upon the side of the majority, pressing on the progress of this measure for the purpose of putting it through by brute force and weight of votes before the people of the United States can think about it and discuss it and express their opinion upon it.

Mr. President, the fact that this measure cannot have that kind of discussion and be passed at this short session consistently with doing the primary work of the session upon the appropriation bills shows that it ought not to pass at this short session. You can pass it, my friends upon the Democratic side of this Chamber. You can pass the bill. You have it in your power. The Senator from Missouri was right when he said: " We have the votes, and will pass it." You can do it because upon this side of the Chamber are men who have grown old in the public service, and whose physical strength makes it impossible for them to do what their sense of duty would dictate. You can pass it, but you do it at the fearful risk of denying to the people of the United States that consideration and discussion and formation and expression of judgment to which they are entitled.

Mr. President, important as this bill is, I am not sure that the subject I am now discussing is not still more important. The modification of constitutional government by practice is a gradual but resistless process. We are all familiar with the change in our constitutional system which practice has made in regard to the election of a President. The electoral college no longer is at liberty to speak its own mind or to act upon the dictates of its own judgment. Gradual progress has nullified the constitutional provision, and has created a new system. That process has taken place in many a land. When Louis XIV declared himself to be the State, it had become the sole function of the Parliament of Paris to register — not to discuss, but to register his decrees. I have seen national legislative bodies which have reached that point. I have seen them, have been present in them, when no voice was clear enough, no courage high enough, to break away from the custom which accepted and registered the directions of the chief executive. It was the result of a gradual process.

Let us not be too confident that we are proof against such a process. We abandon today the performance of our function of so discussing this measure among ourselves that there shall be real deliberation, real consideration, real forming of opinion here, of discussing it so that the people of the country shall follow us in discussing it, in forming and expressing their opinion, and we have taken one step further than ever before in the process which will make us a registering body rather than a legislative body.

I do not mean that it will come tomorrow. I do not mean that other bills may not come, on which there will be discussion; but I mean that we are taking a step in a process which is fraught with danger and with fatal results to representative government. We can justify our existence as a body only by the performance of our duty.

Oh, sir, the liberties of a free people depend upon the courage and persistency of a minority. They depend upon independence of thought and action on the part of all the members of a legislative body. If we are merely to register, if we are to refrain from discussion, if we are to smother our judgment, we are contributing our part toward a process more fatal to our country than any legislation we can devise, more injurious than any benefit we can render will compensate for.

Now, Mr. President, let me turn my attention to the bill itself, and what it does.

It is an emergency measure. It puts in the hands of three members of the Cabinet practically $40,000,000, with power to increase the amount for the purpose of entering into the business of ocean transportation on the part of the Government of the United States.

THE SHIP PURCHASE BILL 351

I looked to see what may have prompted the sponsors of the bill, and I find that in the testimony of the protagonist in its behalf, the Secretary of the Treasury, Mr. McAdoo, the emergency character of the bill is clearly and forcibly stated. I read from his testimony taken on September 1, 1914, before the House committee, the hearing of the Committee on Merchant Marine and Fisheries on House Bill 18518. He says:

> A great many of our commodities and our products are dependent and have been dependent for outlet upon some of the foreign bottoms which are now idle, and that, in turn, has, of course, had an injurious reflex action upon our commerce. The immediate problem confronting us is to provide additional facilities for carrying American products in the foreign trade; and in order to do that, we must depend upon either private capital to make these investments in ships to be sailed under our flag or else the Government will have, as an emergency measure, to come to the assistance of the country.

He says also:

> Of course this measure is designed to be an emergency measure. It never was contemplated that this should be a permanent operation on the part of the Government. Still I think the provision for the disposition of these ships is ample in case the necessity for them shall have disappeared. Therefore the bill was drawn with reference to the immediate emergency that is to be met.

He says also:

> You are facing a situation now where you cannot measure economy against the interests of the American people, and you must assume also, in the discussion of subsidy, which I am opposed to on principle anyway, you must assume that companies are available to take advantage of any subsidy that would be granted. They are not available, and there is no telling how soon they could be organized. It is only by the Government dealing with this question in double-fisted fashion that relief can be given.

There was something said about South American trade, but manifestly that is not an emergency and not any part of the emergency, for every one agrees that there is more shipping to transact the South American business than there is business to be transacted for the present, and there is no emergency there.

I said this puts a large amount of money in the hands of these gentlemen. They are at liberty to subscribe for $10,000,000 of stock. They are bound to subscribe for fifty-one per cent of that. They are to offer the remainder to public subscription; but it is agreed that the business is to be conducted at a certain loss. The Secretary of the Treasury stated that with great frankness in the hearing; and therefore it is assumed by him and by other sponsors of the measure that there will be practically no private subscriptions for stock. It is quite evident that no one would from ordinary and proper commercial motives, subscribe at par for the minority stock of a corporation which is advertised beforehand as a losing venture.

Therefore the Government will subscribe for all the stock under the terms of the bill. They are authorized to sell $30,000,000 of Panama bonds, making $40,000,000. They are authorized to increase the stock indefinitely with the approval of the President.

The newspapers say that in the Democratic caucus an amendment has been adopted which will limit that increase to $10,000,000 more, and I will without dwelling further upon it assume that to be the limit, making $50,000,000. They are to put $50,000,000 into a losing business, the loss upon which will have to be made up from taxation.

Of course, this must be but an emergency measure. Of course, it is only as an emergency measure that anyone would propose to do such a thing at a time when we have had to impose an extraordinary war-revenue tax upon the people of the country because of a deficit in our revenue. Every man who pays his part of that war-revenue tax will be contributing to make up the loss upon the shipping business which is authorized by this bill, and of course it is an emergency measure.

Mr. SIMMONS. Mr. President —

The VICE-PRESIDENT. Does the Senator from New York yield to the Senator from North Carolina?

Mr. ROOT. Yes, I yield.

Mr. SIMMONS. I assume that the Senator from New York does not desire to misrepresent the Secretary of the Treasury with reference to the testimony given by him about the first of September. I read that testimony very carefully last night. I think the Senator is in error when he states that the Secretary of the Treasury admitted that this whole business would be operated at a loss. At one stage of his testimony there was something said by the Secretary which might have had that construction, but later the Secretary made the positive statement that while he was satisfied a part of the ships would be operated at a loss, especially that part engaged on the new routes for the purpose of building up new trade, he was equally satisfied that other of these ships would be operated at a profit; and there is nowhere, I think, in his testimony anything that could be construed as a statement, taken in connection with the qualifications, that there would be a loss upon the entire operation.

Mr. ROOT. The Secretary of the Treasury says in his testimony:

> It is not only a question of establishing these routes, many of which will undoubtedly have to be operated at a loss for a time in order to establish the necessary trade relationships, but the Government will also have the power to establish rates that will be advantageous to American commerce.

He says:

> I think one of the essential requisites is that the Government shall have the power to establish these lines and see that they are operated in such a way, even at a loss, as to benefit the commerce of this country.

There are other expressions at various points in his testimony which leave no doubt whatever that that is his expectation.

We need not rely solely upon his expectations, for we know that as a matter of fact private enterprise operating American ships has been a losing enterprise. Upon good authority it is stated that there are, or there were a few weeks ago, 2,000,000 tons of shipping engaged in the commerce of the world under foreign flags and owned by American citizens. Why? Because the conditions of foreign commerce under the laws of the United States are such as to make profit practically impossible.

The Senator from Massachusetts [Mr. Lodge] has called my attention to a clause in the President's message where he says:

It —

that is, the Government —

> It should take action to make it certain that transportation at reasonable rates will be promptly provided, even where the carriage is not at first profitable; and then, when the carriage has become sufficiently profitable to attract and engage private capital, and engage it in abundance, the Government ought to withdraw.

So the proposal is to go into a losing business, and to go into a losing business at a time when we are making up a deficit by an extraordinary war-revenue tax; and, of course, I say it can be regarded only as an emergency measure.

Now, this bill authorizes the Secretary of the Treasury, the Postmaster-General, and the Secretary of Commerce to buy or build ships. How can the emergency be met? Manifestly, not by building ships. The small fleet of ships which could be procured by the use of this $50,000,000 would require from a year to eighteen months, as I am advised, to build. So that will not meet the emergency. The emergency is the prevalence of high rates for the carriage of American produce to Europe. There is no emergency anywhere else.

It is true all the steamers in the world that are free are coming in to get the benefit of those high rates, and the ordinary working of economic laws is sure to bring the rates down. But for the moment there is the emergency, and but one emergency, and that is high rates of carriage for American produce to Europe.

It is true our farmers are getting $1.40 for their wheat, so that those high rates are paid not by us but by the purchasers abroad. It is true the export of food-stuffs has been greater within the last few months than ever before in our history. Still, there is an emergency. It is true cotton is bringing eight cents, and the interposition of Government which was so strenuously demanded here a few months ago in order to save the cotton producers, proved to be unnecessary. Still the rates of transportation of cotton are high and there is an emergency. But the emergency cannot be met by building ships. We have got to buy them. Now, why?

Mr. SIMMONS. Will the Senator from New York allow me to ask him one more question and then I will not interrupt him again?

Mr. ROOT. Certainly.

Mr. SIMMONS. The Senator says it is proposed that the Government shall go into a losing business. Does the Senator see any particular difference between the Government going into a losing business and the Government inviting private citizens of this country to go into what is admitted to be a losing business with a guarantee that by subsidies that loss will be made up out of the Treasury of the United States?

Mr. ROOT. Oh, Mr. President, I see many differences, but I am not going to discuss them here today. I am speaking upon an entirely different subject. I wish that I could detach the mind of the Senator from North Carolina from certain preconceived ideas which evidently possess it, and get him to attend to the subject that I am talking about.

Mr. SIMMONS. The Senator was just talking upon the subject about which I asked the question.

Mr. ROOT. I have been pressing upon the Senate the emergency nature of this bill, and I had passed on to the question as to how the emergency can be met. I was saying you cannot meet it by building ships because you cannot get them in time to meet the emergency. You have got to buy them. Where are you going to buy them? You meet no emergency by buying ships that are already engaged in transporting our products. You meet no emergency by buying free ships.

A report of a committee of the Chamber of Commerce of New York, presented to that body on the fourth of the present month, makes an observation on that subject which is very pertinent, and it is very good authority. This was a special committee on the American merchant marine in foreign trade, appointed by the chamber of commerce of the greatest commercial city of the country. In their report, which I shall hereafter have occasion to bring to the attention of the Senate at large, they say:

> Government ownership of ocean lines cannot bring to our aid a single vessel except by building. Every steamship in the world is working today except those interned in neutral ports. If these can be transferred to our flag without international complications, there will be no difficulty in financing the transfer of those suitable for freight carrying, for their earnings will justify the purchase.

Now, that is high authority of men who know far more than you and I know about the great complicated worldwide business of ocean freight carriage.

There is left, then, to meet the emergency nothing but the purchase of vessels which are prevented by the conditions of war from engaging in the business of transportation now. I therefore was not surprised in reading the testimony of the Secretary of the Treasury to find that he plainly contemplated meeting this emergency by the purchase of vessels which are, to use the common although not very correct ex-

THE SHIP PURCHASE BILL

pression, interned because of war risks; that is to say, the vessels which are remaining in the ports where they were found at the outbreak of the war, unable or unwilling to put to sea for fear of capture; vessels belonging to one or another of the belligerent powers.

The Senator from Massachusetts [Mr. Lodge] has called attention to the testimony of the Secretary of the Treasury upon this subject; there are but a few words of it, and I wish to call your attention to it again as a part of what I have to say. In this same hearing from which I have quoted this occurred:

Mr. EDMONDS. Will they not be able to get plenty of bottoms when they can make financial arrangements for payment for the cargo?

Secretary McADOO. I do not think so. An immense number of bottoms have been withdrawn from service.

Mr. EDMONDS. There are still quite a number of idle bottoms in New York harbor today.

Secretary McADOO. The number of bottoms that are idle in New York harbor are largely bottoms that cannot be put into service now.

Mr. SAUNDERS. How would this bill add to the number of available bottoms when it proposes to make its purchases from existing bottoms? It will not add to the volume of bottoms.

Secretary McADOO. There is a large number of idle bottoms. They may be purchased.

Mr. SAUNDERS. Chiefly, are not those all German bottoms?

Secretary McADOO. More of those are idle at the moment than any other.

Mr. SAUNDERS. It has been suggested that there would be grave objection to our undertaking to purchase German bottoms.

Secretary McADOO. Why?

Mr. SAUNDERS. The newspapers make the statement that objection has come from the nations concerned in this war.

Secretary McADOO. I shall not attempt to talk of diplomatic matters.

Mr. SAUNDERS. They say that would be equal to furnishing immediate pecuniary aid — that is, to Germany.

Secretary McADOO. That is a question altogether aside, I think, from the issue. I believe that it cannot be successfully disputed by any individual or any nation that this Government or any Government has a right to buy merchant ships, provided it buys them in good faith and for a neutral purpose, and that is exactly what would be done in this case.

The CHAIRMAN. If we should buy some French ships, too, that would alter the situation. In other words, if they had some, as well as Germany, that objection would not be urged?

Mr. SAUNDERS. We would not buy any French ships, because they are not to be bought.

Secretary McADOO. I infer from what you tell me, or from what you have read in the papers, that those ships, if purchased, would be purchased from the German Government. I understand that those ships are simply owned by German companies in which German citizens are stockholders. It does not follow that the proceeds of a purchase from a private corporation of that country would be turned over to the Government.

It is quite plain that Secretary McAdoo took the same view of the way in which it would be possible — the only way in which it would be possible — to utilize this legislation for the purpose of meeting this emergency, that I take; that is, that the only way is to purchase these idle bottoms, to purchase these ships of belligerents which are unable to go to sea because, if they went to sea, they would be captured. It is perfectly evident that that purchase was in the contemplation of the officer who was to be the head of the shipping board, and who came before the committee of the House to explain the bill. He came, having in mind this bill as a bill which would enable him and his associates, when passed into a law, to buy those ships. In the report in the House which followed this testimony, Report No. 1149, Sixty-third Congress, second session, by Mr. Alexander, submitted September 8, 1914, the committee say:

Fears are expressed that we will involve ourselves in complications with Great Britain and France if we buy German ships. That may be. The bill does not direct the shipping board to buy ships of the subjects of any particular nation. They have the widest discretion in the purchase or construction of vessels. We have no reason to believe they will act otherwise than with the greatest care in whatever they may do.

It is perfectly plain that the committee of Congress which reported the bill did it with the understanding that the bill authorizes the Secretary of the Treasury, the Secretary of

THE SHIP PURCHASE BILL

Commerce, and the Postmaster-General to buy these ships, and that they were contemplating the purchase of these ships in a situation that cannot be met in any other way than by the purchase of these ships.

The Secretary of the Treasury made a speech on this subject in Chicago. It is a speech, the central thought of which is one of the most amazing ever proposed by a responsible officer of the Government of the United States. While it is apart from the line of my discussion, I cannot refrain from quoting it. He said:

> The objection that the shipping bill puts the Government in the shipping business is not tenable. Those who urge it seem to forget that it is the duty of the Government to engage in any activities, even of a business nature, which are demanded in the interest of all the people of the country, when it is impossible to engage private capital in such operations.

Do my friends think that that proposition does not need discussion by the Congress of the United States and by the people of the United States, before the man who holds that view has unlimited millions put into his hands with which to put the Government into business?

I will return to the precise line of discussion; and that is the contemplation and the purpose to meet this emergency by the purchase of the belligerent ships that, unless we buy them, cannot go to sea without being captured. In this speech the Secretary further said:

> Some timid people have argued that if the Government is interested as a stockholder in a shipping company, and a ship of such company should be seized by a belligerent and brought into a prize court, the sovereignty of the Government would be involved. There is no ground whatever for this view. If the Government operated ships outright, just as it operates the vessels of our navy, an awkward situation of this character might arise; but where a nation is merely a stockholder, or the sole stockholder, in a private corporation, its sovereignty is not and cannot be directly involved if the ships of such a corporation become the subjects of litigation in a prize court concerning any issue which does not involve the Government itself. The Government would stand in relation to such a corporation exactly

as any individual stockholder does to a corporation in which he is interested. A suit against the corporation does not necessarily involve the shareholders.

You perceive, sir, whenever this subject is suggested and objection is made to the purchase of these ships, it is met by an argument in favor of the purchase of the ships. This is the last argument which has come to my notice from the Secretary of the Treasury, having been delivered on the ninth of this month, after the pending bill was laid before the Senate — an argument, a lawyer's argument, by the man who is to be the head of the shipping board in favor of the power to buy the ships.

The Secretary of Commerce has said in a speech which I have not before me, delivered last Friday, I believe, at St. Louis, that he contemplated the purchase of British ships. Mr. President, there is no difference in principle, and before I get through I think I shall show that there is no difference in the obstacles in the way of purchasing ships of one belligerent as compared with the ships of another belligerent.

I am not talking about this because the ships are German; I am talking about it because they are belligerent ships, and they are liable to be captured on the high seas as belligerents; they are liable to be torpedoed by submarines as belligerents; they are liable to be seized in foreign ports as belligerents; and I am alarmed by the evidences here that the proposed shipping board means to put the Government of the United States in the position of giving the protection of its flag to such ships when they sail out. German, or British, or French, or Austrian, or Russian, or what not, the objection is to the purchase of belligerent ships, and, as I have said, that objection has been met by the argument to which I have referred whenever it has been proposed to the gentlemen whom we are about to endow with these vast powers.

THE SHIP PURCHASE BILL 361

But there is another circumstance more potent in its effect upon my mind than the manifest necessities of the emergency which would require the purchase of belligerent ships, more compelling in my mind than the expressions of the gentlemen who are going to transact the business in favor of the right to purchase belligerent ships, more compelling even than the practical admission that that is what they have in mind, and that is the filing of an opinion by the Solicitor of the State Department in the Senate on the eleventh of August last. The bill to create the shipping board and to endow it with the power to build or buy ships had just been introduced in the House when, on the eleventh of August, a paper was presented by the Senator from New York [Mr. O'Gorman] to be printed, and it was printed as Document No. 563, Sixty-third Congress, second session. That paper contained an opinion by Mr. Cone Johnson, Solicitor of the State Department. In support of the right to buy these ships, he states these conclusions:

1. Merchant ships of a belligerent may be transferred to a neutral after the outbreak of hostilities.

2. If the sale of the ship is made in good faith, without defeasance or reservation of title or interest in the vendor, without any understanding, expressed or tacit, that the vessel is to be retransferred after hostilities and without the indicia or badges of a collusive or colorable transaction.

3. But transfer cannot be made of such vessel in a blockaded port or while *in transitu*.

4. The transfer must be allowable under and in conformity to the municipal regulations of the country of the neutral purchaser.

5. The declaration of the London convention that transfers of an enemy vessel to a neutral during war will not be valid unless it be shown that the same was not made to evade the consequences to which an enemy vessel, as such, is exposed, if it were controlling of the question, relates only to the good faith of the transfer and not to the ulterior motive of the parties to reap the natural advantages to flow from the operation of the vessel under the flag of a country not at war, while it inverts the burden of proof of the good faith of the transaction.

That opinion was dated August 7, 1914. It was presented in the Senate August 11, four days after, almost coincidentally with the introduction of the bill, and it must stand before us as the opinion upon which this legislation finds its claim of right.

Mr. Johnson is a lawyer of character and position, a lawyer of ability, but he says in the conclusion at the close of the opinion:

> This memorandum is hurriedly struck off, and I have not had time or opportunity to revise it; but it is believed that it correctly presents the status of the question involved.

Why " hurriedly struck off " ? What exigency called for haste in the consideration of this vastly important subject ? The answer may be found by sending our minds back to the fact that it was announced and publicly reported that it was intended to put this shipping bill through then, last summer, during the last session; and this hurried memorandum — a lawyer's opinion that it is all right to buy these belligerent ships — is the basis upon which the legislation proceeds.

Mr. SIMMONS. Mr. President, will not the Senator permit me to interrupt him once more ?

The VICE-PRESIDENT. Does the Senator from New York yield to the Senator from North Carolina ?

Mr. ROOT. Certainly.

Mr. SIMMONS. I wish to ask the Senator if, at the time that opinion was presented to the Senate, the Senate was not engaged in the consideration of the ship registry bill, and if it was not with reference to the ship registry bill that that opinion was expressed ?

Mr. ROOT. I do not know. I have not looked to see, and I have not cared to see, what particular thing the Senate was engaged in doing. What I do see is that in great haste, coincidently with the beginning of this movement for the purchase of ships, there is presented to us a lawyer's opinion, that we have a right to buy these belligerent ships. Therefore, Mr. President, I have come to the conclusion that the inter-

THE SHIP PURCHASE BILL 363

national situation is important, that it is serious, that it is our duty to consider it, and that it is my duty to discuss it.

There are two reasons which press that duty upon me with great weight. One is that I find, according to my own opinion, which is fallible, upon which I do not place, I hope, any greater weight than long experience of many errors leaves in my mind, that in the haste which for some reason or other was imposed upon him, the Solicitor of the State Department has failed to consider fully the state of the law regarding which he was writing, and has been led, through the inadvertence of haste, to give radically and seriously incorrect advice upon this important subject.

The other consideration which makes me feel bound to ask for the attention of the Senate to my own views of what is the true state of the law, is the fact that it happened to be my duty to give the instructions for the Government of the United States to the delegates to the London conference, and to direct their action during all the earlier part of the existence of that conference by daily cable communication, and afterwards as a member of the Foreign Relations Committee of the Senate, to discuss and vote favorably upon the report of the conclusions of that conference, and afterwards, as a member of the Senate, to vote to advise the President to ratify. So, when I see that under the law which I am advised we are about to pass it is the intention of the agents whom we shall constitute, to buy these ships; when I see that that purpose has been formed and is liable to be executed under what I believe to be an erroneous opinion as to the state of the law and the international situation which they will meet, I feel bound to give the best I can in the way of expressing and explaining my views of the true conditions of the law.

I am going now to say something which most of you know. Some of you may not have given attention to it, however, and therefore I will state the rudiments of the case.

The London conference was a sequel of the second Hague Conference of 1907. At this second Hague Conference, the delegates of the United States, under the instructions of their Government, pressed strongly for the creation of two judicial tribunals which should pass upon international disputes. One was an international prize court, made up by the representatives of different nations, which should pass upon questions of prize — just such questions as are arising now — so that instead of going to the courts of the captor country, which apply the law of that country, with the disadvantages that a claimant naturally has in going into the country of the captor and arguing his case before a branch of the government that has captured his ship, he would go to an impartial tribunal, selected from the various countries of the world. That court was created by a treaty called " the prize-court treaty." The other court was a general judicial tribunal which should pass upon all justiciable questions arising between nations, to be composed of judges who should devote their entire time to it, and be paid adequate salaries, and be a really judicial tribunal. That court never has been constituted, although provision was made for it.

It was not constituted because there could not be an agreement upon the manner of appointing the judges; but the prize-court treaty was signed, and that has been ratified by the United States. That is to say, the Senate has advised and consented to its ratification. But when it came to the ratification of that treaty by European powers, there arose a question as to what law the court would apply, and it seemed to many representatives of different European countries that there was a long list of disputed questions that a prize court would have to pass upon, and that in order to make the court effective, there must be some agreement upon the law they were to apply — questions relating to blockade, relating to contraband, relating to continuous

THE SHIP PURCHASE BILL 365

voyages, relating to the transformation of merchant ships into warships, relating to the transfer of ships from a belligerent to a neutral flag; and accordingly Great Britain called a meeting of the representatives of the chief commercial powers of the world, to be held in London in December, 1908.

That meeting was attended by the representatives of Great Britain, France, the Netherlands, Germany, Austria, Italy, Spain, Russia, Japan, and the United States. I think I have enumerated them all. There were ten of them. They discussed these difficult questions. There was long discussion upon the question which is raised by the proposal to buy these belligerent ships — that is, the right of transfer of a vessel from a belligerent flag to a neutral flag. The conclusions to which the conference came upon that subject were stated in these words:

TRANSFER TO A NEUTRAL FLAG. ARTICLE 55

The transfer of an enemy vessel to a neutral flag, effected before the outbreak of hostilities, is valid, unless it is proved that such transfer was made in order to evade the consequences to which an enemy vessel, as such, is exposed.

Then follows a clause which is not pertinent here, and the article proceeds:

Where the transfer was effected more than thirty days before the outbreak of hostilities, there is an absolute presumption that it is valid if it is unconditional, complete, and in conformity with the laws of the countries concerned, and if its effect is such that neither the control of, nor the profits arising from the employment of, the vessel remain in the same hands as before the transfer.

Then there is a clause not relevant here, and then follows:

ART. 56. The transfer of an enemy vessel to a neutral flag effected after the outbreak of hostilities is void unless it is proved that such transfer was not made in order to evade the consequences to which an enemy vessel, as such, is exposed.

Then follow some clauses not relevant here.

You have there, sir, three situations stated:

First. If the transfer is effected before the beginning of hostilities it is valid unless it is proved that the transfer was made in order to evade the consequences to which the enemy vessel, as such, is exposed.

Second. If the transfer was effected more than thirty days before the opening of hostilities, there is an absolute presumption that it is valid, even though it was made in order to evade the consequences to which an enemy vessel, as such, is exposed, provided it is unconditional, complete, and there is no interest reserved. Of course, the declaration that a transfer more than thirty days before the outbreak of hostilities is valid if it is unconditional, complete, and in conformity with the laws of the countries concerned, neither the control of nor the profits arising from the employment of the vessel remaining in the same hands as before the transfer, carries by necessary implication the declaration that a transfer made less than thirty days before the opening of hostilities is not valid, although all those conditions exist, provided it was made to evade the consequences to which an enemy vessel, as such, is exposed.

The third situation, is a transfer after the outbreak of hostilities, where the transfer is void, unless it is proved that it was not to evade the consequences to which an enemy vessel, as such, is exposed.

It is the opinion of the Solicitor, who has given that opinion to the State Department, as it has been communicated to us, that these provisions of the Declaration of London do not involve any question as to the motive with which the transfer is made; that when the declaration says the transfer shall be valid before hostilities unless it is proved that it was made in order to evade, and that it shall be invalid after hostilities unless it is proved that it was not made in order to evade, it involves no question of motive. *Prima facie,* one would say that that is all motive; that there is nothing but motive in

THE SHIP PURCHASE BILL 367

that provision. A thing done in order to evade is done with the motive of evading. There would seem to be nothing but motive in this; but the Solicitor does not think so, and he has advised to the contrary.

Now, sir, the question may arise, and naturally would arise, Why should we discuss the Declaration of London? Why should the Solicitor have given an opinion upon the Declaration of London? It has not been ratified. The Senate has advised and consented to its ratification, but before the documents of ratification were ever deposited the war came, and it never has been ratified. The reason why the Declaration of London is subject to consideration although we are not bound by it, is that England and France and Russia have adopted it with some modifications not touching this subject, as their law for the present conflict.

Let me repeat, for the purpose of making myself clear, we are not bound by the Declaration of London because it has not been ratified; that is, we are not bound by it as a convention, as an agreement, whatever effect the steps which led to it may have upon the propriety or wisdom of our conduct. The convention which embodied that agreement has not become a binding convention among the nations of the earth. It receives its importance because England and France and Russia have, by express provision, made it the law of those respective countries, and Germany, in an order to which I shall call your attention later, has in substance done the same thing. Her law for this war in somewhat different phrase, but with the same effect, is made to conform to the terms of the Declaration of London which I have read.

It may be fortunate for us, fortunate for all who wish to secure freedom of trade, that this is so, because when the conference of London met in December, 1908, there was no rule of international law regarding the transfer of a vessel from a belligerent to a neutral flag. International law requires the general acceptance of nations, and there had been no general acceptance of any rule by the nations of the earth.

The first thing that was done in the conference was to call for a statement from the different countries regarding their position upon the various disputed points that the conference sought to settle, and I call your attention now to the rules which were stated by the principal countries concerned in the present war.

I read from the proceedings of the International Naval Conference held in London, December, 1908, to February, 1909, printed by the British Government and called " Miscellaneous No. 5, 1909."

I will say that this report of the proceedings has never been translated from the original French, it is not open to access generally, and I think it must have been that the Solicitor, in the haste of preparing his opinion, has failed to observe the contents of this report, which gives the proceedings, the discussion, and conclusions reached from time to time by the conference. I am sure that if he had read this attentively he would have come to a different conclusion.

I call your attention now to the rules of national law stated by these different nations at the opening of the conference, for that is the background to which we have to go.

France. The change of nationality of ships of commerce effectuated after the declaration of war is null and of no effect.

Russia. The belligerents have the right not to recognize the neutral character of every ship of commerce purchased by neutral citizens from an enemy's state or one of its nationals, unless the new proprietor proves that the acquisition had become definitive before he had knowledge of the commencement of the war.

Germany. The neutral or enemy character of a ship of commerce is determined by the flag that it carries. A ship flying a neutral flag will nevertheless be treated as an enemy ship if up to the opening of hostilities or within the two weeks which have preceded, it has carried the enemy flag.

There are France, Germany, and Russia. Great Britain and the United States presented an entirely different rule, the rule of complete transfer and good faith. The Solicitor for the State Department has substantially stated what the American rule has been and what the British rule has been, subject to some modifications which it perhaps was not necessary that he should state.

In the conference these two different views confronted each other, the view of France and Russia and Germany that a transfer after the opening of hostilities was void and the view of Great Britain and the United States that a transfer, made complete and in good faith, would be recognized.

Mr. President, there being no rule of international law, each country applies its own law in such cases. Indeed, when a capture is made it is always made under the law of the captor. That is our law. Our Supreme Court has decided it. It is the municipal law of the captor that is in force when the capture is made.

The courts of England and America have said that the law of nations is a part of the law of the country, and we enforce the law of nations. But here there was no law of nations because no rule had ever been accepted. So as the law stood when this conference opened, if there had been a transfer of a merchant ship from the flag of a belligerent to the flag of a neutral any time after the opening of hostilities, the armed ships of France, of Germany, and Russia would have ignored the transfer and treated the vessel as an enemy vessel, notwithstanding the transfer.

Mr. President, that was the law of France when her navy rendered us a service more memorable than any other that one nation ever rendered to another, and held the mouth of the Chesapeake and made the surrender at Yorktown possible. That was the law of France then and for all the century and more that has passed. That was the law of Russia on that never-to-be-forgotten day when her fleet sailed into the harbor of New York during the Civil War. That was the law of Germany, whose ships are lying unable to proceed to sea in the harbors of New York, Boston, Philadelphia, and other ports. There was no escape from the capture of any vessel from one of these belligerents by the cruisers of another belligerent which might chance to meet her, notwithstanding the transfer to the American flag, except to compel these great nations to abandon the law they have held for generations.

Mr. WILLIAMS. I should like to ask the Senator from New York a question, if he will yield for that purpose.

Mr. ROOT. Certainly.

Mr. WILLIAMS. Notwithstanding the fact that this was the law of Russia and of France, and it has been the law of those two nations for a long time, have they not agreed during the present war to adopt the Declaration of London as their law?

Mr. ROOT. Mr. President, I have already stated that.

Mr. WILLIAMS. Then if that be true —

Mr. ROOT. I beg the Senator not to draw me on by leading me into a discussion of questions, however interesting they are, which arise in his mind, because if I do what I think I ought I have got to go through a rather complicated subject. As I have already said, the significance of the Declaration of London is that these countries who started with these perfectly strict and unyielding rules have adopted the Declaration of London as their rule for this war.

Mr. WILLIAMS. And have modified their old position to that extent.

Mr. ROOT. They have modified their old position to that extent. So, although the Declaration of London is not binding upon us as a convention, although it was never ratified, if we undertake to protect our flag upon a ship purchased from a belligerent we are driven to the Declaration of London as the basis on which we must proceed. The old law was much more strict and unyielding than the Declaration is, and that is why the Solicitor of the State Department was quite right in giving his opinion regarding the meaning of this provision of the Declaration of London, and that is why I am going on to discuss that meaning. I have taken so much time because I have frequently observed the statement about the Declaration of London, that it is not binding; that it was not ratified. If we could not have recourse to that Declaration of London, these old rules are the only thing we would meet.

We have then reached this position, that these belligerent powers — England, France, Russia, and Germany — will enforce the provision of the Declaration of London, and if we object to their enforcing that we come against still worse rules for neutral trade, that is, the old rules which three of them stated at the beginning of the conference. So their adoption of the Declaration of London is an advantage to us of which we must avail ourselves so far as practicable.

When the different countries had stated their position regarding the transfer of the flag, there was a statement prepared for the use of the conference which undertook to formulate certain propositions for discussion, basing those propositions upon the varied statements of rules by the different countries, and the basis which was formulated for discussion regarding the transfer of the flag I will now read. This is basis 35:

> A ship cannot be transferred to a neutral flag in order to escape the consequences which its quality as an enemy ship draws upon it.
> 36. The transfer effected before the opening of hostilities is valid if it has come about regularly. That is to say if it involves nothing fictitious or irregular which renders it suspicious.
> 37. After the opening of hostilities there is an absolute presumption of knowledge of the transfer which is effected while the ship is in the course of a voyage.

Upon that they proceed to a discussion. After the discussion proceeded for a considerable time these statements were made by the representatives of Germany and Great Britain. Mr. Kriege, the very able and experienced adviser of the German Foreign Office, who was the representative of that country at this conference, said:

> We are in accord with the authors of the summary upon the principle that a ship cannot be transferred to a neutral flag with a view to escape the consequences which its quality as an enemy ship draws on it, but in the point of view of existing rights and for considerations of practical order we wish to see adopted the system of our memorandum which would have the double advantage of facilitating the task of commanders of cruisers and of avoiding consequences to neutral commerce.

Mr. Crowe, one of the English delegates, explained the principle that was intended to be expressed in basis 35 — that is to say, " that a commercial man subject of a belligerent state ought not to escape the consequences of war while transferring his ships under a neutral flag, but the application of this principle it is difficult to find among the memoranda by a rule precise and generally recognized."

There you see that the German and the English representatives were drawing together upon the rule which looked not so much to what we would call good faith, as to the purpose for which the transfer was made.

A short time after, Mr. Kriege, the German representative, stated with great lucidity the actual point of difference which had been reached by the conference. I read from page 183 of this publication of the proceedings:

> Mr. Kriege exposed the manner in which, according to him, this question ought to be treated in the basis of discussion. This exposé, with the motives which have inspired it, is found treated in Annex 73.

A formal paper which he presented. I call your especial attention to it because it was a formal paper and has a very important bearing upon determining the meaning of this declaration. In this paper he says:

THE SHIP PURCHASE BILL 373

I desire to call the attention of the commission to a divergence which appears to exist between the proposition of the United States of America on the one part, and, upon the other part, the propositions of Great Britain and Germany.

Remember that our representatives and the British representatives had presented a rule which called for good faith in the transfer, and now he says:

This is a question of the meaning of the term " good faith." The propositions are, all three, in accord to prescribe that the transfers made during a war or immediately before a war are to be made in good faith.

Only it seems that, in the idea of the delegation of the United States of America, the good faith would exist if the agreement relative to the transfer was genuine and definitive and involved nothing fictitious or irregular. On the other hand the German and Britannic propositions understand by good faith the absence among the motives of the transfer of the intention to withdraw the ship from the effect of the right of capture.

You perceive this is precisely what Mr. Johnson in his opinion says does not exist in the declaration. Let me read it again:

On the other hand the German and British propositions understand by good faith the absence among the motives of transfer of the intention to withdraw the ship from the effect of the right of capture.

In the sense of these propositions as according to the original text of basis 35 the transfer would be null and without effect from the moment when it should have been induced by the desire of the vendor to put himself under protection from the loss which the confiscation of the ship would inflict upon him. The transfer would be, on the contrary, recognized as valid when there was ground to believe that it would have been effected also if the war had not arisen or had not been imminent at the moment of the conclusion of the contract.

After that presentation of the precise point in difference which had been reached between the delegates of the United States on the one hand and the delegates of these other powers, including England and Germany, on the other hand, the subject was submitted to a drafting committee to endeavor to formulate a rule which would be satisfactory, and I now wish to call your attention to the report of that committee. I will say, in order to indicate the materiality of the report, that it contains the rule which now appears in the declaration. It was presented in the ninth session of the commission — that is, with the conference sitting as in committee of the whole — on February 6, 1909. I read the record of proceedings:

> The delegation of the United States of America made a reserve on the subject of the first article of the rule —

which was reported upon the transfer of a flag, and the committee of the whole, the commission, adopted the report with the understanding that the part to which the American delegates objected, upon which they made their reserve, was to be reconsidered, and not deemed as adopted. That reserve of the American delegates appears on page 290 of these proceedings. By reference to it, we find that it related not at all to the transfer of the flag after the opening of hostilities, but related solely to the transfer of the flag before the opening of hostilities. They say:

> The American delegation regrets to find itself obliged to make a reserve upon the first article of the regulation relative to the transfer of flag. It considers that a rule which says, " The transfer to a neutral flag of an enemy ship before the opening of hostilities is valid, unless it shall be established that the transfer has been effected with a view to escape the consequences which the enemy character of the ship draws upon it," is not in accord with the spirit of modern rules adopted at The Hague concerning war, which have for their end to guarantee the security of international commerce against the surprises of war and wishing, conformably to modern practice, to protect as much as possible the operations engaged in in good faith and in course of execution before the beginning of hostilities.

The report was reconsidered upon that reserve. You perceive the American delegates accepted the rule which related to transfers after the beginning of hostilities, but objected to the rule relating to transfers before. A compromise was made. Under that compromise a new provision making a

THE SHIP PURCHASE BILL 375

distinction between transfers thirty days before and less than thirty days before the opening of hostilities, was made. Upon that our delegates agreed; that is to say, they got a rule which made all transfers more than thirty days before the war valid, if they were real; they got a rule which made all transfers at any time valid if they were not made with the motive of avoiding the risk of war. Before thirty days they were valid even though they were made with that motive; after thirty days they were valid unless they had that motive. On that they agreed.

When the drafting committee came to make its report to the committee of the whole, there was a full discussion of the question which Mr. Kriege had brought up by his very lucid statement of the different views as to what constituted good faith. That report leaves no doubt as to the meaning of this regulation, and no doubt whatever that the advice which has been given to the State Department and communicated to us as a basis for this legislation, is erroneous. The report says — I read from pages 326 and 327 of the proceedings of the conference, translating, I hope, with substantial correctness.

The report has just stated the rules as I have read them, the rules as they were finally adopted. The report says of those rules:

> The validity of the transfer is at the beginning subordinated to the accomplishment of certain judicial conditions, having for their object to show that the proprietor has been divested in a definitive manner and without reserve of his title to the ship over which he should preserve no control. If these conditions have not been fulfilled, for example, if the effect of the transfer has been subordinated to the eventualities of the war, the transfer is presumed to have taken place with the intention of shunning the consequences of the war, and it is declared null.
>
> This is simple.
>
> Behold the difficult point. All the juridical conditions have been fulfilled; but the captor is able to establish that the transfer, regular in substance and in form, has been effected with a view to escaping the con-

sequences which the enemy character entails. Will he be permitted to make this proof in order to arrive at the result of declaring the transfer void, or will the intention of avoiding the consequences of the war result only from the failure to accomplish the juridical conditions? It has appeared doubtful to some. It has been recalled that the condition of good faith was exacted in a distinct manner, independently of juridical conditions, and that so, even if these conditions were fulfilled, one could prove that the sale had been made in bad faith; but how is this to be understood? It is a delicate point. The captor evidently will not view " good faith " in the same manner as the vendor. The vendor will consider that he acts honestly if he divests himself regularly and definitively of his ships, because he does not wish to run the risk of losing them by the exercise of the right of prize. The captor will think that there has not been good faith in wishing to escape from the consequences of war. If one considers the simple juridical interpretation, it seems, indeed, that a prize court, in the presence of the proposition reported above, would hold the transfer valid because the juridical conditions had been fulfilled, and would not place itself in the point of view of the captor in order to consider if there had been good or bad faith.

The majority of the committee did not accept this result, and accordingly, desiring an unequivocal formula, the following has been adopted:

The transfer to the neutral flag of an enemy ship effected before the opening of the hostilities is valid, unless it should be established that the transfer has been effected with a view to escape the consequences which the enemy character entails.

There, Mr. President, is a statement as plain as words can make it, that the terms which are used in the rule embraced in the declaration were substituted for the words " good faith " that our delegates were pressing for, in order that the intention to escape the consequences of the right of capture should be a separate and substantive ground for invalidating the transfer. There is no escape from that. There is no man here who could state with greater certainty and lucidity the purpose of the rule than it is stated in this report by Mr. Renault, the greatest of living teachers of international law, and the official adviser of the French foreign office.

That report of the drafting committee was adopted by the committee of the whole; it was made by the committee of the whole to the conference in plenary session, and it was adopted by the conference. If the conference could have heard read the advice given to our State Department and laid before the Senate as the basis of this legislation, it could not have controverted the conclusion of that advice in more positive and more unambiguous terms. I can find no words in which to show that the Solicitor for the State Department was wrong in his advice so clear as the words of Mr. Renault in this report.

Mr. SUTHERLAND. Mr. President, will the Senator permit me to ask him a question?

The PRESIDING OFFICER. Does the Senator from New York yield to the Senator from Utah?

Mr. ROOT. Certainly.

Mr. SUTHERLAND. I understand the Senator from New York to have shown that in addition to there having been payment in consideration and bona fides, in the usual meaning of that term, it must also appear that the ship was not transferred in order that the capture of it might be avoided. If it should turn out that the vendor transferred it with that desire; that is, that he transferred it in order that it might not be captured, and the vendee did not participate in that intention, would that be sufficient to meet the requirements of the rule, or does it require that there should be a participation on the part of both the vendor and the vendee in the desire to avoid capture?

Mr. ROOT. Clearly, Mr. President, the motive is a motive which is ascribed to the vendor. It is he who is seeking to take his ship out of the danger of capture; it is he who will substitute the valuable consideration that is necessary in place of the vessel that he cannot use except at the risk of capture. The vendee prior to the transaction has no motive whatever in regard to the ship. It is the owner of the ship who escapes from the effect that the enemy character of the ship brings upon it.

Mr. WALSH. Mr. President —

The PRESIDING OFFICER. Does the Senator from New York yield to the Senator from Montana?

Mr. ROOT. Certainly.

Mr. WALSH. The distinguished Senator has been giving us the propositions upon this important question submitted by the representatives of the various nations in response to the suggestion of the British Government. As I recall, a statement came from France as well as from Germany. Will the Senator kindly advise us whether the American delegates stated for the benefit of the conference, in response to the invitation, the position of our Government?

Mr. ROOT. Mr. President, the American delegates did not upon this point present any memorandum as to the position of the United States at the outset, but shortly after the discussion began they did present a statement of their views.

Mr. WALSH. They were called upon to make a formal statement of the position taken by their Government, together with the authorities which they desired to submit in support of the view taken. Will the Senator, who then was Secretary of State, advise us as to why our delegates did not comply with that request?

Mr. ROOT. Because the delegates of the United States presented, as the basis of their position upon the whole range of questions, the naval war code and discussions of the Naval War College, and it was deemed wiser, as those discussions covered the entire range, not to attempt to commit them to any more definite and precise statement.

Mr. WALSH. Are we to understand the Senator, then, that they did not make a definite statement on any of the seven propositions submitted by the Government of Great Britain?

Mr. ROOT. I do not remember about the others; I have not examined the facts as to them.

Mr. WALSH. Very well. Will the Senator have the kindness to advise us in that connection if the delegates from Austria-Hungary made a statement as to the position of their Government, and, if it is brief, will he give it to us?

Mr. ROOT. They made a statement, and the representatives of various other countries made statements. The delegates of Austria-Hungary made a statement which was much nearer in its view to the position of Great Britain and the United States than it was to the position of France and Russia.

Mr. WALSH. My recollection is that the delegates from Austria-Hungary made a statement to the effect that the French doctrine was entirely obsolete and had been disregarded by France.

Mr. ROOT. They did not go so far as that. They said in their statement that it was too strict, and that France had modified it or varied from it in the war of 1870; but we can hardly take the statement of Austria-Hungary regarding the position of France as against the formal official statement of France herself.

Now, I want to give credence to what I have said about what happened in this conference, by reading from a distinguished publicist, a professor in the University of Vienna, Professor von Ferneck, who was one of the Austrian delegates to the conference of London. I read from an article by him in the *Handbuch des Völkerrechts*, for 1914. He says, in chapter 5, under the heading "Transfer of the Flag":

> It may well be said that this subject, which is perhaps of much less importance to neutrals than that of contraband or of blockade, was the object of extraordinary attention on the part of the conference.

Omitting some irrelevant remarks, he proceeds:

> For some time it seemed as though an unanimous solution of this question could not be reached. The reason for this was that the interests in the subject on the part of the powers represented at the conference were of

a widely differing character, and that the laws and the customs of different states are dissimilar in important respects. The United States of America, France, Italy, the Netherlands, and Russia recognize without exception the transfer of enemy merchant ships to a neutral flag when the transfer is completed before the outbreak of the war; Germany, France, and Russia declare without exception as null and void any transfer of flag made after the outbreak of the war — these are strict, uncompromising solutions that may indeed be understood from a theoretical point of view, but in practice lead to difficulties.

Several of the powers, among them Great Britain, the American Union, and Germany insisted that in order to be valid in law, the transfer must have been intended in " good faith," and according to the American interpretation " good faith " meant not fictitious, while the other powers understood by " good faith " that the owner himself must not have intended to make it impossible for the opponent to seize the ship.

You will perceive that this statement answers the question put by the Senator from Utah [Mr. Sutherland], and it states in few words just what Mr. Renault's report says.

The other powers —

says Professor von Ferneck —

understood by " good faith " that the owner must not have intended to make it impossible for the opponent to seize the ship.

And so, as Mr. Renault's report said, in order that they might have an unequivocal expression, because there were these two views of " good faith," they put in a rule which states in so many words the second view, according to Professor von Ferneck, that " the owner must not have intended to make it impossible for the opponent to seize the ship." He proceeds:

By a remarkable argument, the American delegation controverted the idea that the shipowner could not protect himself against the prize law by transferring his ship to a neutral flag. . . .

At the second session of the commission, the delegates were evidently eager to reach an agreement that would avoid the harshness of the consequent enforcement of a principle: The transfer of the flag effected before the outbreak of the war should be regarded as valid, the transfer after the outbreak of the war as invalid; in both cases the presumption might be refuted by counter evidence. In the course of the third meeting of the commission the question regarding the elaboration of "special rules regarding the transfer previous and the transfer subsequent to the opening of the hostilities" was referred to the investigating committee. This committee made its report at the ninth session of the commission. The rules which this committee had elaborated met the idea of the agreement, but did not meet with the full approval of the American delegation, for the reason that they did not take into account the thought developed in the declaration referred to above. In order to overcome this difficulty, the representatives of Great Britain proposed at the eleventh session of the commission "in the interest of neutral commerce" to add the following: ". . . there shall be absolute presumption of validity, if the transfer was effected more than thirty days before the opening of the hostilities, provided it is in absolute and complete conformity with the laws of the countries interested, and has for its object that the control over the ship and over the earnings resulting from its use does not remain in the same hands that exercised this control before the transfer." To this the American delegation agreed; it yielded in principle, but obtained a practically important concession. The question of "good faith" might be raised only with regard to such ships as were transferred within the last thirty days before the outbreak of the war.

I find, Mr. President, that Italy upon two occasions since the conference of London has applied the rule. In the *Revue Générale de Droit International Public*, of September-October, 1913, there is a report of the case of the sailing vessel *Vasilios* and of the sailing vessel *Aghios Georghios*, Greek ships, or ships flying the Greek flag, which had been Turkish vessels at the opening of the war between Italy and Turkey, and had been sold to a Greek citizen, admitted to Greek registry, and were flying the Greek flag. The ships were seized, condemned, and sold. So that we may add Italy to the powers which have adopted this rule of the Declaration of London.

Germany has put herself upon the same basis, in terms which leave no possible doubt. I read from the Prize Ordinance of September 30, 1909, published in the *Law Gazette* of the Empire for 1914, No. 50:

I approve the accompanying prize ordinance, and direct that in the enforcement of the prize law my fleet commanders shall, during the war, proceed in accordance with the provisions of the prize ordinance. In so far as it may be necessary to make exception thereto in special cases, you shall make proposition to that end to me. I empower you to give such interpretation to this ordinance and to make such changes thereto as may be necessary, provided they are not of fundamental importance.

In the absence of the Imperial Counselor.
(Signed)   WILHELM.
(Countersigned)   v. TIRPITZ.

Dated September 30, 1909. Promulgated at Berlin, August 3, 1914, the date of the beginning of the war.

The ordinance, section II, is as follows:

Enemy ships and their cargoes. — With the exceptions specified under 6 —

which are not relevant here; they relate to cartel ships, hospital ships, etc. —

With the exceptions specified under 6, enemy ships are subject to capture.

Ships are adjudged enemy or neutral ships by the flag they are entitled to carry.

The flag which a ship is entitled to carry is determined in accordance with the flag law of almost all maritime states from an official document that any merchant ship must have on board.

If the nationality of a ship cannot be readily established, and especially if the document required in accordance with the flag law of the respective state is not in evidence, then the ship shall be considered as an enemy ship.

Ships that after the outbreak of the hostilities have been transferred from the enemy to the neutral flag are also to be considered as enemy ships —

(a) If the commander is not convinced that the transfer would have followed, even if war had not broken out, as, for instance, by succession, or by virtue of a construction contract.

(b), (c), and (d) pertain to matters which are not relevant.

That points to the German understanding of the rule; and I will say that in the final report of the London conference, which is printed in this document containing the solicitor's opinion, an illustration is given of the meaning of the rule — that is, for instance, " in case of inheritance."

Applying these illustrations, the rule becomes plain. The ordinary trade in ships is not to be prevented. Trade in the

THE SHIP PURCHASE BILL 383

ordinary course of business is not to be prevented. The ordinary devolution of property is not to be interfered with. If the owner of a ship belonging to a belligerent dies, the property may devolve upon a neutral. The rule does not prevent it, and the neutral flag will protect it. If you or I have ordered a ship from a shipyard in Germany or Great Britain, and the ship is constructed, and we take it, if the ship was ordered before the war and the transfer was made after the war, that transfer is manifestly in the ordinary course of business, as the German rule says, under a construction contract. But none of these great nations will permit a citizen of an enemy to rob it of its prize by transferring to a neutral the ships it is entitled to capture on the high seas.

Mr. President, we are not bound by that; but that is the state of the law of England, France, Germany, Russia, Italy, and I presume the allies of these countries, and that is what we have to run up against if we buy these belligerent ships; for of course no one will contend for a moment that the Hamburg-American Line or the North German Lloyd Line is selling its ships in the ordinary course of business, or for any reason other than that they cannot go out on the ocean and carry on their business; and no one would doubt it if we were to buy a British ship and put it in the Bremen trade or the Hamburg trade. There can be no purchase now of ships that have been lying idle six months, under the conditions of this war, that is not stamped with a purpose that invalidates the transfer under the rule of the Declaration of London equally with those old and more severe rules which were presented at the beginning of the conference.

But, Mr. President, I have been considering this subject as if an American citizen were to buy. I have said about that, that we are not bound by the rules of these countries. We are at liberty to say: "Our rule is different, and we insist upon its being applied." I have always believed in that rule, sir. I believe in it now. I instructed our delegates to the Second Hague Conference to urge upon the conference the immunity of all private property at sea in time of war. Our delegates fought loyally for the rule which our courts applied, and which is in furtherance of that beneficent and liberal rule. But there is the law of Europe, and against that we will come; and I repeat, it is their law that will be enforced in the treatment of this subject. We should be left to protest and attempt to get them or some court of arbitration to abandon their rule and adopt ours. How easy it would be, sir, for us to bring that about through the voluntary action of any country or the action of any court of arbitration, in view of the fact that they have adopted the rule of the Declaration of London to which our delegates finally agreed, to which our Government agreed in sending it to the Senate for ratification, and to which the Senate agreed by advising and consenting to the ratification, I shall not discuss.

But, says the Secretary of the Treasury, the Government of the United States could not be involved in any difficulty if it were to buy these ships — that is to say, if this proposed corporation were to buy the ships:

> Some timid people have argued that if the Government is interested as a stockholder in a shipping company, and a ship of such company should be seized by a belligerent and brought into a prize court, the sovereignty of the Government would be involved. There is no ground whatever for this view.

I am sorry to write myself down in the category of timid people, but I must, for I do not agree with the Secretary of the Treasury in the idea that there is no ground whatever for this view; and I am filled with apprehension by the idea of putting these vast powers into the hands of a man who thinks there is no ground whatever for that view.

A question was put to the counselor of the State Department, Mr. Lansing, before the Committee on Naval Affairs

THE SHIP PURCHASE BILL 385

of the House. I read from the hearings on Senate Bill 5259 and H. R. 5980, dated August 20, 1914:

> Mr. WILLIAMS. The first question that we want information on, as a legal proposition, is the liability that would attach to this Government if the Government itself was operating a line of steamships engaged in the transportation of goods to South America and to European countries compared with the liability of a steamship company or an individual engaged in the same business. Can you give us some information along these lines?
>
> Mr. LANSING. I suppose you refer to neutrality and to the question of contraband?
>
> Mr. WILLIAMS. Yes, sir.
>
> Mr. LANSING. I think that the transportation of contraband to a belligerent port in a public ship of the United States would go much further than the mere matter of liability, and that it would be regarded as an unneutral act.
>
> Mr. WILLIAMS. That the United States transporting goods to English, French, or German ports would be a violation of neutrality?
>
> Mr. LANSING. I think it might be so regarded.

That is what we have to deal with. That is what the Secretary of the Treasury does deal with in the words I have read from him. He says:

> If the Government operated ships outright, just as it operates the vessels of our navy, an awkward situation of this character might arise; but where a nation is merely a stockholder, or the sole stockholder, in a private corporation, its sovereignty is not and cannot be directly involved if the ships of such a corporation become the subjects of litigation in a prize court concerning any issue which does not involve the Government itself. The Government would stand in relation to such a corporation exactly as any individual stockholder does to a corporation in which he is interested. A suit against the corporation does not necessarily involve the shareholders.

Mr. President, that is not the law as it has been understood by the Government of the United States, or as it has been applied. In the Delagoa Bay case our Government went straight through the legal fiction of a Portuguese corporation and asserted and enforced the rights of American citizens who were stockholders of that corporation, precisely as if they had been the owners themselves. The British Government did the same thing in the same case. Time and again the rule which was established in that case has been applied to the affairs of these legal fictions which give to the real owners of property the municipal right of succession and limitation of liability and the use of a corporate seal, etc. Of course, Mr. President, it stands to reason that a municipal statute giving to A and B and C rights to sue and be sued in corporate form and to have limitation of liability and to act through a seal, is no concern of another Government if A and B and C, through that form, have injured or affected the rights of that other Government. The idea is idle and baseless that the Government of the United States, by the exercise of its vast national power, can wrest enormous funds from its people by taxation, can use those funds to withdraw from Germany's right of capture British ships and from France's and Great Britain's right of capture of German ships, and say: " I cannot be called to account because I have made a statute under which I protect myself by a legal fiction, calling myself a trading corporation." Ah, no! the real and serious affairs of this world are not conducted in that way. Whatever we do through this corporation that we create and own, we do as a government, and are responsible for as a government.

In the case of the *Parlement Belge*, which was referred to the other day by the Senator from Massachusetts [Mr. Lodge], the courts of England were called upon to consider the effects of government ownership. The Government of Belgium owned a boat plying across the Channel from Ostend to some British port, much like our municipal ferries, and the question was raised, whether being a trading boat engaged solely in trading operations, it was to be treated as subject to the laws relating to trading ships or was to have the immunities which pertained to government ships. The court below held that it was subject to the laws relating to trading ships. The court above reversed the decision, and held that,

THE SHIP PURCHASE BILL

being the property of the Government of Belgium, it was immune from the English laws relating to trading ships. The reality of things, sir, prevents us from escaping by any possibility from responsibility for the use of our national power to withdraw any belligerent ships that we may now purchase from the right of capture on the part of the other belligerents, whether we proceed by the fiction of a corporation or directly.

There is only one possible escape from the condemnation and forfeiture of a prize court for every ship of this kind that is purchased. That is the possible protection of the sovereignty of the United States, preferring to occupy the position of violating neutrality rather than to submit to condemnation.

What is the meaning, sir, of the violation of neutrality? It means taking sides in the controversy. It means helping one belligerent against another. It means that after all our proclamations and our efforts, we abandon the attempt to be neutral, and we take sides in the great conflict; and we cannot stop. We cannot measure the number of steps. One unneutral act by us will lead to acts by others that will compel further acts by us, more acts by others and more by us and more by them, until we are in the thick of the controversy.

Remember, sir, the condition of the world today. I am arguing against the Government of the United States buying, not a ship, but an international quarrel with every ship. Somebody said to me: "It is buying a claim, not a ship." No. It is buying a quarrel, not a ship; and I say, remember the condition of the world. Recall to your minds all that you have read during the past six months of the condition of feeling on the part of the people in all these countries — England, Belgium, France, Germany, Russia, Servia, all of them — tense to the highest degree, in that condition of exaltation which holds prudence for naught.

Why, sir, we were ready to fight, from Mason and Dixon's line to Canada, on the instant, when Mason and Slidell were taken from the *Trent*, and Great Britain mobilized her fleet. It was ruin for the North if we fought — certain ruin. We could not stand against the gallant South and against mighty England. Our blockade would be gone; but we were ready to fight, because every heart of the North was full of emotion, and every nature was tense with feeling, and we cared naught for prudence. That is Europe today.

If we are going to maintain our neutrality, we must hold close to it, and keep out of all needless causes of controversy. And let us remember ourselves. We have kept, hitherto, a united America. We have stood behind the President in his neutrality proclamations. Here and there fault has been found on one side or the other, but we have stood by him; but do not forget that there are here millions of Germans who love their Fatherland, and I honor them for it. I should think less of them if their natures were not awakened by the peril and the stress of the land that gave birth to them and their fathers. They are alive and tense. There are millions of men of English blood, born and bred with a love for Anglo-Saxon liberty and the laws that we inherited from England. Do not imagine that they are not thinking and feeling, and if you precipitate this country into a controversy where Europe feels and acts upon the belief that we have taken sides, we shall rend ourselves.

No; the only safe course is to keep out of unnecessary controversial questions with as great care and conservatism and caution as possible, for we never can tell where a controversy will lead us.

Mr. President, I deeply regret that any shade of party politics has fallen upon the consideration of this measure. We have in the Senate long felt that it was our duty to lay aside party when we reach the water's edge. We have considered

THE SHIP PURCHASE BILL 389

the terms of treaties and advised the President, of whatever party, in accordance with the best of our judgment and our conscience. When we have reached the water's edge we have said we leave party.

This bill proposes a business which is all beyond the water's edge — international in its aspect and in its purpose. It is international at a time of intense emotion and certain controversy. I wish we could have considered it — I wish we could consider it now — as Americans earnest for the peace and prosperity of our country, forgetful of party.

Mr. President and Senators, there is no crime against our country so wicked as the crime of conducting our international relations with a view to party popularity. The two considerations are incompatible, and cannot exist at the same time in any mind. He who has charge of our foreign affairs must deal with them regardless of the effect upon his political future or his party's advantage, or he cannot deal with them as the public safety demands. The man who is considering his political future and his party's advantage should keep out of foreign relations. The two cannot coexist.

One incident for which I impute blame to no one has recently happened which illustrates what I say. The note that was sent by our State Department to Great Britain a short time ago regarding the search for contraband, endeavoring to remedy serious evils of delay and perhaps indifference in making the search for contraband, which is admittedly the right of belligerents, was a moderate, a reasonable, and a proper note. No one in the world had a right to find fault with it. But before the note was delivered in Great Britain and before it was made public here, the newspapers were filled by somebody, I do not know whom, with an account of it, far, far from the truth, with an account of it which pictured the Administration as standing up against frightful odds and dreadful danger for a view of American rights which no serious student of international law ever thought of asserting and which the note did not assert. Both this country and England were filled with an erroneous view of that note and that erroneous view persists. It could have been given for no other purpose than a political purpose and it was a crime against the American people and against the peace of the world to misrepresent it.

I will not proceed. I will not specify or illustrate further. I will close what I have to say by expressing the most fervent hope that we may deal both in this great deliberative body and in the executive department of the Government with this serious, grave question as lovers of our country, with all the wisdom and experience and ability that we can bring to our country's service.

THE OUTLOOK FOR INTERNATIONAL LAW

PRESIDENTIAL ADDRESS AT THE NINTH ANNUAL MEETING
OF THE AMERICAN SOCIETY OF INTERNATIONAL LAW
WASHINGTON, DECEMBER 28, 1915

THE incidents of the great war now raging affect so seriously the very foundations of international law that there is for the moment but little satisfaction to the student of that science in discussing specific rules. Whether or not Sir Edward Carson went too far in his recent assertion that the law of nations has been destroyed, it is manifest that the structure has been rudely shaken. The barriers that statesmen and jurists have been constructing laboriously for three centuries to limit and direct the conduct of nations toward each other, in conformity to the standards of modern civilization, have proved too weak to confine the tremendous forces liberated by a conflict which involves almost the whole military power of the world and in which the destinies of nearly every civilized state outside the American continents are directly at stake.

The war began by a denial on the part of a very great power that treaties are obligatory when it is no longer for the interest of either of the parties to observe them. The denial was followed by action supported by approximately one half the military power of Europe and is apparently approved by a great number of learned students and teachers of international law, citizens of the countries supporting the view. This position is not an application of the doctrine *rebus sic stantibus* which justifies the termination of a treaty under circumstances not contemplated when the treaty was made so that it is no longer justly applicable to existing conditions. It is that under the very circumstances contemplated by the treaty and under the conditions for which the treaty was intended to provide the treaty is not obligatory as against the interest of the contracting party.

This situation naturally raises the question whether executory treaties will continue to be made if they are not to be binding, and requires consideration of a system of law under which no conventional obligations are recognized. The particular treaty which was thus set aside was declaratory of the general rule of international law respecting the inviolability of neutral territory; and the action which ignored the treaty also avowedly violated the rule of law, and the defense is that for such a violation of the law the present interest of a sovereign state is justification. It is plain that the application of such a principle to a matter of major importance at the beginning of a long conflict must inevitably be followed by the setting aside of other rules as they are found to interfere with interest or convenience; and that has been the case during the present war. Many of the rules of law which the world has regarded as most firmly established have been completely and continuously disregarded, in the conduct of war, in dealing with the property and lives of civilian non-combatants on land and sea and in the treatment of neutrals. Alleged violations by one belligerent have been asserted to justify other violations by other belligerents. The art of war has been developed through the invention of new instruments of destruction and it is asserted that the changes of conditions thus produced make the old rules obsolete.

It is not my purpose at this time to discuss the right or wrong of these declarations and actions. Such a discussion would be quite inadmissible on the part of the presiding officer of this meeting. I am stating things which whether right or wrong have unquestionably happened, as bearing upon the branch of jurisprudence to which this Society is devoted. It seems that if the violation of law justifies other violations, then the law is destroyed and there is no law; that if the discovery of new ways of doing a thing prohibited justifies the doing of it, then there is no law to prohibit. The basis of such assertions really is the view that if a substantial belligerent interest for the injury of the enemy come in conflict with a rule of law, the rule must stand aside and the interest must prevail. If that be so it is not difficult to reach the conclusion that for the present at all events in all matters which affect the existing struggle, international law is greatly impaired. Nor can we find much encouragement to believe in the binding force of any rules upon nations which observe other rules only so far as their interest at the time prompts them. Conditions are always changing and a system of rules which ceases to bind whenever conditions change should hardly be considered a system of law. It does not follow that nations can no longer discuss questions of right in their diplomatic intercourse, but upon such a basis it seems quite useless to appeal to the authority of rules already agreed upon as just and right and to their compelling effect because they have been already agreed upon.

When we recall Mansfield's familiar description of international law as " founded upon justice, equity, convenience, the reason of the thing, and confirmed by long usage," we may well ask ourselves whether that general acceptance which is necessary to the establishment of a rule of international law may be withdrawn by one or several nations and the rule be destroyed by that withdrawal so that the usage ceases and the whole subject to which it relates goes back to its original status as matter for new discussion as to what is just, equitable, convenient and reasonable.

When this war is ended, as it must be some time, and the foreign offices and judicial tribunals and publicists of the world resume the peaceable discussion of international rights and duties, they will certainly have to consider not merely what there is left of certain specific rules, but also the fundamental basis of obligation upon which all rules depend. The civilized world will have to determine whether what we call international law is to be continued as a mere code of etiquette or is to be a real body of laws imposing obligations much more definite and inevitable than they have been heretofore. It must be one thing or the other. Although foreign offices can still discuss what is fair and just and what is expedient and wise, they cannot appeal to law for the decision of disputed questions unless the appeal rests upon an obligation to obey the law. What course will the nations follow?

Vague and uncertain as the future must be, there is some reason to think that after the terrible experience through which civilization is passing, there will be a tendency to strengthen rather than abandon the law of nations. Whatever the result may be, the world will have received a dreadful lesson of the evils of war. The sacrifice of millions of lives, millions homeless and in poverty, industry and commerce destroyed, overwhelming national debts, — all will naturally produce a strong desire to do something that will prevent the same thing happening again.

While the war has exhibited the inadequacy of international law, so far as it has yet developed, to curb those governmental policies which aim to extend power at all costs, it has shown even more clearly that little reliance can be placed upon unrestrained human nature, subject to specific temptation, to commit forcible aggression in the pursuit of power and wealth. It has shown that where questions of conduct are to be determined under no constraint except the circumstances of the particular case, the acquired habits of civilization are weak as against the powerful, innate tendencies which survive from the countless centuries of man's struggle for existence against brutes and savage foes. The only means yet discovered by man to limit those tendencies consist in the establishment of law, the setting up of principles of action and definite rules of conduct which cannot be violated by the individual without injury to himself. That is the method by which the wrongs naturally flowing from individual impulse within the state have been confined to narrow limits. That analogy, difficult as it is to maintain in view of the differences between the individual who is subject to sovereignty and the nation which is itself sovereign, indicates the only method to which human experience points to avoid repeating the present experience of these years of war consistently with the independence of nations and the liberty of individuals. The *Pax Romana* was effective only because the world was subject to Rome. The Christian Church has been urging peace and good-will among men for nineteen centuries, and still there is this war. Concerts of Europe and alliances and ententes and skillful balances of power all lead ultimately to war. Conciliation, good-will, love of peace, human sympathy, are ineffective without institutions through which they can act. Only the possibility of establishing real restraint by law seems to remain to give effect to the undoubted will of the vast majority of mankind.

In the effort to arrange the affairs of the world so that they will not lead to another great catastrophe, men will therefore turn naturally towards the re-establishment and strengthening of the law of nations. How can that be done? How can the restraints of law be made more effective upon nations?

It is not difficult to suggest some things which will tend in that direction.

Laws to be obeyed must have sanctions behind them; that is to say, violations of them must be followed by punishment. That punishment must be caused by power superior to the law-breaker; it cannot consist merely in the possibility of being defeated in a conflict with an enemy; otherwise there would be no law as between the strong and the weak. Many states have grown so great that there is no power capable of imposing punishment upon them except the power of collective civilization outside of the offending state. Any exercise of that power must be based upon public opinion. It cannot rest merely upon written agreements or upon the accidental dictates of particular interests. It must proceed from general, concurrent judgment and condemnation. When that exists, punishment may be inflicted either by the direct action of governments, forcible or otherwise, or by the terrible consequences which come upon a nation that finds itself without respect or honor in the world and deprived of the confidence and good-will necessary to the maintenance of intercourse. Without such an opinion behind it, no punishment of any kind can be imposed for the violation of international law.

For the formation of such a general opinion, however, questions of national conduct must be reduced to simple and definite form. Occasionally there is an act the character of which is so clear that mankind forms a judgment upon it readily and promptly, but in most cases it is easy for the wrongdoer to becloud the issue by assertion and argument and to raise a complicated and obscure controversy which confuses the judgment of the world. There is but one way to make general judgment possible in such cases. That is by bringing them to the decision of a competent court which will strip away the irrelevant, reject the false, and declare what the law requires or prohibits in the particular case. Such a court of international justice with a general obligation to submit all justiciable questions to its jurisdiction and to abide by its judgment is a primary requisite to any real restraint of law.

When we come to consider the working of an international court, however, we are forced to realize that the law itself is

OUTLOOK FOR INTERNATIONAL LAW 397

in many respects imperfect and uncertain. There is no legislature to make laws for nations. There is no body of judicial decisions having the effect of precedent to declare what international laws are. The process of making international law by usage and general acceptance has been necessarily so slow that it has not kept pace with the multiplying questions arising in the increasing intercourse of nations. In many fields of most fruitful controversy different nations hold tenaciously to different rules, as, for recent example, upon the right of expatriation, upon the doctrine of continuous voyages, upon the right to transfer merchant vessels after the outbreak of a war. Yet any attempt to maintain a court of international justice must fail unless there are laws for the court to administer. Without them the so-called court would be merely a group of men seeking to impose their personal opinions upon the states coming before them. The lack of an adequate system of law to be applied has been the chief obstacle to the development of a system of judicial settlement of international disputes. This is well illustrated by the history of the convention for an international prize court adopted by the Second Hague Conference. The Conference agreed to establish such a court and provided in article seven of the treaty that in the absence of special treaty provisions governing the case presented " the Court shall apply the rules of international law. If no generally recognized rule exists, the Court shall give judgment in accordance with the general principles of justice and equity." When the question of ratifying this treaty was presented to the Powers whose delegates had signed it, some of them awoke to the fact that upon many subjects most certain to call for the action of a court there was no general agreement as to what the rules of international law were, and that different nations had different ideas as to what justice and equity would require, and that each judge would naturally follow the views of his own country. Accordingly the Conference of London was called, and met in December, 1908. In that Conference the delegates of the principal maritime powers came to agreement upon a series of questions and they embodied their agreement in the seventy-one articles of the Declaration of London. If that Declaration had been ratified by all the Powers in the Conference, it would doubtless have been accepted as a statement of the international law upon the subjects covered. But it was not ratified, and so the Prize Court treaty remains ineffective because the necessary basis for the action of the Court is wanting. It is plain that in order to have real courts by which the legal rights of nations can be determined and the conduct of nations can be subjected to definite tests, there must be a settlement by agreement of old disputes as to what the law ought to be and provision for extending the law over fields which it does not now cover. One thing especially should be done in this direction. Law cannot control national policy, and it is through the working of long-continued and persistent national policies that the present war has come. Against such policies all attempts at conciliation and good understanding and good-will among the nations of Europe have been powerless. But law, if enforced, can control the external steps by which a nation seeks to follow a policy, and rules may be so framed that a policy of aggression cannot be worked out except through open violations of law which will meet the protest and condemnation of the world at large, backed by whatever means shall have been devised for law enforcement.

There is another weakness of international law as a binding force which it appears to me can be avoided only by a radical change in the attitude of nations towards violations of the law.

We are all familiar with the distinction in the municipal law of all civilized countries, between private and public rights and the remedies for the protection or enforcement of them. Ordinary injuries and breaches of contract are redressed only at the instance of the injured person, and other persons are not deemed entitled to interfere. It is no concern of theirs. On the other hand, certain flagrant wrongs the prevalence of which would threaten the order and security of the community are deemed to be everybody's business. If, for example, a man be robbed or assaulted, the injury is deemed not to be done to him alone, but to every member of the state by the breaking of the law against robbery or against violence. Every citizen is deemed to be injured by the breach of the law because the law is his protection, and if the law be violated with impunity, his protection will disappear. Accordingly, the government, which represents all its citizens, undertakes to punish such action even though the particular person against whom the injury was done may be content to go without redress. Up to this time breaches of international law have been treated as we treat wrongs under civil procedure, as if they concerned nobody except the particular nation upon which the injury was inflicted and the nation inflicting it. There has been no general recognition of the right of other nations to object. There has been much international discussion of what the rules of law ought to be and the importance of observing them in the abstract, and there have been frequent interferences by third parties as a matter of policy upon the ground that specific, consequential injury to them might result from the breach; but, in general, states not directly affected by the particular injury complained of have not been deemed to have any right to be heard about it. It is only as disinterested mediators in the quarrels of others or as rendering good offices to others that they have been accustomed to speak of it at all. Until the First Hague Conference that form of interference was upon sufferance. In the Convention for the Pacific

Settlement of International Disputes, concluded at that Conference, it was agreed that in case of serious trouble or conflict, before an appeal to arms the signatory powers should have recourse to the good offices or mediation of foreign powers, and article three also provided: "Independent of this recourse, the signatory powers recommend that one or more powers, strangers to the dispute, should on their own initiative and as far as circumstances may allow, offer their good offices or mediation to the states at variance. Powers strangers to the dispute have a right to offer good offices or mediation even during the course of hostilities. The exercise of this right can never be regarded by one or other of the parties in conflict as an unfriendly act." These provisions are a considerable step towards a change in the theory of the relation of third powers to an international controversy. They recognize such an independent interest in the prevention of conflict to be the basis of a right of initiative of other powers in an effort to bring about a settlement. It still remains under these provisions, however, that the other powers assert no substantive right of their own. They are simply authorized to propose an interference in the quarrels of others to which they are deemed to be strangers. The enforcement of the rules of international law is thus left to the private initiative of the country appealing to those rules for protection, and the rest of the world has in theory and in practice no concern with the enforcement or non-enforcement of the rules.

If the law of nations is to be binding, if the decisions of tribunals charged with the application of that law to international controversies are to be respected, there must be a change in theory, and violations of the law of such a character as to threaten the peace and order of the community of nations must be deemed to be a violation of the right of every civilized nation to have the law maintained and a legal injury to every nation. When a controversy arises between two nations, other nations are indeed strangers to the dispute as to what the law requires in that controversy, but they cannot really be strangers to a dispute as to whether the law which is applicable to the circumstances shall be observed or violated. Next to the preservation of national character, the most valuable possession of all peaceable nations, great and small, is the protection of those laws which constrain other nations to conduct based upon principles of justice and humanity. Without that protection, there is no safety for the small state, except in the shifting currents of policy among its great neighbors, and none for a great state, however peaceable and just may be its disposition, except in readiness for war. International laws violated with impunity must soon cease to exist, and every state has a direct interest in preventing those violations which, if permitted to continue, would destroy the law. Wherever in the world the laws which should protect the independence of nations, the inviolability of their territory, the lives and property of their citizens, are violated, all other nations have a right to protest against the breaking down of the law. Such a protest would not be an interference in the quarrels of others. It would be an assertion of the protesting nation's own right against the injury done to it by the destruction of the law upon which it relies for its peace and security. What would follow such a protest must in each case depend upon the protesting nation's own judgment as to policy, upon the feeling of its people and the wisdom of its governing body. Whatever it does, if it does anything, will be done not as a stranger to a dispute or as an intermediary in the affairs of others, but in its own right for the protection of its own interest. Upon no other theory than this can the decisions of any court for the application of the law of nations be respected, or any league or concert or agreement among nations for the enforcement of peace by arms or otherwise be established, or any general opinion of mankind for the maintenance of law be effective.

Can any of these things be done? Can the law be strengthened and made effective? Imperfect and conflicting as is the information upon which conjecture must be based, I think there is ground for hope that from the horrors of violated law a stronger law may come. It was during the appalling crimes of the Thirty Years War that Grotius wrote his *De Jure Belli ac Pacis* and the science of international law first took form and authority. The moral standards of the Thirty Years War have returned again to Europe with the same dreadful and intolerable consequences. We may hope that there will be again a great new departure to escape destruction by subjecting the nations to the rule of law. The development and extension of international law has been obstructed by a multitude of jealousies and supposed interests of nations each refusing to consent to any rule unless it be made most favorable to itself in all possible future contingencies. The desire to have a law has not been strong enough to overcome the determination of each nation to have the law suited to its own special circumstances; but when this war is over the desire to have some law in order to prevent so far as possible a recurrence of the same dreadful experience may sweep away all these reluctances and schemes for advantage and lead to agreement where agreement has never yet been possible. It often happens that small differences and petty controversies are swept away by a great disaster, deep feeling, and a sense of common danger. If this be so we can have an adequate law and a real court which will apply its principles to serious as well as petty controversies, and a real public opinion of the world responding to the duty of preserving the law inviolate. If there be such an opinion it will be enforced. I shall not now inquire into the specific means of enforcement, but the means can be found. It is only when opinion is uncertain and divided, or when it is sluggish and indifferent and acts too late, that it fails of effect. During all the desperate struggles and emergencies of the great war, the conflicting nations from the beginning have been competing for the favorable judgment of the rest of the world with a solicitude which shows what a mighty power even now that opinion is.

Nor can we doubt that this will be a different world when peace comes. Universal mourning for the untimely dead, suffering and sacrifice, the triumph of patriotism over selfishness, the long dominance of deep and serious feeling, the purifying influences of self-devotion, will surely have changed the hearts of the nations, and much that is wise and noble and for the good of humanity may be possible, that never was possible before.

Some of us believe that the hope of the world's progress lies in the spread and perfection of democratic self-government. It may be that out of the rack and welter of the great conflict may arise a general consciousness that it is the people who are to be considered, their rights and liberties to govern and be governed for themselves rather than rulers' ambitions and policies of aggrandizement. If that be so, our hopes will be realized, for autocracy can protect itself by arbitrary power, but the people can protect themselves only by the rule of law.

SHOULD INTERNATIONAL LAW BE CODIFIED?[1]

ADDRESS AT A SESSION OF SECTION SIX OF THE SECOND PAN-AMERICAN SCIENTIFIC CONGRESS MEETING JOINTLY WITH THE AMERICAN INSTITUTE OF INTERNATIONAL LAW AND THE AMERICAN SOCIETY OF INTERNATIONAL LAW, WASHINGTON, DECEMBER 30, 1915

The Second Pan-American Scientific Congress met in the city of Washington, December 27, 1915, and adjourned January 8, 1916. As stated by the preamble to the Final Act of this Congress, it was held " for the purpose of bringing into close and intimate contact the leaders of scientific thought and of public opinion in the American Republics, to the end that by an exchange of views results might be reached of service to the peoples of the American continent, and that by personal intercourse foundations would be laid for friendly and harmonious coöperation in the future."

An elaborate program was prepared by the Executive Committee of the United States dealing with the various phases of science, arranged in nine sections, the Sixth Section being devoted to International Law, Public Law, and Jurisprudence.

I SHALL not at this hour detain you by any extended remarks, and I should apologize for having no prepared address. The subject is one which is very interesting to me and must be very interesting, I think, to every one who thinks about international affairs or who thinks about the possibilities of the future of his country. Should international law be codified? and, if so, should it be done through governmental agencies or by private scientific societies? If that means should we undertake to put the law of nations into a single body which shall be the rule and guide for international relations, I think we must answer " No, that it is impossible at the present time." Mr. Field made a valiant

[1] The reader desiring fully to grasp Mr. Root's views on this subject, should see also his presidential address at the fifth annual meeting of the American Society of International Law, April 27, 1911, on " The Function of Private Codification in International Law," on page 57 of this volume.

attempt, and Bluntschli a great effort, but the formation of international law, still in its infancy, is a process only just begun, and it has not reached a point where the rules can be embodied in a code. On the other hand, codification, considered not as a result but as a process, seems to me plainly should be attempted and pressed forward and urged with all possible force.

It is curious that codification should be especially necessary in a system of law which is based upon custom more exclusively even than municipal law; but that is necessarily so in the case of the law of nations, because there are no legislatures to make the law and there are no judicial decisions to establish by precedent what the law is. One great weakness of international law has been that to ascertain what it was you have to go to text writers, and to a great variety of statements, differing, inconsistent, many of them obscure and vague, capable of different interpretations, so that the instant the occasion for the application of a law arises, there is pressed upon the conflicting or disputing nations the question as to what the law is, without any clear and definite standard from which to ascertain it.

Recent events, or rather the realization of the truth which comes from a great war in Europe, compels us to consider the great shortcomings of what we think of as international law, to consider how narrow the field which it covers, how vague and uncertain it is within that field, and how difficult it is to compel in any way a recognition of its rules of right conduct. There is but one way in which that weakness of international law can be cured, and that is by the process of codification, a process which must extend through long periods, which has been going on very gradually for many years. The Declaration of Paris was a little bit of codification. The three rules of the Treaty of Washington constituted a little bit of codification as between the United States and Great Britain, and they have been in substance accepted and adopted by the nations of Europe at The Hague. The Geneva Convention covered a certain field by codification, and the Hague Conventions a much wider field. So I say, considered as a conclusion, there can be no codification, but, considered as a process, there must be codification, codification pressed forward and urged on by all possible means.

The very fact that there are no courts to establish precedents and no legislatures to make laws makes this necessary. All international law is made, not by any kind of legislation, but by agreement. The agreement is based upon customs, but the ascertainment and recognition of the customs is the subject of the agreement; and how can agreement be possible unless the subject-matter of the agreement is definite and certain?

I say that recent events indicate that we must press forward codification. I can go a step further than that. The changes in the conditions of the earth, the changes in international relations which have been so rapid in recent years, have outstripped the growth of international law. I think it quite right to say that the law of nations does not come so near to covering the field of national conduct today as it did fifty years ago. The development of international relations in all their variety, in the multitude of questions that arise, goes on more rapidly than the development of international law; and if you wait for customs without any effort to translate the custom into definite statements from year to year, you will never get any law settled except by bitter controversy. The pressing forward of the codification of international law is made necessary by the swift moving of events among nations. We cannot wait for custom to lag behind the action to which the law should be applied.

Mr. Chairman, I want to express entire harmony with what Governor Baldwin said a few moments ago upon the other branch of this question, as to whether codification should be by governmental agencies or by private societies. It is not practicable that governments should do the threshing out of questions necessary to reach a definite statement of a conclusion. That has to be done with freedom from constraint by the private individual doing his work in a learned society or in private intercourse. I think it is not generally understood that the first conference at The Hague would have been a complete failure if it had not been for the accomplished work of the Institut de Droit International. The first conference was called by the Czar of Russia to consider and agree upon disarmament. It was called with expressions of the most noble character which, if they could have impressed themselves upon the minds and hearts of Europe, would have rendered impossible the terrible sacrifices that are now going on. The conference was called for the purpose of agreeing upon disarmament, and for the purpose of averting what the Czar saw coming in the future and which has now come. But there were Powers in Europe which would not have it. They refused to enter a conference for the purpose of considering that subject. Something had to be done. Here was a conference called by this great Power about to meet, and something had to be done, so they took the accomplished work of the Institut de Droit International, which had been threshed out through the labors and discussions of the most learned international lawyers of Europe, including most of the technical advisers of the foreign offices of Europe meeting in their private capacity, and embodied it in the conventions of the First Hague Conference. It would have been impossible for the Hague Conference to do that work or one tithe of it if they had not had the material already provided.

So I think it is quite clear that the process of codification, step by step, subject by subject, point by point, must begin with the intellectual labor of private individuals, and it must

CODIFICATION OF INTERNATIONAL LAW 409

be completed by the acceptance of governments. All of the hundreds of thousands of pages that have been written upon international law by the private individuals go for nothing unless governments accept them. A wilderness of text-writers one has to wander through in endeavoring to get at what the law of nations is, and all that they wrote is of no consequence, except as it exercises a force in bringing about action and agreement by the governments of the earth. So, Mr. Chairman, this process must have both private initiative and governmental sanction.

Mr. Chairman, there is one other subject which I think we should consider in dealing with the subject of codification, and that is this: Are the small nations of the earth to continue? Is it to be any longer possible for the little people to maintain their independence? That is a serious question with many of us in this joint meeting of the Society and Subsection Six of the Pan-American Congress and the American Institute. The large nations can take care of themselves by the exercise of power, if they are willing to be armed to the teeth always; but the small countries — what are they to do? There is no protection for them but the protection of law! And there is no protection in law unless the law be made clear and definite and certain, so that a great bully cannot escape it without running into the condemnation of that law. So I say that every dictate of humanity should lead us to urge forward that process by which in its better moments mankind may be led to agree to the setting up of clear and definite and distinct rules of right conduct for the control of the great nations in their dealings with the small and weak.

The presence here of Dr. Maurtua, whom it is a great pleasure for me to hail as a colleague in the Faculty of Political and Administrative Science of the University of San Marcos, at Lima, and of the distinguished Ambassador from Brazil, my old friend from Rio de Janeiro, lead me to say something which follows naturally from my reflections regarding the interests of the smaller nations. It is now nearly ten years ago when your people, gentlemen, and the other peoples of South America, were good enough to give serious and respectful consideration to a message that it was my fortune to take from this great and powerful republic of North America to the other American nations. I wish to say to you, gentlemen, and to all my Latin American friends here in this congress, that everything that I said in behalf of the Government of the United States at Rio de Janeiro in 1906 is as true now as it was true then. There has been no departure from the standard of feeling and of policy which was declared then in behalf of the American people. On the contrary, there is throughout the people of this country a fuller realization of the duty and the morality and the high policy of that standard.

Of course, in every country there are individuals who depart from the general opinion and general conviction, both in their views and in their conduct; but the great, the overwhelming body of the American people love liberty, not in the restricted sense of desiring it for themselves alone, but in the broader sense of desiring it for all mankind. The great body of the people of these United States love justice, not merely as they demand it for themselves, but in being willing to render it to others. We believe in the independence and the dignity of nations. and while we are great, we estimate our greatness as one of the least of our possessions, and we hold the smallest state, be it upon an island of the Caribbean or anywhere in Central or South America, as our equal in dignity, in the right to respect and in the right to the treatment of an equal. We believe that nobility of spirit, that high ideals, that capacity for sacrifice are nobler than material wealth. We know that these can be found in the little state as well as in the big one. In our respect for you who are small, and for you who are great, there can be no element of condescension or patronage, for that would do violence to our own conception of the dignity of independent sovereignty. We desire no benefits which are not the benefits rendered by honorable equals to each other. We seek no control that we are unwilling to concede to others, and so long as the spirit of American freedom shall continue, it will range us side by side with you, great and small, in the maintenance of the rights of nations, the rights which exist as against us and as against all the rest of the world.

With that spirit we hail your presence here to coöperate with those of us who are interested in international law; we hail the formation of the new American Institute of International Law and the personal friendships that are being formed day by day between the men of the North and the men of the South, all to the end that we may unite in such clear and definite declaration of the principles of right conduct among nations, and in such steadfast and honorable support of those principles as shall command the respect of mankind and insure their enforcement.

THE DECLARATION OF THE RIGHTS AND DUTIES OF NATIONS OF THE AMERICAN INSTITUTE OF INTERNATIONAL LAW

PRESIDENTIAL ADDRESS AT THE TENTH ANNUAL MEETING OF
THE AMERICAN SOCIETY OF INTERNATIONAL LAW
WASHINGTON, APRIL 27, 1916

The American Institute of International Law, consisting of five representatives from each national society of international law in each of the twenty-one American republics, was founded on October 12, 1912, and held its first session in connection with and under the auspices of the Second Pan-American Scientific Congress, at Washington, December 28, 1915, to January 8, 1916. On January 6, 1916, the American Institute of International Law, upon the motion of its president, James Brown Scott, adopted a Declaration of the Rights and Duties of Nations, prefixed by a preamble and followed by a commentary upon each article of the declaration. This commentary was based in each instance upon a decision of the Supreme Court of the United States.

WITH this meeting we finish the first decade of this Society. How great is the change of conditions in the field of international law during that period! Ten years ago all the governments of the world professed unqualified respect and obedience to the law of nations, and a very small number of persons not directly connected with government knew or cared anything about it. In this country at least international law was regarded as a rather antiquated branch of useless learning, diplomacy as a foolish mystery, and the foreign service as a superfluous expense. Now that governments have violated and flouted the law in many ways and with appalling consequences, the people of this country at least have begun to realize that observance of the law has a real and practical relation to the peace and honor of their own country and their own prosperity. They are beginning to take an interest in the subject, to discuss it in the newspapers, to inquire how observance of the law may be enforced. There appears a dawning consciousness that a democracy which undertakes to control its own foreign relations ought to know something about the subject. If we had not established this Society ten years ago to study and discuss and spread a knowledge of international law it would surely be demanded now, and we may be certain that our annual public discussions and the publication of the admirable *Journal* which we have always maintained, with its definite and certain information upon international events, its interesting and well-informed discussion of international topics, and its supplements, with their wealth of authentic copies of international documents, have contributed materially towards fitting the people of our country to deal with the international situations which are before them.

Following our example, all the American countries have established similar societies, so that there are now twenty-one such societies on the American continents. In most cases these societies have been organized with the direct approval and sympathy of the government of the country and they include in their numbers a large part of the most eminent leaders of opinion in all the American states. Still another institution has been created in the American Institute of International Law, composed of delegates selected, to a limited number, by each of these national societies. This Institution has been established not as a competitor of the Institut de Droit International, which selects its members from among all the civilized countries, and not with the idea that there is such a thing as American international law to be distinguished from general international law, but with the idea that there may be special American views upon international questions; that the circumstances of the American republics may make it desirable for them to insist upon and press forward the development of particular principles in the law; that there are varieties of opinion upon such subjects which it may be useful to subject to common discussion and comparison of views; that the promotion of the habit of thinking broadly and internationally and not narrowly or locally, and a knowledge in each country of the points of view and habits of thought of each other country, will make all the American states more useful members of the family of nations, more considerate, more tolerant of differences of opinion, and more conscious of the international duties which are correlative to international rights.

The American Institute of International Law held its first meeting in Washington in December last, and, after a discussion in which representatives from all parts of the new world engaged, it adopted as its point of departure for future discussions a declaration of the rights and duties of nations which I commend especially to your attention. The declaration was in these words:

Declaration of the Rights and Duties of Nations

I. Every nation has the right to exist, and to protect and to conserve its existence; but this right neither implies the right nor justifies the act of the state to protect itself or to conserve its existence by the commission of unlawful acts against innocent and unoffending states.

II. Every nation has the right to independence in the sense that it has a right to the pursuit of happiness and is free to develop itself without interference or control from other states, provided that in so doing it does not interfere with or violate the rights of other states.

III. Every nation is in law and before law the equal of every other nation belonging to the society of nations, and all nations have the right to claim and, according to the Declaration of Independence of the United States, " to assume, among the powers of the earth, the separate and equal station to which the laws of nature and of nature's God entitle them."

IV. Every nation has the right to territory within defined boundaries and to exercise exclusive jurisdiction over its territory, and all persons whether native or foreign found therein.

V. Every nation entitled to a right by the law of nations is entitled to have that right respected and protected by all other nations, for right and duty are correlative, and the right of one is the duty of all to observe.

VI. International law is at one and the same time both national and international: national in the sense that it is the law of the land and applicable as such to the decision of all questions involving its principles; international in the sense that it is the law of the society of nations and applicable as such to all questions between and among the members of the society of nations involving its principles.[1]

You will observe that this declaration states in the main familiar principles. We have long been accustomed to such statements in the text books. Indeed the official reporter of the Institute, in his commentary upon the declaration, undertakes to show and does show that every statement, far from being novel, is based upon the decisions of American courts and the authority of American publicists. Yet the declaration was not superfluous or unimportant. There is a vast difference between the occasional decisions of a national court or the opinions of individual students, and a unanimous agreement of representatives of all the sovereign states

[1] Mr. Root quotes only the text of the declaration, and the preamble prefixed to it is here printed for the information of the reader who may desire to have the whole document before him.

Whereas, the municipal law of civilized nations recognizes and protects the right to life, the right to liberty, the right to the pursuit of happiness, as added by the Declaration of Independence of the United States of America, the right to legal equality, the right to property, and the right to the enjoyment of the aforesaid rights; and

Whereas, these fundamental rights, thus universally recognized, create a duty on the part of the peoples of all nations to observe them; and

Whereas, according to the political philosophy of the Declaration of Independence of the United States, and the universal practice of the American Republics, nations or governments are regarded as created by the people, deriving their just powers from the consent of the governed, and are instituted among men to promote their safety and happiness and to secure to the people the enjoyment of their fundamental rights; and

Whereas, the nation is a moral or juristic person, the creature of law, and subordinated to law as is the natural person in political society; and

Whereas, we deem that these fundamental rights can be stated in terms of international law and applied to the relations of the members of the society of nations, one with another, just as they have been applied in the relations of the citizens or subjects of the states forming the Society of Nations; and

Whereas, these fundamental rights of national jurisprudence, namely, the right to life, the right to liberty, the right to the pursuit of happiness, the right to equality before the law, the right to property, and the right to the observance thereof are,

of the western hemisphere upon a statement in definite terms of fundamental principles of international right. A still more important reason for such a declaration lies in the fact that the fundamental principles declared, now stand denied or repudiated by the conduct of nations in the great war that rages in the old world.

This instrument asserts the right of every nation to continued existence, to independence, to exclusive jurisdiction over its own territory, and to equality with every other nation; and it denies the right of any nation to commit for its own protection or preservation, unlawful acts towards innocent and unoffending states. These are the fundamentals of international right. They involve the existence of a democratic community of nations in which each individual nation has the same rights and full liberty for their enjoyment, limited and limited only, by the equal rights of every other member of the community. The body of rules of action which long experience and general consent have worked out for the assertion and preservation of these rights and the application of the universal limitation upon them in the practical relations between nations constitutes international law. This scheme of organization of the civilized

when stated in terms of international law, the right of the nation to exist and to protect and to conserve its existence; the right of independence and the freedom to develop itself without interference or control from other nations; the right of equality in law and before law; the right to territory within defined boundaries and to exclusive jurisdiction therein; and the right to the observance of these fundamental rights; and

Whereas, the rights and the duties of nations are, by virtue of membership in the society thereof, to be exercised and performed in accordance with the exigencies of their mutual interdependence expressed in the preamble to the Convention for the Pacific Settlement of International Disputes of the First and Second Hague Peace Conferences, recognizing the solidarity which unites the members of the society of civilized nations;

Therefore, the American Institute of International Law, at its first session, held in the city of Washington, in the United States of America, on the sixth day of January, 1916, adopts the following six articles, together with the commentary thereon, to be known as its Declaration of the Rights and Duties of Nations.

inhabitants of the earth is sharply distinguished from conditions of tribal hostility which prevailed during all the early part of human history and in which each separate tribe maintained its independence and liberty as best it could by force of arms in a normal relation of hostility to all other tribes; and it is equally distinguished from the condition of subordination and suzerainty in which a single nation, acquiring a preponderance of power, reduces other nations to submission and imposes upon them friendly relations with each other as equal vassals of the superior state. A familiar example of the one extreme is to be found in Europe during the Middle Ages and of the other in the Roman Empire, and upon a smaller scale and for a brief period in the control of Napoleon over a large part of Continental Europe. One condition affords independence to strong, civil societies at the expense of progress in civilization. The other condition fosters the arts of peace at the cost of liberty. The democratic organization of a community of nations, on a basis of acknowledged right, declared and protected by law, seeks to avoid both of these extremes, and the vast progress of civilization since the Peace of Westphalia, with the general advance of mankind in comfort, intelligence, individual freedom and opportunity, testify to the superior merit of the arrangement. Yet just as ordinary democracies composed of natural persons tend, unless continually restrained, to lapse into anarchy on the one hand or to seek security under autocracy on the other, this community of nations has hitherto been in a condition of unstable equilibrium, always in danger of being overturned in one direction or the other. The age-long struggle to maintain the balance of power in Europe, often misguided, as we can see in looking back, often controlled by selfish purposes, often violating the very rights it professed to preserve, has nevertheless been constant effort to counteract these tendencies.

A careful examination of the undisputed facts which show the origin and conduct of the present war leaves no room for doubt that the entire basis of the community organization of nations upon which rests the structure of international law is put at issue in the struggle. The principles of action upon which the war was begun involve a repudiation of every element of fundamental right upon which the law of nations rests. The right of every nation to continued existence, to independence, to exclusive jurisdiction over its own territory and equality with other nations, is denied. The right of any strong nation to destroy all those alleged rights of other nations in pursuit of what it deems to be useful for its own protection or preservation is asserted. Under this view what we have been accustomed to call fundamental rights would become mere privilege to be enjoyed upon sufferance according to the views of expedience held by the most powerful. If this view prevails the whole structure of modern international law will be without foundation; and the discussion of its rules with the nations who maintain this view must now be not a real appeal to any law, but merely a balancing of possible injuries and benefits. So long as these fundamental questions are unsettled all discussion of international law must be hypothetical, as if architects were to discuss the elevation of a building while the ground plan remains undetermined. These propositions are the postulates of all reasoning regarding the rules of international law. All discussion of international right is based upon them, assumes assent to them. To discuss international law with a nation which denies these postulates can be nothing but an unreal and futile appearance of discussing the law. When your major premise is disputed you must establish that before you can go on with your argument.

There is only one real question of international law today, and that is, whether these postulates of the law are to stand or not. As between nations which agree that they should stand there may be discussion as to international rules based upon that hypothesis, but as between nations which assert and nations which repudiate these fundamentals of the law, there can be no real discussion except of expediency. The declaration of the American Institute of International Law arrays the members of all these American countries upon one side of this vital question of principle which is being fought out in the great war. Their act is altogether impersonal. It takes no account of responsibility or blame or racial feelings or friendships or enmities, and it is unmistakable. The representatives of all the American countries affirm the old basis of international right upon which depends the life, the independence and the legal equality of all small nations and the laws which protect them against the arbitrary power of the strong.

It will be useful to remember, however, that to be effective such declarations must be accompanied by conformity in the conduct of the nations adhering to the principles declared. There are some rules of national conduct which flow directly from the principles of national independence and equality, but which do not always coincide with the impulses of sentiment or with the apparent requirements of immediate interest. On the one hand these principles require that nations shall refrain from interference with the internal affairs of other nations. It frequently happens that many persons, in the United States for example, strongly disapprove things that are done in other countries within the jurisdiction and affecting the citizens of those other countries and not affecting any country's international rights. Such acts may run counter to our ideas of liberty, of morality, of humanity, of fair business conduct. The strongest sentiments and interests may urge interference to prevent conduct which shocks or offends us, yet, failing some special and exceptional ground — some recognized international ground for intervention — we have no right to interfere, because interference would be an infringement upon the independent equality of the other state. The peace and order of the world require that each nation shall mind its own business and refrain from attempting to impose its ideas of conduct upon other equal independent states. This is not because the interference in the particular case might not be beneficial so far as that case goes; but because the right to interfere in one case carries with it the right to interfere in other cases; the determination of the question when interference is justifiable would necessarily rest with the interfering power; and in the exercise of such a right all weaker states would become subject to the control of the stronger and ultimately to the control of the strongest. With the great varieties of race and custom and conceptions of social morality in the human family, the right of each nation to conduct its own internal affairs according to its own ideas is of the essence of liberty. The rule which prohibits interference by other nations, with however good a purpose, is a rule against inevitable tyranny. It is not at all uncommon that the best impulses and sentiments of our own people in this country are enlisted in favor of action by our government which would do infinitely more harm than good, by breaking down the barrier which the principle of the independent equality of states presents against the evils of foreign domination.

On the other hand the assertion of the independent equality of states implies an interest on the part of all states adhering to the doctrine in having it preserved, and it follows necessarily that when one sovereign state is dealing not with its internal affairs but with its international relations and violates the rule of right as against another equal and independent state, all other equally independent states have a right to insist that the international rule shall be observed, and such insistence is not interfering with the quarrels of others but is an assertion of their own rights. In each case every state must be guided by its own circumstances and interests in determining how far it will go in supporting its interference. There can, however, be no doubt of the international right to interfere in behalf of the maintenance of the law. So far as it is possible to see now, if the issue of the present conflict leaves the fundamental basis of international law still existent the possibility of securing conformity to the rules of law resting upon that basis will depend upon the recognition by the nations in general of the duty to interfere and insist upon the observance of the law and upon the adoption by them of a practice in conformity with that duty.

The exercise of such an international right was well illustrated when, in November, 1861, the Commander of the United States man-of-war the *San Jacinto* took the Confederate commissioners, Messrs. Mason and Slidell, from the neutral British passenger vessel, the *Trent*. Upon England's demanding the surrender to her of Mason and Slidell, the Prussian Minister of Foreign Affairs, Count Bernstorff, the father of the present German Ambassador to the United States, wrote to the Prussian Minister at Washington for communication to the American State Department a letter, dated at Berlin, December 25, 1861. He said:

> The maritime operations undertaken by President Lincoln against the Southern seceding States could not, from their very commencement, but fill the King's Government with apprehensions lest they should result in possible prejudice to the legitimate interests of neutral powers.
>
> These apprehensions have unfortunately proved fully justified by the forcible seizure on board the neutral mail-packet the *Trent*, and the abduction therefrom, of Messrs. Mason and Slidell by the Commander of the United States man-of-war the *San Jacinto*.
>
> This occurrence, as you can well imagine, has produced in England and throughout Europe the most profound sensation, and thrown not cabinets only, but also public opinion, into a state of the most excited expectation. For, although at present it is England only which is immediately con-

cerned in the matter, yet on the other hand, it is one of the most important and universally recognized rights of the neutral flag which has been called into question.

. . . In the absence of any reliable information we were in doubt as to whether the Captain of the *San Jacinto*, in the course taken by him, had been acting under orders from his Government or not. Even now we prefer to assume that the latter was the case. Should the former supposition, however, turn out to be the correct one, we should consider ourselves under the necessity of attributing greater importance to the occurrence, and to our great regret we should find ourselves constrained to see in it not an isolated fact but a public menace offered to the existing rights of all neutrals.

The French Foreign Office wrote, on December 3, 1861, to the French Minister in Washington:

The wish to contribute to prevent a conflict, imminent perhaps between two powers towards which it is animated by sentiments equally friendly, and duty to maintain certain principles essential to the security of neutrals with the effect of protecting the rights of its own flag from injury, have convinced it (the Government of the Emperor) after matured reflection, that it cannot under these circumstances remain altogether silent.

M. Thouvenel then discusses the merits of the *Trent* affair, and proceeds:

Not wishing to enter into a more thorough discussion of the question raised by the capture of MM. Mason and Slidell, I have said enough about it, I believe, to establish that the Cabinet at Washington would not be able, without infringing upon the principles for which all neutral powers are equally interested in assuring respect or without contradicting its own conduct up to this time, to give its approval to the proceedings of the Commander of the *San Jacinto*.

The Austrian Government instructed its minister in Washington in the same sense.

Here was a case in which these great powers asserted unhesitatingly their interest in maintaining the common right of nations to have the rules of international law maintained. The case happened to be free from those obstacles to frank expression which have been so frequently presented by the delicate adjustments necessary to preserve the balance of power in Europe, and accordingly the powers expressed themselves freely. It never occurred to anybody to deny that they were within their rights. We can hardly doubt that their expressions had a material effect in leading to the action of the American Government in preventing war between Great Britain and the United States, and in making effective a rule of law which protects the rights of all neutrals.

Any nation which adheres to the American Institute's declaration of the rights and duties of nations rests under a duty, whenever the law which declares and protects those rights is clearly violated or threatened, to follow some such course as these continental nations followed in the *Trent* case. This is not a duty created by law or by treaty. There is no legal obligation, but there is a moral obligation, supported by enlightened self-interest, such as urges every member of a civil community who is worthy of respect to give his voice, his influence, his example, towards the preservation of the law through which alone the community can continue to exist. If the nations really wish to have peace and order maintained by law they must take an interest in having the law observed. They must really mean it, and act accordingly.

Furthermore the declaration of the Institute asserts the subordination of nations to the obligations of morality. It denies that any aggregation of human beings in any state, under any form of government, can be superior to the duties of good faith, of justice, and of humanity. I shall not discuss that. No democracy, no republic, no form of government based upon the rights of men, can continue to live in a world which rejects that view. This Republic cannot continue to live in a world which rejects that view.

It is to be observed that this declaration, in which representatives of all the American countries unite, asserts for all the world as a matter of general public right the same principles which, somewhat more narrowly and upon a different ground, the famous declaration of President Monroe asserted in respect of the American republics. The message of Monroe affirmed in effect that all the American states were to be regarded as members of the community of nations; that they were entitled to live, to be independent, to be treated as equals, and to be free from oppression by other powers. He gave notice that the attempt by any European power to override these rights of the American states would be regarded as unfriendly to the United States, because it would be dangerous to the peace and safety of the United States. As we turn from the narrow limits of the Monroe Doctrine to the broader field of universal international right set forth in the declaration of the Institute, with the terrible lesson of the great war in our minds, we may well assert that the repudiation of these principles, the violation of these rules anywhere within the confines of civilization, is dangerous to the peace and safety of the whole community of nations. To the efforts of the community of nations towards defending its peace and safety against the destruction of the fundamental bases of its public right, the often quoted words of Mr. Calhoun regarding the Monroe Doctrine are applicable. He said in the Senate, in 1848:

> Whether you will resist or not, and the measure of your resistance — whether it shall be by negotiation, remonstrance, or some intermediate measure, or by a resort to arms; all this must be determined and decided on the merits of the question itself. This is the only wise course. . . . There are cases of interposition where I would resort to the hazard of war with all its calamities.

Whether the United States will soon have occasion or will long have the ability or the will to maintain the Monroe Doctrine lies in the uncertain future. Whether it will be necessary for her to act in defense of the Doctrine or abandon it, may well be determined by the issue of the present war.

Whether when the occasion comes she will prove to have the ability and the will to maintain the Doctrine, depends upon the spirit of her people, their capacity for patriotic sacrifice, the foresight and character of those to whose initiative in foreign affairs the interests of the people are entrusted.

Whether the broader doctrine affirmed by the American Institute of International Law is to be made effective for the protection of justice and liberty throughout the world depends upon whether the vision of the nations shall have been so clarified by the terrible lessons of these years that they can rise above small struggles for advantage in international affairs, and realize that correlative to each nation's individual right is that nation's duty to insist upon the observance of the principles of public right throughout the community of nations.

FOREIGN AFFAIRS, 1913–1916

ADDRESS AS TEMPORARY CHAIRMAN OF THE NEW YORK
REPUBLICAN CONVENTION, NEW YORK, FEBRUARY 15, 1916

Only those portions of this address which deal with international matters are included in this volume.

WE are entering upon a contest for the election of a president and the control of government under conditions essentially new in the experience of our country. The forms which we are about to follow are old and familiar; but the grounds for action, the demand of great events for decision upon national conduct, the moral forces urging to a solution of vaguely outlined questions, the tremendous consequences of wisdom or folly in national policy, all these are new to the great mass of American voters. Never since 1864 has an election been fraught with consequences so vital to national life. All the ordinary considerations which play so great a part in our presidential campaigns are and ought to be dwarfed into insignificance. . . .

When a president and secretary of state have been lawfully established in office the power of initiative in foreign affairs rests with them. The nation is in their hands. Theirs is the authority and theirs the duty to adopt and act upon policies, subject to such laws as Congress may enact within constitutional limits. Parliamentary opposition can take no affirmative step; can accomplish no affirmative action. The expression of public opinion can do nothing except as it produces an influence upon the minds of those officers who have the lawful power to conduct our foreign relations. Their policy is the country's policy because it is they who are authorized to act for the country. While they are working out their policy all opposition, all criticism, all condemnation, are at the risk of weakening the case of one's own country and frustrating the efforts of its lawful representatives to succeed in what they are seeking to accomplish for the country's benefit. An American should wish the representatives of his country to succeed whatever may be their party unless there be wrongdoing against conscience. However much he may doubt the wisdom of their course he should help them where he can and refrain from placing obstacles in their way. But when the president and secretary of state have acted, and seek a new grant of power, they and the party which is responsible for them must account for their use of power to the people from whom it came, and the people must pass judgment upon them, and then full and frank public discussion becomes the citizen's duty.

The United States had rights and duties in Mexico. More than forty thousand of our citizens had sought their fortunes and made their homes there. A thousand millions of American capital had been invested in that rich and productive country, and millions of income from these enterprises were annually returned to the United States not merely for the benefit of the investors, but for the enrichment of our whole country and all its production and enterprise. But revolution had come, and factional warfare was rife. Americans had been murdered, American property had been wantonly destroyed, the lives and property of all Americans in Mexico were in danger. That was the situation when Mr. Wilson became president in March, 1913. His duty then was plain. It was, first, to use his powers as president, to secure protection for the lives and property of Americans in Mexico and to require that the rules of law and stipulations of treaties should be observed by Mexico towards the United States and its citizens. His duty was, second, as the head of a foreign power to respect the inde-

FOREIGN AFFAIRS, 1913–1916

pendence of Mexico, to refrain from all interference with her internal affairs, except as he was justified by the law of nations for the protection of American rights. The President of the United States failed to observe either of those duties. He deliberately abandoned them both and followed an entirely different and inconsistent purpose. He intervened in Mexico to aid one faction in civil strife against another. He undertook to pull down Huerta and set Carranza up in his place. Huerta was in possession. He claimed to be the constitutional president of Mexico. He certainly was the *de facto* president of Mexico. Rightly or wrongly, good or bad, he was there. From the north Carranza and a group of independent chieftains were endeavoring to pull down the power of Huerta. President Wilson took sides with them in pulling down that power. In August, 1913, through Mr. John Lind, he presented to Huerta a communication which was in substance a demand that Huerta should retire permanently from the government of Mexico. When Huerta refused, the power of the United States was applied to turn him out. Foreign nations were induced to refuse to his government the loans of money necessary to repair the ravages of war and establish order. Arms and munitions of war were freely furnished to the northern forces and withheld from Huerta. Finally the President sent our army and navy to invade Mexico and capture its great seaport, Vera Cruz, and hold it and throttle Mexican commerce until Huerta fell. The government of the United States intervened in Mexico to control the internal affairs of that independent country and to enforce the will of the American President in those affairs by threat, by economic pressure, and by force of arms. Upon what claim of right did this intervention proceed? Not to secure respect for American rights; not to protect the lives or property of our citizens; not to assert the law of nations; not to compel observance of the law of humanity.

On the contrary, Huerta's was the only power in Mexico to which appeal could be made for protection of life or property. That was the only power which in fact did protect either American or European or Mexican. It was only within the territory where Huerta ruled that comparative peace and order prevailed. The territory over which the armed power of Carranza and Villa and their associates extended was the theatre of the most appalling crimes. Bands of robbers roved the country with unbridled license. Americans and Mexicans alike were at their mercy, and American men were murdered and American women were outraged with impunity. Thousands were reduced to poverty by the wanton destruction of the industries through which they lived. The payment of blackmail was the only protection of property against burnings and robbery. No one in authority could or would give protection or redress. It had become perfectly plain that the terms upon which both Carranza and Villa held their supporters, were unrestricted opportunity and license for murder, robbery, and lust. Yet the government of the United States ignored, condoned, the murder of American men and the rape of American women and destruction of American property and insult to American officers and defilement of the American flag and joined itself to the men who were guilty of all these things to pull down the power of Huerta. Why? The President himself has told us. It was because he adjudged Huerta to be a usurper; because he deemed that the common people of Mexico ought to have greater participation in government and share in the land; and he believed that Carranza and Villa would give them these things. We must all sympathize with these sentiments, but there is nothing more dangerous than misplaced sentiment. Of all men in this world, the man who had vested in him the executive power of the United States was least at liberty to sit in judgment of his own motion upon the title of a claimant to the Mexican presidency or to reform the land laws of Mexico.

The results of this interference were most unfortunate. If our government had sent an armed force into Mexico to protect American life and honor we might have been opposed but we should have been understood and respected by the people of Mexico, because they would have realized that we were acting within our international rights and performing a nation's duty for the protection of its own people; but when the President sent an armed force into Mexico to determine the Mexican presidential succession he created resentment and distrust of motives among all classes and sections of the Mexican people. When our army landed at Vera Cruz, Carranza himself, who was to be the chief beneficiary of the act, publicly protested against it. So strong was the resentment that he could not have kept his followers otherwise. When Huerta had fallen, the new government which for the day had succeeded to his place peremptorily demanded the withdrawal of the American troops. The universal sentiment of Mexicans required that peremptory demand, and the troops were withdrawn. Still worse than that, the taking of Vera Cruz destroyed confidence in the sincerity of the American government in Mexico because every intelligent man in Mexico believed that the avowed reason for the act was not the real reason. The avowed purpose was to compel a salute to the American flag. I will state the circumstances: On the ninth of April, 1914, a boat's crew from the *Dolphin* landed at a wharf in Tampico to take off supplies. The use of that wharf had been prohibited, and the Mexican officer in charge of the wharf put the crew under arrest, but a higher officer ordered him to hold the boat's crew at the wharf and await instructions. Within an hour and a half the crew was set free. No injury or indignity was suffered except the fact of the arrest. Immediate amends were made. The Mexican officer in command at Tampico apologized; General Huerta's government apologized; the officer who made the arrest was himself arrested and his punishment promised. The admiral in command of our fleet at Tampico demanded more public amends through a salute to our flag, but there ensued a discussion as to the facts and as to the character of the salute which the circumstances demanded, the number of guns, and how, if at all, the salute was to be returned. While that discussion was pending and avowedly because of that incident the American Government presented a twenty-four hour ultimatum and landed an armed force and captured the city of Vera Cruz. Three hundred Mexicans were reported killed; seventeen United States marines were killed and many were wounded. At that very time Mr. Bryan, with the President's approval, was signing treaties with half the world agreeing that if any controversy should arise it should be submitted to a joint commission and no action should be taken until after a full year had elapsed. This controversy arose on the ninth of April, and on the twenty-first of the same month Vera Cruz was taken. Several times the troops of Carranza and Villa had arrested and imprisoned American consular officers and torn down the American flags from the consulates and trampled them in the mire, with indescribable indignities. The proofs were in our hands and no attention was paid to them. Many times soldiers of the United States, in uniform, on duty, had been shot and killed or wounded by soldiers of Carranza and Villa across the border. More than fifty of them have been killed in this way and no attention has been paid to it. The demand of a salute to the flag was never heard of again after Vera Cruz was captured. There is not an intelligent man in Mexico who believes that the dispute about the salute was the real reason for the capture of Vera Cruz. Is there one here who doubts that the alleged cause was but a pretext and that the real cause was the purpose to turn Huerta out of office ? The people of Mexico, who saw their unoffending city captured by force of arms, three hundred of its people slain, their soil violated, a foreign flag floating over their great seaport, upon what they felt to be a false pretense, were misled into imputing a more sinister purpose still — to secure control of Mexico for the United States; and they believed that when the American troops departed, that purpose was abandoned through fear. With the occupation of Vera Cruz the moral power of the United States in Mexico ended. We were then and we are now hated for what we did to Mexico, and we were then and we are now despised for our feeble and irresolute failure to protect the lives and rights of our citizens. No flag is so dishonored and no citizenship so little worth the claiming in Mexico as ours. And that is why we have failed in Mexico.

Incredible as it seems, Huerta had been turned out by the assistance of the American government without any guarantees from the men who were to be set up in his place, and so the murdering and burning and ravishing have gone on to this day. After Huerta had fallen and the Vera Cruz expedition had been withdrawn, President Wilson announced that no one was entitled to interfere in the affairs of Mexico; that she was entitled to settle them herself. He disclaims all responsibility for what happens in Mexico and contents himself with a policy of Watchful Waiting. But who can interfere in a quarrel and help some contestants and destroy others and then absolve himself from responsibility for the results ? It is not by force of circumstances over which we had no control, but largely because the American Administration intervened by force to control the internal affairs of that country instead of asserting and maintaining American rights that we have been brought to our present pass of confusion and humiliation over Mexico.

And for the death and outrage, the suffering and ruin of our own brethren, the hatred and contempt for our country, and the dishonor of our name in that land, the Administration at Washington shares responsibility with the inhuman brutes with whom it made common cause.

When we turn to the Administration's conduct of foreign affairs incident to the great war in Europe we cannot fail to perceive that there is much dissatisfaction among Americans. Some are dissatisfied for specific reasons, some with a vague impression that our diplomacy has been inadequate. Dissatisfaction is not in itself ground for condemnation. The best work of the diplomatist often fails to receive public approval at the time and must look to a calm review in the dispassionate future for recognition of its merit. The situation created by the war has been difficult and trying. Much of the correspondence of the State Department, especially since Mr. Lansing took charge, has been characterized by accurate learning and skillful statement of specific American rights. Every one in the performance of new and unprecedented duties is entitled to generous allowance for unavoidable shortcomings and errors. No one should be held to the accomplishment of the impossible. The question whether dissatisfaction is just or unjust is to be determined upon an examination of the great lines of policy which have been followed and upon considering whether the emergencies of the time have been met with foresight, wisdom, and decisive courage. If these are lacking as guides, all the learning of the institutes and the highest skill in correspondence are of little avail.

A study of the Administration's policy towards Europe since July, 1914, reveals three fundamental errors. First, the lack of foresight to make timely provision for backing up American diplomacy by actual or assured military and naval force. Second, the forfeiture of the world's respect for our assertion of rights by pursuing the policy of making threats and failing to make them good. Third, a loss of the moral forces of the civilized world through failure to truly interpret to the world the spirit of the American democracy in its attitude towards the terrible events which accompanied the early stages of the war.

First, as to power.

When the war in Europe began, free, peaceable little Switzerland instantly mobilized upon her frontier a great army of trained citizen soldiers. Sturdy little Holland did the same, and, standing within the very sound of the guns, both have kept their territory and their independence inviolate. Nobody has run over them because they have made it apparent that the cost would be too great.

Great, peaceable America was farther removed from the conflict, but her trade and her citizens travelled on every sea. Ordinary knowledge of European affairs made it plain that the war was begun not by accident, but with purpose which would not soon be relinquished. Ordinary knowledge of military events made it plain from the moment when the tide of German invasion turned from the Battle of the Marne that the conflict was certain to be long and desperate. Ordinary knowledge of history — of our own history during the Napoleonic wars — made it plain that in that conflict neutral rights would be worthless unless powerfully maintained. All the world had fair notice that, as against the desperate belligerent resolve to conquer, the law of nations and the law of humanity interposed no effective barriers for the protection of neutral rights. Ordinary practical sense in the conduct of affairs demanded that such steps should be taken that behind the peaceable assertion of our country's rights, its independence and its honor, should stand power, manifest and available, warning the whole world that it would cost too much to press aggression too far. The Democratic government at Washington did not see it. Others saw it and their opinions found voice. Mr. Gardner urged it; Mr. Lodge urged it; Mr. Stimson urged it; Mr. Roosevelt urged it; but their argument and urgency were ascribed to political motives; and the President described them with a sneer as being nervous and excited.

But the warning voices would not be stilled. The opinion that we ought no longer to remain defenseless became public opinion. Its expression grew more general and insistent, and finally the President, not leading, but following, has shifted his ground, has reversed his position, and asks the country to prepare against war. God grant that he be not too late. But the Democratic party has not shifted its ground. A large part of its members in Congress are endeavoring now to sidetrack the movement for national preparedness; to muddle it by amendment and turn it into channels which will produce the least possible result in the increase of national power of defense. What sense of effectiveness in this effort can we gather from the presence of Josephus Daniels at the most critical post of all — the head of the Navy Department; when we see that where preparation has been possible it has not been made; when we see that construction of war ships already authorized has not been pressed, and in some cases after long delay has not even been begun?

If an increase of our country's power to defend itself against aggression is authorized by the present Congress it must be largely through Republican votes, because the representatives of the Republican party in Washington stand for the country no matter who is president; and all the traditions and convictions of that party are for national power and duty and honor.

As to the policy of threatening words without deeds.

When Germany gave notice of her purpose to sink merchant vessels on the high seas without safeguarding the lives of innocent passengers, our Government replied on the tenth of February, one year ago, in the following words:

> The Government of the United States . . . feels it to be its duty to call the attention of the Imperial German Government, with sincere respect and the most friendly sentiments but very candidly and earnestly, to the very serious possibilities of the course of action apparently contemplated under that proclamation.
>
> The Government of the United States views those possibilities with such grave concern that it feels it to be its privilege, and indeed its duty in the circumstances, to request the Imperial German Government to consider before action is taken the critical situation in respect of the relations between this country and Germany which might arise were the German naval forces, in carrying out the policy foreshadowed in the Admiralty's proclamation, to destroy any merchant vessel of the United States or cause the death of American citizens.
>
> . . . If such a deplorable situation should arise, the Imperial German Government can readily appreciate that the Government of the United States would be constrained to hold the Imperial German Government to a strict accountability for such acts of their naval authorities and to take any steps it might be necessary to take to safeguard American lives and property and to secure to American citizens the full enjoyment of their acknowledged rights on the high seas.

By all the usages and traditions of diplomatic intercourse those words meant action. They informed Germany in unmistakable terms that in attacking and sinking vessels of the United States and in destroying the lives of American citizens lawfully travelling upon merchant vessels of other countries, she would act at her peril. They pledged the power and courage of America, with her hundred million people and her vast wealth, to the protection of her citizens, as during all her history through the days of her youth and weakness she had always protected them.

On the twenty-eighth of March, the passenger steamer *Falaba* was torpedoed by a German submarine, and an American citizen was killed, but nothing was done. On the twenty-eighth of April, the American vessel *Cushing* was attacked and crippled by a German aeroplane. On the first of May, the American vessel *Gulflight* was torpedoed and sunk by a German submarine, and two or more Americans were killed, yet nothing was done. On the seventh of May, the *Lusitania* was torpedoed and sunk by a German submarine, and more than one hundred Americans and eleven hundred other non-combatants were drowned. The very thing which our Government had warned Germany she must not do, Germany did of set purpose and in the most contemptuous and shocking way. Then, when all America was stirred to the depths, our Government addressed another note to Germany. It repeated its assertion of American rights, and renewed its bold declaration of purpose. It declared again that the American Government " must hold the Imperial German Government to a strict accountability for any infringement of those rights, intentional or incidental," and it declared that it would not " omit any word or any act necessary to the performance of its sacred duty of maintaining the rights of the United States and its citizens and of safeguarding their free exercise and enjoyment."

Still nothing was done, and a long and technical correspondence ensued; haggling over petty questions of detail, every American note growing less and less strong and peremptory, until the *Arabic* was torpedoed and sunk, and more American lives were destroyed, and still nothing was done, and the correspondence continued until the Allied defense against German submarine warfare made it unprofitable and led to its abandonment, and the correspondence is apparently approaching its end without securing even that partial protection for the future which might be found in an admission that the destruction of the *Lusitania* was forbidden by law. The later correspondence has been conducted by our State Department with dignity, but it has been futile. An admission of liability for damages has been secured, but the time for real protection to American rights has long since passed. Our Government undertook one year ago to prevent the destruction of American life by submarine attack, and now that the attempt has failed and our citizens are long since dead and the system of attack has fallen of its own weight, there is small advantage in discussing whether we shall or shall not have an admission that it was unlawful to kill them.

The brave words with which we began the controversy had produced no effect, because they were read in the light of two extraordinary events. One was the report of the Austrian Ambassador, Mr. Dumba, to his government, that when the American note of February tenth was received, he asked the Secretary of State, Mr. Bryan, whether it meant business, and received an answer which satisfied him that it did not, but was intended for effect at home in America.

The other event was the strange and unfortunate declaration of the President in a public speech in Philadelphia the fourth day after the sinking of the *Lusitania* that " a man may be too proud to fight." Whatever the Austrian Ambassador was in fact told by the Secretary of State, the impression which he reported was supported by the events which followed. Whatever the President did mean, his declaration, made in public at that solemn time, amid the horror and mourning of all our people over the murder of their brethren, was accepted the world over as presenting the attitude of the American government towards the protection of the life and liberty of American citizens in the exercise of their just rights, and throughout the world the phrase " too proud to fight " became a by-word of derision and contempt for the Government of the United States.

Later, in another theatre of war — the Mediterranean — Austria, and perhaps Turkey also, resumed the practice. The *Ancona* and then the *Persia* were destroyed, and more Americans were killed. Why should they not resume the practice? They had learned to believe that, no matter how shocked the American Government might be, its resolution would expend itself in words. They had learned to believe that it was safe to kill Americans, — and the world believed with them. Measured and restrained expression, backed to the full by serious purpose, is strong and respected. Extreme and belligerent expression, unsupported by resolution, is weak and without effect. No man should draw a pistol who dares not shoot. The government that shakes its fist first and its finger afterwards falls into contempt. Our diplomacy has lost its authority and influence because we have been brave in words and irresolute in action. Men may say that the words of our diplomatic notes were justified; men may say that our inaction was justified; but no man can say that both our words and our inaction were wise and creditable.

I have said that this Government lost the moral forces of the world by not truly interpreting the spirit of the American democracy.

The American democracy stands for something more than beef and cotton and grain and manufactures; stands for something that cannot be measured by rates of exchange, and does not rise or fall with the balance of trade. The American people achieved liberty and schooled themselves to the service of justice before they acquired wealth, and they value their country's liberty and justice above all their pride of possessions. Beneath their comfortable optimism and apparent indifference they have a conception of their great republic as brave and strong and noble to hand down to their children the blessings of freedom and just and equal laws. They have embodied their principles of government in fixed rules of right conduct which they jealously preserve, and, with the instinct of individual freedom, they stand for a government of laws and not of men. They deem that the moral laws which formulate the duties of men towards each other are binding upon nations equally with individuals. Informed by their own experience, confirmed by their observation of international life, they have come to see that the independence of nations, the liberty of their peoples, justice and humanity, cannot be maintained upon the good nature, the kindly feeling, of the strong towards the weak; that real independence, real liberty, cannot rest upon sufferance; that peace and liberty can be preserved only by the authority and observance of rules of national conduct founded upon the principles of justice and humanity; only by the establishment of law among nations, responsive to the enlightened public opinion of mankind. To them liberty means not liberty for themselves alone, but for all who are oppressed. Justice means not justice for themselves alone, but a shield for all who are weak against the aggression of the strong. When their deeper natures are stirred they have a spiritual vision in which the spread and perfection of free self-government shall rescue the humble who toil and endure, from the hideous wrongs inflicted upon them by ambition and lust for power, and they cherish in their heart of hearts an ideal of their country loyal to the mission of liberty for the lifting up of the oppressed and bringing in the rule of righteousness and peace.

To this people, the invasion of Belgium brought a shock of amazement and horror. The people of Belgium were peaceable, industrious, law-abiding, self-governing and free. They had no quarrel with any one on earth. They were attacked by overwhelming military power; their country was devastated by fire and sword; they were slain by tens of thousands; their independence was destroyed and their liberty was subjected to the rule of an invader, for no other cause than that they defended their admitted rights. There was no question of fact; there was no question of law; there was not a plausible pretense of any other cause. The admitted rights of Belgium stood in the way of a mightier nation's purpose; and Belgium was crushed. When the true nature of these events was realized, the people of the United States did not hestitate in their feeling or in their judgment. Deepest sympathy with downtrodden Belgium and stern condemnation of the invader were practically universal. Wherever there was respect for law, it revolted against the wrong done to Belgium. Wherever there was true passion for liberty, it blazed out for Belgium. Wherever there was humanity, it mourned for Belgium. As the realization of the truth spread, it carried a vague feeling that not merely sentiment but loyalty to the eternal principles of right was involved in the attitude of the American people. And it was so, for if the nations were to be indifferent to this first great concrete case for a century of military power trampling under foot at will the independence, the liberty, and the life of a peaceful and unoffending people in repudiation of the faith of treaties and the law of nations and of morality and of humanity — if the public opinion of the world was to remain silent upon that, neutral upon that, then all talk about peace and justice and international law and the rights of man, the progress of humanity and the spread of liberty is idle patter — mere weak sentimentality; then opinion is powerless and brute force rules and will rule the world. If no difference is recognized between right and wrong, then there are no moral standards. There come times in the lives of nations as of men when to treat wrong as if it were right is treason to the right.

The American people were entitled not merely to feel but to speak concerning the wrong done to Belgium. It was not, like interference in the internal affairs of Mexico or any other nation, for this was an international wrong. The law protecting Belgium which was violated was our law and the law of every other civilized country. For generations we had been urging on and helping in its development and establishment. We had spent our efforts and our money to that end. In legislative resolution and executive declaration and diplomatic correspondence and special treaties and international conferences and conventions we had played our part in conjunction with other civilized countries in making that law. We had bound ourselves by it; we had regulated our conduct by it; and we were entitled to have other nations observe it. That law was the protection of our peace and security. It was our safeguard against the necessity of maintaining great armaments and wasting our substance in continual readiness for war. Our interest in having it maintained as the law of nations was a substantial, valuable, permanent interest, just as real as your interest and mine in having maintained and enforced the laws against assault and robbery and arson which protect our personal safety and property. Moreover, that law was written into a solemn and formal convention, signed and ratified by Germany and Belgium and France and the United States in which those other countries agreed with us that the law should be observed. When Belgium was invaded that agreement was binding not only morally but strictly and technically, because there was then no nation a party to the war which was not also a party to the convention. The invasion of Belgium was a breach of contract with us for the maintenance of a law of nations which was the protection of our peace, and the interest which sustained the contract justified an objection to its breach. There was no question here of interfering in the quarrels of Europe. We had a right to be neutral and we were neutral as to the quarrel between Germany and France, but when as an incident to the prosecution of that quarrel Germany broke the law which we were entitled to have preserved, and which she had agreed with us to preserve, we were entitled to be heard in the assertion of our own national right. With the right to speak came responsibility, and with responsibility came duty — duty of government towards all the peaceful men and women in America not to acquiesce in the destruction of the law which protected them, for if the world assents to this great and signal violation of the law of nations, then the law of nations no longer exists and we have no protection save in subserviency or in force. And with the right to speak there came to this, the greatest of neutral nations, the greatest of free democracies another duty to the cause of liberty and justice for which America stands; duty to the ideals of America's nobler nature; duty to the honor of her past and the hopes of her future; for this law was a bulwark of peace and justice to the world; it was a barrier to the spread of war; it was a safeguard to the independence and liberty of all small, weak states. It marks the progress of civilization. If the world consents to its destruction the world turns backwards towards savagery, and America's assent would be America's abandonment of the mission of democracy.

Yet the American Government acquiesced in the treatment of Belgium and the destruction of the law of nations. Without one word of objection or dissent to the repudiation of law or the breach of our treaty or the violation of justice and humanity in the treatment of Belgium, our government enjoined upon the people of the United States an undiscriminating and all-embracing neutrality, and the President admonished the people that they must be neutral in all respects in act and word and thought and sentiment. We were to be not merely neutral as to the quarrels of Europe, but neutral as to the treatment of Belgium; neutral between right and wrong; neutral between justice and injustice; neutral between humanity and cruelty; neutral between liberty and oppression. Our Government did more than acquiesce, for in the first *Lusitania* note, with the unspeakable horrors of the conquest of Belgium still fresh in our minds, on the very day after the report of the Bryce Commission on Belgian Atrocities, it wrote these words to the Government of Germany:

> Recalling the humane and enlightened attitude hitherto assumed by the Imperial German Government in matters of international right, and particularly with regard to the freedom of the seas, having learned to recognize the German views and the German influence in the field of international obligation as always engaged upon the side of justice and humanity, etc.

And so the Government of the United States appeared as approving the treatment of Belgium. It misrepresented the people of the United States in that acquiescence and apparent approval. It was not necessary that the United States should go to war in defense of the violated law. A single official expression by the Government of the United States, a single sentence denying assent and recording disapproval of what Germany did in Belgium would have given to the people of America that leadership to which they were entitled in their earnest groping for the light. It would have ranged behind American leadership the conscience and morality of the neutral world. It would have brought to American diplomacy the respect and strength of loyalty to a great cause. But it was not to be. The American Government failed to rise to the demands of the great occasion. Gone were the old love of justice; the old passion for liberty; the old sympathy with the oppressed; the old ideals of an America helping the world towards a better future; and there remained in the eyes of mankind only solicitude for trade and profit and prosperity and wealth.

The American Government could not really have approved the treatment of Belgium, but under a mistaken policy it shrank from speaking the truth. That vital error has carried into every effort of our diplomacy the weakness of a false position. Every note of remonstrance against interference with trade, or even against the destruction of life, has been projected against the background of an abandonment of the principles for which America once stood, and has been weakened by the popular feeling among the peoples of Europe, whose hearts are lifted up by the impulses of patriotism and sacrifice, that America has become weak and sordid.

Such policies as I have described are doubly dangerous in their effect upon foreign nations and in their effect at home. It is a matter of universal experience that a weak and apprehensive treatment of foreign affairs invites encroachments upon rights and leads to situations in which it is difficult to prevent war, while a firm and frank policy at the outset prevents difficult situations from arising and tends most strongly to preserve peace. On the other hand, if a government is to be strong in its diplomacy, its own people must be ranged in its support by leadership of opinion in a national cause worthy to awaken their patriotism and devotion.

We have not been following the path of peace. We have been blindly stumbling along the road that continued will lead to inevitable war. Our diplomacy has dealt with symptoms and ignored causes. The great decisive question upon which our peace depends, is the question whether the rule of action applied to Belgium is to be tolerated. If it is tolerated by the civilized world, this nation will have to fight for its life. There will be no escape. That is the critical point of defense for the peace of America.

When our Government failed to tell the truth about Belgium, it lost the opportunity for leadership of the moral sense of the American people, and it lost the power which a knowledge of that leadership and a sympathetic response from the moral sense of the world would have given to our diplomacy. When our Government failed to make any provision whatever for defending its rights in case they should be trampled upon, it lost the power which a belief in its readiness and will to maintain its rights would have given to its diplomatic representations. When our Government gave notice to Germany that it would destroy American lives and American ships at its peril, our words, which would have been potent if sustained by adequate preparation to make them good, and by the prestige and authority of the moral leadership of a great people in a great cause, were treated with a contempt which should have been foreseen; and when our Government failed to make those words good, its diplomacy was bankrupt.

Upon the record of performance which I have tried to describe, will the American people say that the Democratic party is entitled to be continued in power?

INDEX

INDEX

Abdul-Aziz, sultan of Turkey (1861–1876), 283, 284.
Acapulco, 229, 299.
Adams, President John Quincy, 120, 223; on South American independence, 114.
Adrian, *see* Hadrian.
Agadir, 165.
Aggression, intentional, pretext always sought for, 166.
Aix-la-Chapelle, Congress of (1818), 106.
Alabama Claims, arbitration of the, at Geneva, 66 f., 213, 291, 301.
Alaska, 299; boundary dispute, 301.
Alexander II, emperor of Russia (1855–1881), 93.
Alexander, Joshua W., American congressman, 358.
Alexandria, 101.
Algeciras, Conference of (1906), 46, 165.
Aliens, rights of, under treaties, 7–23.
Altruism, defects and merits of, 132 f.
Ambassador from Brazil, *see* Gama.
American Institute of International Law, the, 405, 411; its Declaration of the Rights and Duties of Nations, 412–426.
American Peace Society, the, 63.
American people, the, characterized, 133 f., 440 f.
Americans, killing of, thought safe, 440.
American Society for Judicial Settlement of International Disputes, 145, 150, 151 f.
American Society of International Law, 3, 7 f., 72, 89, 124, 126, 154, 404, 413.
Amos, Sheldon, on Lieber, 94.
Anarchy, tendency of democracies to lapse into, 418; condition of, in Mexico, 333 f., 430.
Ancona, the, destroyed, 439.
Anglo-Saxon liberty, 388.

Antioquía, Colombian state, 191.
Arabic, the, torpedoed, 438.
Arbitral Justice, Court of, proposed, 86, 364.
Arbitral tribunals, characteristics of, 148.
Arbitration, international, 31 f., 33–42, 57, 135, 140 ff., 144, 147 ff.; principle of, the United States committed to, 232–238, 332, 432; vital questions of public policy cannot be submitted to, 165 f.
Arbitrations, tendency of, 83 f., 140 f.
Ardila, Panaman notable, 196.
Argentina, 115, 120, 253 ff.
Argentine Confederation, Argentine Republic, *see* Argentina.
Armaments, limitation of, 137 f.
Arosemana, Justo, Panaman notable, 196.
Arosemana, Pablo, Panaman legislator, 196.
Arthur, President, 237.
Ashburton, Lord, 4.
Asser, T. M. C., of Holland, 165.
Association for the Reform and Codification of the Law of Nations, 63 f.
Atmosphere of the court room, importance of, 37.
Austria-Hungary, 71, 78, 99, 170, 176, 283, 308, 319, 365, 379, 439.

Bacon, Lord, saying of, 157.
Bahamas, the, 210.
Bailey, Joseph Weldon, American senator, 321, 322.
Balance of power, the, in Europe, 111, 165, 395, 418.
Baldwin, Simeon Eben, governor of Connecticut, 407 f.
Balkans, the, 174.
Baltic ports, the, of Russia, 299.

452 INDEX

Baltimore, 299.
Bancroft, George, American diplomat and historian, 97; negotiates treaties with the German states, 319 f.
Bar, Ludwig von, professor of criminal law at Göttingen, 164.
Bard, Thomas Robert, American senator, 221.
Bayard, Chevalier de, 174.
Bayard, Thomas Francis, American statesman and diplomat, 301 f.
Beaupré, Arthur Matthias, American diplomat, 198 f.
Belgium, 170, 176, 319, 386, 387; invasion of, 441–447.
Belize, *see* British Honduras.
Bentham, Jeremy, 62.
Bentwich, Norman, remarks of, in the *Fortnightly Review*, 82 f.
Berlin, entry of Napoleon into (1806), 96.
Berlin Decree, the (1806), 75.
Bermuda, 210.
Berne, meeting of economists and publicists at, 169 f.
Bernstorff, Albrecht, Count, Prussian minister, 422.
Bernstorff, Johann Heinrich, Count, German diplomat, 422.
Biddle, Nicholas, American financier, 97.
Binney, Horace, American lawyer, 91.
Black, Jeremiah Sullivan, attorney-general of the United States, 317.
Black Sea, the, neutralization of, 180.
Blaine, James Gillespie, American statesman, 222, 237, 262 f., 278.
Blockades, in the Declaration of Paris, 78.
Blücher, Prussian general, 96.
Bluntschli, Johann Kaspar, publicist, 62, 99, 406; comments of, on Lieber's work, 94 f., 101 f.
Bogota, capital of Colombia, 187, 192, 193, 194, 195, 197, 198, 199.
Bolivar, Colombian state, 191.
Boston, 16, 97, 294, 370.
Bourbons, restored to the throne of France, 106.

Boxer Rebellion, the, in China (1900–1901), 47, 205.
Brandegee, Frank Bosworth, American senator, 240.
Brazil, 52 f., 120.
Bremen trade, the, 385.
Brest, 75.
British Guiana, 210.
British Honduras, 210.
Brussels Conference, the (1874), 93.
Bryan, William Jennings, American politician, 432, 439.
Bryce Commission on Atrocities in Belgium, the, 445.
Buchanan, James, 110, 317.
Buchanan, William Insco, American diplomat, 176.
Buffalo, 294.
Buffer states, establishment of, 111.
Bunau-Varilla, Panaman diplomat, 175, 243.
Bureau of International Peace, the, 63.
Burritt, Elihu, 'the Learned Blacksmith,' 63.
Burton, Theodore Elijah, American senator, 345.

Cadwalader, American general, 90.
Calhoun, John Caldwell, American statesman, 110, 425.
California, 9–23, 154, 209.
Calvo, Carlos, publicist, 34.
Canada, 213 f., 269, 299, 388.
Canal Zone, the, 207, 225 ff., 241, 243, 285, 296.
Canning, George, English statesman, 106, 114.
Cape Horn, perils of navigation around, 179.
Capital, accumulation of, 45.
Caribbean Sea, the, 121, 179, 226, 410.
Carnegie Endowment for International Peace, the, 124 f., 126, 154.
Caroline Islands, the, 299.
Carranza, Venustiano, Mexican chief, 429–432.
Carson, Sir Edward, 391.

INDEX 453

Cartago, Costa Rica, permanent court for the Central American states established at (1908), 154.
Cases: the *Adela*, 41; the *Aghios Georghios*, 381; Baldwin v. Franks, 17; Chirac v. Chirac, 19; the *Circassian*, 41; Costello (1866), 318; the *Dashing Wave*, 40; Delagoa Bay, 385 f.; Ernst, 317; Fairfax v. Hunter, 19; Geofroy v. Riggs, 14 f.; the *Georgia*, 40; the *Hiawatha*, 41; the *Isabella Thompson*, 40; Olsen v. Smith, 298; the *Parlement Belge*, 386 f.; Tiburicio Parrot, 17; the *Pearl*, 41; the *Peterhof*, 40; the *Science*, 41; Shank v. Dupont, 316; the *Sir William Peel*, 41; the *Springbock*, 41; the *Vasilios*, 381; the *Volant*, 41; Ware v. Hylton, 18; Warren (1866) 318; Williams (1797), 315 f.
Cass, Lewis, on the scope of the Monroe Doctrine, 117; on the isthmian route, 188 f., 224; on canal privileges, 222, 258, 262.
Cauca, Colombian state, 191.
Caucuses, place of, 348.
Cavour, Italian statesman, 174.
Central America, 47, 189, 210, 211, 224, 236, 258, 261, 410.
Central American Peace Congress, the (1907), 153 f.
Central Office of International Institutions, the, at Brussels, 64.
Chaffee, Adna Romanza, American general, at Peking, 205.
Chamber of Commerce of New York, 356.
Channel, English, 386.
Charleston, 16.
Chesapeake Bay, 369.
Chicago, 359.
Chile, 120.
China, 46, 47, 48, 176, 205, 272 ff.
Chinamen, mobbed, 52.
Chinese children, separate schools for, in California, 10.
Chinese policy, the, of America, 321 f.
Chiriqui, province, 191.

Choate, Joseph Hodges, American diplomat, 145, 247 f., 256, 259, 263, 272, 276, 279, 280, 281, 286 f., 288, 294 f., 307 f.
Christian Church, the, 395.
Christiania, Norway, 154.
Civilization, advances of, 139, 418.
Civil War, the, 66, 75 f., 89-95, 370.
Clay, Henry, American statesman, 120, 223, 260 f.
Clayton, John Middleton, American politician, 110, 210, 211.
Cleveland, President Grover, on the Monroe Doctrine, 108; on differential tolls at Canadian canals, 213 f.; on the neutrality of interoceanic routes, 224, 264; on arbitration, 238.
'Coasting trade,' 'coastwise trade,' use of the terms, 227 f., 298 f.
Codification of international law, 405-411; private, 57-72, 408 f.; private codification goes for nothing unless accepted by governments, 408 f.
Coercion, to be avoided by peace conferences, 143.
Colberg, city in Prussia, 96.
Collegium, 8.
Colombia, 228 f., 230, 268 f., 295 f., 299, 309; relations of, with Panama and the United States, 175-206.
Colon, city, 194, 202, 203, 204, 205.
Colonies, growth of, 29.
Colonization, right of, in America, no longer asserted, 107.
Colt, Le Baron Bradford, American senator, 295, 296.
Columbia College, Lieber at, 90, 97.
Colunje, Gil, Panaman legislator, 196.
Confederate archives, classified and arranged by Lieber, 98.
Confederate cruisers, fitted out in the ports of Great Britain, 76.
Confederation of the Rhine, the, 96.
Conference of Teachers of International Law and Related Subjects (1914), 125.
Conflict of treaties and state laws, 17-20.
Conformity, impulse of, 28.

INDEX

Constantinople, Convention of (1888), 219, 220, 221, 229 ff., 245, 249, 264 f., 282–285, 290, 295, 296.
Constantinople, Treaty of, *see* Constantinople, Convention of.
Constitution, American, 39 f., 51.
Constitutional government, modification of, by practice, 349.
Constitutional provisions, reason for, 61.
Continental Congress, treaty-making power exercised by, 15 f.
Contraband, search for, 389 f.
Contract debts, ordinary, of governments, not to be collected by force, 139 f.
Control of American nations by the United States, not involved in the Monroe Doctrine, 119 f.
Conventions: for the International Protection of Industrial Property (1883) 65; for the Protection of Submarine Cables (1884), 65; for the Exchange of Official Documents (1886), 65; for the Publication of Customs Tariffs (1890), 65; for the Prohibition of the Use of Explosive Bullets (1868), 65; Geneva Convention relating to the Treatment of the Wounded of Armies in the Field, (1864), 65; for the Pacific Settlement of International Disputes (1899), 399 f.
Costa Rica, 176, 190, 211, 220, 264, 299.
Crete, 180.
Crimean War, the, 318.
Crowe, English delegate, 372.
Cruelty, now shocks the sensibilities, 172.
Cuba, 110, 153, 176, 206.
Cullom, Shelby Moore, American senator, 281, 288, 295.
Cummins, Albert Baird, American senator, 215 f., 305, 345.
Cundinamarca, Colombian state, 191.
Cushing, the, attacked by an aeroplane, 437.
Cynics, attitude of, 87.

Daniels, Josephus, secretary of the navy, 436.

Danubian principalities, 180.
Dardanelles, the, 180.
Darien, Isthmus of, 258. *See* Panama.
Davis, Bancroft, 16.
Davis, Cushman Kellogg, American senator, 215, 220, 229, 264, 288.
Declaration of Independence, the, 28, 32, 209, 416.
Declaration of the Rights and Duties of Nations, the (Jan. 6, 1916), 413–426.
De Jure Belli et Pacis, by Grotius, 156, 402.
De Lesseps Company, *see* Panama Canal Company.
Democracy, dangers of, as respects international relations, 7 f., 22 f., 127 f., 310 f.; tendency of democracies to lapse into anarchy, 418; what the American democracy stands for, 440 f.
Democracy in America, by de Tocqueville, 310.
Democratic party, the, 435, 436, 447.
Denmark, 170, 176, 319.
Denver, 52.
Devonshire, Duke of, on the Monroe Doctrine, 109.
Diplomacy, former character of, 135; present relation of, to moral standards, 135; American, has lost authority and influence, 440.
Discussion in legislative bodies, uses of, 339 f., 347–350.
Disraeli (Earl of Beaconsfield), 283.
Distribution of powers, 14.
Dolphin, the, American naval vessel, 431.
Don Pacifico case, the, 49.
Drago, Luis Maria, Argentine publicist, 34, 115.
Drago Doctrine, the, 139 f.
Droit oblige, 102.
Dufour, Guillaume Henri, Swiss general, 101.
Dumba, Konstantin Theodor, Austrian diplomat, 439.
Duplessix, French publicist, 63.
Duties, to be kept in mind as well as rights, 102, 127 f.

INDEX 455

Eastern Question, the, 165.
Ecuador, 190.
Edmonds, George Washington, American congressman, 357 f.
Edward VII, king of England (1901–1910), 274.
Egypt, 180, 229, 230 f.; British occupation of, 121.
Elba, Napoleon's escape from, 96.
Elbe, the, 75.
Electoral college, the, 178, 349.
El Relator, newspaper of Bogota, quoted, 195 f.
Ems, the, 75.
Encyclopaedia Americana, the, 97.
Enforcement of laws conditional upon public opinion, 27 f.
England, *see* Great Britain.
Erie Canal, the, 200.
Erwin, Mississippi, 52.
Europe, quarrels of, to be kept from America, 121 ff.; armaments of, 138.
European War, the (1914–), 154; relation of, to the Ship Purchase Bill, 337–390; relation of, to international law, 391–420; and the administration of President Wilson, 434–447.
Everett, Edward, American statesman, 97, 317.
Expatriation, right of, 166 f., 313–326.
Explosivistas, 303.
Ezuero, province, 191.

Falaba, the, torpedoed, 437.
Faultfinders, perennial, an incident of free institutions, 177.
Federalist, The, 39.
Federation of the world, dreams of, 143 f.
Feeling, matters of, as causes of war, 147, 324 f.
Ferdinand VII, king of Spain (1814–1833), 106.
Ferneck, Alexander von, professor at Vienna, 379 ff.
Feudal system, the, in Japan, 22.
Field, David Dudley, American jurist, 62, 63, 100, 405 f.

Fiore, Pasquale, Italian publicist, 62 f.
Fish, Hamilton, American statesman, 52 f.
Fisheries arbitration, the, 296 f.
Fletcher, Duncan Upshaw, American senator, 339, 342, 343, 345.
Force, world said to be ruled by, 135.
France, 71, 78, 106, 107, 109, 110, 114, 170, 176, 258, 308, 316, 320, 332, 358, 365, 367, 368, 369, 370, 371, 378, 379, 380, 383, 386, 387, 443.
Franco-German War of 1870, the, 93, 94.
French Company, the, *see* Panama Canal Company.
French Revolution, inspires a conception of popular liberty, 95 f.; remark of Lieber concerning, 102.
Friedland, battle of (1807), 96.

Galileo, apocryphal exclamation of, 174.
Gallinger, Jacob H., American senator, 305 f., 345.
Gama, Domicio da, Brazilian diplomat, 409 f.
Gardner, Augustus Peabody, American congressman, 436.
General Order No. 100 of 1863, 66, 67, 89–95.
Geneva Conventions, the, 173, 407.
Germany, 78, 109, 111, 117, 126, 165, 170, 176, 228, 272, 273, 299, 308, 332, 365, 367, 368, 369, 370, 371, 372, 373, 378, 380, 381 f., 383, 386, 387; idle German ships in American harbors, 357 f., 370; submarine warfare of, 436–440, 447; attack upon Belgium, 440–446.
Ghent, 63, 101.
Golden Rule, the, as a guide of American diplomacy, 109.
Grant, President, 236.
Great Britain, 66 f., 71, 75 f., 76, 80, 82 f., 111, 170, 176, 316, 318, 319, 320, 332, 358, 365, 367, 369, 371, 372, 373, 378, 379, 380, 383, 385, 386, 387, 388, 422, 424; relations of, to the Monroe Doctrine, 106, 107, 109, 112, 117, 181 f.;

456 INDEX

to Germany, 111; attitude of, regarding Agadir, 165; and the question of Panama tolls, 207–312; and the question of contraband, 389 f.
Great Lakes, the, 213, 267.
Greece, 96, 97, 180; cases of the *Vasilios* and the *Aghios Georghios*, 381.
Greek War of Independence, the, 96 f.
Grey, Sir Edward, British minister, 77, 207, 230 f., 249 f., 300.
Greytown, *see* San Juan de Nicaragua.
Grotius, Hugo, Dutch jurist, 100, 101, 156, 402.
Guatemala, 176.
Guerillas, Lieber on, 90.
Gulflight, the, torpedoed, 437 f.

Hadrian, Roman emperor (117–138), 101.
Hague, The, conferences at, 30, 93 f., 102, 103, 107, 147, 160, 162 f., 407; First, in 1899, 65, 67 f., 73, 126, 129, 135, 144, 159, 234, 399, 408; Second, in 1907, 68 f., 70, 78, 84, 107, 129–144, 145, 161, 234, 238, 292, 364, 384, 397; Third, proposed, 69, 163.
Hague Convention, the, for the Pacific Settlement of International Disputes, 118, 119, 159, 315, 399 f.
Halifax, Nova Scotia, 229, 299.
Halleck, American general, 90, 91.
Hamburg-American Line, the, 383.
Hamburg trade, the, 383.
Hamilton, Alexander, 33 f., 39.
Handbuch des Völkerrechts, 379.
Hanna, Marcus Alonzo, American senator, 216.
Hanover, 317.
Harrison, President Benjamin, 53, 237.
Harte, Bret, 51.
Hartsuff, American general, 90.
Hawaii, 299.
Hay, John, American statesman, 153, 175, 198, 201, 234 f., 247 f., 256, 257, 259, 263, 264, 271, 272 ff., 275, 276, 279, 280, 281, 286 f., 288, 294, 295, 307, 308, 309, 311 f.

Heis, American diplomat, 211.
Henry IV, king of France (1589–1610), 136.
Hilliard, Francis, American jurist, 97.
Hipsang, sinking of the, 76.
History, rewriting of, 173.
Hitchcock, American general, 90, 91.
Hohenzollern candidature for the Spanish throne, the (1870), 111.
Holland, 170, 435. *See* Netherlands.
Holy Alliance, the, 106 f.
Honduras, 299.
Hong-Kong, 299.
House of Commons, resolution of, in favor of arbitration (July 16, 1893), 235, 238.
Huerta, Victoriano, Mexican ruler, 327–335, 429–433.
Hughes, William, American senator, 346.
Humanitarianism, defects and merits of, 132 f.
Humanity, sentiment of, as a leading power, 133 f.
Hungary, immigration from, 320.
Hurtado, Panaman diplomat, 196.

Idaho, 209.
Idealism, strain of, in the American nature, 134, 440 f.
Impartiality, not to be expected from executive and administrative officers, 36 f., 132.
Independent sovereignty, the fundamental principle of international law, 113; practical limitations of, 115 ff., 180 f.
Indian children, separate schools for, 10.
Innes, Mitchell, 300.
Institut de Droit International, *see* Institute of International Law.
Institute of International Law, the, 63, 68, 93, 101, 102, 408, 414.
Insults, as causes of personal and national quarrels, 324 f.
Intelligence, general diffusion of, 44.
International Bureau of Weights and Measures, establishment of (1875), 65.
International Committee of Geneva, 101.

INDEX

International conduct, standard of, 35 f.
International court, proposed, 396–402.
International law, private codification of, 57–72; independent sovereignty the fundamental principle of, 113; limitations on this principle, 115 ff., 180; study of, necessary to avert dangers of democratic control, 5 f., 163 ff.; international school of, to be established at The Hague, 164 f.; outlook for (1915), 391–403; Declaration of the Rights and Duties of Nations (1916), 413–426. See Law of nations.
International Law Association, 63 f.
International Naval Conference, see London, Conference of.
International police force, idea of a, 157.
International Prize Court, Convention for, 70, 72–78, 82–87.
International public opinion, 28–32. See Opinion.
International societies, multiplication of, 64 f.
Ireland, 317.
Ismail Pasha, khedive of Egypt (1863–1879), 283, 284.
Isolation, breaking down of, 29, 166 f., 171.
Italians, lynched, 52, 53.
Italy, 71, 78, 117, 170, 176, 308, 320, 332, 365, 380, 381.

Jamaica, 210.
Japan, 8–23, 46, 71, 76, 78, 154, 170, 176, 365.
Jefferson, Thomas, on the Monroe Doctrine, 108.
Jena, battle of (1806), 96.
Jena, university of, 96.
Jews, 313, 321.
Johnson, Cone, solicitor of the American State Department, 361 f., 363, 366, 367, 368, 369, 371, 373.
Jomini, Baron, Russian delegate, 93.
Judicial Arbitral Court, creation of, recommended, 84.
Judicial v. diplomatic action in arbitration, 142.

Justice, revered by the founders of the American Union, 40; conformity to, the unquestionable standard of international conduct, 35 f.
Justinian, 91.

Kent, James, American jurist, 316.
Kenyon, William Squire, American senator, 304 f.
Khedive, the, see Ismail Pasha.
King, American diplomat, 192, 194.
Knight Commander, sinking of the, 76.
Korea, American force in (1904), 205.
Korean children, separate schools for, in California, 10.
Kriege, Johannes, German delegate, 372 f., 375.
Kurihama, town in Japan, 22.

Labor, fluidity of, 44.
Labrador, 209.
La Fontaine, Henri, director of the International Bibliographical Institute at Brussels, 167.
Lake Mohonk Conference, the, 3.
Lansdowne, Lord, British minister, 247 f., 256, 280, 295, 307 f.
Lansing, Robert, 384 f., 434
Laodicea, 101.
Law of nations, 58; new era in, 69; formerly existed for Europe alone, 107; described by Lord Mansfield, 161 f., 393; assertion of Sir Edward Carson concerning, 391; violated by the attack on Belgium, 442–447. See International law.
Lawrence, William Beach, American jurist, 63.
Laybach, Congress of (1821), 106.
Leeward Islands, the, 210.
Lesseps, Ferdinand de, 185.
Liberalism, reaction against, in Europe, 106.
Lieber, Francis, 66, 67, 89–103.
Lincoln, Abraham, 66, 89, 93, 94, 174, 259, 422.

458 INDEX

Lind, John, agent of President Wilson, 429.
Lodge, Henry Cabot, American senator, 304, 318, 327, 333, 341, 345, 354, 357, 386, 436.
Lövland, president of the Nobel Prize Committee, 153.
L'Office Central, the, at Brussels, 167.
London, 299.
London, Conference of (1908), 70 f., 78–87, 363, 364, 365, 367 ff., 382, 398.
London, Declaration of (1909), 79–87, 365–384, 398.
Louis XIV, king of France (1643–1715), 349.
Lowell, James Russell, American author and diplomat, 222.
Lusitania, the, torpedoed, 437 f., 439, 445.

McAdoo, William Gibbs, American cabinet officer, 351, 352, 353, 357 f., 359, 360, 384, 385.
McCumber, Porter James, American senator, 282.
McKinley, President William, 153, 175, 238, 309.
McLean, George Payne, American senator, 257.
McLean, Thomas Chalmers, American naval officer, 204.
Magdalena, Colombian state, 191.
Mallarino, New Granadan diplomat, 181 f., 186.
Mansfield, Lord, 58, 161 f., 393.
Marcy, William Learned, American statesman, 317.
Marne, battle of the (1914), 435.
Marroquin, José Manuel, Colombian ruler and savant, 197, 198.
Marshall, John, American jurist, 19.
Martens, Frederick de, Russian publicist, 320; on Lieber, 94.
Martindale, American general, 90.
Maryland, 15, 19.
Mason, James Murray, Confederate commissioner, 80, 388, 422, 423.
Massachusetts, 16, 40.

Maurtua, Peruvian savant, 409.
Media sententia, 81.
Mediation, right and duty of, 118 f., 401.
Mediterranean, the, extension of Russian power towards, 111; submarine attacks in, 439.
Mexican Claims Commission, the, 98.
Mexican Resolution, the (1914), 327–335.
Mexicans, lynched, 52.
Mexican War, the, 209.
Mexico, 109, 110, 114, 117, 153, 174, 199, 209, 228 f., 299, 442; American relations with, 1913–1916, 327–335, 428–434.
Michigan, Lake, 268.
Middle Ages, the, 418.
Milan Decree, the (1807), 75.
Miles, James B., secretary of the American Peace Society, 63.
Minority, courage and persistency of a, the bulwark of liberties, 350.
Mobility of mankind, the new, 29, 44, 166 f.
Mobilization as a justification for immediate war, 111.
Mob violence, outrages on foreigners by, 50.
Moe, secretary of the Nobel Prize Committee, 153.
Mongolian subjects of Russia, 323.
Monroe Doctrine, the, 165, 180 f., 182, 189, 425 f.; defined, 105–123.
Monroe, President James, 109, 112, 113, 120, 121, 122, 425; his message of Dec. 2, 1823, 105 f.
Moral isolation, dread of, by governments, 30 f.
Morality, obligations of, nations must submit to, 424.
Morocco, 46, 111, 165.
Mosquito Coast, British protectorate over the, 210, 211, 212, 216.
'Most favored nation' provision, the, 16, 252 f., 254, 255, 259 f.
Mouravieff, Count, Russian minister, 67.
Municipal law, codification of, 59.

INDEX 459

Namur, battle of (1815), 96, 103.
Napoleon, 75, 96, 418.
Napoleonic wars, the, 435.
Nashville, the, at Colon, 202, 203.
Nations, law of, *see* Law of nations.
Naval Conference of London, *see* London, Conference of.
Naval War College, the, 378.
Netherlands, the, 71, 78, 176, 365, 380. *See* Holland.
Neutral flag, in the Declaration of Paris, 78.
Neutralization, of the Suez and Panama canals, 219 f., 244 f.; of the Panama canal, 274–279.
Neutral merchandise, in the Declaration of Paris, 78.
Neutral territory, inviolability of, 392.
New Brunswick, 209.
Newfoundland, 209, 297, 301.
New Granada, 181–184, 189, 190 f., 216, 217, 243, 266. *See* Colombia.
New Orleans, 52, 53.
New York, city and port, 16, 97, 101, 294, 299, 356, 370.
New York, state, 16, 40, 200; Republican state convention of 1916, address of Mr. Root at, 427–447.
New Zealander, the typical, 178.
Nicaragua, 176, 211, 220 f., 224, 264, 268, 295, 299.
Nicaragua Canal route, the, 210, 268, 295.
Nicholas II, czar of Russia (1894–), 67, 136, 408.
Niebuhr, Barthold Georg, German diplomat and historian, 97.
Nippold, Otfried, German scholar, 164.
Nobel, Alfred, Swedish scientist, 153, 154, 172.
Nobel Institute, the, at Christiania, 153, 154.
Nobel Prizes, the, 153.
North German Confederation, the, 319.
North German Lloyd Line, the, 383.
North Germany, 100.
Norway, 176, 319.

Notes, of the American government to Germany, 436–440, 445–447.
Nova Scotia, 209.
Nunez, Rafael, Colombian statesman, 192 ff.
Nys, Ernest, on Lieber, 95.

O'Gorman, James Aloysius, American senator, 256, 361.
Oliver, George Tener, American senator, 347.
Olney, Richard, American secretary of state, 217, 271, 301 f.
'Open door,' the, in China, 272 f.
Opinion, power of, 135, 167 ff., 396, 402 f.
Orders in Council, the, 75.
Oregon, 209.
Oregon boundary, the, 209.
Orient, passage to the, sought by early navigators, 179.
Oriental Public School, the, in San Francisco, 10.
Ostend, 386.
Ottawa, 303.

Pacific railroad companies, bonds of, 249.
Palmerston, Lord, 49, 210, 261.
Panama, city, 194, 202, 203, 204.
Panama, republic, 230; revolt of, from Colombia, 175–206; treaty with the United States (1903), 224, 225 ff.
Panama, Bay of, 121, 179.
Panama Canal, the, 121, 154; and the Panama revolt, 175–206; the question of tolls, 207–312.
Panama Canal Act, the (Aug. 24, 1912), 207–312.
Panama Canal Company, the, 185, 187, 188, 189, 258, 263.
Panama Congress, the (1826), 223.
Panama Railroad, the, 176, 185, 202 ff., 247, 262.
Panama Railroad Company, the, 247, 249, 262.
Pan-American Bureau, the, 153.
Pan-American Conference, *see* Pan-American Congress.

460 INDEX

Pan-American Congress, First, at Washington, 234, 236, 237.
Pan-American Congress, Second, at Mexico, 234.
Pan-American Congress, Third, at Rio de Janeiro, 114 f., 153, 234, 410.
Pan-Americanism, 153.
Pan-American Scientific Congress, Second, 124, 405, 409 ff., 413.
Paris, Declaration of (1856), 66, 78, 162, 406.
Paris, Parliament of, 349.
Paris, Peace of (1856), 66, 99.
Parliament of man, dreams of, 143, 157.
Patriotic societies, in Germany, 96.
Pauncefote, Julian, British diplomat, 140, 257, 271 f., 276, 280, 288.
Pax Romana, 395.
Peaceful interpenetration, 45.
Peace-loving and peace-keeping character, steady development of, 144.
Peace propaganda, methods of, 155.
Peace, universal, the object of the Hague conferences, 144.
Peking, 47, 205.
Pennsylvania, 16, 40.
Permanent Court, the, at The Hague, 159 ff.
Permanent judges, court of, needed for arbitration, 142, 145, 149-152.
Perry, Matthew Calbraith, American naval officer, 22.
Persia, the, destroyed, 439.
Personal rights, how limited, 115.
Peru, 176.
Philadelphia, 16, 294, 299, 370.
Philip II, king of Spain (1556-1598), 179.
Philippines, the, 153, 206.
Phillips, William, American diplomat, 300.
Pike County Ballads, by John Hay, 259.
Pilotage regulations, 298.
Pitt, William, the younger, 75.
Polemon of Laodicea, traveling professor in the second century, 101.
Poles, the, 195.

Policy, questions of, as causes of war, 146, 165-168, 394, 398.
Polk, President James Knox, 182; states a corollary to the Monroe Doctrine, 112; on the New Granadan treaty of 1846, 183, 266.
Portland, Maine, 229, 299.
Portland, Oregon, 229.
Portugal, 176; the Delagoa Bay case, 385 f.
Practical administrator, value of the, 132 f.
Privateering, abolished by Declaration of Paris, 78.
Prize Court Bill, rejected, 83.
Professors, under the Roman empire, 101.
Protection, national, problem of, 122.
Protection to citizens residing abroad, 43-56.
Prussia, 16, 96, 97, 100.
Prussian Decree, the (1806), 75.
Public opinion, education of, 8, 164.

Quebec, province of, 209.

Race prejudice, 170, 321-323.
Rayner, Isidor, American senator, 314, 318, 321.
Rebus sic stantibus, 391.
Red Sea, the, 231.
Renault, Louis, professor o' international law at Paris, 165; report of, 80 f., 375 ff., 380.
Republican party, the, 436.
Reyes, Rafael, Colombian general, 198 f.
Right and duty, connection of, 102, 127 f.
Rio Grande, the, 209.
Rives, William Cabell, American diplomat, 210, 215, 261.
Robber baron, days of, have passed, 166.
Rock Springs, Wyoming, 52.
Rolin-Jaequemyns, circular letter of, 101.
Roman Empire, the, 418.
Roman proconsul, days of, have passed, 166.
Rome, 101.

INDEX

Roosevelt, Theodore, 85, 153, 201, 224, 262, 263, 265, 276, 289, 309, 436; on the Monroe Doctrine, 114 f.; on arbitration, 238, 303, 305; on the Hay-Bunau-Varilla Treaty, 257 f., 259.
Rouse, Colorado, 52.
Rush, Richard, American diplomat, 106, 120.
Russia, 71, 76, 78, 99, 111, 176, 272, 299, 308, 365, 367, 368, 369, 370, 371, 380, 383, 387; claims of, in America, 106, 107; treaty of 1832 with, 313-326.
Russia, czar of, *see* Nicholas II.
Russia, emperor of, *see* Alexander II, Nicholas II.

St. Clair Flats Canal, the, 213.
Saint Kilda, sinking of the, 76.
St. Lawrence, river, 267, 268.
St. Lawrence Canal, the, 213.
St. Lawrence, Gulf of, 209.
St. Louis, 360.
Salisbury, Lord, 257, 259, 264; on arbitration, 140 f.
Salute, demanded from Mexico, on account of Tampico affair, 329-335, 431 f.
Sanclemente, M. A., Colombian president, 197, 198.
Sanction of international law, the, 25-32.
San Francisco, 154, 299; and the Japanese question, 9-23.
San Jacinto, the, 422, 423.
San Juan, island of, 301.
San Juan, river in Central America, 210.
San Juan de Nicaragua, or Greytown, 210.
Santander, Colombian state, 191.
Sault Sainte Marie, canal at, 246, 294.
Saunders, Edward Watts, American congressman, 357 f.
Savagery, 139, 444.
Sawyer, Justice, 17.
Scharnhorst, Prussian statesman, 96.
Schill, Prussian officer, 96.
Schools of California, Japanese in, 9-23.
Scott, James Brown, 125, 126, 129, 145, 413.

Scott, Winfield, American general, 91.
Seattle, 299.
Self-protection, national right of, 111.
Sentiment, in international relations, 112, 430.
Separatist policy of Washington, importance of, 122.
Servia, 387.
Seward, William Henry, American statesman, 110, 114, 117, 268.
Ship Purchase Bill, the, 337-390.
Ship registry bill, the, 362.
Ship subsidies, 249 f., 351, 355.
Shively, Benjamin Franklin, American senator, 335.
Siberian ports, the, of Russia, 299.
Sidney, Sir Philip, 174.
Simmons, Furnifold McLendel, American senator, 257, 353, 355, 362.
Sims, Thetus Wilrette, American congressman, 208.
Slidell, John, Confederate commissioner, 80, 388, 422, 423.
Smyrna, 101.
Smyth, American citizen, injured by a mob in Brazil, 52 f.
Soil, severance from the, 29, 44, 166 f.
Solicitor of the State Department, the, *see* Johnson, Cone.
Sosa, Panaman savant, 196.
South America, struggle for independence in, 107, 112; misunderstanding of the attitude and purposes of the United States in, 114; importance of the Monroe Doctrine to, 122 f.; development of arbitration in, 142, 236; visited by Secretary Root, 153, 410; trade with, 351 f., 385.
South Carolina, 16.
South Carolina College, Lieber at, 97.
Sovereign rights, how limited, 115 ff., 180.
Spain, 71, 78, 106, 109, 111, 117, 179, 283, 365.
Spanish provinces in America, revolt of, 106.
Spanish War, the, 153, 263.

'Spheres of influence,' 272 f.
Spooner, John Coit, American senator, 216, 309.
Squier, Ephraim George, American author and diplomat, 211.
Stanton, Edwin McMasters, American statesman, 90.
Stein, Prussian statesman, 96.
Stimson, Henry Lewis, American cabinet officer, 436.
Stone, William Joel, American senator, 339, 342, 343, 344, 349.
Story, Joseph, American jurist, 19, 97, 98, 316.
Strasburg, 101.
Sturdza, Demetrius, Roumanian scholar, 164 f.
Submarine warfare, 436–440, 447.
Suez Canal, the, 219, 245, 265, 282 ff., 299.
Suez Convention, *see* Constantinople, Convention of.
Sultan, the, *see* Abdul-Aziz.
Sumner, Charles, American statesman, 97, 99, 100.
Supreme Court, the, 17, 18, 19, 40 f., 369.
Survival of the fittest, law of the, 156.
Sutherland, George, American senator, 289, 290, 304, 377, 380.
Sweden, 176, 319.
Switzerland, 170, 176, 435.
Sympathy, in international relations, 112.

Taft, President, 249, 303, 304, 313.
Tallulah, Louisiana, 52.
Tampico, 299, 329–335, 431 f.
Tehuantepec, isthmus of, 212, 277.
Texas, 209.
Thayer, Martin Russell, American jurist, 100, 102.
Thirty Years' War, the, 402.
Thouvenel, Édouard Antoine, French minister, 423.
Thucydides, remark of, on property at sea, 100.
Tilsit, Peace of (1807), 96.

Tirpitz, Alfred von, German admiral and minister, 382.
Tocqueville, Alexis de, French statesman and writer, 310.
Tolima, Colombian state, 191.
Tolls, Panama Canal, question of, 207–312.
'Too proud to fight,' 439.
Torres, Colonel, Colombian officer, 203.
Torture, of witnesses or of criminals, now unthinkable, 173.
Traité de droit international, by Martens, 320.
Transportation, cheapness and ease of, 44.
Trave, the, 75.
Treaties: of Berlin (1878), 111; the Prize Court Treaty, 364, 397 f.; of San Stefano (1878), 111; on the Slave Trade (1890), 65; the Ship Canal Treaty (1909), 175; of the United States of America, with the Argentine Confederation (1853), 253 ff.; with Austria-Hungary (1870), 319; with China (the Burlingame Treaty, 1868), 16 f.; with Colombia (1868), 268 f.; (1870), 269; (Hay-Herran), 295 f.; with Denmark (1872), 319; with France (1778), 15 f.; with Great Britain (1783), 18; (1818), 297; (Webster-Ashburton, 1842), 4, 209; (Clayton-Bulwer, 1850), 210–213, 214–219, 222, 223, 224, 225, 244, 248, 256, 261, 262, 264, 266 f., 271 f., 274 f., 277–282, 300, 307; (of reciprocity, 1854), 267 f., 294; (May 13, 1870), 319; (of Washington, 1871), 66 f., 68, 213 f., 269 f., 291, 294, 406 f.; (Hay-Pauncefote, 1901), 207, 217–235, 243–312; (of arbitration, 1908), 232, 300; (1909), 294; with Japan (1854), 21 f.; (1894), 7–23; with Mexico (Guadalupe-Hidalgo, 1848), 209; with the Netherlands (1782), 16; with New Granada (1846), 182 ff., 185, 216, 224, 243, 262, 266; with Nicaragua (Heis), 211; (Squier), 211; (1867), 268, 295; with Panama (Hay-Bunau-Varilla, 1903), 224, 225

INDEX 463

ff., 243 f., 257, 296, 309; with Prussia (1786), 16; with Russia (1832), 313–326; with Sweden and Norway (1869), 319.
Treaty-making power, the, in the United States, 11–23.
Trent affair, the, 80, 99, 422 ff.
Trinidad, 210.
Tripartite Agreement, the, failure of., 175, 309.
Tripoli, 174.
Turkey, 46, 48, 229, 230 f., 284, 295, 296, 381, 439.

United States of America, the, 66 f., 71, 78, 85 f., 94, 97, 100, 126, 170, 406, 410, 420, 422 ff.; and the Monroe Doctrine, 105–123, 165, 425 f.; and the Panama revolt, 175–206; obligations of, as to Panama tolls, 207–312; relations with Russia, 313–326; with Mexico, 327–335, 428–434; the Ship Purchase Bill, 337–390; foreign affairs, 1913–1916, 427–447; relations to the European war, 434–447; the question of Germany, 436–447; need of military and naval preparation, 434 ff., 447; a government 'too proud to fight,' 439; the true spirit of the American democracy, 440 f.

Vancouver, British Columbia, 299.
Varilla, *see* Bunau-Varilla.
Venezuela, 109, 117 f., 119 ,176, 190; boundary controversy, 263, 301 f.
Vera Cruz, 229, 299, 330, 335, 429, 431, 432 f.
Veraguas, province, 191.
Veritas carissima, 102.
Verona, Congress of (1822), 106.
Victoria, British Columbia, 229.
Villa, Francisco, Mexican chief, 430, 432.
Virginia, 18, 19, 40.

Walsh, Thomas James, American senator, 338, 378 f.

War, continual recurrence of, 155; universally increasing preparations for. 155; avenue to all that mankind desired, 156; causes of, classified, 146 f.
War of 1812, the, 75.
Washburn, Emory, American statesman, 63.
Washington, state, 209.
Washington, George. 114, 122, 174, 291; Farewell Address of, 121.
Watchful Waiting, policy of, 433.
Waterloo, battle of (1815), 96.
Weak states, protection of, against the strong, 113, 115, 132, 401, 409.
Webster, Daniel, 4, 317; on the Monroe Doctrine, 108.
Weeks, John Wingate, American senator, 345.
Welland Canal, the, 213.
Weser, the, 75.
West Indies, the, 47.
Westlake, John, remarks of, in the *Nineteenth Century*, 81 f.
Westphalia, Peace of (1648), 418.
White, Andrew Dickson, American educator and diplomat, 100, 125, 126, 273.
White, Henry, American diplomat, 256 f., 259, 263, 264, 271.
Wilkes, Charles, American naval officer, 80, 422, 423.
William II, German emperor (1888–), 382.
William the Silent, 174.
Williams, John Sharp, American senator, 248, 284, 285, 305 f., 308, 345, 370.
Williams, William Elza, American congressman, 385.
Wilson, President Woodrow, 207 f., 303 f., 354; and the Mexican Resolution (1914), 327–335; foreign policy of (1913–1916), 427–447.
Windward Islands, the, 210.
Woolsey, Theodore Dwight, American educator, 63, 98.

Yorktown, 369.
Yucatan Bill, the (1848), 110.

ST. MARY'S COLLEGE OF MARYLAND LIBRARY
ST. MARY'S CITY, MARYLAND

33332

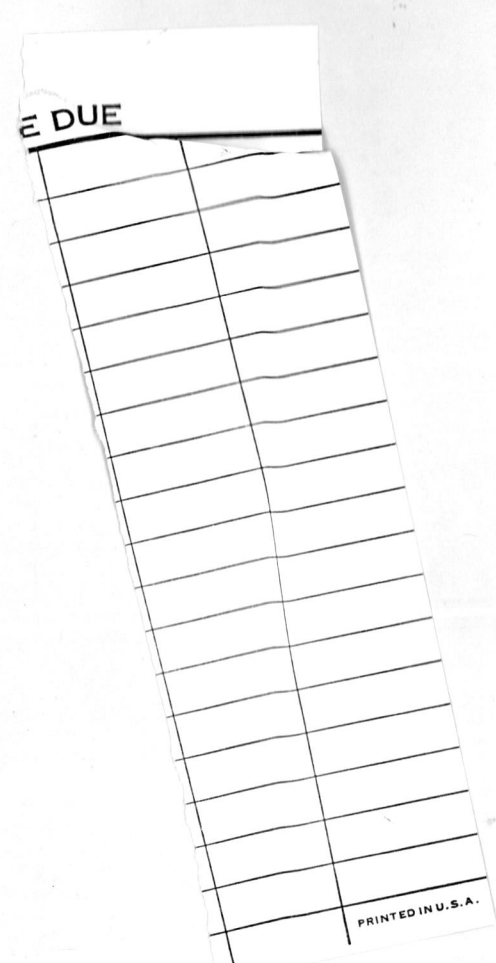